Marianne Jewell Memorial Library
Baker Coll
Muskegon,

Financial Reporting
and Corporate Governance

Financial Reporting and Corporate Governance

THOMAS A LEE

University of Alabama

John Wiley & Sons, Ltd

Marianne Jewell Memorial Library
Baker College of Muskegon
Muskegon, Michigan 49442

Copyright © 2006   John Wiley & Sons Ltd, The Atrium, Southern Gate, Chichester,
West Sussex PO19 8SQ, England

Telephone (+44) 1243 779777

Email (for orders and customer service enquiries): cs-books@wiley.co.uk
Visit our Home Page on www.wiley.com

All Rights Reserved. No part of this publication may be reproduced, stored in a retrieval system or transmitted in
any form or by any means, electronic, mechanical, photocopying, recording, scanning or otherwise, except under
the terms of the Copyright, Designs and Patents Act 1988 or under the terms of a licence issued by the
Copyright Licensing Agency Ltd, 90 Tottenham Court Road, London W1T 4LP, UK, without the permission in
writing of the Publisher. Requests to the Publisher should be addressed to the Permissions Department, John
Wiley & Sons Ltd, The Atrium, Southern Gate, Chichester, West Sussex PO19 8SQ, England, or emailed to
permreq@wiley.co.uk, or faxed to (+44) 1243 770620.

This publication is designed to provide accurate and authoritative information in regard to the subject matter
covered. It is sold on the understanding that the Publisher is not engaged in rendering professional services. If
professional advice or other expert assistance is required, the services of a competent professional should be
sought.

Other Wiley Editorial Offices

John Wiley & Sons Inc., 111 River Street, Hoboken, NJ 07030, USA

Jossey-Bass, 989 Market Street, San Francisco, CA 94103-1741, USA

Wiley-VCH Verlag GmbH, Boschstr. 12, D-69469 Weinheim, Germany

John Wiley & Sons Australia Ltd, 42 McDougall Street, Milton, Queensland 4064, Australia

John Wiley & Sons (Asia) Pte Ltd, 2 Clementi Loop #02-01, Jin Xing Distripark, Singapore 129809

John Wiley & Sons Canada Ltd, 6045 Freemont Blvd, Mississauga, ONT, L5R 4J3, Canada

Wiley also publishes its books in a variety of electronic formats. Some content that appears
in print may not be available in electronic books.

Library of Congress Cataloging-in-Publication Data

Lee, T. A. (Thomas Alexander)
  Financial reporting and corporate governance / Thomas A. Lee.
    p. cm.
  ISBN-13: 978-0-470-02681-6 (pbk. : alk. paper)
  ISBN-10: 0-470-02681-2 (pbk. : alk. paper)
  1. Financial statements. 2. Corporate governance. I. Title.
  HG4028.B2B427 2006
  657′.3—dc22
                                    2006017991

British Library Cataloguing in Publication Data

A catalogue record for this book is available from the British Library

ISBN-13: 978-0-470-02681-6
ISBN-10: 0-470-02681-2

Typeset in 10/12pt Times by Laserwords Private Limited, Chennai, India.
Printed and bound in Great Britain by Scotprint, Haddington, East Lothian
This book is printed on acid-free paper responsibly manufactured from sustainable forestry
in which at least two trees are planted for each one used for paper production.

As always to my loving and very patient wife, Ann

Contents

Lessons

Glossary of Terms

Abbreviation	Term
AA	Arthur Andersen
AIA	American Institute of Accountants
AICPA	American Institute of Certified Public Accountants
AP	Accounting profit
APB	Accounting Principles Board
ASB	Accounting Standards Board
ASSC	Accounting Standards Steering Committee
AUPB	Auditing Practices Board
BCCI	Bank of Commerce and Credit International
BPC	British Printing Corporation
CEO	Chief executive officer
CFA	Cash flow accounting
CFO	Chief financial officer
CL	Coopers & Lybrand
COGS	Cost of goods sold
COO	Chief operating officer
CR	Cash resources
DC	Dividend cover
DPS	Dividend per share
DRR	Dividend rate of return
DTI	Department of Trade and Industry
EPS	Earnings per share
EU	European Union
FASB	Financial Accounting Standards Board
FCF	Financial cash flow
FRC	Financial Reporting Council
FRRP	Financial Reporting Review Panel
FRS	Financial Reporting Standard
GAAP	Generally accepted accounting principles
GAAS	Generally accepted auditing standards
GP	Gross profit
GPM	Gross profit margin
IASB	International Accounting Standards Board
ICAEW	Institute of Chartered Accountants in England and Wales
ICF	Investment cash flow
ISB	Independence Standards Board
MC	MiniScribe Corporation
MCC	Maxwell Communications Corporation
MGN	Mirror Group Newspapers

NASDAQ	National Association of Securities Dealers
NP	Net profit before or after tax
NPM	Net profit margin
NYSE	New York Stock Exchange
OCF	Operating cash flow
PCAOB	Public Company Accounting Oversight Board
PER	Price earnings ratio
PLC	Public limited company
PP	Pergamon Press
PWC	Price Waterhouse & Company
ROI	Return on investment (or capital employed)
SEC	Securities and Exchange Commission
SPE	Special purpose entity
SSAP	Statement of Standard Accounting Practice
UK	United Kingdom
US	United States of America
VP	Vice president
WC	Working capital
WCM	WorldCom

About the Author

Tom Lee has taught and researched mainly in the area of financial accounting and reporting for more than 40 years. He has been a professor of accounting at the Universities of Liverpool, Edinburgh, and Alabama, and held visiting professorships in Australia, England, Scotland, and the United States. He is retired and Emeritus Professor of Accountancy at the University of Alabama. Tom has written several well known textbooks on corporate auditing, corporate financial reporting, income and value measurement, and cash flow accounting. His research also covers these areas as well as accounting history, and he has published numerous research texts, papers, and other contributions to the literature. Tom received the Burnum Award in 1997, the University of Alabama's premiere honour for scholarship, and the British Accounting Association's Lifetime Achievement Award in 2005. He is a former Council member of the Institute of Chartered Accountants of Scotland and a past President of the Academy of Accounting Historians.

About the Book

Corporate accounting, financial statements, and auditing are typically seen as technical matters of interest only to specialist accountants and accounting students. However, in corporate business today, it is impossible for non-accountants to avoid the presence of audited financial statements as part of daily management and decision making. Corporate directors and senior executives are legally responsible for the content and quality of financial statements addressed to shareholders and long-term lenders. The job performance of senior and junior managers is judged in part on the basis of the financial results reported in these statements. Investors, lenders, and other stakeholders learn about companies and their managers through financial statements. The content of these statements is used as a basis for a variety of financial decisions. It is therefore imperative that non-accountants access financial reports with a reasonable degree of confidence and understanding. Proper use of financial results in management and decision making improves the quality of management and decisions.

This book has been written for non-accountants with an interest in corporate financial reports. It is intended to give non-accountants an ability to use corporate financial statements with confidence and understanding. In turn, the objective is to improve the quality of management and decisions related to reporting companies. The book aims to provide corporate directors and senior executives with an understanding of the nature and role of the reporting function for which they are legally responsible. It also focuses on providing shareholders, lenders, and investors with a knowledge base about accounting and reporting that permits the extraction of key data from corporate financial reports that can be used in investment, lending, and other decisions. The book does not attempt to make non-accountants into accounting specialists. Instead, it provides non-accountants with the knowledge necessary to access financial statements without the fear, uncertainty, and scepticism that too often causes financial results to be misinterpreted, misused and, more often, ignored.

The book is therefore intended as a primary text for non-accounting students who need some understanding of accounting. The students can be majoring in business either as undergraduates or graduates, or in non-business areas such as engineering, law, and the media. The book can be used as a self-contained text to support a specific course or course module. However, it is designed so that it can be built on in more advanced courses on the subject. For this reason, it may be used by specialist accounting students in introductory courses.

A unique feature of the book is that its accounting, reporting, and auditing contents have been written within the context of the related subject of corporate governance. Over several decades in the UK and elsewhere, it has become apparent that companies need to be governed properly by their directors and senior executives, and that there need to be adequate means of holding these individuals accountable for their actions on behalf of shareholders and other stakeholders. In many countries, there have been investigations, recommendations, and provisions to improve the quality of corporate governance. These include matters relating to financial reporting and auditing. The text incorporates appropriate explanations and discussions.

The book is intended primarily for United Kingdom (UK) readers and readers with corporate financial reporting systems similar to those of the UK. The explanation and discussion of topics is therefore focused on UK legislation and regulation affecting corporate financial reports. However, corporate financial statements and auditing in the UK are also influenced by other regulatory systems. For example, the UK is part of the European Union (EU) and is therefore subject to EU requirements for financial reporting (e.g. the use of International Accounting Standards Board [IASB] accounting standards by listed companies). In addition, UK companies listed on United States (US) stock exchanges are subject to US accounting and auditing standards. US accounting standards and those of the IASB are intended to be compatible. For these reasons, the book deals with EU, IASB, and US provisions for corporate financial reporting when these are relevant, and recommends US reading when this is appropriate.

The book has been written as simply and clearly as possible. It does not provide the detail expected in a specialist text and therefore permits a more relaxed and straightforward coverage of the material. There are ten chapters in total. The first three chapters set the scene in the sense of providing introductions to later material and dealing with the subject of corporate governance as it relates to financial reporting and auditing. The next four chapters cover the main and supplementary financial statements that comprise the annual financial report. There is then a chapter on corporate auditing, followed by one on creative accounting practices that undermine the quality of corporate financial statements. The final chapter deals with the use of corporate financial statements and particularly the calculation and interpretation of accounting ratios.

Throughout the text there are a number of features designed to assist the learning process. These include:

- Abbreviating key terms and names to aid reading. A glossary of such terms is provided on pages xv and xvi.
- Learning lessons throughout the text in which a summary is made to reinforce meaning and significance. Numbered lessons are the stepping stones of each chapter.
- Exercises are listed at the end of each chapter and should be regarded as means of building on the contents of each chapter as well as reinforcing points made in it. Answers are provided on the publisher's website.
- Additional reading of an equivalent level to the text in order to expand on points made in each chapter and present an alternative perspective on the topics covered.

Acknowledgments

The author has been able to write this book because of thousands of hours spent in the classroom with numerous generations of accounting and non-accounting students. This experience has given him a sense of what is and is not possible in a text such as this. It is too easy to provide content that is too simple for the specialist student and too difficult for the non-specialist. Striking a balance is essential. Working with students over many years has given the author a sense of where that balance should lie. Whether it has been achieved in this book has to be judged by the reader.

The book has also benefited from numerous conversations between the author and academic colleagues concerning the subjects of financial accounting and auditing. These conversations have included concerns about the state of accounting and auditing, and how to communicate on a technical subject to readers who are not going to specialize with it. Grateful thanks are therefore due to colleagues and friends such as Bob Sterling, Lee Parker, Peter Wolnizer, and Paul Williams.

Particular thanks on this project go to Steve Hardman and Mark Styles of Wiley, and the text's reviewers.

All reasonable efforts have been made to trace the copyright owners of third party material included in this book. In the event of any omission of acknowledgment, copyright owners are invited to contact the Higher Education Division at John Wiley & Sons Ltd, so that they can be acknowledged in future editions of the book or request that such material be removed from future editions.

CHAPTER 1

Corporate Financial Reporting

Learning Objectives

This chapter is an introduction to corporate financial reporting. By the end of the chapter you should be able to identify and understand:

- The corporate environment in which financial reporting takes place.

- The main statements that comprise a corporate financial report.

- The content of the main financial statements as sets of related accounting numbers.

- Those individuals involved in the preparation, verification, use, and regulation of corporate financial reports.

- Corporate financial reporting as part of the broader process of corporate governance.

- Corporate financial reporting as a source of stability in capital markets.

- The general content of legal requirements for reporting corporate financial statements.

At the end of this chapter, please refer to these learning objectives again before moving on to Chapter 2 on corporate governance.

INTRODUCTION

This chapter introduces most of the topics that are explained and discussed in later chapters. It uses a simple illustration of a corporate situation based loosely on real events in order to identify the main elements of corporate financial reporting (Illustration 1). Any resemblance to an actual company, board of directors, management team, or auditor is coincidental.

ILLUSTRATION 1 GOOD NEWS AT FLASH BANG WALLOP PLC

Picture the following scene in a conference room of a luxury London hotel. Joe Gucci, the chief executive officer (CEO) of Flash Bang Wallop (FBW), a market leader in internet services, faces members of the press to announce record financial results for the year 2006. Using a computer presentation, he reveals that, compared to 2005, sales have increased by 50%, profits by 120%, and total assets by 80%. The dividend to shareholders will improve from 2005 by 75%. Joe also discloses his 2006 bonus as CEO. Based on the reported profits

1

for 2006, it is £1.2m. Joe reports in more detail on the increases he has announced and then opens the meeting for questions. A journalist suggests that the CEO's bonus is excessive in a year when the non-managerial staff of FBW had a 3% increase in wages. Joe answers by saying that the £1.2m bonus is consistent with the terms of his contract and the board of directors of FBW approved his contract. Joe also adds that five other senior executives of the company earned large bonuses in 2006. The skills and hard work of the FBW management team have increased the share price of the company by 45% during the year, he adds as an after-thought.

There are several other questions relating to the prospects for FBW in 2007 to which Joe Gucci gives brief and guarded responses, and the conference soon ends with drinks and a buffet. The share price of FBW rises rapidly on publication of its 2006 financial results and quickly hit a peak of £65—about thirteen times their value when the company went public four years ago. Press coverage of Joe Gucci's comments is generally positive and a week after the London press conference he receives the *Financial Journal* award for 2006 as Young Business Manager of the Year.

BAD NEWS AT FLASH BANG WALLOP PLC

The scenario described above suggests that all is well at FBW. Substantial increases in sales, profits, assets, and dividend indicate a healthy performance and condition—similar to health indicators such as heart beat, blood pressure, and cholesterol level for a patient who has been medically examined. In the case of FBW, however, there is also bad news. Six months later, Joe Gucci addresses the financial press again—this time to announce a restatement of FBW's 2006 financial results due to what he describes as accounting "errors." He discloses that reported sales for 2006 have been reduced by 20%, profits by 50%, and total assets by 33%. The proposed dividend will now only be a modest 10% greater than last year. The company's share price quickly drops to £23 and there is critical comment about what financial journalists call creative accounting practices at FBW. Joe Gucci and his management colleagues are accused of "cooking the books." There is no response to this from FBW or Joe Gucci.

Two months later, the investor relations department at FBW issues a press release. It reports that there will be accounting restatements of sales, profits, and total assets for each of the years 2004 and 2005 as a result of an investigation by an independent firm of public accountants. Joe Gucci leaves the company—his lawyer states Joe's need to spend more time with the Gucci family—and he receives £3m as compensation for the loss of his contract. The Financial Reporting Council (FRC) announces a formal investigation into FBW's financial affairs and its share price trades at an all-time low of £2. A prominent London law firm, Sue, Plead, and Settle, issues a multi-million pound lawsuit on behalf of the company's shareholders for alleged damages by FBW, its senior executives, and the company's auditor Delighted, Pleasing & Grinning (DPG), Chartered Accountants. DPG issues a press release stating that FBW's accounting procedures have been consistent with generally accepted accounting principles (GAAP) and that the firm is co-operating fully with the FRC. It is also confident that the FRC investigation will exonerate it from any wrongdoing. The government's Minister for Trade and Industry comments in a Radio 4 interview that cases such as FBW are rare in the UK and that, in any case, there are legislative and regulatory provisions to deal with these matters. FBW's customers, however, begin to cancel their internet contracts. DPG resigns as auditor. Joe Gucci and his family remain on holiday in Barbados. He refuses to discuss the "wild speculation in the press" about FBW's accounting practices. He confidently expects it to have a bright future in the global telecommunications industry.

FINANCIAL PLAY WITH ACTORS AND PLOT

The two-part FBW case is similar to a play with two acts. The first act is about a young and dynamic company battling for customers in an emerging and highly competitive market. The company's charismatic leader announces news of the commercial battles he and his managerial generals have fought and won on behalf of their shareholders. Managerial efforts have resulted in considerable spoils of victory—increased dividends and share price appreciation for the shareholders and large bonuses for the managers. The former have high expectations of considerable financial returns on their investment if FBW is successful. For the risk they are taking by investing in FBW, they anticipate levels of profit sufficient to generate not only dividends but also rapid growth in the company and its share price. To assist in this process, senior managers have contractual incentives to share in FBW's financial success through enhanced compensation. The first act in the play therefore indicates that shareholder expectations have been met and managerial incentives have worked. In other words, the capitalist system of financial risks and returns appears to have worked well.

The second act of the play tells a different story. Somehow, the charismatic leader and his staff at FBW have overstated the accounting for the spoils of victory in the war of commerce. The calculations have to be reduced following a recount by an independent investigator. At first the recount is limited to the most recent battles and victories but quickly extends to previous events in earlier years. Soon the credibility of the accounting numbers and the managers is being questioned and the value of the company tumbles. Unsurprisingly, shareholders seek recompense. The most senior manager moves on. The company begins to dissolve. The state moves in to investigate and hopes that the unfolding events will be isolated instances. There is then a third act to the play—whether FBW survives and prospers or eventually liquidates its remaining assets and dies.

LESSONS TO BE LEARNT

At this point, it is useful to reflect on what has been learnt from the FBW example. These lessons are reinforced in more detail in later chapters but need to be identified at this point before moving on. The key features are as follows.

Legal structure

Business takes place in organizations called companies (e.g. FBW). These are legal structures that permit investor principals (i.e. shareholders) to provide funds to allow managers (e.g. Joe Gucci) to do business on their behalf.

Managerial agents

Company managers act as agents for shareholders and periodically have to account for their actions and performance in business (e.g. the FBW press conferences and releases).

Financial indicators

The performance of the company and its managers is described in terms of indicators produced from a system of accounting that generates numbers to report to shareholders (e.g. FBW sales, profits, and total assets).

Accounting subjectivity

Accounting numbers are subjective and can be affected by error and adjustment (e.g. the FBW restatements of previously reported numbers). Accounting adjustments can lead to the accusation of manipulation in order to enhance the performance of the company and its management (i.e. creative accounting). Such an accusation is understandable in a situation where managers are remunerated in part on the basis of the accounting numbers they report to shareholders (e.g. profit-related bonuses).

Audit

The quality of reported accounting numbers is verified by an auditor (e.g. the DPG firm) on behalf of the shareholders. The process of verification is called an audit.

Legal protection

Shareholders can use the legal system to seek compensation for any damages caused by managers when they produce misleading accounting numbers.

Role of the state

The state can interfere in corporate matters when it believes there has been a serious abuse of shareholder trust in managers (e.g. the investigation of FBW by the FRC).

Each of the above matters is now briefly expanded on in the context of FBW and as a foundation for later detailed explanations and discussions.

COMPANIES

FBW is a relatively new company. It was formed in 1990 and came to the London Stock Exchange in 2003 as a listed company. It has particular features that are common to most companies in the UK.

Legal entity

Companies such as FBW are legal structures created by registration with an appropriate government agency (e.g. the Registrar of Companies in the UK). The existence of FBW as a legal entity is recorded with the Registrar and enables FBW to enter into business contracts and be managed in the absence of its owners. The FBW registration includes the company's name, various written rules concerning the nature of its business and the way it would be governed (i.e. what are called the memorandum and articles of association), and the identity of its promoters (i.e. those persons who formed it). Its annual accounting period is also notified to the Registrar.

Shares

The owners of FBW are called shareholders. They own the capital of the company in the form of shares or units of capital which have a designated monetary amount. In FBW's case, the company has issued two million shares of £1 each.

Limited liability

FBW shareholders have a limited liability to its creditors should the company fail. Shareholder can only lose the shares they hold and normally cannot be asked to contribute more funds if the company becomes bankrupt.

Listed company

FBW was created in 1990 as a limited liability company (i.e. FBW Ltd). At this point, it was a private company with a small number of shareholders and no public trading of its shares. As it grew, it became a public limited company (plc) (renamed FBW plc) with a large number of shareholders and could publicly trade its shares. In other words, FBW is permitted to offer its shares for sale to the public. However, it is also required to file its annual financial report with the Registrar of Companies and this makes its financial information public. FBW became a listed company when its shares were traded on the London Stock Exchange.

Corporate legislation

FBW is subject to corporate legislation—currently the Companies Act 1985 amended by the Companies Act 1989. These Acts provide the basic rules of corporate governance, including the requirement to keep proper accounting records, the publication of specific financial statements, the minimum content of each financial statement, and the audit of the statements. There are separate disclosure provisions for different sizes of company.

Other regulation

As a stock exchange-listed company, FBW is subject to regulation by the FRC, a legally-mandated body responsible for financial reporting standards and enforcement. A subsidiary body of the FRC, the Accounting Standards Board (ASB), is responsible for producing the accounting standards that companies in the UK must adhere to when producing their financial statements. However, as a listed company within the EU, FBW is required by the FRC to adhere to the accounting standards of the International Accounting Standards Board (IASB). The IASB has a set of accounting standards that are used by listed companies in numerous countries throughout the world.

FBW's main business is a communications service in great demand and relies on cutting-edge technology. The market for FBW's services is highly competitive and many of its internet service competitors have failed to survive. In fact, more have failed than succeeded. The financial rewards are therefore considerable for any company that survives long enough to provide internet access efficiently and speedily at an affordable price to the customer.

Because of the high financial risks involved, shareholders who invest in FBW expect high financial returns. These risks, however, are not just because the internet service market is very competitive. For example:

(1) Customers of companies such as FBW are notoriously fickle and not particularly loyal to brand names.

(2) The computer technology and software developed and used by FBW is fallible and constantly evolving.

(3) The company's senior managers are relatively untested as a team, although several have experience in other retail areas.

(4) There is no long-term history of financial performance with which to judge FBW—either in terms of its own track record or in comparison with competitors.

FBW is therefore in a situation of considerable uncertainty that demands investor caution and care. It requires FBW to supply good quality information to its shareholders, and therefore, to capital markets. Reliable financial information is the lifeblood of such markets as investors seek to find winners and avoid losers. Many of these investors are professional firms with skilled resources to use this information in their investment decisions (e.g. as in pension funds or investment trusts).

Lesson 1.1 Nature of company
A company represents a deliberate collaboration between investors with funds to invest in business and managers with skills to operate that business on behalf of investors. The collaboration exists within a legal structure that is subject to legislative requirements concerning its governance. The success of this governance depends on a flow of regular and reliable financial information from managers to investors.

CORPORATE MANAGERS

Joe Gucci and his senior management colleagues at FBW form a team of talented but inexperienced computer scientists and experienced retailers from other areas. The scientists typically graduated recently from university. They therefore have a short-term track record for imagination and creativity in the manufacture of internet service provision. The company's salesmen, however, are much more experienced and have a longer-term record of being able to market retail services to the public.

As previously mentioned, the senior managers of FBW are agents for the company's shareholders. The latter are the principals and provide the initial funding to do business but do not wish to manage the company. Instead, they employ Joe Gucci and his colleagues to manage on their behalf and offer them contractual incentives to perform well. It is a win-win situation if the principal-agent relationship works. Joe and his colleagues can work hard to generate profits that reward not only the shareholders but also themselves.

More generally, the corporate management structure of a company such as FBW consists of several layers connected by established lines of communication, responsibility, and accountability. The overall structure is outlined below. The relative size of each layer depends on the nature of the business and its management style—some companies, for example, have few middle managers.

(1) Employees and staff work within designated areas and specialist tasks, and are supervised by:

(2) Junior and middle managers with particular skills and experience who report to:

(3) Senior managers such as the CEO who are contracted to be responsible for the overall management of the company and are accountable to:

(4) The board of directors that is the main governance structure in the company and which directs the company on behalf of its shareholders.

> **Lesson 1.2 Principal-agent relationship**
> The principal-agent relationship is fundamental to the corporate system of business and should be beneficial to both shareholders and managers. The relationship is monitored and directed by the board of directors.

CORPORATE GOVERNORS

The principal-agent relationship at FBW (and every other company), consists of trust and risk. Shareholders trust managers to work effectively on their behalf. However, they assume a risk that senior managers may take advantage of the situation to abuse that trust. It is a relationship that has existed since the mid nineteenth century and, with exceptions, has worked reasonably well.

A major reason for the success of the principal-agent relationship is the existence of corporate governance mechanisms to monitor and control management. These mechanisms attempt to ensure that senior managers are working in the best interests of the company and its shareholders and not just for themselves. As mentioned above, a large part of corporate governance takes the form of the company's board of directors. This body exists to supervise and regulate management on behalf of its shareholders. In the case of FBW, the board of directors comprises:

(1) Its chairman Lord William Pendleton, a former senior civil servant in the Department of Trade and Industry, Dame Jill Roman, a leading ballet dancer, and Willy Golightly, the CEO of FBW's supplier of computer hardware. These are the external, non-executive members expected to bring independence to the board's work. They bring a variety of skills and experiences as well as name recognition to the company and are intended to enhance its public image.

(2) Joe Gucci, the CEO, and Stan Armani, the chief financial officer (CFO). These are internal members working full time as FBW managers.

To be effective as a corporate governance mechanism, the board of FBW needs to be competent and independent enough to hold Joe Gucci and his colleagues accountable. This is difficult with Joe and Stan on the board as they have inside knowledge about FBW. In the case of FBW, the board meets quarterly to:

(1) Review company operating and financial performance.

(2) Consider corporate strategy, planning, and decision making.

(3) Approve financial information for publication.

(4) Consider reports from board committees dealing with board nominations, managerial compensation, and audit.

Joe Gucci chairs a nomination committee that has never met. FBW's audit committee is chaired by Dame Jill Roman and has rarely met since its inception in 2004 as it does its business by telephone conferences twice a year with Stan Armani and DPG the auditor. The compensation contracts of the senior managers of FBW are dealt with by the compensation committee chaired by Willy Golightly whose philosophy is that the more the compensation, the harder the executive manager works.

The restatements in the accounting results for 2004, 2005, and 2006 did not arise because of the actions of the board or any of its committees. Instead, a member of Stan Armani's accounting department, Sarah Collins, a chartered accountant, informed the FRC towards the end of 2006 about her concerns over FBW's misuse of GAAP in producing its financial statements and lack of oversight by the audit committee and the board of directors. As soon as the FRC notified Joe Gucci of its investigation of the financial affairs and statements, Sarah was fired by Stan Armani. She is currently suing the company for unfair dismissal.

> **Lesson 1.3 Corporate governance**
> The success of a company based on the principal-agent relationship is dependent on the effectiveness of its corporate governance—particularly the competence and independence of its board of directors and various subcommittees.

CORPORATE FINANCIAL STATEMENTS

Because the shares of FBW trade on the London Stock Exchange, its shareholders are a mixture of large institutional investors (such as the British Universities Pension Fund) and individual investors. As a company with publicly listed shares, FBW is required by legislation, stock exchange regulation, and accounting standards regulation to produce and file regular reports on its financial performance. These reports are addressed to its shareholders and include an annual set of financial statements. The annual statements focus on three aspects of FBW's financial performance—i.e. profitability, cash flow, and financial position.

Profitability

The 2006 statement of profitability describes the total accounting profit earned by FBW during the year. Accounting profit is broadly defined by GAAP as the difference between the company's sales revenues recognized in 2006 and the various costs associated with these revenues. In the UK, the statement of profitability is called either income statement (for listed companies) or profit and loss account (for non-listed companies).

Cash flow

FBW's statement of cash flows for 2006 reconciles the change in the company's cash resources over the year to a combination of specific cash flows i.e. cash flows from the company's trading activities; cash received from new borrowing from the company's bankers; and cash spent on new equipment. In the UK, the statement of cash flows is usually called a cash flow statement.

Financial position

The statement of financial position at the end of 2006 reports FBW's total assets—i.e. recorded resources used in the company's trading activities; total liabilities—i.e. recorded obligations to lenders and bankers who have financed the company's trading activities; and shareholder capital including undistributed profits—i.e. capital of the company owned by its shareholders. In the UK, the statement of financial position is called a balance sheet.

The annual financial report for 2006 issued by the FBW board of directors states that each of these statements has been prepared in accordance with the rules of GAAP. As a listed company in the EU, FBW is subject to GAAP rules mandated by the IASB and its compliance is regulated by the FRC. GAAP standards issued by the IASB deal with the rules of accounting that are expected to be applied to specific financial statement matters such as the recognition and calculation of sales and costs, or the classification of cash flows. If FBW was a non-listed company, GAAP rules would be those of the ASB. These are reasonably consistent in purpose and detail with those of the IASB.

FBW's annual financial report also contains other quantitative and narrative statements designed to support, explain, and expand the main financial statements. Some of these statements are legislated and subject to audit and others are voluntary and disclosed unaudited. For example, there are required subsidiary financial statements explaining gains and losses other than those reported in the income statement, and the overall change in shareholders' funds in the balance sheet. Additional audited statements include descriptions of the various accounting conventions and standards applied in the preparation of the main financial statements. Unaudited statements include the report by the chairman of the company. Statements reviewing company operations and finances, and corporate governance are also part of the corporate financial report of a company such as FBW.

> **Lesson 1.4 Main financial statements**
> The principal components of a corporate financial report comprise several statements including the income statement or profit and loss account, the cash flow statement, and the balance sheet. These statements are mandatory, their content is governed by prescribed rules of accounting, and they are supported by a variety of other explanatory and review statements.

ACCOUNTING NUMBERS

Each of FBW's financial statements comprises a set of accounting numbers calculated by the company's accountants and based on the business transactions recorded in the company's transactions database during 2006. Each transaction contracted by FBW is recorded in the database according to a centuries-old procedure called double-entry bookkeeping. The procedure is relatively standard across the world and therefore relatively uncontroversial. The recorded transactions are suitably collated within the database according to type, and then subjected to the accounting rules specified in GAAP standards. These rules transform the bookkeeping numbers into accounting numbers that describe FBW's profits, cash flows, and financial position. Accounting numbers are therefore generated in the following sequence:

(1) Business contracts give rise to individual transactions with monetary amounts.

(2) These monetary amounts are recorded according to transaction type in a book-keeping database.

(3) The bookkeeping database is periodically accessed to identify specific transaction totals again according to type.

(4) Transaction totals are related to one another by the rules of GAAP.

(5) GAAP-determined transaction relationships are disclosed in the appropriate financial statements (together with additional explanatory notes when required).

The precise magnitude of individual accounting numbers is therefore a combination of the monetary amounts of contracted business transactions; procedures of double-entry book-keeping; and rules of GAAP standards.

Although bookkeeping procedures and GAAP standards are rule-based, the rules of GAAP allow discretion and therefore an element of subjectivity. It is therefore possible for a given set of contracted business transactions, with indisputable monetary amounts, to result in different possible accounting numbers to describe profits, cash flow, and financial position. This explains why FBW reported one set of accounting numbers for each of the years 2004, 2005, and 2006, and then later reconsidered the application of the GAAP rules and restated the numbers.

> **Lesson 1.5 Accounting numbers**
> The content of the financial statements of a company is numerical. The numbers are calculated by applying a combination of bookkeeping procedures and generally accepted accounting rules to the monetary amounts of business transactions.

CREATIVE ACCOUNTING

The fact that known business transactions of a company such as FBW can generate a range of possible accounting numbers to describe profits, cash flow, and financial position appears counter-intuitive. Numbers are meant to be exact and suggest that a given set of business transactions should generate a unique set of financial results. That this is not the case presents problems for shareholders and other users of financial statements when trying to assess the financial performance of a company such as FBW and its management. Using accounting numbers in this context is similar to measuring height with a piece of elastic.

Lesson 1.6 Accounting calculation

Accounting involves the calculation of monetary numbers but these calculations are not exact, can generate a range of possible financial statements, and depend on arbitrary rules that permit discretion and subjectivity in their application by accountants.

The ability to use accounting procedures to generate a range of accounting numbers based on the same set of economic circumstances also presents a hazard within the principal-agent relationship of shareholder and manager. The manager can use the flexibility of accounting practice to manipulate accounting numbers to overstate profits, cash flow, and financial position to the shareholders. Such manipulation is called creative accounting. The manager creatively describes the company's financial performance to reflect well on his performance and to improve contracted compensation if it is linked to reported profits. This is probably what happened with Joe Gucci and FBW. The whistleblower triggered an investigation that led to restatements of previously reported accounting numbers. This in turn triggered a market reaction to the deception.

Lesson 1.7 Creative accounting

Creative accounting generates accounting numbers intended to deceive shareholders and other users. It damages the credibility of the company and its managers, and can financially damage shareholders and other users who rely on them in their decisions. Creative accounting effectively destroys the trust on which the principal-agent relationship needs to be based and can de-stabilize capital markets.

CORPORATE AUDITING

The case of FBW and its restated accounting numbers raises a question about what the audit firm DPG had done before the publication of the original 2006 financial results. Joe Gucci and his senior management colleagues were in a powerful position with respect to the FBW shareholders. The managers were trusted by the shareholders to operate the company on their behalf and required by law to self-report on their financial performance. This is a situation described by economists as a moral hazard—where senior managers can take advantage of the shareholders' absence by misusing or misappropriating company assets and misreporting to cover their actions. To counter the moral hazard, legislators in countries such as the UK require companies to have their accounting systems and financial statements audited by a competent and independent public accountant such as DPG. The auditor uses generally accepted auditing standards (GAAS) to verify the quality of the accounting numbers recorded, calculated, and reported by Stan Armani and his department on behalf of the FBW board of directors. GAAS in the UK is regulated by the Auditing Practices Board (AUPB) of the FRC.

DPG gave a written opinion on the accounting and reporting quality of the financial statements to FBW's shareholders in terms that state the statements provide a true and fair view of profits, cash flows, and financial position. No definition has ever been given to the term true and fair view, although it is usually taken to mean the statements are of sufficient quality to be used with confidence by shareholders and other users. More particularly, the DPG audit confirmed:

Compliance

The accounting numbers in the financial statements of FBW related to its profits, cash flows, and financial position, and complied with acceptable double-entry bookkeeping procedures, the standardized rules of GAAP (as in the accounting standards of the IASB), and the disclosure requirements of the Companies Acts 1985 and 1989.

Misstatement

Assuming the auditor's suspicions had not been aroused to the contrary, the financial statements did not contain significant accounting misstatement—i.e. deliberate manipulations of accounting numbers intended by senior management to deceive shareholders about the profits, cash flows, and financial position of FBW.

The audit by DPG is therefore a form of deterrent to any possible accounting misstatement by Joe Gucci and his senior management team. It is a means of protecting FBW shareholders from deceptive and misleading reporting. The problem in the case of FBW is that, following the DPG audit, the company revised its reported accounting numbers for 2004, 2005, and 2006. Such restatement after the audit opinion had been given does not give the shareholders confidence that their investment has been effectively protected by DPG. This lack of trust has resulted in the shareholder lawsuit for damages.

> **Lesson 1.8 Corporate audit**
> Because the principal-agent relationship in corporate business can be abused by senior managers, the corporate audit by an independent public accountancy firm is a vital means of protecting shareholders from potentially misleading accounting numbers. The auditor is therefore a significant means of providing confidence and stability in capital markets.

PROBLEMS FOR PUBLIC ACCOUNTANTS

The case of FBW highlights a familiar problem for auditors such as DPG as well as for regulators of corporate business. Auditors are charged by regulators with the responsibility of determining the quality of the accounting numbers supplied to the shareholders of FBW. The quality of these numbers is crucial to these investors when they make decisions about buying, holding, or selling shares in the company. They do not want to be misled or deceived by the audited financial statements. Reliable accounting numbers, of course, do not necessarily mean shareholders make rational or successful decisions—merely that the decisions are made on the basis of financial information of reasonable quality. The problem in this context for public accountants acting as auditors is that the notion of quality in accounting is different from that possible with more precise and objective measurements and tolerances in number-based systems such as engineering or architecture. Accounting numbers can be relatively fuzzy.

The calculation of accounting numbers is not made on the basis of a universally agreed measurement system where measurements depend on a standardized scale (as in height, weight, distance, and volume). Instead, it concerns the application of GAAP rules that, despite agreement and acceptance, permit deviations and exceptions in specific circumstances. Even when properly applied, GAAP rules produce subjective accounting numbers.

Lesson 1.9 Accounting subjectivity
All accounting numbers are subject to a degree of arbitrary judgment and estimate in their calculation. There is no unique set of accounting numbers to describe a given set of business transactions. Both the calculation and the audit of accounting numbers have to cope with this subjectivity. Accounting does not produce precise numbers.

FINANCIAL STATEMENT USERS

Corporate financial reports are addressed to the shareholders of companies such as FBW. They are the group that legislators for more than 150 years believe is at most risk from abuses of the principal-agent relationship. However, particularly in larger companies, and most specifically in listed companies such as FBW, there are other individuals and organizations with a financial stake in the company that may be damaged by inappropriate managerial behaviour and accounting misstatement. These include:

Investors and analysts look for suitable companies in which to buy shares. These individuals and organizations are potential shareholders and do not contribute funds to a company as they are interested in buying and selling "second-hand" shares in it. Their financial information requirements, however, are similar to existing shareholders.

Lenders (including banks) provide long-term funding to the company. They are entitled to interest payments and repayment of the debt is contracted at specific dates. They are often given security for the debt by a right of repayment from specified assets of the company should it not meet its repayment schedule. Lenders require financial information to assess the risks associated with interest and capital payments by the company and the value of the security provided over the debt.

Creditors supply goods and services to the company on credit. They usually contract with the company to be repaid at the end of a short period of time (e.g. 30 days). There may be contracted interest penalties should the company not meet its repayment obligation on time. Creditors require financial information to judge the ability of the company to meet its short-term obligations to them.

Customers enter into contracts with the company either for cash or on credit terms. These individuals and organizations are interested in the long-term well being of the company for reasons such as warranties on goods or services, services paid for in advance of receipt, and continuity of receipt of further goods and services (i.e. customers are often buying goods and services for their business activities).

Employees invest their time and skills in a company and are remunerated for their efforts— different skills requiring different remuneration. Success achieved by the company typically means security of employment and failure can result in the opposite end-result. Employees are also concerned about the company's long-term survival for career purposes and future pension entitlements.

The state in the form of legislators and government departments is interested in a company—e.g. for purposes of levying tax or monitoring corporate regulations. Financial information is used to determine corporate tax liabilities. It can also be used to assess such commercial matters as product pricing and inflation, and monopoly profits.

There are many other potential users of corporate financial reports—e.g. financial journalists writing about individual companies. All, however, have a stake in the company—some directly (e.g. shareholders, lenders, creditors, and employees) and others more indirectly (e.g. government departments, analysts, and journalists). All may or may not make use and rely on the financial information disclosed by companies. All stakeholders may therefore depend on the quality of the accounting numbers reported by corporate senior managers and the audit opinions on these numbers. Because accounting is an arbitrary process, there is a probability that, despite the presence of an auditor such as DPG, accounting numbers may mislead and even deceive shareholders and other stakeholders in a company such as FBW. This is what this book terms the ugly side of accounting and financial reporting. It recognizes that such ugliness exists and that preparers, auditors, and users of corporate financial information need to be able to cope with it.

> **Lesson 1.10 Stakeholders**
> There are many possible users of corporate financial reports because there are many different stakeholders associated with companies. These user stakeholders require financial information of sufficient quality to permit use in decision making with confidence.

GENERAL PURPOSE FINANCIAL INFORMATION

Although there are various stakeholder groups in a company, each with different interests in its business activities (some direct, some indirect; some short-term, some long-term), the corporate financial report is designed, predominantly, to meet the needs of shareholders. This means that other stakeholder groups have to make use of the report as best they can. The information content of the report, however, comprises what accountants have termed general purpose financial information—i.e. information that is capable of satisfying a general range of user needs rather than just the specific needs of shareholders. This is one of the greatest strengths of the corporate financial report (satisfying many needs). It is also a major weakness in the sense that the report has become a package of statements that may not completely satisfy the needs of any specific stakeholder group (including shareholders).

GENERAL LEGAL REQUIREMENTS IN UK

The reporting of corporate financial statements is usually provided for by legislation or state regulation. In the UK, the primary mandate comes from the Companies Act 1985. Specific provisions vary from time to time. However, the following are the main general requirements. It should be noted that, as this is a text for non-accounting specialists, detailed citations to specific provisions of legislation and regulation of companies are not given. Only the broad terms of these matters are explained for readers as a background to their understanding of corporate financial reporting. They are repeated later where relevant in the context of specific financial statements and their audit.

Public or private

As previously stated, companies are classified as public companies (i.e. their regulations permit the acquisition of their shares by members of the public) or private companies (i.e. companies other than public entities). Public companies are denoted as such with the prefix "plc" (e.g. Public Company plc). Other companies use the prefix "Ltd" (e.g. Private Company Ltd).

Financial information

The board of directors of a company must provide its shareholders annually with a profit and loss account or income statement and balance sheet. A cash flow statement is also required under regulations of the IASB for a listed company.

Audit report

The reported financial statements must be accompanied by a relevant auditor's report and a report of the board of directors.

Accounting period

The annual period attributable to the reported financial statements is mandated as 31 March unless the company has notified a different year-end to the Registrar of Companies.

Registrar of Companies

Each annual package of financial statements and reports must be delivered to the Registrar of Companies. Private companies, however, can deliver modified or summary financial statements. Filed financial statements are available for access by members of the public.

Report deadline

Annual financial statements and reports must be provided to shareholders within ten months of the year-end for private companies and seven months for public companies.

Exemptions

As indicated above, defined small and medium-sized private companies are exempt from reporting fully to the Registrar of Companies and, instead, deliver a summary financial statement—unless they are banks or insurance companies.

Disclosure

The form and content of the required financial statements must comply with the disclosure provisions specified by legislation. There are also other disclosure requirements mandated in the accounting standards of the ASB for non-listed companies and the IASB for listed companies.

True and fair view

The required financial statements and their content should provide a true and fair view of the profitability and financial position of the reporting company. As previously mentioned, there is no statutory definition of a true and fair view and this quality is determined by the specific circumstances of each reporting company. For listed companies, EU regulations require their financial statements to be fairly presented. Again, there is no statutory definition of fair presentation.

Report format

Specific legislative provisions cover the choice of financial statement format (typically either reporting the main accounting numbers in a single vertical column or in several adjacent horizontal columns), the minimum disclosed content of statements, and certain general principles of accounting. It should be noted that the financial statements in this text follow a vertical format throughout as this is the common form in practice.

Group statements

The reporting company must report consolidated or group financial statements (subject to the same provisions as for a single company) when it controls other companies. Control in this respect is defined in terms either of voting shares (more than 50% is held) or the board of directors (i.e. control can be exercised by board membership).

Audit

The audit of reported financial statements is governed by various legislative provisions. These relate to the qualifications, appointment, removal, duties, and rights of the auditor.

In summary, the above provisions reveal a financial reporting system that, as compensation for limited liability for obligations, the public receives protection through public access to financial information. The amount of information available in this way depends on the extent to which the public is involved in the ownership of a company and its corporate structure in terms of entities controlled by it. In all cases, the public is given protection through a minimum requirement for disclosure of specific information and a professional and independent audit of the financial statements and the underlying accounting process. Corporate financial reporting is therefore an important part of a wider process of accountability and governance that is explained in more detail in Chapter 2.

LEARNING OBJECTIVES

Please review the learning objectives at the beginning of this chapter and ensure they have been achieved before proceeding to Chapter 2 on corporate governance and its relationship to corporate financial reporting.

Exercise 1   FBW and Enron

In order to reinforce the learning lessons of this chapter, please read the following summary of the case of the American company Enron in 2001. Compare and contrast it to the case of FBW in this chapter and prepare notes of similarities and dissimilarities. Although it is a US corporate situation, Enron captures universal problems for accountants and auditors. Its impact was global.

In late 2001, Enron, one of the largest companies in the US, announced a third-quarter loss of more than $600m and a $1b write down of assets connected to partnerships controlled by the company's CFO, Andrew Fastow. An investigation by the Securities & Exchange Commission (SEC) was announced into possible conflicts of interest resulting from these partnerships. The company disclosed a downwards restatement of its published earnings from 1997 to 2001 inclusive of $587m. An $8b merger with another large company Dynegy was called off and Enron entered bankruptcy protection. A criminal investigation started and Enron's auditors, Arthur Andersen (AA), and its engagement partner, David Duncan, were found guilty of obstruction of justice. AA admitted shredding audit working papers relating to Enron. AA liquidated in 2003, following a rapid loss of other clients. Enron is a global energy trading company, formed in Houston in 1985 by the merger of two energy suppliers. AA was its auditor but not the auditor of the partnerships associated with Enron. Enron began trading in energy units in 1994 following 1992 legislation that allowed the company access to the wholesale energy market and the 1993 removal of oversight of energy commodity trading. In 1994, Enron was exempted by the SEC from federal energy regulation. Three years later, it formed Energy Services to sell energy contracts in a deregulated market started in Texas in 1999 by then Governor George W Bush. Enron's chairman and CEO from 1986 was Kenneth Lay, a friend of Governor Bush and a substantial contributor to the Republican Party. Its chief operating officer (COO) was Jeffrey Skilling from 2001. In the same year, AA partners discussed dropping Enron as an audit client. The company's vice president (VP), Thomas White, had become Secretary of the Army. Enron's energy contracts included many with the Army. In 2001, Lay and Skilling sold Enron shares for more than $30m. Shortly after the Enron collapse in 2001, Skilling resigned and Lay replaced him as COO. Enron VP, Sharon Watkins, internally recorded her concerns about accounting irregularities relating to loans from banks flowing through the partnerships to Enron which had been wrongly treated either as share capital or cash flow from trading operations. Lay and Skilling continued to sell Enron shares. Lay resigned in 2002 and the New York Stock Exchange removed Enron's shares from the board at a price of 67 cents (compared to a 2001 high of $83) and an estimated $60b capitalization. Watkins testified to the House Energy & Commerce Committee. Her evidence suggested Lay did not understand Enron's trading and accounting practices and that Skilling and Fastow managed in an intimidating style. Jeffrey McMahon replaced Lay but resigned after a few months. Also in 2002, a class action lawsuit started on behalf of Enron shareholders between 1998 and 2001 because of false reporting and insider trading. Lay and other defendants appear to have sold Enron shares worth more than $1b. To date, there have been a number of court decisions and settlements. AA settled for damages of $40m. Bankers J P Morgan Chase and Citigroup settled with various bodies for more than $580m in response to accusations of assisting Enron to account for orally agreed loans as cash flows from operating activities or share capital. Enron's Treasurer, Ben Glisan, has been found guilty of fraud and fined for manipulating the company's earnings. Chief accountant, Richard A Causey, has been indicted on five counts of fraud. Andrew Fastow has been charged with 78 counts of fraud, as have nine other executives. Causey and Fastow entered into plea bargains—Fastow will serve ten years in prison. Three UK bankers from Greenwich Nat West Bank are facing charges of fraud. Lay and Skilling have exercised their Fifth Amendment rights to remain silent during Congressional hearings on the scandal. Both were found guilty of multiple charges of fraud and related offences following a trial in 2006. Available documents suggest that public relations consultants were used by accused executives to lay the blame for the manipulated profits with others. Documents also suggest the company was deliberately manipulating the energy market, particularly in California.

Exercise 2   Limited liability companies

Explain in general terms the nature and purpose of limited liability companies. More specifically, explain the major advantages and disadvantages of such entities. Students should also discuss with their instructor other situations in modern life in which a privileged position is granted and mechanisms are in place to ensure undue advantage is not taken of that privileged position.

Exercise 3   Corporate managers and governors

Compare and contrast corporate management executives and directors in terms of the nature and purpose of their roles. Given corporate managers are responsible for company operations, why is it necessary to have corporate directors? Students should also discuss with their instructor whether the private-public company distinction is reasonable in practice.

Exercise 4   Accounting numbers

What are the advantages and disadvantages of representing corporate activities in the form of accounting numbers? Students can discuss with their instructor the problems of compressing a considerable volume of business activity into a relatively few accounting numbers.

Exercise 5   Shareholders and stakeholders

Explain and contrast shareholders and stakeholders in corporate activity and explain why such a distinction is important to the task of reporting financial statements. Students should discuss with their instructor the varying risks taken by individuals and organizations with respect to a company and whether each is worthy of equal protection.

Exercise 6   Auditors

Explain in general terms the nature and purpose of the auditor in corporate activity. Students can also discuss with their instructor other situations in modern life in which a verification process is necessary to provide protection.

ADDITIONAL READING

For a fuller review of the case of Enron in the context of corporate governance, read J Solomon and A Solomon (2004), *Corporate Governance and Accountability*, John Wiley & Sons Ltd, Chichester, West Sussex, 31–43.

A further example of a large company producing misleading accounting numbers to its shareholders is telecommunications giant WorldCom (now MCI). Details of the MCI case are contained in K E Zekany, L W Braun, and Z T Warder (2004), "Behind Closed Doors at WorldCom: 2001," *Issues in Accounting Education*, 19 (1), 101–17.

There is a special report "Crying Over Spilt Milk" on the Italian fraud in Parmalat ($10b of missing assets) in *Accountancy*, February 2004, 27–36.

Read the following chapters in a 1973 professional text on the objectives of financial statements. The words may be more than 30 years old but the message remains relevant today—i.e. financial statements exist to inform a variety of economic decisions. Study Group on the Objectives of Financial Statements (1973), "Objectives of Financial Statements," *Report of the Study Group on the Objectives of Financial Statements*, American Institute of Certified Public Accountants, New York, 13–20.

A more recent review of corporate financial reporting—from the perspective of attempting to meet the decision-based needs of report users—is found in Special Committee on Financial Reporting (1999), *Improving Business Reporting—A Customer Focus. Meeting the Information Needs of Investors and Creditors*, American Institute of Certified Public Accountants, New York.

R Paterson (2002), "Better Standards After Enron?," *Accountancy*, April, 100; and (2003) "Slipping Standards," *Accountancy*, December, 84–5 argues for improved and simpler accounting standards.

CHAPTER 2

Corporate Governance

Learning Objectives

This chapter reviews the nature and purpose of corporate governance and demonstrates how corporate financial reporting is a significant part of effective governance. By the end of the chapter, you should be able to identify and understand:

- Corporate governance in the context of the needs and rights of shareholders and stakeholders.
- The objectives of corporate governance.
- The evolution of corporate governance from its nineteenth century roots to the present day.
- The main processes of corporate governance.
- Recent regulatory provisions for corporate governance in the UK.
- The place of financial reports in the corporate governance function.

At the end of this chapter, please refer to these learning objectives before moving on to Chapter 3 on the nature and purpose of corporate financial reports.

INTRODUCTION

Chapter 1 introduces the financial report in a context of corporate senior managers acting as agents for shareholder principals in a business structure governed by legislation. The situation is one of potential hazard to shareholders and requires various mechanisms to be in place in order to ensure that the managerial agents perform in ways that are compatible and consistent with the interests of the shareholder principals. These mechanisms are collectively described as corporate governance—a term that is both familiar and typically undefined in the literatures of business management and accounting.

Financial reports are an integral part of corporate governance as they contain a set of audited financial statements to shareholders. These statements comprise accounting numbers describing the financial results of business activity supervised by a team of senior managers and a board of directors. The accounting numbers are prepared using mandatory procedures contained in a regulated process of accounting standards. For this reason, corporate governance needs to be explained in detail in this chapter before dealing in later chapters with specific aspects of individual financial statements, accounting standards, and limitations of accounting numbers.

DEFINING CORPORATE GOVERNANCE

Because it is a familiar and usually undefined term, it is unsurprising that corporate governance appears to have as many meanings as it has users. In an everyday sense, the verb to govern is typically defined as ruling by authority. It is commonly associated with the activities of the state (e.g. national or federal government). In the corporate sense, however, corporate governance seems to be a term used almost universally in a less stringent sense of directing, regulating, or controlling. With this in mind, it is therefore relevant to ask:

- What corporate activities are directed, regulated, or controlled?
- Why is directing, regulating, or controlling corporate activities necessary?
- How is directing, regulating, or controlling corporate activities conducted?

These questions are answered in this chapter. But before proceeding to answers, however, it is helpful to have a clear definition of corporate governance. The definition offered is a broad one that attempts to reflect the modern company as an organization managed on behalf of a variety of stakeholders including its shareholders—i.e. a company such as FBW or Enron in Chapter 1. The reason for taking this broad approach is that it is consistent with a cultural awareness in the UK in recent times that protecting only the narrow principal-agent relationship in corporate activity ignores other vital contributions of groups in society. Companies are dependent on a complex inter-relationship of vested interests and not just on one particular group of suppliers of funding or resources such as shareholders. The success or failure of a company depends on how well these various interests combine in what economists describe as a nexus or bonding of legal contracts. For this reason, corporate governance is defined in this text as the formal mechanisms of direction, supervision, and control put in place within a company in order to monitor the decisions and actions of its senior managers and ensure these are compatible and consistent with the specific interest of shareholders and the various other interests of stakeholders who contribute to the operations of the company.

ACCOUNTABILITY OR STEWARDSHIP

The above definition of corporate governance indicates that formal mechanisms of direction, supervision, and control are intended to hold senior managers accountable to shareholders and other stakeholders. Accountability in this sense means that these managers are expected to provide a regular reckoning or account of their decisions and actions. In other words, having been given responsibility by its shareholders for managing the company, senior managers are held responsible for that management. This means that, within a company, there are various connected lines of responsibility, from employees and staff to junior managers to senior managers to the board of directors to the shareholders and, more indirectly, to other stakeholders.

Accountability is not a new idea. It is a modern equivalent of the centuries-old notion of stewardship. The practice of absentee owners delegating managerial duties to an agent is as old as the history of property ownership. For example, the owners of medieval estates or manors employed stewards to look after their land, buildings, animals, and crops in their absence (e.g. when on military service for the king). On return, they required a formal accounting of the steward's management. These accounts were given either orally or in writing and were the forerunners of modern financial reports and audits.

LEGISLATIVE DEVELOPMENTS IN CORPORATE GOVERNANCE

The principle-agent relationship is well-established historically in economic activity. Its modern form of companies, shareholders, and managerial executives is a natural extension resulting from the capitalist system generally and capital markets particularly. From the European Renaissance onwards, a combination of invention, adventure, and desire for profit led to exploration, colonisation, and international trade. These factors generated short-term venture partnerships that eventually transformed to became long-term business organizations requiring permanent funding. In the UK, companies such as the East India Company in 1600 and the Hudson Bay Company in 1670 were formed by Act of Parliament or royal charter as international trading monopolies. From these early corporate organizations came the practice of buying and selling shares without having to liquidate the company, the establishment of capital markets and stock exchanges to facilitate these activities, and boards of directors to govern corporate activities.

However, the moral hazard of the principal-agent relationship endured into the corporate era. Frauds such as the South Sea Company led to government legislation such as the Bubble Act of 1720 to regulate or govern corporate activity. Gradually over several centuries, a complex structure of corporate governance regulation was formed with one consistent objective—to hold senior corporate managers accountable to shareholders through the board of directors. The following is a brief UK timeline containing many of the predecessors of contemporary corporate governance, particularly as it relates to financial reporting and auditing:

Companies Act 1844

The Companies Act 1844 permitted companies to be incorporated but with unlimited liability only. Shareholders were responsible for meeting all debts of the company if it liquidated. The Act also required boards of directors to provide shareholders with annual audited balance sheets. However, the audit was typically conducted by a shareholder who was not an accountant and therefore had limited value.

Companies Act 1856

The Companies Act 1856 introduced limited liability for shareholders—i.e. they could only be asked to contribute to the liabilities of the company to the extent they had contracted to pay for its shares. The Act also removed the 1844 reporting requirements on the grounds that such matters were for the discretion of boards of directors. This led to numerous court cases in which senior managers and boards were accused of defrauding shareholders and reporting misleading financial statements (e.g. in railway and banking companies).

Companies Act 1900

Compulsory audits were re-introduced by the Companies Act 1900 but there was no requirement for the auditor to be suitably qualified. The auditor was appointed by the shareholders and expected to give them a written opinion on the truth and correctness of the balance sheet. This term, and subsequent versions, was undefined and created problems of interpretation.

Companies Act 1929

The Companies Act 1929 introduced the requirement for companies to report a profit and loss account in addition to a balance sheet. Boards of directors had previously claimed that the disclosure of a company's profit would benefit competitors. This was the start of expanding the supply of financial information into the complex package of disclosure that is typical today.

Companies Act 1948

The Companies Act 1948 required all companies to be audited by a professionally qualified accountant. The Act also significantly expanded the amount of disclosure in financial statements. This included the financial statements of groups of companies—i.e. where an individual company had control of other companies, the financial results of all companies were reported as if they were one entity. The auditor was required to give a written opinion on the quality of the financial statements in the (undefined) terms of truth and fairness. This form of opinion persisted to very recent times—not only in the UK but also in the EU and many Commonwealth countries. The current EU equivalent and undefined term is fair presentation.

Companies Act 1981

The Companies Act 1981 standardized the format of corporate financial statements as required under EU legislation. There were less onerous disclosure requirements for defined small and medium-sized companies. For the first time in the UK, the 1981 Act legislated for certain general accounting practices. The report of the board of directors was required to be audited for the first time, and to contain comment on the future development of the company.

Companies Act 1985

The present governing Companies Act 1985 is a consolidation of several pieces of corporate legislation since 1948 and has been amended by the Companies Act 1989. It is supported by the accounting standards of the ASB that apply to non-listed companies. From 2005, for listed companies, EU countries such as the UK are required to follow the accounting standards of the IASB and to word audit opinions in terms of an undefined fair presentation. In the UK, despite this EU quality mandate, the FRC expects all corporate financial statements to provide the legislated true and fair view of profitability, cash flows, and financial position.

These brief historical notes illustrate how senior managers in companies have increasingly become more accountable to shareholders via the board of directors and through the publication by the board of financial statements, the disclosure of accounting information, and the audit of this information. The general trend has been the disclosure of more detailed and extensive financial information about the performance of the company and its management, and for professional audits of this information.

Lesson 2.1 Corporate legislation

Corporate governance measures in the form of boards of directors, financial reporting, and auditing have been consistently legislated by Acts of Parliament in the UK.

Lesson 2.2 Government response

Corporate financial reporting and auditing provisions in Acts of Parliament have typically been government responses to corporate scandal involving fraudulent activity. In order to protect the public interest in a capitalist economy, government has from time to time felt the need to interfere in capital markets.

Lesson 2.3 Audit

Audited accounting information in financial statements has been a principal tool of corporate governance for more than 160 years.

Lesson 2.4 Report quality

The quality of the accounting information in corporate financial statements has been reported by the auditor consistently in undefined terms mandated by law—e.g. truth and correctness and truth and fairness.

Lesson 2.5 Audit opinion

The mandatory requirement for a professionally qualified accountant to report an opinion on the quality of the financial statements reported by senior managers to shareholders has a relatively short legislative history in the UK since 1948.

NON-ACCOUNTING REGULATIONS IN CORPORATE GOVERNANCE

As previously stated, the governance of an individual company in the UK is specified by the memorandum and articles of association registered on its formation. These are the basic rules of engagement that a board of directors must follow. They will vary from company to company in their detail, but the following are the general areas specified by company legislation.

Memorandum of association

This is the more general of the two sets of rules and deals with matters such as the name of the company, where its registered office or "home address" is, whether or not it has limited liability (some companies can have unlimited liability or liability limited to a guaranteed amount), and its trading objectives specifying the type of business it is in.

Articles of association

These are more detailed and specific rules of governance. They include the rights of shareholders concerning voting and repayments on liquidation; the transferability of shares (particularly relevant in a private company); the powers and duties of the board of directors (central to the corporate governance of the company); the requirement to report financial statements and have them audited; the rights of shareholders to dividends (there are different classes of shareholder with different rights to dividends and votes at meetings); and the requirements to call regular and extra-ordinary meetings of shareholders.

ACCOUNTING REGULATIONS IN CORPORATE GOVERNANCE

Corporate governance in the UK does not depend entirely on legislation from government. There is also a regulatory system dealing with the accounting practices used in the production of corporate financial statements. In most Western countries like the UK, legislators prefer to leave accounting matters to public accountants and their institutions. Whereas Companies Acts contain detailed provisions relating to the type of accounting information to be disclosed to shareholders, they do not usually prescribe all the specific accounting practices to be adopted in preparing such information. As a consequence, the public accountancy profession and its institutions have gradually developed a system of accounting standards that mandate particular ways in which accounting numbers are to be calculated. The evolution of this process has been as follows:

Laissez faire

From mid nineteenth century to mid twentieth century, corporate accounting practices evolved in a laissez faire environment in which the professional accountancy bodies preferred not to provide guidance or prescription. Practices developed through the experiences of individual accountants and the lessons of various court cases that challenged the validity of practices used in specific circumstances. This was a muddled period because it meant that lawyers untrained in accounting were attempting to formulate what was acceptable accounting practice.

Guidance

From 1942 to 1970, British public accountants were guided in corporate accounting practice by a series of *Recommendations on Accounting Principles* by the largest professional body, the Institute of Chartered Accountants in England and Wales (ICAEW). These recommendations were voluntary but undoubtedly brought some uniformity and greater appropriateness to accounting practice.

Mandate

In 1970, as a result of several corporate accounting scandals, the ICAEW formed the Accounting Standards Steering Committee (ASSC) and began to publish *Statements of Standard Accounting Practice* (SSAP) on particular problem areas of corporate accounting practice. A year later, other major bodies joined the ASSC and introduced a unified and national approach to voluntary guidance on accounting practice.

GAAP

By 1972, SSAPs were expected to be followed by all members of the participating bodies in the ASSC. This brought compulsion or mandate to accounting standards applied to corporate financial statements in the UK. These standards increasingly were considered as GAAP, although it is difficult to determine what constitutes general acceptance when standards are largely prepared by public accountants.

Independence

Through a series of developments the ASSC evolved into a quasi-governmental body separate from the institutions of public accountancy. Today, the regulatory system dealing with accounting standards to apply when preparing financial statements is managed by the FRC. This body has an overall supervisory function with respect to the formulation and application of accounting standards. The FRC was formed in 1990 by a provision of the Companies Act 1989 that removed accounting standard setting from the professional accountancy bodies. The main arm of the FRC is the Accounting Standards Board (ASB) that is responsible for prescribing *Financial Reporting Standards* (FRS) that now replace SSAPs. FRSs are required to be followed by all professional accountants in the UK and deal with the main areas of corporate accounting practice. These standards therefore affect all UK non-listed companies. It is much easier to acknowledge the idea of general acceptance in GAAP through these arrangements as non-accountants are involved in the accounting standards process. As previously mentioned, as from 2005, UK listed companies must follow the International Financial Reporting Standards (IFRS) of the IASB. The FRC is responsible for monitoring this in the same way as for FRSs. It is likely, however, that at some time in the near future all UK companies will need to comply with IFRS and that the FRC and ASB effectively use the accounting standards of the IASB.

Monitoring

Another arm of the FRC is its Financial Reporting Review Panel (FRRP) that is responsible for investigating specific instances of companies deviating from prescribed accounting standards. The FRRP has the power to take companies to court if they refuse to restate their financial statements when there have been unacceptable deviations from required standards.

Lesson 2.6 Reporting regulation
In the UK, the financial reporting dimension of corporate governance is regulated in two ways. The first form is company legislation passed by Parliament and the second form is an

independent regulator of accounting standards. The public accountancy profession contributes to both forms—most specifically in its membership and staffing of the FRC and its constituent bodies. There is involvement of non-accountants such as preparers and users in the accounting standards process. UK listed companies require to adhere to international accounting standards.

AUDITING AND CORPORATE GOVERNANCE

Undoubtedly one of the most important elements of modern corporate governance is the external audit function. It is conducted in the UK and other countries by firms of professionally-qualified accountants that adhere to a set of GAAS prescribed by public accountancy bodies. The auditor has a role of verifying the quality of the accounting numbers reported by corporate management and the board of directors in the financial statements to shareholders. The intention is to protect shareholders directly, and other stakeholders indirectly, from sub-standard accounting by senior managers. Such protection is aimed at giving shareholders and others confidence to use the financial statements in their various decisions. In turn, this confidence is expected to feed into capital markets and assist in their efficient operation and stability.

The most significant characteristic of the external corporate audit is that the auditor (i.e. the firm's partners and staff) is independent of the client. An independent auditor is expected to be capable of giving an objective opinion on the quality of the financial statements being verified. Objectivity in the audit enhances the credibility and therefore the value of the audit. Auditor independence is typically associated with the following conditions:

Independence of mind

The auditor must have the ability to be independent in mind as well as in appearance—i.e. the auditor must be independent in his mental reasoning and be seen to be independent. It is therefore important that the auditor is trained to think objectively but is also free of relationships and associations that give the impression of lack of objectivity.

Conflicting relationships

The auditor must therefore be free from conflicting relationships and associations with the client company—i.e. he cannot be a manager or shareholder, or be related to a manager or shareholder.

Conflicting contracts

The auditor must not have conflicting contracts with the company. This is not a universally held condition. For example, in the US, there is a legislative provision that the auditor cannot audit and provide non-audit services (e.g. management consultancy). The philosophy behind this prescription is that an auditor cannot remain objective when auditing the consequences of prior or parallel consultancy services (e.g. preparation of accounting information or internal audit). Such a legislative provision does not exist in the UK.

Competence

The auditor must have sufficient competence not to be dependent on management for answers to significant audit questions—i.e. the auditor must be able to ask the right questions and interpret the managerial responses correctly.

> **Lesson 2.7 Auditor independence**
> The value of the corporate audit is directly related to the independence of the auditor. The less independence the auditor has, the less value can be associated with the audit.

The objective of the corporate audit is to provide an expert opinion on the quality of reported financial statements. According to current professional thinking, it is not aimed at detecting fraudulent accounting misstatement (i.e. the deliberate misreporting of accounting numbers in order to misstate the performance of the company or cover up missing assets). However, current auditing standards require the auditor to assess the risk of misstatement and plan the audit accordingly—i.e. the greater the risk of accounting misstatement, the greater the need to put audit procedures in place to detect it.

> **Lesson 2.8 Fraud detection**
> The corporate audit is not intended by public accountants to be a fraud detection audit. This can lead to different expectations of the audit by auditors and its beneficiaries. Such differences are called expectations gaps.

The main procedures of the corporate audit are as follows:

Risk assessment

Assessing risks associated with the potential corporate client and then signing the audit contract if they are acceptable. There are situations where the risk of accounting misstatement is so high that auditor will not wish to be associated with a company. For example, in the case of Enron, its auditor AA seriously considered terminating the audit contract prior to the public exposure of the fraud.

Familiarity

Getting to know the client company and its business operations, management, and staff. It is also necessary to be familiar with the client's internal control system and accounting records system. Such familiarity is essential to making sense of the accounting numbers that describe corporate performance and position.

Tests

Testing the client company's internal controls and accounting record procedures. These tests confirm whether the systems and procedures are working as planned.

Verification

Verifying the assets and liabilities of the client company according to GAAS. This includes tests to confirm the existence of assets and liabilities as well as the appropriateness of the accounting numbers that describe them.

Consistency with GAAP

Verifying that the processing of recorded accounting numbers is consistent with GAAP and resolving any differences with client senior managers. This is the most subjective and contentious part of the audit and, given, the inherent flexibility of GAAP, the most difficult to resolve.

Opinion

Coming to an opinion on the quality of the financial statements and reporting this to the shareholders following a discussion of the audit and its findings with the audit committee. It must be remembered that the audit report is an expert opinion and not a certificate or guarantee.

> **Lesson 2.9 Audit process**
> The corporate audit comprises several stages involving examinations, assessments, and reports. Each of these stages involves the use of relevant expertise and professional judgment in evaluating audit evidence.

OTHER CORPORATE GOVERNANCE DEVELOPMENTS

There have been several developments in corporate governance in the UK since 1992. Each has had governmental support but not resulted in corporate legislation. Unlike the corporate governance matters of financial reporting and auditing, these developments have been introduced as voluntary or recommended practices. The evidence, however, is that most large companies have adopted them.

As a result of two substantial financial scandals in 1991, the FRC, the London Stock Exchange, and the accountancy profession formed the Cadbury Committee in 1991 to review financial reporting and accountability in the context of corporate governance. The first scandal involved a massive fraud at the Bank of Credit and Commerce International (BCCI) that had global effects and implications for corporate governance and remains on-going in the form of court cases. The second scandal was Maxwell Communications Corporation (MCC) involving not only accounting misstatement but also the fraudulent misappropriation of corporate assets (including employee pension funds). The following are brief descriptions of both BCCI and MCC.

BCCI

In 1991, BCCI closed with the discovery of a fraud involving billions of dollars of lost or fictitious assets. It is difficult to determine the exact size of the fraud. But it is estimated there were $13b of missing assets and original claims of creditors totalled $16b. By 2003, three-quarters of these claims were settled for nearly $6b. In 1998, the auditor, Price Water-house & Company (PWC) paid £117m in an out-of-court settlement and without admitting liability. The most comprehensive account of the fraud is in a US Senate's report in 1992. BCCI was founded in 1973, based in Luxembourg, and had close financial links with the Sheikh of Abu Dhabi. It was banker for the United Arab Emirates. BCCI activities from 1973 until 1991 became global and its operations included Europe, Africa, Asia, and the Americas. BCCI entered the US banking system by acquiring banks there and became banker for governmental funds of many nations, largely through bribery of politicians and key officials. Its main activities were money laundering, drug and arms dealing and traf-ficking, fraud, extortion, and bribery. The Bank of England was taken to court because it was alleged it was slow to investigate BCCI when warned to do so. The accounting fraud involved fictitious lending and other transactions, bad loans and investments, stolen deposits and investments, and unrecorded deposits. The US Senate report accused PWC of failing to protect BCCI depositors and creditors when it had been aware of its accounting practices.

MCC

Robert Maxwell entered publishing in 1946 and purchased Pergamon Press (PP) in 1951. He became a Member of Parliament in 1964. In 1969, he attempted to sell PP using false financial information. A report from Department of Trade & Industry (DTI) inspectors in 1973 stated that Maxwell was not to be relied on to exercise proper stewardship of a public company. A year later, he re-entered publishing and acquired the British Printing Corporation (BPC) (named MCC) in 1986. Two years earlier, he purchased the Mirror Group Newspapers (MGN) for £93m. He unsuccessfully attempted to dominate the tabloid press with this investment and went public with MGN in 1991, the year in which the financial collapse of MCC occurred. Maxwell died in the same year and his companies filed for bankruptcy in 1992. Three years later, his two sons were tried for fraud and a DTI report was published in which it was stated that the primary responsibility for the fraud lay with Robert Maxwell. The fraud involved the misappropriation of funds and false financial reporting, achieved through a complex private ownership of more than 400 Maxwell companies. MGN was part of this empire and Maxwell used its cash flow to fund his other businesses. This cash included the MGN pension funds. In effect, all parts of MCC, including its pension funds, were treated by Maxwell as one entity. By 1991, missing pension fund assets totalled £458m. The senior audit partner on the MCC engagement was censored and fined for admission of 59 errors of professional judgment.

The Cadbury Committee reported in 1992 and produced a *Code of Best Practice* that was adopted by most public companies. The Code has several recommendations currently in place:

Separations

There should be separation of the CEO from the chair of the board of directors in order to improve the independence of the board. Robert Maxwell, for example, was CEO and chair-man of the MCC board. In such a position, and with a dominant personality, he controlled the board, thus preventing the senior managers of MCC from being held accountable by the board and the shareholders.

Independence

There should be greater independence for the board of directors by including non-executive (outside) directors with no relationships to the company that would interfere with their judgment as directors. Companies for many years have claimed an independent element on their boards because the latter included outside directors. However, if these directors were also senior managers of companies doing business with the company concerned, at the very least the appearance of independence and objectivity was damaged.

Nominations

New board appointments should be recommended to the board by a nominations committee comprised mainly of non-executive directors—thus preventing senior managers influencing such appointments. From the point of view of maintaining shareholder confidence in the board of directors, it is essential that there is a mechanism to prevent senior managers influencing the composition of the board membership.

Compensation

The compensation of senior managers who are directors should be recommended by a remuneration or compensation committee comprised mainly of non-executive directors. This provision attempts to prevent senior managers negotiating excessive compensation packages. For many years, there has been considerable concern about the contractual terms associated with the compensation of senior managers—particularly profit-related bonuses and share options, and termination payments when contracts are ended (often when the performance of the company has been poor).

Disclosure

The compensation of the board of directors should be fully disclosed in the financial statements to the shareholders. Companies have previously not disclosed this compensation to shareholders.

Audit committee

An audit committee should review the financial statements and related audit prior to publication of the statements and audit report to the shareholders. This committee should comprise mainly non-executive directors and represents the formal placement of the financial reporting and auditing functions in the corporate governance structure.

Internal control

The board of directors should report in their annual financial report on the effectiveness of the internal control system. Again, this strengthens the formal inclusion of the financial report into corporate governance. The reliability of the bookkeeping and accounting involved in producing financial statements depends greatly on the effectiveness of internal controls.

Going concern

The board of directors should report in the financial statements on whether it regards the company as a going concern. This is a vital piece of information for shareholders and stakeholders—the term states the company's ability to meet its contracted obligations in the foreseeable future (i.e. whether or not it has the funding necessary to pay its bills).

The Cadbury Report was followed by a succession of other reviews of corporate governance. These dealt with the detail of various Cadbury recommendations. For example, the Rutteman Committee in 1994 reported on the internal control recommendation. A year later, the Greenbury Committee reported on directors' compensation. The Hampel Committee in 1998 dealt with the implementation of Cadbury and Greenbury, and resulted in the publication of the *Combined Code* in the same year. In 1999, the Turnbull Committee advised on internal control matters. The effectiveness of non-executive directors was examined by the Higgs Committee in 2003 and the Smith Committee reviewed audit committees, also in 2003. The current *Combined Code on Corporate Governance* incorporated most of the advice of these various committees in 2003. The recommendations are similar in nature to those of Cadbury above, but with specific details from each of the later reviews. For example:

Non-executive directors

The board of directors should contain a minimum of three non-executive directors comprising no less than one-third of the board. The majority of non-executive directors should be independent.

Nominations committee

The nominations committee should comprise a majority of non-executive directors and its membership should be disclosed in the annual financial report.

Remuneration committee

The remuneration committee should comprise independent non-executive directors.

Audit committee

The audit committee should have at least three non-executive directors and the majority of these should be independent. Again, the entire audit committee membership should be disclosed in the annual financial report.

Lesson 2.10 Board of directors

UK corporate governance focuses on the board of directors as the main mechanism, with specific sub-functions relating to board nominations, managerial compensation, and audit and reporting.

Lesson 2.11 Board independence

The guiding principle underlying the board of directors and its subcommittees is the need for independence in order to bring objectivity to the tasks of directing, regulating, and controlling the executive functions of company management—i.e. for the purpose of making senior managers accountable to owners.

Lesson 2.12 *Combined Code*

The *Combined Code* is not mandatory on companies, although most public companies follow its recommendations. Given the mandatory nature of corporate legislation, this is inconsistent.

AUDIT COMMITTEES

One of the important elements in a system of corporate governance is the audit committee. This is a subcommittee of the board of directors and it is charged with the responsibility of monitoring the accounting (including internal controls), financial reporting, and auditing systems of the company on behalf of the board. It reports on these matters to the board—particularly prior to the release of financial information to shareholders and the wider public. The audit committee is not a new idea. It existed in nineteenth-century companies in the UK and US and typically comprised a small group of shareholders given the task of reviewing their company's balance sheet on behalf of all shareholders. This was a form of rudimentary audit before the introduction of professional audit—although some audit committees employed public accountants to assist them. The modern audit committee, however, is a corporate initiative of the 1970s and its existence has expanded gradually to the present day. The composition and remits of audit committees has been relatively stable over the years and consistent with the current *Combined Code* provisions.

(1) The audit committee typically comprises non-executive directors. The present requirements are focused on independent members.

(2) The work of the audit committee is usually concerned with financial statements and audit. The Code's provisions are specific about this—e.g. monitoring the quality of financial statements; reviewing the effectiveness of internal controls and internal audit; recommending the appointment, remuneration, and terms of engagement of the auditor; and recommending non-audit services offered by the auditor.

A major problem for audit committees not addressed in the *Combined Code* is the competence of committee members. It is important that they are knowledgeable about the business of the company and that they can conduct the work of the committee with objectivity (i.e. because they are free of any relationships or associations with the company that have the potential to erode their independence). However, knowledge and independence in this sense mean little if members of the audit committee are lacking competence (i.e. skills and experience) to deal effectively with the subject matter they are reviewing and reporting. The underlying argument is that, unless audit committee members have sufficient competence, they cannot be truly independent.

Lack of appropriate accounting skills and experience mean that audit committees may not ask appropriate questions of the company's senior managers and auditor about internal controls, internal audit, financial statements, and external audit. In addition, even if committee members do ask the right questions, they may not be able to properly assess the reliability or accuracy of the responses. They may have to rely too much on the explanations of senior managers and the auditor, and therefore lose their independence. It is unnecessary for all audit committee members to have accounting and auditing skills and experience. However, at least one member should have this background in order to guide the committee as a whole in its review of internal controls, financial statements, and audit. Such a position has been recognized in the US and audit committees there are required to have at least one member with what are called financial skills.

> **Lesson 2.13 Audit committee competence**
> The work of the audit committee centres on accounting and auditing matters and it makes sense to ensure that at least one of its members is qualified to examine these matters competently in order to maintain the objectivity of the committee on behalf of the board of directors.

INEFFECTIVE AUDIT COMMITTEES

The previous section looks at the audit committee from the perspective of the ideal committee. In order to understand a less than ideal committee, it is useful to examine one in the context of corporate governance. The example below is the 1989 American case of the MiniScribe Corporation of Longmont in Colorado.

MiniScribe

The MiniScribe Corporation (MC) was formed in 1980 to manufacture cheap hard disks for personal computers. It traded uneventfully until a crisis in 1984 when Quentin T Wiles, chairman of the venture capital firm that financed it, became its CEO. Wiles instituted a reorganization, including the segmenting of MC into 20 divisions. However, the company had no systems of internal control and no internal audit department. Sales, profits and shareholders' capital grew rapidly until 1989 when the company disclosed that its financial statements for 1986 and 1987 should not be relied on and that shareholders' capital of more than $140m was a substantial negative figure. An investigation by the SEC revealed considerable overstatement of MC's profits. The company's CFO attempted to conceal missing unsold inventory from the auditor by a variety of techniques. Sales were inflated or invented and unsold inventory was overstated by including scrap parts as fully operational packages or filling crates with bricks. The external auditor was Coopers & Lybrand (CL) and its files were broken into by MC's senior managers in order to inflate or adjust inventory numbers. The company was quoted on the NASDAQ Security Exchange. It had an audit committee from 1985 but it rarely met, had no accounting or auditing expertise in its membership, and all its members had business relationships with the company. MC filed for bankruptcy in 1990 and liquidated in 1991. Its shareholders and lenders received approximately $550m of damages and CL settled out of court for nearly $50m. Wiles was convicted of securities fraud in 1996 and appealed unsuccessfully in 1999.

US DEVELOPMENTS IN CORPORATE GOVERNANCE

Corporate governance, financial reporting, and auditing are matters of an increasing global nature in recent years. The ability of companies to trade internationally and raise finance in different national capital markets means that an international perspective to corporate governance, and therefore to corporate financial reporting and auditing, is essential. In the US, for example, the following brief timeline is relevant to an understanding of the current situation. It is given in this text as it contains issues and practices relevant to the current UK position.

NYSE/AIA

In 1926, the New York Stock Exchange (NYSE) recognized the need to monitor the quality of the financial reporting of its listed companies. As a result, in 1934, the NYSE and the American Institute of Accountants (AIA) recommended five general accounting practices and a standard audit report. The NYSE mandated an audit for its listed companies from 1933. In 1934, the Securities Exchange Act required all companies quoted on US stock exchanges to file financial statements with the newly-formed SEC. From that time, the SEC has pronounced on accounting and reporting matters but relied largely on the AIA and its successor, the American Institute of Certified Public Accountants (AICPA), to set the actual standards expected.

AIA/AICPA

From 1939, the AIA issued various *Accounting Research Bulletins* recommending accounting practices. Twenty years later, the AICPA formed its Accounting Principles Board (APB) to recommend accounting practices. The pronouncements of the APB were adopted as the authoritative source for accounting by American public accountants and the SEC.

SEC/NYSE

In 1940, the SEC recommended audit committees of outside directors to improve financial reporting. In 1956, the NYSE required each listed company to have at least two outside but not necessarily independent directors on its board. In 1978, the NYSE required audit committees comprised of undefined independent directors.

APB/FASB

The APB was replaced in 1973 by the independent Financial Accounting Standards Board (FASB) and the standards of the FASB were regarded by the SEC as authoritative. This position persists at the present time.

NYSE/NASDAQ

In 1999, the NYSE and the National Association of Securities Dealers (NASDAQ) mandated independent audit committees for their listed companies. They defined independence in terms of the company and previous employment, family relationships, and business associations.

SEC

In 2003, the SEC adopted the NYSE and NASDAQ proposals for a majority of board members to be independent and for independence to be defined in terms of such matters as previous employment, family relationships, and business associations.

The relevance of these American events is that they have also eventually influenced the UK position. For example, the increasing role of the SEC in corporate accounting and auditing matters has been mirrored in the UK by the FRC. It is difficult to envisage this transatlantic influence not continuing in the area of corporate governance.

> **Lesson 2.14 Transatlantic contrasts I**
> Both in the UK and the US, corporate governance provisions have centred on the board of directors and its subcommittees (particularly the audit committee). In the UK, the structure has largely been by recommendation and adopted by most large companies. In contrast in the US, developments have used a variety of regulatory bodies, been quicker than in the UK, relied on mandatory prescription, and sought greater and more explicit independence in boards of directors.

> **Lesson 2.15 Transatlantic contrasts II**
> So far as financial reporting and accounting are concerned, the US approach to corporate governance is similar to the UK—i.e. general legislation requiring reported financial statements, and standards for accounting practice set, initially, by public accountancy bodies on a voluntary basis and, then, by an independent body with mandatory provisions. The main differences between the two countries are timing (the evolution was quicker in the US) and the existence of the SEC in the US. This body supervises the overall governance of companies (unlike the FRC in the UK) and acts as an influential pressure on public accountants to reform their practices).

In 2002, the FASB and the IASB (formed in 1973) agreed to produce compatible accounting standards. The EU (including the UK) then agreed to use IASB standards from 2005. This means that, to all intents and purposes, corporate accounting practice throughout most of the world will comply with one set of accounting standards. In addition, for non-US companies quoted in the US, recent American developments in corporate governance have become relevant. Following the financial scandals and reporting frauds of Enron and WorldCom in 2001, the US federal government passed the Sarbanes-Oxley Act in 2002. The Act's primary objective was to improve the corporate governance of American companies but non-US companies quoted on the NYSE and non-US auditors auditing in the US are also affected. For this reason, it is relevant in this text to explain briefly the Act's main provisions as follows:

PCAOB

The Public Company Accounting Oversight Board (PCAOB) is responsible for registering, inspecting, and disciplining public accountancy firms offering external audit services, including non-US firms auditing American companies. The PCAOB is also responsible for determining standards for auditing and the auditor, although it may adopt existing standards of public accountancy bodies. There is no body in the UK or the EU with such widespread powers.

SEC

The SEC has general oversight over the work of the PCAOB. The implication of this is that the US government has a means of controlling not only corporate financial reporting but also auditing. Again, the powers of the SEC exceed those of comparable bodies such as the FRC in the UK.

GAAP

The SEC is authorized to recognize the accounting standards of established standard setting bodies as GAAP. This ensures that the standards of the FASB in the US and the IASB elsewhere remain the primary sources of what is regarded as good accounting practice. As the accounting standards of the IASB are mandatory on UK listed companies, and could soon affect all British companies, it is clear that GAAP issues as dealt with by the FASB in the US are significant in any study of UK corporate governance and financial reporting.

Audit independence

It is unlawful for public accountancy firms registered with the PCAOB and offering audit services to also offer non-audit services to these corporate clients. The idea behind this provision is to improve the independence of auditors and therefore enhance the quality of corporate governance. This position goes beyond that of the AUPB in the UK.

Auditor rotation

The partner of an SEC-registered public accountancy firm acting as an auditor and in charge of the audit cannot remain in that position for more than five years. Again, the idea is to improve the independence and objectivity of the auditor and the quality of corporate governance. A similar provision has been in operation in the UK since 2003.

Audit committee

Each member of an audit committee must be independent—i.e. not receive payments for services other than as a member of the board of directors, and not be affiliated in any way to the company. In the UK, from 1998, listed companies must have audit committees comprising at least three independent directors.

Responsibility for statements

The CEO and CFO must acknowledge responsibility for the reported financial statements and the underlying accounting practices used in their preparation. Under the Companies Act 1985 in the UK, the board of directors must approve the annual financial statements and acknowledge this with a signature on the balance sheet.

Responsibility for internal control

Senior management must acknowledge in the annual financial report its responsibility for the system of internal control and must also report to the shareholders on the effectiveness of the system. The auditor is required to give an opinion on this report. There is no similar mandatory provision in the UK, although larger companies follow the relevant recommendation in the *Combined Code* of 2003.

These US provisions are similar in many respects to requirements in the UK. But they also contain mandatory matters that are unique to the US—e.g. the prohibition of non-audit services, and acknowledging responsibility for internal control. In particular, however, in both countries there is a clear recognition of the importance of an independent auditor and an effective audit committee in corporate governance.

Lesson 2.16 Government regulation
There is evidence in recent times, particularly in the US after a number of financial scandals, of government becoming more involved in the oversight and control of the corporate audit function. There is a pronounced movement toward more independent auditors and a clearer distinction with respect to corporate governance between the roles of corporate senior management and the auditor.

INTERNAL CONTROL AND INTERNAL AUDIT

Recent American developments in corporate governance contain an aspect of the topic that is vital to its credibility and has been explicitly acknowledged in legislative provisions. This relates to corporate management's responsibility for ensuring the company has an effective system of internal control and for reporting on its effectiveness to the shareholders. For purposes of understanding this section of the text, the meaning of internal control should be taken as those controls put in place in the company by its senior managers in order to improve the integrity and effectiveness of its operations with respect to mistakes (i.e. errors) and falsities (i.e. fraud). Internal control therefore includes all aspects of the company's operations and includes accounting controls as well as other business controls. The idea is to minimize the negative affects of human frailty. Internal controls are therefore an obvious benefit in the overall function of corporate governance—i.e. the better the system of internal control, the less error and fraud, and the greater the effectiveness of corporate governance. The *Combined Code* of 2003 in the UK recommends and the Sarbanes-Oxley Act of 2002 in the US requires boards of directors to, first, accept responsibility for the overall system of internal control and, second, to annually review it and report on it to the shareholders in the annual financial report.

Internal control has been defined in a variety of ways over many years. However, for purposes of this text, the following are given as its main features:

Policies and procedures

A system of internal control comprises all policies and procedures put in place by the board of directors and senior managers to facilitate effective and efficient business operations of the company, safeguard its assets, detect and prevent fraud and error, and assist the keeping of proper accounting records and preparation of financial statements of sufficient quality.

Risk management

At the heart of a system of internal control is the need for the board of directors and senior managers of a company to manage the risks associated with doing business. Risk is associated with uncertainty that actual events will not be as planned or expected. Internal control attempts to reduce uncertainty and therefore minimize risk.

Segregation of duties

A system of internal control is based on an appropriate segregation of staff and managerial responsibilities; competent and reliable personnel; proper authorization, documentation, and backup; control over computer and related procedures; and physical controls to safeguard assets.

Internal checks

A system of internal control should be based on a number of internal checks, in which the work of one employee is automatically and independently checked by the work of another employee.

Audit reliance

A sound system of internal control is of considerable assistance to an external auditor who can rely on it to produce reliable accounting information as well as protect assets. The sounder the system, the greater the reliance of the external auditor on it, the less detailed checking of the accounting process is required by the auditor.

Larger companies extend their system of internal control to include the function of internal auditing—i.e. the employment of internal auditors to verify policies, procedures, and controls within the company. Such verification normally includes the accounting system but invariably has expanded to cover other aspects of the business including operational controls and managerial efficiency. The internal audit department is a key tool in the management of risk. Internal audit staff members are dedicated to observing systems of control at work, assessing whether or not they are operating to plan, and taking corrective action if they are not. Internal auditors are often professionally qualified and trained to act objectively. However, they are employees of the company, subject to objectives determined by senior managers, and typically report to a senior manager such as the CFO. They are not as independent as the external auditor and, in particular instances, may not audit the accounting system and financial statements. External auditors rely on internal audit in situations where the latter covers the accounting system and, increasingly, internal audit has been outsourced to firms of public accountants. This becomes a corporate governance issue when the firm of public accountants also serves as external auditor. At the very least, this dual role compromises the appearance of auditor independence.

> **Lesson 2.17 Internal control**
> Corporate governance is assisted generally by an effective system of internal control. More specifically, it is enhanced by an internal audit function—although the internal auditor may be

constrained by the tasks set by senior managers and the need to report to the latter. External auditors should not undertake the provision of internal audit services for the same company client.

LEARNING OBJECTIVES

Please review the learning objectives at the beginning of this chapter and ensure they have been achieved before proceeding to Chapter 3 on corporate financial reporting objectives and regulations.

Exercise 1   WorldCom

In order to reinforce the learning lessons of this chapter, please read the following summary of the case of the American company WorldCom in 2002. Compare and contrast it to the case of Enron in Chapter 1 and prepare notes of similarities and dissimilarities.

Enron shocked the global financial community with the scale of the accounting misstatement by dominant senior managers in the presence of auditors. However, as the facts of Enron emerged, another company became major news. WorldCom (WCM) was one of the largest US corporations in 2002 when it collapsed with $11b of accounting misstatement. Its communications systems handled one-half of the world's e-mail traffic and it was the second largest US long-distance phone carrier. The company entered bankruptcy protection in 2002 with $41b of debt and was renamed MCI. By 2003, MCI had returned to profitability.

To date, two reports about WCM have been given to the bankruptcy court in the US. Their findings are that the fraud was associated with dominant senior managers, and there were two sets of accounting records, lax internal controls, and poor governance by the board of directors. The accounting problems included inflated sales revenue, treating maintenance costs as capital expenditure, and failure to write off bad debts. The company's auditor was AA which ceased practicing in 2003 following revelations about another corporate client, Enron. CEO Bernie Ebbers was recently found guilty and imprisoned for fraudulent activity. He sold $70b of WCM stock prior to the collapse. CFO Scott Sullivan pled guilty to securities fraud, conspiracy, and reporting false information to the SEC. He and Ebbers ran the company virtually unchecked. The company's controller and directors of general accounting, management reporting, and legal entity accounting pled guilty to fraud charges. The company initially admitted hiding more than $1b of losses by accounting misstatements and restated its financial results for 2001 and the first quarter of 2002. Later disclosures revealed further accounting misstatements in excess of $7b and led to restatement of the 2000 financial results. Most recent disclosures added a further $4b of accounting misstatement. WCM has settled its fraud case with the SEC and been fined.

Although these are US cases, they reveal universal characteristics pertaining to fraudulent situations. In this respect, students can expand the topic by discussing the problem of dominant senior managers in companies and their potential impact on financial reports.

Exercise 2   Corporate governance

Compare and contrast the related terms of corporate governance, stewardship, and account-ability. Students should also discuss with their instructor situations in daily life in which there is a need for governance, accountability, and stewardship.

Exercise 3   Corporate legislation

Within the UK context, explain how legislation has provided a structure for the governance of companies. Students are invited to think of what corporate activity might be like if there was no legislation in place to provide governance mechanisms. Are there sufficient incentives to trigger voluntary governance mechanisms?

Exercise 4   Accounting regulation

Explain how accounting regulators have strengthened legislative requirements for corporate governance. Students should discuss with their instructor other professions that have to deal with the state in the form of legislation and regulation. Are there similarities with accountants?

Exercise 5   Role of auditor

What does the auditor do in the context of corporate governance? More specifically, students should discuss with their instructor the utility of the modern audit as an effective corporate governance mechanism.

Exercise 6   Board of directors

Explain the central role in corporate governance of the board of directors. Students can also discuss with their instructor the need for non-executive directors. Are they truly independent if they are also senior executives in other large companies? Do they have the expertise to carry out their governance function effectively?

Exercise 7   Audit committee

What role does the audit committee play in corporate governance? Students should discuss with their instructor the issue of competence in relation to audit committees. If these bodies are required to review financial reports and audits, should their members be professionally-qualified accountants?

Exercise 8   Internal control

Why is internal control such an important issue in the general area of corporate governance? Students should discuss with their instructor other areas of modern life in which control procedures exist in order to reduce the chance of errors and misbehaviour.

ADDITIONAL READING

For a general introduction to corporate governance, its evolution in the UK, and the role of the board of directors, read J Solomon and A Solomon (2004), *Corporate Governance and Accountability*, John Wiley & Sons Ltd., Chichester, West Sussex, 11–30, 45–64, and 65–87.

For a review of stewardship in the context of corporate financial reporting, read P Rosenfield (1974), "Stewardship," in J J Cramer and G H Sorter (editors), *Objectives of Financial Statements: Volume 2, Selected Papers*, American Institute of Certified Public Accountants, New York, 123–40.

The collapse of the Barings Group in 1995 due to lack of meaningful corporate governance is examined in W P Hogan (1997), "Corporate Governance: Lessons from Barings," *Abacus*, Vol. 33 (1), 26–47. It contains a glossary of terms to assist the reader unfamiliar with banking terminology.

To appreciate changes in the role of the audit committee, read Z Rezaee and L E Farmer (1994), "The Changing Role of the Audit Committee," *Internal Auditing*, Spring, 10–20. This is an American article but it describes activities of audit committees that are now common in many other countries such as the UK.

A general introduction to the nature and role of external auditing is contained in T A Lee (1993), *Corporate Audit Theory*, Chapman & Hall, London, 19–25.

Internal controls in relation to the external auditor are defined and reviewed in B Porter, J Simon, and D Hatherly (2003), *Principles of External Auditing*, John Wiley & Sons Ltd., Chichester, 237–50.

Read about the role of the internal auditor in K H S Pickett (2003), *The Internal Auditing Handbook*, John Wiley & Sons Ltd., Chichester, 237–47.

Another US article reviews more recent developments there in relation to corporate governance mandates in light of scandals such as Enron and WorldCom—A Klein (2003), "Likely Effects of Stock Exchange Governance Proposals and Sarbanes-Oxley on Corporate Boards and Financial Reporting," *Accounting Horizons*, Vol. 17 (4), 343–55.

CHAPTER 3

Corporate Financial Accounting

Learning Objectives

This chapter deals with the main objectives, uses, characteristics, and regulations of corporate financial accounting. By the end of the chapter, you should be able to identify and understand:

- The corporate governance context for corporate financial accounting.

- The major decisions and decision-makers that a set of corporate financial statements assist — particularly investors and lenders.

- The time periods covered by the financial information regularly reported by companies to shareholders.

- The subjective nature of the accounting process that produces corporate financial statements.

- The main accounting conventions used in the production of corporate financial statements.

- The general terms of the various legislative and regulatory provisions governing the production of corporate financial statements.

At the end of this chapter, please refer to these learning objectives before moving on to Chapter 4 on the nature and purpose of the corporate profit statement.

INTRODUCTION

Chapters 1 and 2 provide an introduction to corporate financial reporting and financial statements. The primary focus is the need for companies to be properly governed in a legal structure that separates owners from managers and creates the potential for moral hazard—i.e. the possibility of senior managers taking advantage of the absence of shareholders from the daily management of the company. Corporate governance mechanisms centre on the board of directors as the principal tool of direction, regulation, and control of the decisions and actions of senior management. The intention is to hold senior managers accountable for their decisions and actions on behalf of shareholders in a contemporary form of the age-old function of stewardship. Regular financial reports comprising statements of profitability, cash flows, and financial position are an important and long-standing means of making senior managers accountable to shareholders via the board of directors. The purpose of this

Marianne Jewell Memorial Library
Baker College of Muskegon
Muskegon, Michigan 49442

chapter is to develop these ideas and explanations by exploring the reporting function in more detail. In particular, the chapter reminds the reader that the corporate financial report is a comprehensive package of related financial statements designed to satisfy the need for financial information of shareholders and other stakeholder groups.

The chapter identifies:

Uses

The main uses to which reported financial statements are put. The analysis also identifies the principal user groups. It assumes a stakeholder focus rather than the narrower shareholder view of governance.

Decisions

The potential to inform a variety of decisions is a principal feature of reported financial statements. Whatever the type of user, financial statements can be used to provide knowledge about the reporting company that assists in the prediction of possible outcomes inherent in every decision.

Numbers

The major characteristics of the accounting numbers reported in the financial statements. These involve several conventions adopted over many decades by accountants preparing accounting numbers for reporting in financial statements. These conventions assist in identifying the relative strengths and weaknesses of the accounting numbers disclosed in financial statements.

Requirements

The current requirements for corporate financial reporting as these relate to the UK. Such requirements include relevant provisions of the Companies Act 1985 and prescribed accounting standards. With respect to the latter, the relevant material relates mainly to the standards of the IASB rather than the UK's ASB. As mentioned in Chapter 2, the EU (which includes the UK) decided that listed companies follow the accounting standards of the IASB from 2005. It is likely that this approach will be extended to all companies in due course.

COMPREHENSIVE PACKAGE

A corporate financial report is not a single audited financial document. Nor is it a set of statements comprising accounting numbers. Instead, it is a comprehensive package of statements—some quantitative, others with a narrative focus; some audited, others not audited—designed to inform shareholders and other users about the reporting company's financial performance and condition over a specified annual period. For companies listed on a recognized stock exchange, the annual package is supplemented by unaudited quarterly financial statements, largely concerned with sales and profits from trading operations. The overall package can be broken down into the following components. These will be explained in more detail in later chapters.

Main financial statements

These relate to profitability, cash flows, and financial position. They are audited and mainly numerical in content.

Statement of profitability   This statement (called the income statement or profit and loss account in the UK) reports the net gains and losses earned by the company from its operating activities. Profits in this sense are the residue of an accounting process of matching sales revenues with their associated expenses.

Cash flow statement   This statement reports the net cash flows from operating, investing, and financing activities of the company. The aggregation of cash flows reconciles to the periodic change in the company's cash resources.

Balance sheet   This statement reports the company's assets at the end of the reporting period, and the various short-term and long-term obligations of the company (including debt and shareholders' capital).

Subsidiary financial statements

These support the main statements. They are audited and also mainly numerical in content. They include:

Statement of total recognized gains and losses   This statement reports all profits and losses earned by the reporting company during the period—i.e. trading profits and losses, and other gains and losses not reported in the income statement or profit and loss account (e.g. on foreign currency transactions).

Statement on historical cost profits and losses   This statement explains accounting numbers in the main statements that are not based on the original cost of the transactions—e.g. when an asset is revalued.

Movements in shareholders' funds   This statement reconciles the funds of shareholders at the beginning and close of the reporting period—e.g. in terms of undistributed profits and new capital received from shareholders.

Explanatory statements

These support the main financial statements. They are audited and contain a mixture of quantitative and narrative material.

Accounting policies   Particularly for expert users of financial statements, it is important to disclose the main accounting conventions and practices (as contained in prescribed standards) that have been applied to the preparation of the accounting numbers in the main financial statements.

Notes to financial statements   Many of the accounting numbers in the main financial statements are complex calculations and require further explanation as to their nature and composition. This statement provides this explanation and therefore prevents the main financial statements from becoming unreadable due to excessive detail.

Statement of principal subsidiaries   The financial results reported by a company are often a combination of several companies—i.e. typically when the reporting company owns 50% or more of the voting capital of other companies. In these situations, this statement lists these share ownerships. The statement also lists investments of between 20% and 50%. The financial results of these associated companies are not combined into the main statements but, nevertheless, may represent interests in considerable amounts of profits, cash flows, and financial positions that shareholders ought to be aware of.

Other statements

These provide support and amplification to the main financial statement. They are typically unaudited and predominantly narrative in style.

Statement of chairman   This is a voluntary statement, often called the chairman's report, and has a long history in the UK. It is used by the chairman of the board of directors to provide a broad review of the reporting company's financial results in the context of its trading and related activities.

Directors' report   This is a legally required statement by the board of directors and includes a mixture of prescribed and voluntary information.

Operational and financial review   This is a voluntary statement and explains the main features of the financial results disclosed in the main financial statements in a narrative style. It has two sections. The first deals with operating matters relating to profits and cash flows. The second concerns financial funding activities such as share capital and long-term loans.

Review of trading activities   This is a statement that expands on the broad review typically given in the chairman's statement. It is usually contained in the operating and financial review.

Corporate governance   In recent years, companies have published this statement as a condition of stock market listing of their shares. It attempts to explain the philosophy and mechanisms of corporate governance to shareholders and particularly addresses the issue of compensation for senior managers and members of the board of directors. The statement is typically contained in the directors' report.

Auditor's report   This is a legally required statement by the auditor in which the directors' responsibility for the main financial statements and the basis for the audit are broadly described, and the audit opinion on the quality of the main financial statements is given.

Statement of directors' responsibility   Although the responsibility of the board of directors for the main financial statements is identified in the auditor's report, companies are also required to make a more detailed statement separately—usually in the directors' report. The statement includes maintenance of adequate accounting records and use of appropriate accounting standards.

Companies also produce other more quantitative statements on a voluntary basis to expand on financial information disclosed in prescribed and voluntary statements. These statements include multi-year presentations of key financial results relating to profitability, cash flows, and financial position.

> **Lesson 3.1 Financial statements**
> The annual financial report, particularly for larger companies, consists of a considerable number of financial statements. Some of these statements are primary and others secondary. Some are numerical and others use a narrative form. Many are prescribed by legislation or regulation, others are voluntary. The main financial statements would not make much sense without the other supporting statements.

INVESTMENT DECISIONS

Because companies are owned by the shareholders who invest in them, it is sensible to begin an explanation of corporate financial report users by examining the financial information needs of investors. For purposes of this section, investors are defined as two groups. The first group contains existing shareholders. These include private individuals and commercial organizations such as pension funds and investment fund managers. Existing shareholders own shares in the company because they either invested directly in it (e.g. on its formation or initial market listing) or bought shares in it through a recognised stock exchange (i.e. second-hand shares). The second group also comprises private individuals and commercial organizations but they do not currently hold shares in the company—i.e. they are potential shareholders who are interested in it from the perspective of becoming shareholders.

Both investor groups have a need for financial information about specific companies and therefore should make use of corporate financial reports. However, such a need is conditioned by the level of expertise of the individual or organization. Some investors (e.g. investment managers and analysts employed by investment managers) are professional investors and make considerable and regular use of financial and other information in their daily decision making processes. They are trained investors and their use of accounting numbers is expected to be skilled. Private investors, on the other hand, typically lack relevant training and skills in the use of corporate financial reports and their need for financial information is necessarily more basic and less extensive than that of professional investors.

> **Lesson 3.2 Investors**
> The investor group of financial statement users consists of a heterogeneous mixture of individuals and organizations. Their use of financial statements is varied according to their degree of interest and level of expertise in accounting and financial matters. A small minority of investors make

considerable, expert, and direct use of financial statements. The large majority, however, make little or no direct use of them, preferring to rely on professional analyses of reported accounting numbers that appear in newspapers and similar publications.

For purposes of this text, however, all investors are treated as a homogeneous group of interested and expert users whose financial information needs relate to two separate but related functions:

Managerial stewardship

The first financial information need concerns managerial stewardship. As explained in Chapter 2 in the context of corporate governance, existing shareholders need financial information in order to (a) monitor the performance (i.e. decisions, actions, and results) of senior managers, and (b) inform their decisions on the membership and performance of the board of directors. The board is the principal corporate governance device with respect to senior managers and shareholders require from time to time to make decisions regarding the appointment and re-appointment of members of the board (and therefore indirectly of the board's audit, nomination, and remuneration committees). The financial information in corporate reports provides knowledge not only of the performance of senior managers but also of the effectiveness in governing of the board of directors. For example, poor reported profits can signal poor operational decisions and actions by senior managers and inadequate internal controls of operating activities.

Investment decision making

The second financial information need concerns investment decisions. The latter relate to the buying, holding, or selling of shares in a company. The most fundamental characteristic of the investment decision is its comparison of the current market value of a share unit (not always known unless there is an established market for it and a stock market quotation) and the value the investor believes it to be worth (i.e. its intrinsic or present value). If the perceived present value of a share is greater than or equal to its market value then it would be rational for an investor to decide to buy the share or hold it (if it is currently owned). On the other hand, if the share's present value is less than its market value, then a rational decision would be to refrain from buying it or to sell it (if it is currently held).

Lesson 3.3 Present value
In a rational economic world, a marketable object such as a share unit should only be held by its owner or bought by a potential owner if its intrinsic or present value is believed to be at least equal to the price that is being asked for it. Only in these circumstances can the investor avoid making an economic loss.

The present value of a share in a company is a financial number that has to be calculated by an investor and therefore is unique to that individual. It is dependent on the investor's perceptions of the company's future based on financial information published about its past.

The present value of a share is essentially a fuzzy concept in the mind of an investor that may not be formally expressed in the form of a calculated number because of inherent difficulties of prediction—i.e. trying to quantify the uncertainties associated with the future of the company. For this reason, and for purposes of explanation in this text, the calculation of the present value that follows is intended as a formal description for learning purposes of a subjective and informal mental process in practice.

A present value is computed using an arithmetical technique called discounting which is the opposite of compounding of interest. The process involves:

Prediction

Predicting a future stream of dividends expected to be received from owning a share unit in a company. The stream includes the predicted final dividend in the form of the sale proceeds of the share when it is disposed.

Discounting

Discounting each individual predicted dividend to its current present value at a rate of interest commensurate with the level of risk that the investor associates with holding the share. This means the higher the perceived risk, the higher the interest rate used to discount forecast dividends (e.g. the rate applied to gold mining shares is much higher than that for supermarket shares because of the risks associated with the industries). To understand the discounting process, it is useful to think first of its compounding opposite which should be more familiar. For example, take £1 and compound it at 5% for three years—i.e. £1 at 5% gives £1.05; £1.05 at 5% gives £1.10; and £1.10 at 5% gives £1.16. In other words, the compounded number of £1.16 is the predicted value of £1 in three years time if the interest rate is 5% throughout. Now think about reversing this process (i.e. discounting)—£1.16 received at 5% means £1.10 invested a year earlier; £1.10 received at 5% means £1.05 invested a year earlier; and £1.05 received at 5% means £1 invested a year earlier. In other words, the discounted number of £1 is the present value of the aggregate predicted receipts in the three-year sequence—again assuming a 5% interest rate throughout.

Aggregation

Aggregating the discounted present values of predicted receipts and comparing this with the current market value. Then deciding whether or not to buy, hold, or sell depending on the relationship between the two values. For example, if the investor subjectively calculates that the present value of a share in a company is £13 and its market value is £15, then a rational decision would be not to invest. He would pay £15 and receive back only £13 in today's terms. Alternatively, if the present value was £13 and the market value £8, investment would be a prudent decision with the possibility of earning a gain of £5 in current terms.

Lesson 3.4 Subjectivity and uncertainty
The present value of a share is a very subjective and uncertain calculation based on estimations of investment periods, future receipts, and rates of return. It is the perfect model of the investment

decision—i.e. perfect in the sense of the investor being certain about all the information required to make the decision. In practice, however, the investor relies on less precise knowledge when making an investment decision. This reasoning is no different from buying any economic good or service. It only makes sense to buy if the value of the good or service to the buyer is believed to be at least equal to the purchase price asked. The problem for the buyer or seller is one of trying to estimate the present value. More often than not, this boils down to a gut feeling about the worth of the good or service.

It is useful to reinforce these aspects of the investment decision by using a quantified illustration (Illustration 2).

ILLUSTRATION 2 WHAT-A-PICTURE LTD

Jimmy Click, a photographer, inherits £1,000 from an aunt and considers buying 200 shares in What-a-Picture Ltd, a manufacturer of camera equipment. The current market value of the company's shares is £5 per unit. Jimmy's brother, Fred is an investment manager and gives the following advice to Jimmy. The investment should not be held for more than three years because of uncertainty about the speed of technological change in the camera industry. On the basis of observations of this market, Fred estimates dividends from What-a-Picture for the next three years on 200 shares of £100, £100, and £200 respectively. He believes the value of the shares will be £6 per unit at the end of three years. Investors in this industry typically expect a 10% annual return because of the investment risk involved. To simplify matters, Fred ignores taxation and transaction costs. He calculates the present value of 200 shares in What-a-Picture as follows (numbers are rounded up to the nearest £):

Year-End	Receipt	Discount Rate	Calculation	Present Value
	£	%	£	£
1	100	10	$100 \div (1.1)$	91
2	100	10	$100 \div (1.1)(1.1)$	83
3	200	10	$200 \div (1.1)(1.1)(1.1)$	150
3	1,200	10	$1,200 \div (1.1)(1.1)(1.1)$	902
Total	1,600			1,226

Note To reinforce understanding of the calculation of the discounted values in the right-hand column, take each of them and multiply by the discount rate on a compound basis for the period concerned. In each case, you should get a total equal to the equivalent receipt column figure. For example, £902 invested for a year at 10% is £992; £992 invested for a year at 10% is £1,091; and £1,091 invested for a year at 10% is £1,200.

The calculated present value of an investment of 200 shares in What-a-Picture Ltd for three years is £1,226 compared to a current market value of £1,000. Assuming each prediction is realized and interest rates do not change, there will therefore be a net gain of £226 in present value terms if Jimmy invests. If, however, the estimated present value had

Illustration 2 What-a-Picture Ltd ● **51**

been, say, £900 then an estimated loss of £100 (£900 − 1,000) suggests that it would not be wise to invest in the shares. In addition, it should be noted that:

Estimates

Present values are based on estimates of predicted cash flow returns. How accurate these are will not be known until the dates of the dividend receipts and the final disposal. Changes in the prediction of the amount and timing of the dividends and final sale proceeds will alter the present value, its relationship to current market value, and therefore the investment decision.

Discount factor

The discount factor is 10%. Again, this is a subjective estimate and can vary from investor to investor dependent on individual tolerance to investment risk. A higher tolerance and a lower rate give a higher present value (e.g. £100 in a year's time at 8% is £93). A lower tolerance and a higher rate have the opposite effect—e.g. £100 in a year's time at 15% is £87.

There is also the question of the financial information needed so that the investor can base these estimates of future cash flows and interest rates on some known numbers. The reported financial statements of the company's profitability, cash flow, and financial position are a major source of this information. Past dividends can be observed in these financial statements, as can the company's ability to generate profits on which dividends are based. The availability of cash to fund the company's dividends can also be monitored. Thus, the main financial statements provide profit, cash flow, and cash resource numbers to assist the investor to predict future dividends. More generally, the contents of the annual report provide a basis to assess the investment risks associated with the company and therefore the investment return or discount rate commensurate with that risk.

As previously stated, the task of using a complex set of accounting numbers in order to predict several years ahead is not only uncertain and subjective, it also requires skills and expertise. This suggests that processing of the type above is typically confined to the professional investor or investment analyst. The process requires caution and care. It is not one in which accuracy can be expected. Matters such as past profitability and cash flows are not necessarily going to be repeated in the future. A lot depends on the stability of the company and its industry. The more stable it is, the easier it is to predict the amount and timing of future cash flows such as dividends. The less stable it is, the greater the uncertainty about the future, and the more difficult the predicting.

Lesson 3.5 Investment decision making
When buying, holding, or selling shares in companies, investors require financial information to make predictions about future returns that determine formal or informal present values. The corporate financial report provides financial information about the past of the company and is a basis for these predictions. Companies rarely disclosed predicted financial information other than managerial expectations of increased sales and profitability in the most general form—e.g. the CEO informing professional financial analysts and journalists that his company hopes profits next year will continue to rise.

SHARE CAPITAL

So far in this chapter, the share units owned in a company have been described generically and without explanation. Before proceeding further, it is necessary to expand on previous descriptions. Most generally, shares are issued by a company in designated units (e.g. 10p, £1, or £50) for either cash or in exchange for purchased shares in another company or for non-monetary assets. For example:

On-the-Button Ltd forms in 2006 with a maximum (or authorized) share capital of £100,000 in £10 units. It issues 5,000 units to Jim Button and his family for cash, 1,000 units to acquire Jim Button's previous company, and 2,000 units in exchange for plant and equipment owned by Button's uncle. The total issued capital is 5,000 + 1,000 + 2,000 or 8,000 units of £10 each, i.e. £80,000. The assets of the new company include £50,000 of cash, a £10,000 investment in another company, and £20,000 of plant and equipment, giving a total of £80,000. There are 2,000 share units not issued (10,000 − 8,000). These are available for future issues for either cash or exchange.

In practice in the UK, there are two main classes of share that companies issue to their shareholders. These are ordinary and preference shares. Each class of share has a different set of rights.

Ordinary share capital

This is the capital held by shareholders who own the company because ordinary units typically are issued with voting rights to exercise at shareholder meetings. Ordinary shareholders are always the last to receive a dividend return on their investment and to be repaid on liquidation of the company. Their dividends vary according to the level of profit earned by the company. Of all the providers of corporate finance, ordinary shareholders are at greatest risk of losing their investment. However, if the company is successful, they receive the largest returns to providers of finance.

Preference share capital

This is a form of capital held by shareholders who do not normally have a vote in the decisions of the company at shareholder meetings. The preference of these shareholders is to receive a fixed rate of dividend that must be paid before any dividend to ordinary shareholders. Preference shareholders also receive priority over ordinary shareholders on liquidation of the company.

In the balance sheet of a company, ordinary and preference capital issued are part of a general category of obligation of the company that is reported as shareholders' funds. For listed companies, this is termed shareholders' equity. For other companies, it is called share capital and reserves. Shareholders' funds represent in accounting terms the obligation of the company as a legal entity to its shareholder owners. In addition to capital issued, the figure includes accumulated and undistributed profits and gains (net of losses) of the company. These are often described as reserves. Shareholders' capital and reserves or equity is in fact a residual accounting number and should not be interpreted as representing the current value of the shares owned in the company. It can, for example, be very different from the stock market valuation of these shares which results from daily trading by investors in them. For example:

Assume On-the-Button Ltd is operating ten years from its foundation. Plant and equipment is recorded at £10,000 but would realize £5,000 if sold today. There is cash of £35,000 and property recorded at £105,000 (with a current market value of £190,000). There are therefore total assets of £150,000 (£10,000 + 35,000 + 105,000)—equivalent to shareholders' capital and reserves of the same amount (i.e. 8,000 units or £80,000 of issued capital and £70,000 of undistributed profits). These accounting numbers suggest that each share unit issued at £10 ten years ago is now worth £18.75 (£150,000 ÷ 8,000). However, if the assets were realized for their current market value of £230,000 (£5,000 + 35,000 + 190,000), each share unit is worth £28.75 (£230,000 ÷ 8,000).

Lesson 3.6 Accounting precision

Accounting numbers disclosed in the main financial statements of a corporate annual report appear precise but, in fact, can be one of several ways of representing numerically a particular object. For example, shareholders' equity in the balance sheet of a listed company can be very different from the current market value of the shares concerned. This will be a lesson that is revisited throughout the text.

LONG-TERM LENDING DECISIONS

Long-term lenders and shareholder investors have similar characteristics because both groups provide capital sums to a company for use over long periods of time. Each group is therefore concerned with the financial progress and health of the company over a significant future period. Lenders provide capital to finance a company over contracted periods of specific time (e.g. 5, 10 or 20 years). Consequently, unlike shareholders, long-term lenders contract with the company to have their capital repaid. Repayment can either be in instalments over an agreed period for the loan or in one sum at the end of the period. Occasionally, the loan agreement permits renewal of the loan for a further period (i.e. as a form of rolling over of the loan). In the UK, long-term loans are often described as debentures and lenders as debenture-holders. For companies with stock market listings, debentures can be traded in the same way as shares. Debenture-holders and other long-term lenders such as banks often have security provisions built into their loan agreement. These provisions stipulate that the contracted loan is either secured over specific or all assets of the company, or company directors guarantee to personally repay the loan should the company fail to do so. Long-term lenders have a right to receive a fixed rate of interest and usually receive the annual financial report.

Long-term lending is a form of investment in a company and therefore has risks associated with the receipt of interest and repayment of capital when due. However, such risk is less than that of shareholder investors in the company for a number of reasons:

(1) A long-term lender knows what the financial return will be over the life of the loan due to the right to receive a fixed rate of interest payable before any proposed dividend to shareholders.

(2) A long-term loan has to be repaid or renewed at a known future date unlike shareholder capital which may never be returned to shareholders.

(3) When secured, a long-term loan has preference over other obligations of a company in relation to specific or all of its available assets.

What this means is that long-term lenders such as debenture-holders do not have to cope with the same degree of uncertainty about investment recovery and return as do shareholder investors. Instead, in most cases, the long-term lender can predict the expected cash flows over time and has preference over shareholders with respect to interest and capital payments.

Despite this reduced risk and uncertainty, long-term lenders have distinct financial information needs:

Ability to pay

For an actual or potential long-term lender, uncertainty is not about the amount of the capital and interest repayments associated with a long-term loan but, instead, the probability of these repayments being made in full and on time. This is a matter closely associated with the company's ability to pay and therefore with its available cash resources and cash flow related to these resources. For this reason, an actual or potential long-term lender requires information describing cash flow and resources, and the cash flow statement should be helpful in this respect.

Cash flow

Cash or liquidity is the primary information focus for the long-term lender. However, cash flow is the end result of a sometimes long transaction process for the company (i.e. from buying goods and services, through to their sale, and then on to the eventual realization of cash proceeds from sale). During this process, the company buys, pays, manufactures, markets, sells, and collects to earn profits that translate to cash flow. For this reason, the actual or potential long-term lender to the company should be interested in its profitability and requires information about this dimension of its financial affairs from the profit statement.

Realizable values

As stated previously, long-term loans are typically contracted with the amount leant secured over specific assets of the company. The realizable value of these assets determines whether the contracted security will be sufficient to repay any loan repayments and interest over which the company has defaulted. For this reason, an actual or potential long-term lender to the company will be interested in the financial position of the company generally and the condition of the secured assets particularly. As is explained later in the text, information about assets contained in corporate financial statements is not produced on a basis that provides knowledge about the realizability of all assets. However, use by the long-term

Illustration 3 Down-the-Plughole Ltd ● **55**

lender of the balance sheet particularly provides a limited indication of the financial health and condition of its asset structure.

> **Lesson 3.7 Long-term lenders**
> Long-term lenders have a specific need for financial information about the ability of the company to generate cash sufficient to enable it to meet its loan obligations in full and on time. They also have a more general need for information about the profitability and financial position of the company as indicators of its wider financial health.

The following illustration (Illustration 3) highlights some of the respective risks and uncertainties of long-term lenders and shareholders.

ILLUSTRATION 3 DOWN-THE-PLUGHOLE LTD

Down-the-Plughole Ltd retails bathroom accessories. It has been in business for five years and its financial statements for each of these years have included the following data (ignoring taxation).

Year	1	2	3	4	5
	£	£	£	£	£
Profit before loan interest	1,000	2,000	3,000	2,000	1,000
Cash flows from operating activities	800	1,200	1,800	2,000	1,500
Loan interest	2,000	2,000	2,000	2,000	2,000
Loan repayment due	20,000	20,000	20,000	20,000	20,000
Recorded value of available assets	50,000	52,000	55,000	60,000	58,000
Realisable value of available assets	30,000	27,000	28,000	30,000	29,000
Other obligations	15,000	17,000	19,000	24,000	23,000

The company earned profits over the five years—i.e. £9,000 in total before deducting loan interest in total of £10,000. Therefore, profits have been insufficient to cover interest expense. There is an overall short-fall of £1,000 (£9,000 − 10,000). In addition, cash flows from operating activities total £7,300 revealing that not all earned profit has been realized in cash. The cash available to pay interest of £10,000 over five years was £7,300. The deficit of £2,700 would have been funded by bank overdraft (included in the figures for "other obligations"). Interest, therefore, was paid but there was no profit or cash flow available to justify any proposal for a dividend to the shareholders. In each year, there are sufficient realizable assets available to meet the loan repayment of £20,000. But the position of shareholders is poor. For example, assuming the stated position of Down-the-Plug Ltd at the end of year 1, the loan instalment of £20,000 would be repaid out of realizable assets of £30,000, leaving £10,000 to meet other obligations of £15,000 and leaving nothing for the shareholders. Similarly, at the end of year 5, realizable assets

of £29,000 cover a loan repayment of £20,000 and only partially cover other obligations of £23,000. Shareholders would again be left with nothing for dividends. In other
words, profits, cash flows, and realizable assets are sufficient to cover long-term loan
repayments, inadequate to meet other obligations, and non-existent for returns to shareholders.

OTHER DECISIONS

Following the stakeholder approach to the corporate governance and financial reporting of
companies, there are a variety of different financial information needs to be satisfied other
than those of investors and long-term lenders. These range from the customers of the company to government departments. The following notes are a summary of their needs. They
are not presented in any predetermined order of importance. In the stakeholder approach,
all stakeholders are assumed to contribute to the wellbeing and survival of the company and
all deserve access to relevant financial information with which to monitor and assess their
respective stakes.

Customers have two specific interests in a company. Both are associated with its ability to
stay in business over the long term. The first interest concerns future trading between the
company and the customer. Customers should be concerned that the company will continue
in business and therefore provide a continuous and regular supply of goods or services.
Obviously, there are customers who enter into a single transaction with a company, but
the large majority have repeat transactions. These are often part of a contract of supply
over a relatively long period of time. The second interest concerns customers who have
contracts containing warranty conditions should goods or services provided by the company be substandard. Again, customers need to know whether or not the company will
remain in business and therefore be available to honour the warranty. For these reasons,
customers (particularly business customers requiring continuity of supply) need financial
information with which to assess the prospects of the company surviving over the long
term. Such information includes all the major statements of profitability, cash flow, and
financial position.

Suppliers of goods and services to the company (i.e. its creditors) have an obvious interest
in the short term ability of the company to meets its obligations to them—i.e. pay the
amounts due at the end of the term of credit agreed. The need for financial information in
this case focuses on cash resources and cash flow. The company needs cash flow to generate
cash resources to repay creditors. The cash flow statement is the most relevant financial
statement in this respect. In addition, suppliers have a similar interest in the company to
customers—i.e. whether it is likely to remain in business in the long term and therefore
provide continuity of business to the suppliers. It is rare that suppliers will enter into a single
transaction with a company. Continuity of supply generates a need for financial information
centred on all the main financial statements of profitability, cash flow, and financial position.

Bankers to the company can be separated from long-term lenders when they provide short-
term credit facilities such as a bank overdraft. Their major concern is the company's ability
to repay the overdraft (and the accumulating interest) under the terms of the agreement.

Cash flows are the most obvious financial information with which to assess the company's ability to repay when due.

Employees are often forgotten as a major stakeholder group in a company and have relevant financial information needs. The latter may be formally articulated through the employee representations of trade unions that negotiate over wage claims with corporate senior managers. The stake of employees in a company can be evidenced in different ways—e.g. short term payment of wages and benefits for services provided; the longer term provision of employment and career development; and the most long term provision of pension and health care benefits on retirement. The ability of the company to pay its employees suggests a need for information about cash flow and resources. The longer term provisions focus on a wider range of information concerning profitability, cash flow, and financial position.

Government departments and bodies need to monitor and examine the financial affairs of the company. The government can be a major customer of the company (e.g. when it buys goods and services in the area of defence contracting). In these cases, the financial information needs are similar to those of other customers (above). Government departments may wish to monitor significant companies in particular industries (e.g. oil and gas, defence, and banking) in order to assess conditions as part of an economic review or for developmental decisions (e.g. in particular regions). The complete package of financial statements has a potential use in such circumstances. A further governmental use of financial information from companies is the widespread one of determining the liability for corporation tax. The basis for this tax is the profit statement and adjustments to accounting profit to arrive at taxable profit require information from the balance sheet.

Others There are a variety of other users of corporate financial statements. Professional analysts, for example, make constant use of available information on behalf of the groups they serve—e.g. investors and lenders. Their needs and interests are compatible with those of these groups. Competitors and rivals also seek financial information about companies in order to assess relative strengths, weaknesses, and opportunities. Finally, members of the general public may from time to time have a specific interest in the activities of a particular company and its management and use its financial statements as an information source.

> **Lesson 3.8 Information needs of stakeholders**
> There is a variety of different stakeholder groups who have financial information needs satisfied by the annual financial report to shareholders. Although stakeholder interests vary, they can be broken down into two types of information need—short-term (which typically require information on cash flow and resources) and long term (which typically suit a more complete range of statements of profitability, cash flow, and financial position). Despite the diversity of interest, the annual financial report is capable of satisfying different stakeholders because of the range of financial information it contains.

OVERVIEW OF INFORMATION NEEDS

The most obvious conclusions from the above review of specific needs for corporate financial information are as follows:

Prediction

Most groups (with the possible exception of the government when assessing tax) appear to require information that assists in predicting the future of the company (e.g. future dividends, interest payments, custom, supplies, wages, and economic prospects). Companies do not provide predictive information and, instead, disclose accounting numbers that describe past profitability, cash flow, and financial position. Users of corporate financial information therefore take information about a company's past as a basis for generating predictions about its future—e.g. past profits and cash flows to predict future dividend payments.

General purpose information

Most groups have an obvious interest in the overall corporate financial report which discloses information about profits, cash flows, and financial positions. This suggests that the current corporate financial report should be considered to be a source of general purpose information rather than a source that can satisfy the needs of only one group. The annual financial report designed to meet the needs of shareholders therefore has become an exceedingly versatile source of information about a company.

TIME AND CORPORATE FINANCIAL REPORTS

Corporate financial reports contain several financial statements of accounting numbers. The statements are all associated with the same annual period. However, the numbers are generated from transactions of several past periods and calculated with reference to future periods. This makes the preparation and use of corporate financial statements difficult because of the mix of time periods inherent in the accounting numbers. This problem can be explained in a number of ways:

Defined period

Each of the main financial statements describes in accounting terms the economic consequences of past business transactions—i.e. the profit and loss account or income statement describes the total profits of a defined past period (e.g. a year); the cash flow statement describes various cash flows relating to the same past period; and the balance sheet describes the various assets and liabilities of the company that exist at the end of the same past period. In other words, the main reporting package is focused on a defined past period and past business activities and events. This period can be a month, a quarter, a year, or several years. For purposes of this text, the time period is typically the annual one.

Time mix

In order to produce the accounting numbers contained in each of these financial statements, their preparers use a mixture of past transactions, current conditions, and future events. Accounting is therefore not just a matter of identifying a past business transaction. For example, one of the accounting numbers in the profit statement is the depreciation of long-lived assets such as plant and equipment. In order to calculate the depreciation number for a particular past year, the accountant requires the following information—(a) the past acquisition cost of the plant, (b) its current condition and anticipated use in terms of future years, and (c) its anticipated sale value at a future date of sale. In other words, the accounting depreciation number incorporates three time dimensions. The following is an illustration of such a calculation.

Don Romanes is the CFO of Do-You-Know Ltd, a printer of children's books. The company purchased a book-binding press in January 2002 for £30,000. Don is preparing the company's financial statements for the calendar year 2006 and is calculating the depreciation of the press attributable to the year's printing operations. He follows prescribed accounting practice in this respect and uses the same method he has used in each of the years 2002, 2003, 2004, and 2005. The method is to spread the cost evenly over the estimated useful life of the machine, allowing for any anticipated sale proceeds when its useful life ends. The following elements contribute to the calculation:

(1) The cost of £30,000 spent five years ago in 2002.
(2) The estimated useful life of ten years which means the final sale is expected in a further five years in 2011.
(3) The anticipated final sale proceeds of £2,000 in 2011.

Don Romanes takes each of these elements to calculate the depreciable net cost to the company of £30,000 − 2,000 or £28,000 and applies this to the ten-year period by dividing by 10 to give an annual depreciation expense number of £2,800. In other words, an accounting number of a current year (2006) has been based on a cost incurred in a past year (2002) and related to an estimated number of years of life (some of which have expired) and a forecast value in a future year (2011).

Forecasting

Users of financial statements are expected to use financial information about past business activity in order to forecast profits, cash flows, and positions that relate to their various current or potential stakes in the company. Thus, standing at a specific point in time, a report user has to rely on financial information about the past in order to make a current forecast and decision about the future.

ACCOUNTING NUMBERS

Throughout the text to this point there has been continuous mention of accounting numbers. In Chapter 1 and Lesson 1.9, for example, the content of financial statements was described as numerical—i.e. each statement contains a set of accounting numbers derived from a process of bookkeeping and accounting standards application. The numerical nature of financial statements, however, requires further explanation in order to comprehend the nature and limitation of accounting numbers and therefore of financial statements. The most general point to make is that the production of accounting numbers is a process of quantification. This therefore suggests:

Objects

There are corporate objects with identifiable characteristics to quantify in accounting terms. For example, a company may have plant and equipment, cash, or a contracted debt. Each of these is an object for purposes of accounting. The identifiable characteristic in each case for quantification is monetary in nature (e.g. the cost of buying the plant was £1,000; the cash now available in the bank account is £2,000; and the debt owed by a customer is £4,000). The monetary unit (i.e. the £) is therefore a key tool in the accounting quantification process.

Representation

There are processes to quantify and represent the characteristics of objects. In general terms, these are the practices of bookkeeping and the rules of accounting standards that not only identify the monetary characteristics of objects but also use accounting quantifications to derive other quantifications. For example, the company's accounting system separately quantifies a sale of goods to a customer at £1,800 and the purchase cost of these goods from a supplier at £1,500. It then deliberately links these two numbers to derive a third—i.e. by subtracting the second from the first to obtain the profit number of £300.

The overall process of accounting quantification is a system that involves (a) recognizing objects and (b) representing them in numerical terms. It therefore appears similar to processes of measurement in other areas of human activity that depend on quantification (e.g. in the sciences). Measurement rules, scales, and tools seem appropriate. However, accounting quantification is very different from scientific measurement. For example, there are no accounting scales. Instead, it is a process of calculation that involves subjectivity and approximation because the quantification rules (as expressed in GAAP) permit individual interpretations and exceptions. For this reason, accounting numbers cannot be described as accurate representations of a recognized object as occurs, for example, when measuring height, volume, weight, and distance. It is therefore necessary for users of accounting numbers to realize that they can be inherently approximate and imprecise because their calculation relies on a combination of known transactions and subjective estimates and adjustments.

> **Lesson 3.9 Accounting recognition and representation**
> Accounting numbers represent objects relating to the financial affairs of a company. These objects are derived from the business transactions of the company. They are recognized in monetary terms by the accounting system when the transactions take place. Once recognized, the accounting system applies various flexible rules in order to represent the objects appropriately in the financial statements of the company.

An illustration (Illustration 4) emphasizes these points.

ILLUSTRATION 4 RAMBLING-SID-DELI LTD

Ed Rambling is the CFO of Rambling-Sid-Deli Ltd (RSD) and is visiting his family doctor for a check up. The nurse measures his height at 175 centimetres and weight at 70 kilograms. She takes his blood pressure at 120 over 80. Following further examinations by the doctor,

Ed is pronounced fit and healthy and returns to work where he is preparing RSD's financial statements. The company has 1,200 ready-to-eat meals in store. These have been counted by the food preparation manager. Ed estimates that each meal has cost £8 to prepare—an estimated £3 of food content and £5 of preparation time (i.e. because of employee wages and business overheads). Each meal will sell for £10, giving an estimated profit margin of £2. For purposes of preparing the financial statements, the inventory of meals is recognized as 1,200 units and represented in accounting terms at a cost of £9,600 (1,200 multiplied by £8). GAAP then uses an accounting rule to determine the appropriate accounting number for inventory—the accounting number for inventory has to be the lower of its cost (£9,600) or its market value (1,200 multiplied by £10, or £12,000). The number to represent inventory in the financial statements would therefore be £9,600. If the sale value of the inventory had been £5 per unit or £6,000 in total, then the financial statement number would be £6,000—the lower of £9,600 or £6,000.

The illustration demonstrates several things about accounting numbers:

Measurement

Each of Ed Rambling's health measurements is subject to a universal measurement system using calibrated measurement tools. Subject to errors in measuring or in the measurement tool (e.g. a tape or scales), each measurement should be regarded as accurate and different measurers of the same object should be expected to arrive at the same measurement (at least within accepted tolerances).

Measurement deviation

In contrast, the inventory accounting number is subject to permissible measurement deviations. In the case of the physical quantity of meals, there should be no deviation unless there has been a miscount. However, the accuracy of the accounting number that represents inventory is a different matter as Ed Rambling has to estimate two major costs for each unsold meal. Different estimates by different accountants can provide different numbers. In addition, the cost estimate is the number used in the financial statements even though it does not represent the current condition of the object recognized (i.e. its saleability). The total sale value of £12,000 represents this current state but GAAP does not permit its use (unless it is lower than the total cost).

> **Lesson 3.10 Poor representation**
> Accounting numbers in financial statements may represent appropriate objects but do not necessarily recognise their current condition. The required use under conventional practice of past costs means that accounting numbers reflect past rather than current events and characteristics of objects represented in the financial statements.

ACCOUNTING COSTS AND FAIR VALUES

Lesson 3.10 raises an important issue concerning accounting numbers in corporate financial statements. The main point is that they do not depend on a single calculation basis. Instead, GAAP—as expressed in written accounting standards throughout the world—stipulates that reported numbers depend on several bases:

Cash paid or received at the date of a business transaction—which can be several years in the past in the case of some long-lived business assets. An example is the inventory in Illustration 4 which affects both the profit statement and the balance sheet. Another example is the comparison of expenses and sales in a profit and loss account or income statement. A sale of a good can take place in an immediate past period. Its purchase and cost may have occurred in an earlier period.

Fair values (typically market values) at the date of reporting. An example of this is the reporting of investments in market securities in the balance sheet. Most accounting legislation or regulation requires the disclosure of market values for this type of asset.

Arbitrary amounts estimated by the preparers of financial statements. An example is the depreciation number in Illustration 2 which affects the profit and loss account or income statement and the balance sheet. The number depends on predictions and an arbitrary allocation basis.

These points are emphasized in Illustration 5 and will be elaborated in later chapters.

ILLUSTRATION 5 BALANCE SHEET NUMBERS

Ed Rambling produces a draft balance sheet with a page devoted to RSD's assets as they existed on 31 December 2006.

	£	£
Assets		
Plant and equipment purchased in 2004 for		5,000
Less: depreciation estimated to date of		2,000
Plant at net recorded value of		**3,000**
Inventory at its estimated cost of	9,600	
Investments at their market value of	1,000	
Cash in bank of	2,000	12,600
Total assets		**15,600**

In the above balance sheet there are four types of asset. Each type varies according to its realizability (e.g. cash is immediately realizable and plant may have limited realizability). Each is represented in different accounting terms. Plant is disclosed at its actual past cost reduced by an arbitrary annual allocation of that cost as expense. Inventory is shown at an estimated past cost. Investments are at their current market value. Cash is stated at the current amount in the bank. The total is an aggregate of these different accounting representations. This leaves a question mark about the meaning of such a total—it is neither a total cost nor a total sale value.

> **Lesson 3.11 Accounting inconsistency**
> Accounting numbers reported in corporate financial statements do not use a universal and consistent system of monetary representation. Consequently, aggregations of numbers such as the total assets number above do not have a meaning that is easily explicable. More particularly, in the

case of the balance sheet, which reports accounting representations at a specific point of time, several of these representations (e.g. plant and inventory above) do not represent conditions or characteristics pertaining at that date.

ACCOUNTING CONVENTIONS

The previous sections in this chapter attempt to provide an overview of the corporate financial report. In particular, they begin to reveal one of the major limitations of financial accounting—that it does not use a precise calculation system to produce accounting numbers and that the meaning of these numbers varies according to what characteristics are recognized and what accounting basis is used to represent these characteristics. Accounting totals in the financial statements are particularly difficult to interpret. From this brief review, it is clear that accounting number production is based on a series of conventions accepted by accountants and built on over many years. These conventions exist as a result of custom and habit, convenience, and expediency. For example, double-entry bookkeeping developed in the fourteenth century and has always focused on the monetary value of the recorded business transaction at the time it was contracted (e.g. the actual cost of a good purchased or an expense incurred). Also, although many accountants would prefer to use market values as the basis to represent such objects as assets, market values can vary according to location and circumstances and may not exist for many assets. Thus, it is not surprising to see a system of accounting that uses a mixture of bases for calculation of numbers. The following are some of the more familiar and long-lived conventions that govern the recognition and representation processes in accounting. They are not presented in any particular order of importance.

Entity

All corporate financial statements describe a specific entity or economic enterprise. The latter is the object of reporting in terms of its business transactions, profitability, cash flow, and financial position. The entity can be either a single company or a group of companies. But identifying it for reporting purposes is not always straight forward. For example, when a company has also invested in other companies, there is a need to determine whether these investments are controlled by the company. This is usually taken to mean the ability of the latter to govern the operating and financial activities of the other company—i.e. by owning or controlling either more than 50% of the voting rights in its shares or controlling its board of directors. The financial results of all controlled companies are then aggregated as if they were a single entity—i.e. as a group. A major problem in recent times with defining the group entity concerns major non-controlling investments made by several companies in long-term business partnerships or short-term ventures (e.g. companies A, B, C, and D each owning 25% of a non-corporate partnership). This means significant profits, cash flows, and assets and liabilities can remain hidden from the shareholders of A, B, C, and D as the financial statements of the partnership are not subject to the disclosure requirements of corporate legislation or regulation.

> **Lesson 3.12 Group accounting**
>
> According to typical legislative provisions, the corporate financial report should disclose the financial results not only of the reporting company but also of all the other companies it controls. However, this does not mean that the report discloses all the financial results of all the entities in which it has a substantial investment.

Monetary unit

All accounting numbers in financial statements depend on the use of a monetary unit—in the UK, the £ and in the US, the $. This permits accounting representations to be manipulated arithmetically in terms of additions and subtractions—e.g. plant of £1,000 + inventory of £2,000 + cash of £3,000 gives total assets of £6,000. However, this creates a problem in that these monetary units may not be the same unit in economic terms. They may appear to be a single unit (e.g. all £s) but, in fact, they can be three or more different units depending on when the underlying object (i.e. the plant, inventory, or cash) was recognized for accounting purposes. In other words, they may be £s of different times. The monetary unit is a means of economic exchange and has a fluctuating value in terms of its purchasing power at the time of the business transaction to which it relates. A £ of 2003 does not necessarily buy the same amount of goods or services as a £ in 2006. Thus, if the plant above was purchased in 2003, inventory in 2005, and cash is of 2006, adding these different £ units provides a £ total that is a confusing aggregate of three different £s with different purchasing powers. The total asset £ is therefore not a £ unit of a single period. The problem here is equivalent to adding 1,000 millimetres, 2,000 centimetres, and 3,000 metres and pretending that the total is an aggregate of 6,000 millimetres, centimetres, or metres instead of converting them to a single unit (e.g. metres).

> **Lesson 3.13 Monetary unit**
>
> Corporate financial statements disclose accounting numbers calculated in terms of what appears to be a common monetary unit. However, because that unit has a fluctuating value as a means of economic exchange, the accounting convention of aggregating different units in the financial statements as if they were a single monetary unit produces totals that are impossible to give meaning.

Historical cost

The calculations in accounting originate with individual business transactions predominantly to do with the purchase and sale of goods and/or services. These transactions are expressed in terms of the value contracted in the economic exchange. In the context of a sale transaction, this is typically not a problem and the sale is recorded as the net sale proceeds (the cash collected or to be collected minus any discounts or commissions). However, with purchases of goods and services (whether for resale or for use in the business), the problem is that the net cost of the transaction at the point of purchase becomes dated so long as the object concerned (e.g. plant or inventory) is held by the company. For example, assume that inventory purchased on 1 January 2004 for £5,000 has an equivalent purchase price at 31

December 2006 of £7,000 and a resale value of £10,000. If the inventory is reported in the financial statements on 31 December 2006 at £5,000, this number does not appear to be a reasonable representation of its condition at this date. Nevertheless, this is what GAAP requires companies to do—to account for and disclose inventory at its original or historical cost (unless its market value is less than cost). GAAP also requires other transactions to be recorded, accounted for, and disclosed at their historical cost with the exception of objects where a reliable current value is possible (e.g. with stock market investments).

Lesson 3.14 Problem of historical cost

Commonsense suggests that, if accountants disclose an accounting number as representing an object such as an asset at a particular point of time, the representation should reflect the condition of the object at that point. Instead, accountants are required by GAAP to follow the convention of representing most objects in the financial statements in terms of their historical cost—i.e. the transaction value at the time of the initial transaction and not at the time of reporting.

Realization

There is a further accounting convention followed by accountants in their adherence to GAAP and this is, in effect, the mirror image of the historical cost convention. Realization means that, for most transactions, despite changes in the current value of the object concerned since the date of the original business transaction, accountants continue to use its historical cost for accounting purposes. In other words, any increase in value is not recognized until there is a realization by sale of the object concerned. Paradoxically, however, GAAP permits the recognition of any decrease in value as soon as it occurs. For example, assume a good for resale is purchased by a company for £500. Its resale value is £600. So long as the good is not sold to a customer, it is represented in the company's financial statements at £500. Suppose, however, it continues to be unsold for a period of time when its resale value increases to £700. It continues to be reported to shareholders at £500. The unrealized profit of £200 is therefore hidden from them. Then, suppose the same item was held for the same period and its resale value dropped to £400. Under GAAP, the company reports it to the shareholders at £400 and also discloses the unrealized loss of £100. This is the realization convention in practice.

Lesson 3.15 Inconsistency in accounting

Under the realization convention, and assuming increasing prices, companies report their assets at the understated value of historical cost and fail to report known but unrealized profits. Assuming decreasing prices, however, companies report the assets concerned at their current market value and disclose unrealized losses. Accounting is therefore not a consistent practice.

Conservatism

The historical cost and realization conventions are long-standing aspects of corporate financial reporting. In fact, they originate from reporting abuses committed by senior managers and boards of directors throughout the nineteenth century and early twentieth century. These abuses related to the overstatement of reported profits and assets in order to cover up for mismanagement or misappropriation of assets or to justify the payment of dividends to shareholders. These experiences caused accountants to be cautious about the reporting of profits and assets and to prefer to understate rather than run the danger of overstating these matters. Consequently, the GAAP conventions of historical cost and realization generally, and the lower of cost or market rule particularly, suited this reporting strategy—which has come to be known as the conservatism convention in accounting. It is a convention that permeates current reporting practice although recent years have seen an increase in what is known as fair value accounting or mark-to-market accounting. Such accounting relates mainly to assets held in the short-term that are readily realizable (e.g. financial assets such market securities and tradable contractual rights called financial instruments).

Lesson 3.16 Cautious accounting
Modern corporate financial reporting is based on a nineteenth century practice of cautious accounting amended by more recent awareness of the need to incorporate profits and losses before realization if realizable values can be determined with some degree of accuracy. Financial statements therefore use a mixture of historical costs and market values to report profitability and financial position.

Going concern or continuity

There is a conventional assumption that underlies all accounting practice as it relates to businesses. It is called the assumption of going concern or continuity and means that the accountant assumes the business for which the financial statements are being prepared will continue to trade indefinitely. Put differently, the assumption is that the company is not about to go out of business in the short-term. The assumption is necessary because it permits the accountant to use the previous conventions such as historical cost and realization. The company's assets are held for purposes of long-term trading and therefore for future use (in the case of assets such as plant) and future resale to customers (in the case of inventory). If the company was assumed not to be a going concern, then the use of historical costs would be inappropriate and the use of realizable values necessary. For example, plant reported at a cost of £2,000 less depreciation to date of £500 (a net recorded cost of £1,500) can be interpreted as signalling one-quarter of its useful life is over and three-quarters have yet to expire.

Lesson 3.17 Trading indefinitely
The accounting numbers reported in corporate financial statements are intended to convey a message to shareholders that senior managers and the board of directors expect it to continue to trade indefinitely and not cease to trade in the near future.

Periodicity

Corporate financial statements relate to a specific and stated period of business trading. The conventional period is one year irrespective of the nature of the business operated by the company. Companies with stock market quotations for their shares also report on a half-yearly or (e.g. in the US) quarterly basis. However, these financial statements are abbreviated versions of the annual statement, subject to a great deal of estimation, and are not audited. They therefore require to be treated with caution by shareholders and other stakeholders. Half-yearly or quarterly statements have the advantage of giving reasonably up-to-date financial information about the company which can be used for decision making. Annual statements, on the other hand, are considerably detailed and subject to legislative or regulative requirements for disclosure. They are also audited. However, the financial information they convey is relatively out of date as it may take several months from the year-end before they can be released to shareholders. Annual financial statements do not take into account the different operating cycles of companies. For example, retail clothing stores operate in quarterly seasons and their regular reporting could adopt a quarterly basis with full disclosure and audit. Builders of power stations, on the other hand, manage operating cycles of up to seven years and fully disclosed and audited financial statements of periods greater than one year may be more appropriate for their shareholders.

> **Lesson 3.18 Periodicity problems**
> Annual financial statements from companies have the advantages of full disclosure and audit and the disadvantage of being outdated. Half-yearly or quarterly financial statements have less disclosure and no audit but are reasonably up-to-date.

LEGAL AND REGULATORY REQUIREMENTS

These are two types of corporate financial reporting requirements. These relate to the provisions of legislation (in the UK under the Companies Acts of 1985 as amended by the Companies Act 1989) and regulations produced by standard setters (in the UK under the ASB for non-listed companies or the IASB for listed companies). The following is a brief summary of the main provisions. In the case of accounting standards, those of the IASB are used. From 2005 onwards in the UK, listed companies must use IASB standards and ASB standards for non-listed companies must be consistent with those of the IASB.

Companies Act 1985 and 1989

The 1985 and 1989 Acts provide for the publication of audit financial statements by individual companies and groups of companies. In the Companies Act 1985, the various main provisions are as follows:

Accounting records

The board of directors must keep accounting records that are sufficient to show and explain business transactions and enable the financial statements to be prepared and disclosed.

Financial statements

The board of directors must produce for shareholders, debenture-holders (i.e. long-term debt), and the government's Registrar of Companies, a profit and loss account or income statement and balance sheet for the company and, where relevant, group of companies. These financial statements should provide a "true and fair view" of profitability and financial position and comply with the format and disclosure requirements listed in the Act. Should such compliance not provide the required "true and fair view," the board is required to disclose this and reasons for it. No definition is made of "true and fair view."

Board approval

The board of directors must approve the financial statements and they must be signed by a director on behalf of the board.

Audit

The auditor reports on the audit of the financial statements by giving an opinion on whether or not a true and fair view has been given, adequate accounting records have been kept, the financial statements are consistent with these records, and the statements have been properly prepared in accordance with the Companies Act 1985. The Act requires the statements to comply with applicable accounting standards.

Shareholder approval

The shareholders of the company must approve of the auditor's appointment.

Right of information and to be heard

The auditor has the right to receive access to all information required for the audit and to attend and be heard at meetings of shareholders.

Audit provisions

Further audit provisions are contained in the Companies Act 1989—the auditor can be an individual or firm and must be a professionally qualified public accountant registered with a qualifying professional body. The auditor is prohibited from being an officer or employee of the company (or related to an officer or employee).

These various provisions can be seen to focus on the basic principles of corporate governance explained in Chapter 2. First, the board of directors has responsibility for producing a package of financial statements for shareholders (and another key stakeholder group, debenture-holders). Second, the required package is defined and its content specified in detail. Third, shareholders are responsible for appointing the auditor and this matter is therefore separated from the duties of the board. The quality of the required financial statements is specified in the undefined terms of a true and fair view. This may appear not to be helpful to preparers, auditors, and users of financial statements as it is left to the discretion of the preparers and auditors particularly and there is also provision for departures despite compliance with legislative provisions and accounting standards. Nevertheless, the lack of definition can be argued to have a distinct advantage. It accommodates the flexible nature of prescribed accounting standards and recognizes that each corporate situation is unique in terms of its business activities. The lack of definition also allows courts of law to interpret reporting quality when required in terms of individual circumstances rather than trying to fit these circumstances to inflexible accounting and disclosure formulae. The true and fair view has become the overriding quality standard for corporate financial reporting in the UK—irrespective of the EU requirement for listed companies to present fairly.

Lesson 3.19 Legislative requirements
Legislative requirements for corporate financial reporting in the UK make clear it is seen as an important element of corporate governance by boards of directors in association with auditors. The legislative prescriptions are detailed and specific yet permit the individual circumstances of companies to play their part in the production of financial statements of an acceptable quality.

ASB accounting standards

The ASB has produced numerous accounting standards that apply in the UK to non-listed companies. As explained previously, because the accounting standards of the ASB must be consistent with those of the IASB, listed companies adhere to IASB standards, and in order to simplify the explanation in this book, the remaining text deals with IASB statements (as in the next subsection).

IASB accounting standards

There are numerous accounting standards prescribed by the IASB. They include a *Framework for the Preparation and Presentation of Financial Statements* published originally in 1989 and adopted by the IASB in 2001. Individual standards cover a range of topics including, for example, accounting for inventory, cash flow statements, income taxes, leases, sales, retirement benefit plans, intangible assets, and financial instruments. It is not possible or appropriate to cover the detail of these standards in this text. Instead, this section deals particularly with the main features of the 1989 *Framework* as this constitutes the general foundation on which the individual standards are based. They are similar to the ASB's *Statement of Principles for Financial Reporting* (1999). The main sections of the *Framework* are as follows:

Objectives of financial statements are stated to relate to the provision of information on financial position, performance, and changes in financial position to assist in a range of economic decisions. These decisions are explained in terms of various stakeholder groups (as explained previously).

Assumptions underlying financial statements include accruals (business transactions are accounted for as they arise and do not wait until their completion by the payment or collection of cash—e.g. a sale on credit is recognized as a sale before the customer eventually pays for it); and going concern (dealt with above).

Qualitative characteristics of financial statements are described. These include understandability (i.e. the capacity of the financial statements to provide information that is comprehensible to its users); relevance (i.e. the capacity of the financial statements to provide information capable of informing the economic decisions of users); reliability (i.e.

whether the financial statements faithfully represent profitability, cash flows, and financial position); and comparability (i.e. the capacity of the financial statements to provide information that can be compared from period to period or company to company). Constraints on financial statement quality are explained.

Elements of financial statements include financial position, assets, liabilities, equity, profit, revenue, and expenses. These are explained in various chapters that follow in this text.

Recognition and measurement of financial statement elements will be explained in relevant chapters that follow in the text.

Present fairly is the term used by the IASB to describe the overall quality of corporate financial statements of listed companies prepared under its standards. No definition of this term is offered by the IASB. The FRC in the UK has recently stated that, although listed companies and their auditors are required to describe whether or not financial statements have been fairly presented, the true and fair view remains the overriding quality standard for corporate financial statements in the UK. This is exceedingly confusing in the case of listed companies as it suggests that fair presentation and true and fair view can be different quality standards. Yet neither is defined. This places considerable pressures on preparers and auditors of financial statements to determine when the latter have met the required quality standard.

LEARNING OBJECTIVES

Please review the learning objectives at the beginning of this chapter and ensure they have been achieved before proceeding to Chapter 4 on the nature and purpose of the corporate profit and loss account or income statement.

Exercise 1   Investment decision

You are contemplating investing in shares in order to save for the purchase of a house in three years' time. A friend has suggested that you read the personal investment and finance section of a leading Sunday newspaper. The section's writer is advising investment in a manufacturing company and provides information that its dividends per share have averaged £10 over the last four years without any major fluctuation and the rate of investment return received by investors in the industry is 8%. You have £2,000 to invest and the quoted price per share is £20. The price was £30 three years' ago. Note the estimates and calculations you should record in order to make a decision to invest. Should you invest your money in this company? State the reason(s) for your decision. Students can also discuss with their instructor what would change in these calculations if the estimated realizable value of the shares in three years was, say, £300 or £3,000, and what would happen if the expected investment return was, say, 6% or 10%.

Exercise 2   Lending decision

You are a bank manager and have been approached by the CFO of a company for a loan of £100,000. What financial information will you require from the CFO prior to considering his request? Students should be prepared to expand in detail on each point made—e.g. the specific information required from the profit statement.

Exercise 3   Time and accounting

How does time affect the preparation, audit, and use of corporate financial information? Students should discuss with their instructor each point made in greater depth—e.g. the problem of maintaining the quality of the audit when under time pressure to provide an opinion.

Exercise 4   Recognition and representation

Wally Summer, CFO of the family-owned manufacturing company Summers Forever Ltd, presents the annual financial statements to the board of directors. His mother, Holly Summer the company's CEO, asks him to explain the following accounting numbers in the balance sheet. Prepare notes for Wally that would let Holly know what was being recognized and represented by each accounting number.

- (1) Plant and equipment at cost £150,000 less depreciation written off to date £60,000. Last year, the equivalent numbers were, respectively, £150,000 and £30,000.
- (2) Inventory of raw materials, semi-processed goods, and finished goods (less provision for damaged items) £320,000.
- (3) Investment securities £16,000.

Students should also be prepared to discuss with their instructor the problems in every-day life of recognizing objects and representing them in some form for purposes of understanding, enjoyment, entertainment, etc. (e.g. the painting of an artist).

Exercise 5   Accounting conventions

The CEO of a company is interviewed by a financial journalist at the time of the publication of the company's annual financial report. The journalist's notes contain the following:

- (1) JB Tee Shirt Company Ltd: year to 31 December 2006
- (2) Profit before tax £151,000
- (3) Sales increased by 13%
- (4) Total assets £1,600,000
- (5) Inventory £230,000

What are the accounting conventions signalled by these notes? Students should discuss with their instructor the meaning given to conventions used by accountants and the reasons for their importance in accounting (e.g. the use of monetary amounts to facilitate arithmetical calculations and associations for purposes of presenting numerical statements).

ADDITIONAL READING

A brief review of the fundamental features of financial statements by an accounting standard setter is given in IASB (2001), *Framework for the Preparation and Presentation of Financial Statements*, International Accounting Standards Board, London, paragraphs 9–11. These features include statement users, objectives, qualitative characteristics, and elements.

A more specific review of the UK position on accounting principles is contained in a simple question and answer document from the Accounting Standards Board (ASB) (1999), *An Introduction to the Statement of Principles for Financial Reporting*, Accounting Standards Board, Milton Keynes.

A description and explanation predominantly of investor and lender information needs in relation to their economic decisions as seen in the US is given in G H Sorter, (1974), "Economic Decision-Making and the Role of Accounting Information," in J J Cramer and G H Sorter (editors), *Objectives of Financial Statements: Volume 2, Selected Papers*, American Institute of Certified Public Accountants, New York, 66–79. There is no reason to doubt that this US perspective is not relevant to the UK.

The UK equivalent to the above is contained in Accounting Standards Steering Committee (ASSC) (1975), *The Corporate Report: A Discussion Paper*, Institute of Chartered Accountants in England and Wales, London, 15–27.

R J Chambers (1991), *Foundations of Accounting*, Deakin University Press, Geelong, 77–90, provides a detailed review of what is meant by measurement as it relates to accounting. It particularly deals with the problems of approximation and accuracy in accounting.

A useful article dealing with most of the topics in this chapter is R Skinner (1995), "Judgment in Jeopardy: Why Detailed Rules Will Never Replace a Chartered Accountant's Professional Judgment in Financial Reporting," *CAmagazine*, November, 14, 16–21. Skinner is a retired practitioner in Canada where the approach to corporate financial reporting is a mixture of ideas from the UK and the US. The article deals with the problem of judgment in preparing financial statements and, particularly, reasons why reliance on judgment rather than rules is necessary.

An argument for a simpler accounting standards structure is given by a leading accounting standard setter of the 1980s and 1990s—D R Beresford (1999), "It's Time to Simplify Accounting Standards," *Journal of Accountancy*, March, 65–7.

There are a number of sources dealing with the related issues of accounting standards and the quality of reported information in terms of a true and fair view. These are a selection:

Anonymous (2005), "Adoption of IFRs," *Corporate Reporting*, October, 3–8. This uses real-world examples to illustrate.

Anonymous (2005), "Invoking the True and Fair View Override," *Corporate Reporting*, May, 3–8. This uses real-world examples to illustrate. See also February 2003, 3–8.

L Evans (2004), "Problems with Fairness," *Accountancy*, October, 81. Evans considers the confusion over "fair presentation" and "true and fair view."

R H Parker (2005), "Have IFRSs Conquered the World?" *Accountancy*, November, 97. Parker looks at the problem of local versus global standards under the IASB.

B Shearer (2005), "In Support of a GAAP Gap," *Accountancy*, September, 96–7. This article questions the appropriateness of IASB standards to UK companies.

A Wilson (2002), "True and Fair: the Lost Dimension," *Accountancy*, April 97. Financial reporting is more than rule compliance.

CHAPTER 4

Corporate Profit Statement

Learning Objectives

This chapter explains the main objectives, uses, conventions, and regulations affecting the corporate profit and loss account or income statement. As previously explained, the statement of profitability of listed companies in the UK is called an income statement. That of a non-listed company is called a profit and loss account. For purposes of simplicity in this chapter, however, a composite term of profit statement is used throughout the text with appropriate titles used in numerical illustrations. By the end of the chapter, you should be able to identify and understand:

- The purpose of the corporate profit statement as part of an annual financial report.
- The major decisions assisted by a corporate profit statement — particularly those of corporate investors and lenders.
- The time period covered by the corporate profit statement.
- The structure and main sections and components of the corporate profit statement.
- The basic matching relationship inherent in accounting numbers reported in the corporate profit statement.
- The subjective nature of the accounting process underlying the preparation of the accounting numbers reported in the corporate profit statement.
- The main conventions used in the production of the accounting numbers in the corporate profit statement.
- The use of creative accounting practices by senior corporate managers to inflate or deflate reported profits.
- In general terms, the legislative and regulatory provisions governing the production and content of the corporate profit statement.

At the end of this chapter, please refer to these learning objectives before moving on to Chapter 5 on the nature and purpose of the cash flow statement.

INTRODUCTION

As previously mentioned, the annual corporate financial report has three main financial statements—i.e. the profit statement, the cash flow statement, and the balance sheet. Because of the way in which financial statements are constructed by relevant accounting procedures, each statement is connected to the other two. For this reason in this chapter, the profit statement is explained in the context of suitable contrasts with cash flow and balance sheet information. Such contrasts assist in understanding the following explanations of profit statements and provide a basis for understanding cash flow statement and balance sheet explanations in Chapters 5 and 6.

BALANCE SHEET OR PROFIT STATEMENT APPROACH

Before proceeding in this chapter to an explanation and discussion of the profit statement, and similar commentaries in Chapters 5 and 6 on the cash flow statement and balance sheet, it is necessary to contrast two different ways of approaching the accounting for these financial statements. The differences have been inherent in financial accounting thought for many decades but were clarified in the mid 1970s in the US by the FASB and reinforced in the 1980s and 1990s by the ASB in the UK and, more widely, by the IASB. The issue concerns whether an accountant should produce a set of corporate financial statements by, first, producing the opening and closing balance sheets for the reporting period and, second, deriving the profit statement as the difference between the balance sheets. This is called the assets and liabilities approach and is suggested in order to enable the accountant to use current values such as replacement costs and market values when producing asset numbers for the balance sheet. The alternative method of accounting is called the revenue and expenses approach, in which the profit statement is produced and based on the historical costs of business transactions and the balance sheet becomes a residue statement following the production of the profit statement. In essence, the revenue and expenses approach favours historical cost accounting and downplays the use of current values.

The asset and liabilities approach is recommended in *Framework for the Preparation and Presentation of Financial Statements* published originally in 1989 and adopted by the IASB in 2001. It is also the basis for the ASB's *Statement of Principles for Financial Reporting* (1999). In practice, no consensus has been achieved and companies use a mixture of historical costs and current values in their financial statements as will become clear in this and later chapters (particularly Chapter 6). Although it is not an issue that needs to be dealt with further in this text, it should be noted that the sequencing of financial statements in this and later chapters (i.e. profit statement, cash flow statement, and balance sheet) should not be taken as a preference for the revenue and expenses approach. The reason for starting with the profit statement in this chapter is due entirely to the fact that corporate financial statement users place primary emphasis on the reporting of profits and cash flows.

THE PROFIT STATEMENT

The profit statement describes the profits and losses earned by the reporting company over a twelve-month period of business trading. In all cases, the statement compares the reporting company's sales with its associated expenses. Then, in the case of a non-listed company, after deductions for tax on profits and proposed dividends to shareholders, the residue (termed retained profit) is added to shareholders' capital and reserves reported in the company's balance sheet. In the case of a listed company, only tax is deducted in the profit statement to provide a figure of profit for the year. This is added to shareholders' equity and any dividend paid during the year is deducted from equity. In this way, the profit statement contains a large part of the explanation for any periodic change in shareholders' capital and reserves (or equity). The following is an outline profit statement of a small retail company for an annual period.

	£	£	Note
Sales		130,000	**1**
Less:			
Cost of sales	49,000		**2**
Wages	34,000		**3**
Overheads	12,000	95,000	**4,5**
Profit before tax		**35,000**	**6**
Less: taxation		10,000	**7**
Profit after tax		**25,000**	**8**
Less: dividend proposed		5,000	**9**
Profit retained		**20,000**	**10**

What this profit statement discloses to its reader is:

(1) The company sold goods to customers for £130,000 during the year.

(2) These goods were purchased by the company for £49,000 during the year.

(3) Employees of the company earned £34,000 of wages and benefits during the year.

(4) There were overheads for the year of £12,000 incurred by the company.

(5) In total for the year, the company had expenses of £95,000 to match against sales.

(6) The difference between sales and expenses gave the company an earned profit before tax for the year of £35,000.

(7) The company estimated tax due on the profit of £35,000 was £10,000.

(8) This left the company £25,000 of profit after tax.

(9) The company proposes to make a dividend payment to its shareholders of £5,000.

(10) This leaves the company a retained profit of £20,000 to add to its shareholders' capital and reserves at the end of the year.

The related cash flow statement, on the other hand, describes the various cash inflows and outflows realized by the company over the annual period. The difference between these inflows and outflows reconciles to the increase or decrease in the company's cash resources reported in its balance sheet. The cash flows and inflows are rarely the same as the revenues and expenses reported in the profit statement due to the latter allowing for such matters as unpaid and unreceived transactions during the year. For example, the cash flow statement that relates to the above profit statement is as follows:

	£	£	Note
Cash receipts from customers		118,000	1
Less:			
Cash payments to suppliers	46,000		2
Wages paid	34,000		3
Overheads paid	11,000	91,000	4,5
Cash flows from operating activities		**27,000**	6
Less: tax paid		7,000	7
		20,000	8
Less: dividend paid during period		1,000	9
Increase in bank account		**19,000**	10

The cash flow statement is reporting that:

(1)   Although sales by the company were £130,000, it received £118,000 from its customers by the end of the year. The difference is due to amounts yet to be received from customers in the next year.

(2)   The company paid £46,000 to its suppliers although it sold goods that cost £49,000. The difference is partly due to goods purchased and unsold by the year-end, and partly because of amounts due to suppliers at the year-end.

(3)   Wages of £34,000 were paid in full by the company during the year.

(4)   Overheads of £12,000 were incurred by the company during the year and £11,000 of these were paid for by the year-end.

(5)   Total cash outflows from operating activities by the company for the year were £91,000.

(6)   This gave the company pre-tax cash flows from operating activities of £27,000 compared to an equivalent profit figure of £35,000.

(7)   Actual tax paid by the company during the period was £7,000, compared to a total liability of £10,000. The difference is due to an amount due to the tax authorities at the year-end.

(8)   After-tax, the remaining cash flow of the company for the year was £20,000

(9)   The dividend paid by the company during the year was £1,000. This was a partial payment of the proposed dividend of £5,000.

(10)   The net cash surplus of £19,000 increased the company's bank account by this amount.

The company's balance sheet describes its assets (including cash resources), liabilities and shareholders' capital and reserves (including undistributed profits) at the end of the year. The basic relationship is one of total assets equating in numerical terms with the combination of reported liabilities and shareholders' funds. Amounts in the balance sheet often explain differences between accounting numbers in the profit and cash flow statements. Using the above accounting numbers for the profit statement and the cash flow statement, the balance sheet is as follows:

	£	£	Note
Unsold inventory		6,000	1
Amounts due by customers		12,000	2
Bank account		31,000	3
Total assets		**49,000**	4
Amounts due to suppliers	9,000		5
Amount due for overheads	1,000		6
Amount due for tax	3,000		7
Amount due for dividend	4,000		8
Total liabilities		**17,000**	9
Share capital	12,000		10
Retained profits	20,000		11
Shareholders' capital and reserves		**32,000**	12

The balance sheet reveals:

(1) The company had an inventory of unsold goods that cost £6,000. In the UK, this is described as stock in non-listed companies and inventory in listed companies.

(2) There was uncollected cash from the company's customers of £12,000. These are described by accountants in the UK as debtors (for non-listed companies) and trade receivables (for listed companies).

(3) Cash in the company's bank account was £31,000.

(4) The total recorded assets of the company amounted to £49,000.

(5) The company was due cash to suppliers of £9,000. This amount is described by accountants in the UK as creditors (for non-listed companies) and trade payables (for listed companies).

(6) The company owed suppliers £1,000 for overheads. These are usually disclosed separately from creditors (or trade payables).

(7) The company owes tax of £3,000. This is usually disclosed as a separate liability.

(8) The company owes dividends of £4,000 to shareholders. This is usually disclosed as a separate liability.

(9) The total recorded liabilities of the company amounted to £17,000.

(10) The company's total assets minus its total liabilities reconcile to its share capital of £12,000 and the retained profit of £20,000.

(11) The combination in (10) gives shareholders' capital and reserves of £32,000 at the year-end.

Lesson 4.1 Financial statement relationships
Each of the main financial statements provides financial information relating to a different dimension of a company's financial performance and condition. Although these are different dimensions, they are linked in accounting terms within an overall financial structure. The annual profit statement and cash flow statement provide different reports of what has happened during the year. The balance sheet portrays the position at the end of the year.

The purpose of this chapter is to explain in more detail the nature and purpose of the profit statement. Chapters 5 and 6, respectively, explain the related cash flow statement and the balance sheet in greater detail. In the UK, the profit statement is reported by the board of directors to the company's shareholders and debenture-holders (as required by the Companies Act 1985, amended by the Companies Act 1989). The profit statement is audited and the auditor is required to report an opinion to the shareholders on whether the profit statement gives a true and fair view of the company's profitability (as required under the Companies Act 1985). Alternatively, under EU regulations relating to IASB accounting standards, the auditor of a listed company reports that there has been a fair presentation of profits in the profit statement.

IMPORTANCE OF PROFIT STATEMENT

During the early history of corporate financial reporting, and certainly until the 1930s, the emphasis in accounting disclosure to shareholders was on the balance sheet. The reason for this was to demonstrate to the shareholders that the reporting company had sufficient assets to meet its liabilities—i.e. it was able to repay its creditors and lenders, and had funds to pay its proposed dividends to shareholders. For many decades, senior managers and boards of directors were left to manage their companies without having to disclose detailed financial information on profitability. Indeed, disclosure on corporate profitability was regarded by shareholders, directors, and senior managers alike as an unnecessary way of revealing secrets to business competitors.

However, by the end of the 1920s in the UK, attitudes to corporate financial disclosure were changing and the Companies Act 1929 required the reporting of profit statements for the first time. This mandate therefore started a process that continues to the present day of corporate managers, boards of directors, and shareholders emphasizing profitability as the key ingredient in their decisions, actions, and announcements. Gradually, professional and private investors began to closely scrutinize the profit statement for information likely to influence and assist their decisions and, just as methodically, senior managers and boards of directors reacted to this emphasis on profits by careful consideration of how much they were going to reveal about profitability in the profit statement. In other words, at least from a managerial perspective, the tradition of corporate secrecy with respect to financial results has never fully disappeared. This is a matter that is returned to when looking at the topic of creative accounting.

Investors were and remain particularly concerned about profits being available to justify dividends and influence share prices in capital markets. Managers and directors, on the other hand, were and remain concerned to avoid reporting falling or fluctuating profits for fear of precipitating a financial crisis and instability in relations with customers, suppliers, and bankers. The ideal scenario for managers and directors is, whenever possible, to disclose increasing profits. This becomes especially important to managers when their employment contracts contain provisions for bonuses based on reported profits or beneficial share purchase options (i.e. buying shares at a low price and selling them at a higher price). It is therefore unsurprising that managers look for ways to manipulate reported profits and to disregard the ethics of disclosing what has actually happened during the reporting period. This problem is discussed further in Chapter 8.

EARNINGS PER SHARE

In order to enhance understanding of the importance of the corporate profit statement and its content, it is useful at this point in the text to consider briefly the use of information about company profitability. This involves an introduction of financial ratios as profit indicators and is a subject dealt with in more detail in Chapter 10. More specifically, in this chapter profitability is examined by means of the ratio earnings per share (EPS).

Corporate profitability as reported in the profit statement is analyzed in considerable detail by a variety of corporate report users. However, one profit indicator above all others dominates the attention of shareholder investors. That indicator is EPS. In the UK, consistent with specific accounting standards of the ASB and IASB, EPS is reported as part of the profit statements of companies with publicly traded shares. The standards define EPS in its most basic form as reported profits after tax divided by the number of ordinary share units issued by the reporting company. They also define a more complex variant that allows for possible increases in the number of ordinary share units issued.

Taking the basic definition of EPS given above, suppose reported profit after tax is £150,000 and there are 300,000 ordinary share units issued. Basic EPS is £0.50 or 50 pence (i.e. £150,000 ÷ 300,000)—a financial ratio stating how much of reported profit is attributable to each ordinary share unit. In this case, for example, if a shareholder owns 10,000 ordinary share units, then £5,000 (i.e. 10,000 units multiplied by the EPS of 50 pence) is the after-tax profit attributable to that shareholder.

The reasons behind the considerable shareholder investor emphasis on EPS can be summarized as follows:

Investment indicator

EPS is an investment indicator that has the apparent advantage to an investor of reducing the financial complexity of corporate economic activity over a twelve-month period to a single accounting number. Few investors are fully literate in accounting terms and a single figure to indicate corporate performance has obvious appeal.

Subjective

EPS appears simple and straightforward as a corporate performance indicator. It can be used comparatively over time and between different companies. The formula does not change. However, there is a significant health warning to be attached to its use. EPS depends on a complex and subjective accounting process and the number is not as concrete as it appears. In other words, any subjectivity and any managerial manipulation in the production of the profit statement will translate to the EPS number.

Dividend return

Corporate profits have been used throughout corporate history by managers and boards of directors as a numerical basis for decisions on dividend payments to shareholders. Proposed dividends are typically calculated as a proportion of available after-tax profits disclosed in the profit statement. EPS is therefore a potential indicator to an investor of dividend per share (DPS) used in determining returns to investors on shares held in the company. For example, if a company typically distributes as a dividend one-third of its profits after tax, then one-third of its EPS (say 60 pence) will give an investor an estimated DPS (i.e. 20 pence).

EPS is not just an indicator of performance in its own right. It can also be used as a basis for calculating a return on investment (ROI) for shareholder investors. The calculation is called the price earnings ratio (PER) and it is possible to obtain it when there is a quoted or estimated share price. More specifically, EPS is divided into the quoted share unit price to get the PER. For example, if EPS is 50 pence and the share price is £5 per unit then the PER is 10 (i.e. £5.00 ÷ £0.50). What the PER indicates in this case is that the quoted share price of £5 represents ten years of reported annual earnings or profit-after-tax of 50 pence. Put differently, buying a share for £5 in this company is equivalent to buying ten years of its current profit-after-tax.

An alternative way of looking at the profit-based ROI calculation is to invert the PER and convert it to a percentage. In this case, £0.50 ÷ 5.00 × 100 gives an ROI to the shareholder of 10%. This calculation implies that the shareholder investor at this time is receiving a 10% investment return as a reward for the risk taken in investing in the ordinary shares of the company. The investor can then compare the ROI with that for investments involving similar risks and judge its adequacy.

In other words, profit reported in a profit statement can be extracted from it and used in a numerical calculation of investment return that provides information about the risk involved in an investment.

Lesson 4.2 Investment indicators

Accounting numbers such as profit are only useful if they can be extracted from the financial statement in which they are reported and related to other numbers in a way that provides indicators of performance of relevance to their user. In other words, financial statements such as the profit statement are a source of information and need to be related to other information in order to provide knowledge that is relevant to a user's decisions (e.g. EPS to market price to derive PER).

Because of the importance of the EPS and PER ratios to shareholders and other investors, the profit statement is a crucial source of financial information. It contains the accounting numbers that provide the single profit-after-tax number in the EPS calculation. However, if its users are to make any sense of EPS, they need to understand the content and composition of the profit statement. Unfortunately, investors and investment analysts have tended to focus in recent times too much on EPS (called "the number" in US capital markets) and ignore or fail to comprehend the underlying subjectivity of the accounting numbers used to calculate it. The following sections attempt to provide some understanding of the basic issues in this area of corporate reporting. Chapter 8 expands on these issues in greater depth.

Lesson 4.3 Dangers of a single number

Focusing on a single number as a basis for assessing performance has the merit of simplicity and possible comparability but the disadvantage of missing other relevant signals. It also contains a danger of the single number being based on subjective data that are open to manipulation.

Illustration 6 Jam-Today Ltd ● **81**

For example, in the area of health assessment, a medical practitioner will not make a diagnosis on the basis of a single number such as temperature or heart beat. Instead, he or she uses a range of indicators that are either measured (e.g. height and weight) or calculated (e.g. blood pressure or cholesterol level) and arrives at an opinion based on a combination of several signals of the patient's health. Accounting numbers such as EPS are problematic because, as indicators of corporate financial health, they are calculations rather than measurements and can be readily manipulated by the senior managers or directors of a reporting company.

BASIC RELATIONSHIP AND CONVENTIONS

The most basic accounting relationship described in the profit statement is that between sales and expenses. The comparison of total sales and total expenses for a defined period provides either a profit (when sales are greater than expenses) or a loss (when expenses exceed sales). A company can survive in the short-term if it is earning losses. However, in the longer-term, survival and growth depend on the generation of profit. The following example (Illustration 6) illustrates this point.

ILLUSTRATION 6 JAM-TODAY LTD

Jam-Today Ltd (JT) was formed at the beginning of 2005 with share capital of £20,000. It buys farm produce for cash and sells it at farmers' markets, for cash. The company has two employees, who are also its shareholders, and each receives an annual salary of £15,000. The only asset owned by JT is a truck purchased for £10,000 in cash when the company was formed. The following are the recorded sales and costs of the farm produce for the years 2005 and 2006. The truck has an estimated useful life of five years and will have a negligible salvage value at the end of its life.

Year	Sales £	Produce Costs £
2005	140,000	116,000
2006	147,000	120,000

From these accounting numbers, the following profit statements can be produced for 2005 and 2006:

Jam-Today Ltd
Profit and Loss Account for Year to 31 December 2006

	2005 £	2005 £	2006 £	2006 £
Sales		140,000		147,000
Less:				
Cost of produce	116,000		120,000	
Wages	30,000		30,000	
Depreciation of truck	2,000	148,000	2,000	152,000
Loss		*8,000*		*5,000*

What these accounting numbers are saying is that JT started business in 2005 with cash invested by the two shareholders of £20,000. The truck was bought for £10,000. This left £10,000 available to fund operational losses of £8,000 in 2005 and £5,000 in 2006. In these circumstances, the losses exceed the available cash resources by £3,000 (£10,000 − 8,000 − 5,000). It is probable that, in the absence of further investment by the shareholders, JT would attempt to borrow £3,000 to stay in business in 2007 and beyond. However, whether a bank would lend to the company with a record of losses is questionable. In any case, JT cannot borrow indefinitely to fund losses. Debt and interest must be paid and shareholders also expect a return on their investment. No bank would lend to a company to permit dividends to be paid even if there were profits earned that justified a dividend proposal.

BASIC ELEMENTS OF PROFIT STATEMENT

The JT example demonstrates two basic elements in the profit statement:

Sales

This accounting number represents the proceeds of sales made to the company's customers at farmers markets, during 2005 and 2006. Sales can be either on credit terms or for cash. In the case of JT, the basis is cash only which means that the company has no debtors (i.e. amounts due by customers for past sales). The most fundamental accounting convention associated with sales revenue is that each sale recorded must reflect a genuine legal contract and an economic exchange—i.e. goods or services given to the customer in return for a promise to pay in cash (i.e. credit) or immediate cash. In the case of JT, the convention appears to have been followed with farm produce exchanged for cash. However, in many other business situations, the application of the convention in practice is not as straightforward as with JT. For example, a publisher of journals may offer a subscription service in which the customer pays in full by cash (e.g. by credit card) when entering the contract and receives the journals issue by issue over the subscription period. Suppose, for example, that mid way through the business year, the publisher receives an annual subscription of £100 for 12 monthly issues. This sum cannot be treated as sales revenue in its entirety because only six issues will be delivered during the year. Thus, £50 would be accounted for as a sale and the remaining £50 as a prepayment by the customer and therefore an amount due by the company. These adjustments appear in the balance sheet as creditors. In the following business year, the second £50 becomes a sale when the remaining six issues are delivered to the customer and the amount due is extinguished.

> **Lesson 4.4 Sales**
> In accounting, contracted sales are not always recorded and processed immediately as sales. Only when there has been an economic exchange of goods or services can the transaction (or part of the transaction) be recorded as a sale for accounting purposes.

Expenses

In a profit statement, sales revenue is matched with the expenses associated with the generation of the sales. In other words, in the typical case when a sale is transacted, various expenses will have been incurred by the company in order to enable the sales transaction to take place (e.g. the purchase of a good, the payment of employee wages, or the payment of overheads such as utilities and advertising). In the case of JT above, the expenses of sale include the cost of the farm produce sold, the wages of the employees doing the buying and selling of produce, and the depreciation of the truck that took the produce from the farms to the markets (i.e. one fifth of the truck's cost assuming a five-year life). In other situations, there are expenses called overheads. These include rent, property taxes, utilities such as heat and light, and insurance. The cost of these items is normally invoiced to the company and processed through its accounting system. However, occasionally, it may be necessary to estimate these expenses, in which case the cost appears in the profit statement and also as a creditor in the balance sheet. These estimates are called accruals by accountants. On other occasions, a company may pay for overheads in advance of the service provided (e.g. rent paid for a future period beyond the end of the reporting period). In these circumstances, only the cost attributable to the service provided appears in the profit statement. The remainder (termed a prepayment by accountants) is included in the balance sheet as a debtor (recognizing the cost of a service yet to be provided).

Matching

The basic accounting convention in the above circumstances is called matching—i.e. the contrasting of sales revenue with the expenses attributable to the sales. Matching, however, is not as easy in practice as it appears from this example. There may be various costs that cannot be directly associated with sales with any degree of accuracy. For example, in the case of JT, the depreciation expense of £2,000 is based on the assumption that the truck was and will be used evenly throughout its useful life—i.e. in each year such as 2005 or 2006 the mileage is the same and justifies an annual allocation of £2,000 for five years. In practice, this may not be the case. For example, suppose the total five-year mileage is estimated at 80,000 miles (10,000 in 2005 and 20,000 in 2006, and estimates of 15,000 in 2007 and 2008, and 20,000 in 2009). This would suggest depreciation should be allocated as follows:

2005   £1,250 or 10,000 ÷ 80,000 × £10,000
2006   £2,500 or 20,000 ÷ 80,000 × £10,000
2007   £1,875 or 15,000 ÷ 80,000 × £10,000
2008   £1,875 or 15,000 ÷ 80,000 × £10,000
2009   £2,500 or 20,000 ÷ 80,000 × £10,000

These calculations are appropriate in retrospect when the mileage is known for each of the five years. However, in practice, a financial statement such as the profit statement is produced annually and estimates need to be made. For example, in 2005, the mileage will be known but that for later years is unknown. Thus, the accountant prefers to use a simplistic calculation of equal annual use despite knowing that this is not what is likely to happen. Dividing the cost of £10,000 by five is an easy, subjective, and inaccurate way of accounting for the expense. The matched depreciation expense for 2005 of £2,000 may appear accurate. In reality, it is an estimate.

Lesson 4.5 Realistic matching
Accounting for profit depends on a realistic matching of sales with the expenses attributable to these sales. Some matching is routine and can be done with reasonable accuracy and objectivity. Other matching depends on estimates and is necessarily subjective. The result is that the profits reported by a company in its profit statement is rather like measuring a distance with a piece of elastic. Its "length" depends on how much the elastic is stretched or contracted. Profit is a very approximate accounting number for use in assessing corporate financial performance.

The basic elements of a profit statement can be decomposed to various sub-elements that describe each step in the disclosure of accounting information about profit. There are in fact eleven basic elements described in this section and these are seen in Illustration 7.

ILLUSTRATION 7 GIVE-ME-A-BREAK LTD

The board of directors of the travel goods firm Give-Me-A-Break Ltd (GMAB) has received from its accountant the following draft profit statement for the year 2006. The board has asked the accountant to provide notes to explain to its members each of the main elements of the statement.

Give-Me-A-Break Ltd
Profit and Loss Account for Year ended 31 December 2006

	£	£
Sales		865,000
Less: cost of sales:		
Opening inventory	73,000	
Add: purchases of inventory	409,000	
	482,000	
Less: closing inventory	85,000	397,000
Gross profit for year		**468,000**
Less: other expenses:		
Wages, salaries, and benefits	194,000	
Overheads	63,000	
Interest on loans	15,000	
Depreciation of equipment	27,000	299,000
Net profit for year		**169,000**
Add: income from market securities		5,000
Profit before tax		**174,000**
Less: taxation on profits		50,000
Profit after tax		**124,000**
Less: dividend proposed		31,000
Retained profit		**93,000**

Sales

The accounting number of £865,000 represents the sales revenue earned from the continuous trading operations of GMAB during 2006 and recognizes contracted economic exchanges of goods for credit or cash between GMAB and its customers—i.e. travel goods have been

Illustration 7 Give-Me-A-Break Ltd ● **85**

contracted for and delivered to customers in exchange for promises to pay the cash due. Sales are disclosed in the GMAB profit statement minus any returns of goods during the period by its customers. Returns occur because the wrong goods are delivered or customers are dissatisfied with the quality or amount of goods delivered.

Cost of sales

In the case of a company selling goods such as GMAB, this accounting number represents the cost of the travel goods sold (COGS) to its customers during 2006. It therefore does not represent the cost of all goods purchased in the period by the company or payments made to suppliers of goods—only those goods delivered to customers because of orders contracted by them. For this reason, the number is calculated as follows:

> Total cost (or sale value if less than cost) of inventory of unsold goods as at 1 January 2006
>
> +
>
> Total cost of the goods purchased by the company during 2006
>
> −
>
> Total cost (or sale value if less than cost) of inventory of unsold goods as at 31 December 2006

Thus, using the figures for GMAB above, the COGS is:

> Opening inventory of £73,000
> + goods purchased of £409,000
> − closing inventory of £85,000
> = COGS of £397,000.

In other words, although the total of travel goods purchased during 2006 cost £409,000, only £397,000 can be matched against sales of £865,000.

Lesson 4.6 Cost of sales
When goods are sold by a company, the expense to match against sales is not the total purchases of the period. Instead, it is the cost of only those items sold. Unsold items at the beginning and the end of the period need to be taken into account to get the appropriate net cost to match against sales.

Gross profit

Once sales and COGS are matched in the accounting process, the net difference is determined. This accounting number is called gross profit (GP) and represents the profit margin earned by the company on its sales for the period—i.e. the proportion of each sale that represents profit to the company. In the case of GMAB, the GP is £468,000 and is the margin of profit on sales of £865,000. This can be converted to a percentage of sales—i.e. £468,000 ÷ 865,000 × 100 or 54%. In other words, for the year 2006, GMAB has earned a GP margin (GPM) of 54% on its sales. This represents a GP of 54 pence on every £1 of sales. The significance of the GPM to investors and other users of the profit statement is that it provides a signal of what corporate managers have achieved in buying and selling goods. Different businesses have different GPMs and GMAB can be compared not only with itself in previous periods but also with competitors and the industry as a whole. For example, suppose the following GPMs are available to an analyst interested in travel goods firms:

Year	GMAB %	Competitor %	Industry %
2004	56	52	53
2005	55	50	52
2006	54	49	51

These comparative margins signal that GMAB is outperforming not only its main competitor (e.g. in 2006 a margin of 54% against 49% which is an additional 5% or five pence of GPM on each £1 of sales) but also the industry average (e.g. in 2006 54% against 51% or an additional three pence on each £1 of sales). In addition, the numbers reveal that this position existed in both 2004 and 2005. However, for GMAB, its major competitor, and the industry as a whole, the trend of GPMs over the three years shows that margins are decreasing—in the case of GMAB by two pence per £1 of sales from 56% in 2004 to 54% in 2006, for the competitor from 52% to 49%, and for the industry from 53% to 51%. This suggests that the travel goods industry is finding margins are being squeezed because of customer resistance to higher prices or higher supplier costs or a mixture of both. Whatever the reason, the profit statement provides a key accounting indicator of corporate managerial performance for its users.

> **Lesson 4.7 Gross profit margin**
> The GPM is one of the most important indicators of managerial performance in corporate activity. However, as with the EPS number, the GPM should not be used in isolation. Instead, it should be used in conjunction with other accounting indicators to assess corporate performance.

Other expenses

The COGS is not the only business expense for a company such as GMAB. There are various other expenses that companies incur and many of these cannot be associated directly with the goods or services recognized during a defined period. For this reason, these other expenses are grouped together and deducted from the GP in the profit statement. In the case of GMAB, these expenses include:

- Wages, salaries, and benefits to employees £194,000.
- Various overhead expenses such as rent, business rates, utilities, repairs and maintenance, office expenses, and advertising and marketing £63,000.
- Interest paid to lenders £15,000.
- Depreciation of equipment £27,000.

Illustration 7 Give-Me-A-Break Ltd ● **87**

There are, however, types of business (e.g. in manufacturing) where a proportion of "Other Expenses" can be attributed to the COGS when calculating the GPM (e.g. wages of manufacturing employees and overheads such as utilities and repairs directly associated with the manufacturing process). In these situations, the COGS is calculated as follows:

Total cost (or sale value if less than cost) of semi-processed and unsold goods (raw material costs plus manufacturing wages and overheads attributable to these items) at the beginning of the period

+

Total cost of raw materials, wages and overheads attributable and allocated to the manufacturing process incurred during the period

−

Total cost (or sale value if less than cost) of semi-processed and unsold goods (raw material costs plus manufacturing wages and overheads attributable to these items) at the close of the period

In these circumstances, the remainder of the wages and overheads not directly attributable and not allocated to the manufacturing process and goods is therefore treated for accounting purposes as "Other Expenses."

The processes of allocation of costs in this way between goods and services sold and unsold and what amount to other expenses is complex and arbitrary. The detail of these processes is beyond the objectives of this text because they form part of the instruction of specialist accountants. However, users of accounting numbers such as those reported in the profit statement should appreciate that these numbers may appear precise but are dependent on judgments that are subjective but hopefully reasoned and consistent. Without such reason and consistency, the accounting process lacks credibility and cannot be relied on.

Lesson 4.8 Accounting consistency

The information provided in the profit statement is dependent on a number of operational associations and subjective allocations made by accountants in preparing numbers such as COGS, GP, and other expenses. Different accounting associations and allocations create different costs and margins. Comparisons of these accounting numbers over time and between companies must be made on the basis that the associations and allocation methods are comparatively similar and consistently applied. If they are not, then profit numbers, and their derivatives such as EPS, cannot be trusted.

Net profit

Once the GP and other expenses numbers have been determined, they can be matched and deducted from one another in order to calculate net profit (NP). In the case of GMAB, the NP number is £169,000—i.e. GP of £468,000 minus other expenses of £299,000. NP represents the profit earned for the period by the company after deduction of all expenses reasonably associated with the sales recognized for the period. For this reason, as with GP, it can be converted to a ratio and used as an indicator of managerial performance. The ratio is NP to sales—i.e. £169,000 ÷ 865,000 × 100 or 19.5%. What this ratio signals in this case is that for every £1 of sales in the period, GMAB generated 19.5 pence of NP. As with GP, NP can be used by investors and others to compare with similar ratios in previous years for the company, its major competitors, and the industry as a whole. Also as with GP, the NP number can only be used meaningfully if its components are calculated using similar accounting methods—i.e. with reason and consistency.

Other income

A company may have income other than that generated from its business operations. For example, it can receive dividends and interest on money invested in other companies and business ventures. If these income sources exist, the income concerned is usually reported separately and added to NP. In the case of GMAB, this additional income is £5,000 from investments in stock market securities. Such investments are not usually part of the business operations of a company. Instead, they typically represent the investment of cash that is not required in the foreseeable future for the renewal or expansion of business operations. Other income increases GMAB's profits to £174,000.

Profit before tax

Pre-tax profits are the arithmetical combination of GP minus other expenses plus other income. They are the basis for the calculation of corporate taxation due on corporate profits. It can also be used as a basis for calculating ROI—i.e. relating the pre-tax profit to current market price or a figure for shareholders' equity reported in the accompanying balance sheet.

Taxation

Companies are required to pay tax on their profits and the basis for this calculation is the pre-tax profit number—usually NP. The latter is adjusted suitably according to the rules of the applicable tax code that vary from time to time. For example, in the UK, depreciation expense in the profit statement is substituted in the tax calculation by an equivalent figure using formulae permitted by the tax code. Similarly, if the company incurs expenses that are not for the purposes of the business then these are not permissible as deductions in arriving at taxable profit. Once the latter number has been computed, the appropriate tax rate is applied to it, and the resultant tax liability calculated and deducted from profit before tax. It should be noted that the rules for computing taxable profit are just that—rules. They are legislated to provide governments with the tax revenues required to fund public expenditure. They therefore may not coincide with accounting practices and vary from one tax regime to another.

Profit after tax

This accounting number is the basis for the EPS and PER calculations explained previously in this chapter. It is also the basis for senior managers and board of directors deciding on

Illustration 7 Give-Me-A-Break Ltd ● **89**

the amount of dividend to provide for payment to shareholders. Dividends are typically a proportion of the profit after tax figure, with the remainder retained in the company for purposes of survival, renewal, and growth.

Proposed dividend

Shareholders and other users of the profit statement can take the proposed dividend number and use it in the calculation of two other financial ratios of use in assessing the performance of the company and its management.

The first ratio is called the dividend cover (DC) and it is a comparison of the profit-after-tax number and the proposed dividend. It represents the number of times the dividend is covered by available profits and indicates the degree of risk associated with the dividend—i.e. the greater the DC, the more profit is being retained in the business for its survival, renewal, and growth. For example, assume a company has profit after tax of £60,000 and proposes to pay a dividend of £20,000. The DC in this case is 3 (£60,000 ÷ 20,000)—i.e. the dividend is covered three times and two-thirds of the profits are retained. Suppose, on the other hand, that profit after tax is £30,000 and the dividend is £28,000 then virtually all available profits are used to reward the shareholders and there is little to retain in the business.

The second dividend ratio relates the proposed dividend to the number of share units issued to calculate the dividend per share (DPS) in the same way as EPS. For example, assume dividends of £40,000 and share units of 10,000 then DPS is £4 (£40,000 ÷ 10,000). The DPS can then be used in association with the current share unit price to calculate a dividend-based ROI—i.e. the dividend rate of return (DRR). Suppose the share price is £10 per unit and the DPS is £4 then the DRR is 40% (£4 ÷ 10 × 100). As with EPS and PER, DPS and DRR can be used to compare with previous years or with comparable companies.

Profit retained

This accounting number is the residue of the profit after tax and dividends that is retained in the company for purposes of maintaining, renewing, or expanding its operations. The number is added to the shareholders' equity reported in the company's balance sheet.

> **Lesson 4.9 Profit statement ratios**
> The profit statement is the source of a number of different if related accounting numbers that users can use to prepare various financial ratios to assess the performance of the company and its senior managers.

It should be noted that Illustration 7 deals with the profit statement of a non-listed company in the UK. If GMAB had been a listed company (i.e. GMAB plc), then its profit statement (i.e. income statement) discloses all of the information stated as for GMAB Ltd with the exception of the proposed dividend and retained profit, and some repositioning and rewording. The profit statement of GMAB plc appears as follows:

Give-Me-A-Break plc
Income Statement for Year ended 31 December 2006

	£	£
Sales		865,000
Cost of sales	*397,000*	
Wages, salaries, and benefits	*194,000*	
Overheads	*63,000*	
Depreciation of equipment	*27,000*	*681,000*
Operating profit		**184,000**
Finance income		5,000
Finance expense		*15,000*
Profit before tax		**174,000**
Less: taxation on profits		*50,000*
Profit for the period		**124,000**

Expenses are typically shown in italic script or with parentheses. Details of COGS are not usually disclosed and, instead of NP, profitability is termed operating profit. Loan interest and investment income are combined as finance items before arriving at profit before tax. Profit after tax is described as profit for the period and added to shareholders' equity in the balance sheet. Dividends paid during the year are deducted from shareholders' equity.

EXCEPTIONAL EVENTS AND TRANSACTIONS

The business activity of companies largely comprises routine contracts and transactions with customers and suppliers of goods and services, regular employment of staff and managers, and ordinary use of various assets such as plant and equipment. This activity generates the accounting numbers from which the profit statement can be prepared. Occasionally, however, a company experiences an event or enters a transaction that is not routine, regular, or ordinary and which has a significant effect on financial matters such as profitability. When the matter is a regular transaction but is unusually large then accountants have described it in the past as exceptional. When it is not regular and is significant, they termed it extra-ordinary. Until recently, companies in the UK were required to separate exceptional or extra-ordinary effects in the profit statement from ordinary matters. This continues to be legislated for in the Companies Act 1985 with its requirement to separate reported profits from ordinary activities from extra-ordinary profits and losses. However, in practice, the ASB and IASB have virtually proscribed such reporting because of its potential to overstate ordinary profitability by separating disclosing exceptional or extra-ordinary gains and losses due to events such as a major part of a company's operations ceasing because of a fire or natural disaster; a factory contributing significantly to a company's production output closing because products are no longer economically viable or found to be environmentally unsafe;

or a company receiving a large order from a foreign government for goods or services that is unlikely to be repeated.

These separations were regarded for many decades as useful to shareholders and other users of financial statements attempting to predict future profits and dividends on the basis of routine and regular events and transactions. However, in 1993 in the UK, the ASB (and the IASB in 2004) removed the distinction between ordinary and extra-ordinary profits and losses on the basis that all events and transactions should be treated as part of the normal business risk of a company—e.g. closing an operational facility is not unusual because it is likely to happen from time to time in the normal course of business. The ASB and IASB therefore require no separation of ordinary from exceptional or extra-ordinary gains and losses in the profit statement. However, companies are sensitive to the issue that fluctuations in profitability reported in this way may be due to unusual single events and transactions and, from time to time, may make appropriate additional and voluntary disclosures. Users of the profit statement therefore must make their own judgments about how to treat these matters when attempting to assess the past profitability of a reporting company and predict its future profitability.

> **Lesson 4.10 Unusual events and prediction**
> Financial statement users typically identify reported accounting numbers such as profit after tax as a basis for predicting future results. Past numbers, however, can be distorted by unusual events or transactions and therefore provide a poor basis for predicting future numbers. Users therefore may prefer to exclude exceptional or extra-ordinary items when trying to predict matters such as profitability. Accounting standard setters, however, require all events and transactions to be treated as ordinary as this prevents corporate managers and directors using the notion of exceptional or extra-ordinary events to present a more favourable disclosure of profitability. This is a regulatory policy that creates problems for financial statement users when they attempt to determine what is usual and what is unusual in reported accounting numbers.

OTHER PROFIT STATEMENT MATTERS

The previous sections of this chapter outline the structure, components, and accounting associated with the corporate profit statement. Two other matters require explanation. The first is comparative figures and the second is notes to the profit statement.

Comparative figures

The Companies Act 1985 requires companies in the UK to disclose comparative figures for the year previous to that being reported. The objective is to provide the reader of the profit statement with a basis for questioning any significant changes in accounting numbers in the profit statement. Comparative figures are given in the example below which is based on the profit statement in Illustration 7 above.

Give-Me-a-Break Ltd
Profit and Loss Account for Year to 31 December 2006

2005 (£)			£	£
801,000		Sales		865,000
		Less: cost of sales:		
69,000		Opening inventory	73,000	
373,000		**Add**: purchases of inventory	409,000	
442,000			482,000	
73,000	369,000	**Less**: closing inventory	85,000	397,000
	432,000	**Gross profit**		**468,000**
		Less: other expenses:		
181,000		Wages, salaries, and benefits	194,000	
57,000		Overheads	63,000	
14,000		Interest on loans	15,000	
29,000	281,000	Depreciation of equipment	27,000	299,000
	151,000	**Net profit**		**169,000**
		Add: income from market		
	4,000	securities		5,000
	155,000	**Profit before tax**		**174,000**
	45,000	**Less**: taxation on profit		50,000
	110,000	**Profit after tax**		**124,000**
	29,000	**Less**: dividend proposed		31,000
	81,000	**Retained profit**		**93,000**

With the disclosure of comparative accounting numbers for 2005, the reader of GMAB's profit statement for 2006 is able to observe that there has been an increase in most figures—i.e. sales and related cost of sales, other expenses, and other income. The result is a £19,000 or 12% increase in pre-tax profit. This has been reduced by increases in tax and dividends, resulting in a £12,000 or 15% increase in profit retained. None of the increases is unusual or extra-ordinary.

Notes to profit statement

The Companies Act 1985 and other regulations require companies to report specific information that can be disclosed as part of the profit statement—e.g. sales revenue, cost of sales, and depreciation. However, the Act also requires disclosure of more specific information and this is normally presented in the form of notes to the profit statement. The specific nature of this additional information varies over time as corporate legislation changes. However, in broad terms, it would currently include details of any additional voluntary information required to give a true and fair view or fair presentation of profitability, particulars and reasons for any departures from mandatory requirements for reporting on profitability, staff numbers employed and related emoluments and pension benefits, emoluments and benefits of directors, and detailed information regarding cost of sales, distribution and administration costs, interest payable, and other income received (if not disclosed within the profit statement).

CREATIVE ACCOUNTING

One of the most persistent features of corporate financial reporting since the middle of the nineteenth century has been the temptation for senior managers and boards of directors to take advantage of their position of influence in a company to distort the financial results they report to shareholders and others. This is typically done by using accounting to exaggerate the profitability and financial position of the company. Occasionally, managers and directors will attempt to reduce or increase reported profits. The activity has come to be known as creative accounting. The reasons for manipulating financial results in this way are reasonably constant over time:

Hiding reality

Senior managers or directors use accounting to inflate profits and assets and reduce liabilities because they believe they need to hide the reality of the poor profitability and financial position of the company from shareholders. In these circumstances, creative accounting occurs in the belief that it is good for the company while it goes through a sticky patch towards economic recovery. Mostly, however, managers and directors become creative with accounting practices because they want to hide the financial effects of substandard management.

Secret reserves

There may be circumstances in which managers and directors wish to deflate profits and assets and increase liabilities in order to hide profits for a future period in which profitability is less than at present. In other words, at times of high profits, there is a temptation to keep a proportion in reserve and reintroduce it at a future date when profitability is low. This practice was a familiar part of corporate accounting and reporting prior to the 1940s and came to be known as secret reserve accounting. In the UK, it persisted for several decades beyond that time with the blessing of legislators in the case of banks and insurance companies where it was believed that it prevented instability in profit reporting that could have negative effects on their business—e.g. bank depositors panicking at low profits or losses, withdrawing their funds, and precipitating a banking collapse.

Missing assets

There may be missing company assets due to fraudulent activity by senior managers or directors and creative accounting practices attempt to cover up the fraud by creating and reporting fictitious assets and profits.

Debt

Senior managers and directors can damage the health of a company by contracting for more debt than it can afford to fund. The result is that the company becomes crippled with interest charges and debt repayments. In these situations, senior managers and directors have been found to concoct elaborate organizational structures to remove company debt from financial statements to shareholders and place it "off-balance sheet" in entities that are not reported to shareholders.

Executive compensation

Senior managers may have compensation contracts with the company that contain provision for considerable financial bonuses based on reported profits. There is therefore a very obvious economic incentive for these managers to inflate reported profits in order to trigger bonus provisions.

Creative accounting can take many forms and ought to be discovered by a competent audit. It can only happen with the knowledge of senior managers and directors because it requires systems of internal control to be overridden or for junior managers and accountants to be persuaded or bullied into making appropriate accounting adjustments. The following are some of the more popular creative accounting practices of recent years.

Dubious transactions

Senior managers instruct junior colleagues to create fictitious business transactions that nevertheless look legitimate. For example, assume a company that has experienced poor profitability during the year 2006. In November, its CEO instructs sales staff to deliver goods in inventory to large customers even though the latter have not ordered the goods. The goods are delivered and invoiced and the appropriate sales entries are made in the company's accounting records. In other words, goods are delivered, and delivery notes and invoices are prepared and mailed. Profits on these sales are included in the total profit for 2006 that is disclosed to shareholders. The issue with this situation is that, when it happens, many of the customers receive and pay for the goods because they have weak systems of internal control that do not detect the lack of a prior order. The fictitious sales then become real sales with real cash flows. Other customers may be more diligent and return the goods in the next period of 2007 and the reported profits have to be reversed in the accounting records of that period. However, the sales and the profits are reported in 2006. This is creative accounting at the borderline of legitimacy.

Fictitious transactions

Senior managers can construct bogus business transactions, including false purchases and sales. This is fraud and there is an obvious consequence that a false sale is never going to result in an equivalent cash inflow (and vice versa with a false purchase). There are accounting techniques that can delay the mismatch between false sales and purchases and subsequent cash inflows and outflows. However, in the long-term, the situation is not sustainable. For example, assume goods are purchased for £80 and a false credit sale transaction of £100 is recorded with a bogus customer AB. The false sale of £100 is recorded, the cost of the goods is paid for by cash of £80, and the profit of £20 is recognized. The goods are apparently no longer in inventory, although in reality they are. The cash flow situation is a negative £80 because there can be no cash inflow of £100. However, suppose another credit customer CD pays the company £100 for an amount owed and suppose this is deliberately but incorrectly attributed to the false debt of AB. The result is a cash inflow of £100 and the cancellation of the false debt of AB. However, the debt of CD still remains in the company's records despite the fact that it has been paid. To sustain the fraud, £100 from yet another customer will need to be diverted to the CD debt, and so on in a never-ending game of catch-up until the numbers are unsustainable. Such a fraud is called "carry over" in the UK and "teeming and lading" in the US.

Misclassification

Senior managers can interfere in the accounting system so that business transactions are misclassified before they are recorded—e.g. treating an operating expense as if it were a depreciable asset. Suppose in 2006 a company pays a supplier £100,000 for the maintenance of its equipment. This should be recorded as an operating expense and reduce 2006 profits by £100,000. Instead, the CFO classifies the transaction as new equipment with a five-year life. The amount would appear in the balance sheet as an asset (less depreciation of one-fifth) of £80,000. In the profit statement, profits would reduce by the depreciation number of £20,000 in stead of the expense of £100,000. Overall, the misclassification has resulted in the overstatement of profits in 2006 by £80,000 ($£100,000 - £20,000$).

Over-optimism

Over-optimistic estimates can be made by senior managers concerning the condition of a company's assets that result in inflated profits. For example, assume that a company has plant that cost £60,000 at the beginning of 2006. Given the use to which it is put, the manufacturers and suppliers of the plant estimate it will have a three-year life. Using the simplest depreciation method, depreciation in 2006 should be £20,000 (i.e. $£60,000 \div 3$). However, the CEO wishes to boost profits and suggests to the CFO that the useful life should be five years. This reduces the depreciation expense in the profit statement to £12,000 ($£60,000 \div 5$) and increases reported profit by £8,000 ($£20,000 - 12,000$). A similar effect can be had by misstating closing inventory of unsold goods. For example, suppose the cost of closing unsold goods is £210,000, opening inventory is £190,000, purchases of goods are £519,000, and sales are £655,000. Also suppose that one-third of the closing inventory is not saleable and has a spare parts value of £25,000. The CEO instructs the CFO to account for all closing inventory at cost despite the problem with unsaleable items. The following alternative profit figures result:

	Unadjusted Profit		Adjusted Profit	
	£	£	£	£
Sales		655,000		655,000
Less: cost of sales:				
Opening inventory	190,000		190,000	
Add: purchases	519,000		519,000	
	709,000		709,000	
Less: closing inventory	210,000		165,000	
		499,000		544,000
Gross profit		**156,000**		**111,000**

The closing stock at cost of £210,000 should be reduced to £165,000 (i.e. £210,000 minus unsaleable inventory of £70,000 plus its scrap value of £25,000). In other words, one-third of the closing inventory (£70,000) has a resale value of £25,000, giving a loss to the company of £45,000 (£70,000 − 25,000). By not making this adjustment, the CFO and the CEO have wrongly inflated profit by £45,000 of creative accounting (i.e. £156,000 − 111,000).

Creative accounting sets out to mislead users of corporate financial statements and particularly affects the profit statement because of the contemporary focus on profit-related indicators such as EPS and PER, and the link between reported profits and managerial compensation. The auditor is expected to identify creative accounting and prevent its effects in the financial statements reported to shareholders. However, creative accounting schemes are, by definition, deliberately creative in the sense they exploit the subjective nature of the accounting process and its standards. For example, in the illustrations above, it is difficult to challenge senior managers about sales made without customer orders if the customers concerned accept the goods and pay for them. Fictitious business transactions are difficult to detect if they are kept to a minimum among a considerable number of similar but genuine transactions and are supported by documentation. The estimated working life of plant or the resale value of unsold inventory is exceedingly difficult to evidence objectively. Given the persistent existence of creative accounting practice throughout the history of corporate financial statements, even in the presence of reputable and skilled auditors, the financial statement user must be prepared to cope with it from time to time and be alert to signals of its existence.

CORPORATE GOVERNANCE AND PROFIT STATEMENT

The corporate profit statement discloses the financial returns generated from business activity managed on behalf of shareholders by management executives and supervised by a board of directors. It is part of the overall accountability of senior managers to shareholders. More specifically, it is a means of allowing senior managers to report the financial returns generated for shareholders in compensation for the investment risk they are taking. It is therefore vitally important that the profits disclosed in the profit statement are a proper representation of a company's profitability. Acceptable accounting for profit is an essential part of the overall system of corporate governance. Unfortunately, accounting for profit is not a precise measurement process and shareholders must understand that the accounting numbers they use to generate indicators of corporate investment performance such as EPS and PER are subjective and can be manipulated by management. In this sense, corporate governance, as expressed through the profit statement, is not an exact science.

OTHER LEGISLATIVE AND REGULATIVE REQUIREMENTS

As previously mentioned, the structure and content of the reported profit statement is governed by various legislative (e.g. the Companies Act 1985 as amended by the Companies Act 1989) and regulative provisions (e.g. ASB accounting standards for non-listed companies and IASB standards for listed companies). The specific details of these provisions vary from time to time as legislators and regulators respond to financial reporting problems. The previous sections in this chapter therefore follow the general principles inherent in the current provisions. The following subsections deal specifically with the profit statement and also with related accounting provisions introduced previously in Chapter 3 but not explained in detail in the text. They also inevitably cover several associated balance sheet matters where relevant and therefore have relevance to Chapter 6.

Accounting and reporting

The Companies Act 1985 deals with accounting and reporting provisions of a general nature affecting the production of the profit statement and balance sheet. There are three main provisions.

The first provision outlines the requirement for each company to maintain a system of accounting records to provide the data on which the profit statement and balance sheet are based. It also prescribes the location for these records (usually the company's registered office), access by the company's officers, and retention length (three years for a private company and six years for a public company).

The second provision specifies the requirement to define the accounting year (called the reference period) and notify any changes to that specification. This provision defines the period for the profit statement and the date of the balance sheet.

The third provision is a major one as it deals with the annual duty to prepare a profit statement and balance sheet for the company, and of any group of companies under its control, and specifies the expected quality of these statements in terms of an undefined true and fair view of profitability and financial position.

There are exemptions permitted to these main reporting requirements for small and medium-sized companies, and for dormant companies. If a company produces a summary profit statement and balance sheet for public consumption, however, there are also provisions to govern this. In addition, there are exemptions regarding the timing of the delivery of the profit statement and balance sheet to the shareholders and its presentation at a general meeting of shareholders. Other specific provisions cover such matters as approval of the financial statements by the board of directors and acknowledgment of this with a signature of a director on the balance sheet; delivery of the statements to the Registrar of Companies; post-publication revisions to the statements; and powers of the Secretary of State and other authorized persons should the company fail to produce the required statements. The previous sections of this chapter, and the numerical illustrations used in it, are compliant with the Companies Act 1985 as it relates to the profit statement.

Formats

The Companies Act 1985 permits a profit statement format choice of two types. The first type is a vertical format in which the profit statement starts with sales and deductions such as COGS, other expenses, taxation, and dividends are listed vertically as in all the examples and illustrations in this text. This is the most commonly used system in the UK. The second type is a horizontal format—sales and other income are placed in one column adjacent to a parallel column listing COGS, other expenses, taxation, and dividends.

Abbreviations

As mentioned above, private companies defined as small or medium sized are permitted under the Companies Act 1985 to report their profit statements in modified form—i.e. without the amount of detail required by legislation as minimum disclosure. Size definitions are given in terms of the amount of sales, gross assets, and employee numbers. The Registrar of Companies must be notified if the profit statement is modified and whether it is audited. Banking, insurance, and shipping companies are not permitted to modify in this way.

Groups

Also as mentioned above, when a company controls another company, it is required under the Companies Act 1985 to prepare what is described as a consolidated profit statement in which the sales, COGS, other expenses, and taxation of the controlling and controlled companies are combined as if they were the financial results of a single entity. If control is less than 100%, then the appropriate proportion of the combined profit is recognized as a deduction from total profit and described as attributable to minority interests (i.e. the other shareholders in the controlled company). The combined NP is typically disclosed in two parts—profit of the holding (controlling) company and profit of the subsidiary (controlled) company.

Accounting practices

A combination of Companies Act legislation and ASB or IASB regulations determines the accounting principles and practices specifically used in the production of each corporate profit statement. There are five accounting principles currently specified by the Companies Act 1985. Some relate inevitably to both the profit statement and the balance sheet due to accounting connections between the two statements. All principles are explained at this point in the text.

The first principle concerns both the profit statement and the balance sheet and requires the accounting practices used by the reporting company to be based on the presumption that it is a "going concern." In other words, the company is assumed to be financially viable and is not expected to fail in the foreseeable future. This permits the use of historical costs to account for asset numbers in the balance sheet and related profit statement numbers (e.g. in the depreciation of fixed assets).

The second principle also affects the profit statement and balance sheet and expects accounting practices to be used consistently from period to period in order to permit legitimate comparisons of reported accounting numbers. Inconsistency in accounting from period to period creates differences when comparing accounting numbers that are due to accounting practice rather than economic activity.

The third principle is "prudence" which means that only realized profits are included in the profit statement and all liabilities are accounted for in the balance sheet (including those that become apparent between the reporting date and the date of publishing the financial statements). This is the convention of conservatism that seeks not to overstate reported profitability and financial position.

The fourth principle requires all sales and expense transactions incurred in the period to be included in the profit statement even if cash has not flowed. This is effectively the accruals basis of accounting in which transactions are accounted for prior to their completion in the form of a cash receipt or cash payment.

The fifth principle affects the balance sheet and mandates that asset and liability aggregates are computed from numbers for individual assets and liabilities. In other words, the accountant is required to compute numbers for each asset and liability to be reported by the company and for these numbers to be aggregated appropriately.

Departures from these prescribed principles are permitted but required to be disclosed in an appropriate note to the profit statement or balance sheet. The IASB's *Framework for the Preparation and Presentation of Financial Statements* (1989), the ASB's *Statement of Principles for Financial Reporting* (1999), and various specific accounting standards contain similar principles.

LEARNING OBJECTIVES

Please review the learning objectives at the beginning of this chapter and ensure they have been achieved before proceeding to Chapter 5 on the nature and purpose of the corporate cash flow statement.

Exercise 1   Profit statement

Explain what a profit statement is and discuss its importance to shareholders and other users of corporate financial reports. Students can also discuss the importance of an abstract notion such as profit in a capitalist economy. Contrast its importance in an alternative economy. If the profit number in the profit statement is an accounting representation then what is the recognized object that it is representing?

Exercise 2   Earnings per share and price earnings ratio

Describe what is meant by the EPS and PER ratios. Explain their importance to shareholders and other investors. Students should also discuss with their instructor reasons why indicators such as EPS and PER have become so important to shareholders—often to the point that other performance indicators are either ignored or downgraded to a secondary status. In doing so, students should think more generally about the use of numerical indicators of performance in human affairs.

Exercise 3   EPS and PER calculations

Here are some basic data. Identify the missing number.

PER is 10 and the share price per unit is £20. What does PER represent? Can it be expressed in a different form? If so, what is that form?

EPS is £8 and share price per unit is £16. What does EPS represent? What are its advantages and disadvantages?

Students can also discuss with their instructor the proposition that the share price represents so many years' purchase of EPS and therefore is indicative of the risk of the investment. In other words, think about the link between investment risk and return.

Exercise 4   Cost of goods sold

What is meant by COGS in the profit statement? If COGS is £25,000 and opening and closing inventory is £3,000 and £4,000 respectively, what is the missing number? If sales are £66,000 and COGS is £37,000, what accounting number can be calculated from these data? What is that number's significance to users of the profit statement? To consolidate understanding of this topic, students can substitute different numbers for opening and closing inventory and purchases.

Exercise 5   Gross profit margins

You are a shareholder reviewing the profit statement of a company. You have been doing this for a number of years and have extracted the following GPMs for the last four years. Review these numbers and explain what you believe they are saying.

Year	Company %	Competitor %	Industry %
2003	12	12	12
2004	14	14	12
2005	18	15	13
2006	13	15	13

Students can reinforce understanding of this topic by substituting different sequences of GPM in each of the columns.

Exercise 6   Type of company

Differentiate the profit statements of a service-providing company and a manufacturing company.

Exercise 7   Exceptional and extra-ordinary items

Describe what is meant by the terms exceptional and extra-ordinary items as they relate to a corporate profit statement and explain the arguments for and against reporting them separately from the financial results of its normal or ordinary operations. Students can discuss with their instructor whether any business transaction or event can realistically be labelled as exceptional or unusual.

Exercise 8   Creative accounting

Explain what is meant by creative accounting and how it relates to the reporting of corporate profits in the profit statement. Students can also discuss more generally the existence of creativity with respect to the presentation of numbers for public consumption. In other words, is accounting unusual in this respect?

ADDITIONAL READING

Additional descriptions and explanations of the profit statement and related matters can be found in a number of introductory accounting texts. One that is relevant to most readers of this text is M Jones (2006), *Accounting*, John Wiley & Sons Ltd., Chichester. The specific parts of Jones relevant to this chapter are pages 74–91. These include discussion topics comparable to the exercises in this chapter.

An institutional view of the profit statement can be found in the IASB's (2004) "Presentation of Financial Statements," *International Accounting Standard 1*, International Accounting Standards Board, London, paras. 78–95 and in the Appendix.

In order to understand the importance of the profit statement in corporate activity generally, and capital markets particularly, it is necessary to realize how shareholder investors became fixated about a single accounting number—i.e. the profit or earnings per share unit. This single-minded phenomenon of the 1980s and 1990s is described in A Berenson (2003), *The Number: How America's Balance Sheet Lies Rocked the World's Financial Markets*, Simon & Schuster, London. This book can be read over three or four weeks in conjunction with this and the following two chapters. The book has appendices that explain in simple terms profit statements, cash flow statements, and balance sheets.

Analyses of specific profits-related issues can be found at a website *Corporate Reporting* (www.corporatereporting.com)—e.g. earnings per share (October 2004, 3–8); goodwill amortization (March 2004, 3–8); research and development (September 2002, 3–8; September 2003, 3–8; and November 2005, 3–8); revenue recognition (March 2002, 3–8; April 2002, 3–8; October 2003, 3–8; November 2003, 3–8; and April 2005, 3–8); and segmental reporting (March 2003, 3–8).

The following contributions are suggested to cover specific aspects of accounting for and reporting on corporate profits.

P R Brown (1999), "Earnings Management: A Subtle (and Troublesome) Twist to Earnings Quality," *Journal of Financial Statement Analysis*, Winter, 61–3. This paper discusses the use of creative accounting as a deliberate corporate strategy.

W J Bruns and K A Merchant (1990), "The Dangerous Morality of Managing Earnings," *Management Accountant*, August, 22–5. This is a rare glimpse into the thinking of corporate senior managers with respect to creative accounting—what is sometimes called the management of reported earnings.

A Buchanan (2003), "Recognising Performance," *Accountancy*, April, 76–7. This reviews the problem of revenue recognition with respect to corporate performance.

D R Carmichael (1999), "Hocus-Pocus Accounting," *Journal of Accountancy*, October, 59–65. This article reviews the impact of sales revenue recognition practices on reported profits.

K Lever (2004), "Would Pacioli Turn in His Grave?" *Accountancy*, July, 76–7. This is an article that argues against the idea of comprehensive income and financial gains and losses being reported.

A Levitt (1998), *The Numbers Game*, American Accounting Association, Rutgers University, New York. The serious consequences of the so-called accounting numbers game is emphasised in this publication by a leading US corporate regulator.

J L Morris (2005), "The Change Game," *Journal of Accountancy*, December, 67–73. This article deals with the requirement to account for the effect on past reported profits of a change in accounting practice in the current reporting period.

R Paterson (2003), "What's It All About?" *Accountancy*, October, 88–9. This article looks at the problems of matching in order to calculate accounting profit numbers.

P Rosenfield (2000), "What Drives Earnings Management?" *Journal of Accountancy*, October, 106–10. Reasons for earnings management by corporate managers and directors are discussed by a leading standard setter in the US with the conclusion that it is mandated accounting standards.

CHAPTER 5

Corporate Cash Flow Statement

Learning Objectives

This chapter explains the main objectives, uses, conventions, and regulations affecting the corporate statement of cash flows or cash flow statement as it is called in the UK. By the end of the chapter, you should be able to identify and understand:

- The purposes of the corporate cash flow statement.

- The major decisions assisted by a corporate cash flow statement.

- The time period covered by the corporate cash flow statement.

- The main sections and components of the corporate cash flow statement, including those containing operating, financing, and investing cash flows.

- The accounting basis used in the preparation of the cash flow statement and its relationship to the profit statement.

- The subjective nature of accounting for cash flows.

- The accounting convention used in the production of the corporate cash flow statement in practice — i.e. the indirect method.

- In general terms, the regulatory provisions governing the corporate cash flow statement.

- The relationship of the cash flow statement to corporate governance.

At the end of this chapter, please refer to these learning objectives before moving on to Chapter 6 dealing with the corporate balance sheet.

INTRODUCTION

The profit statement describes profits recognized and earned by a company over a defined period of time such as a year. Acceptable accounting procedures as described in GAAP match sales and expenses in a process that is inherently subjective and dependent on a combination of conventions, rules, and estimates. Within this process, there are three fundamental features of accounting for profit:

Credit and cash

The accounting used in the profit statement involves a mixture of credit and cash transactions. In particular, the sales and expense accounting numbers are based on a combination of business transactions where there is either an immediate flow of cash (e.g. goods purchased for cash) or a delay in the flow of cash due to contractual terms (e.g. goods sold on credit with the expectation of payment at the end of an agreed period).

Accruals

Accrual accounting adjustments are made to the cash and credit transactions included in the calculation of profit. These accruals include provisions for expenses incurred but not yet invoiced or paid (e.g. electricity, gas, or telephone services consumed prior to billing), and sale transactions where goods or services are to be delivered in a future period (e.g. a magazine subscription).

Allocations

Allocation accounting adjustments are also involved in profit calculations. Accounting allocations are calculated proportions of past business transactions that affect company operations over several periods (e.g. as in the depreciation of a long-lived asset).

In summary, therefore, accounting profit is a mixture of cash and credit transactions adjusted by relevant accruals and allocations. It is not what is intuitively believed by non-accountants—i.e. that profit is the difference between cash coming into the company and cash going out. This may be the case in the simplest business activity (e.g. a trader's stall at a country market) but it rarely happens in corporate organizations. For this reason, it is important to understand what is meant by cash flow accounting (CFA) and the cash flow statement.

The cash flow statement is prepared using CFA procedures that match associated cash inflows and outflows. At its most basic, CFA identifies recorded cash inflows and outflows in a defined period and reconciles the difference between these flows to the periodic change in cash resources disclosed in the balance sheet. CFA only deals with cash transactions. It does not include credit transactions or accrual and allocation adjustments that typically affect the profit statement. The cash flow statement is therefore a numerical explanation of periodic changes in cash resources and is useful for assessing the capacity of a company to pay its day-to-day business expenses and longer-term obligations when due; maintain and expand business operations by long-term investment in operational facilities for trading or manufacture; raise long-term finance to fund continuing business operations and new investments and projects; and provide dividend returns to shareholders.

Lesson 5.1 Cash flow statement
The cash flow statement contains accounting numbers and numerical relationships that are very similar to those used in day-to-day domestic activity. Few individuals prepare profit statements and balance sheets to describe their financial affairs. However, most adults in a developed economy receive monthly bank statements describing various receipts and payments over a monthly period. The bank statement is a form of cash flow statement. What it lacks is the classification of the different types of cash flow described below.

Illustration 8 Would-You-Believe-It Ltd ● **105**

The cash flow statement provides financial information about whether a company is better or worse off as a result of managed business operations that generate over a defined period of time either a net increase or decrease in cash resources (ΔCR) from a combination of cash flows from operating activities (OCF), financing activities (FCF), and investing activities (ICF). This relationship can be seen in Illustration 8.

ILLUSTRATION 8 WOULD-YOU-BELIEVE-IT LTD

Would-You-Believe-It Ltd (WYBI) is a retail store specializing in religious literature and music. It has been in business for a number of years and the year 2006 has been a period of expansion in markets and investment in new stores. WYBI's 2006 cash flow statement is as follows. To simplify the explanation, the illustration ignores interest payments and receipts, taxation, and dividends.

Would-You-Believe-It Ltd
Cash Flow Statement for Year Ending 31 December 2006

Cash Flows	£	£
Cash received from customers		1,312,000
Less: cash paid to suppliers of goods and overheads		*978,000*
Cash flows from operating activities		**334,000**
New long-term loan received from bank	100,000	
Less: final repayment on old loan from bank	*20,000*	
Cash flows from financing activities		**80,000**
Cash paid for new stores and related equipment	*566,000*	
Less: sale of store and used equipment	121,000	
Cash flows from investing activities		***445,000***
Net reduction in cash resources		***31,000***
Opening cash assets	67,000	
Less: closing cash assets	36,000	
Change in cash resources		***31,000***

OCF

This is the net cash flow resulting from a matching of inflows representing cash receipts from customers, and outflows representing cash payments for supplies of goods and services, wages, salaries, and benefits, and overheads such as insurance. OCF is positive when inflows exceed outflows and corporate managers should aim to achieve this condition over the long-term if the reporting company is to survive and prosper. OCF is negative when outflows exceed inflows. This condition occurs from time to time during the typical economic cycle of a company and is not unusual. It does not mean the company is failing any more than a cash deficit for an individual in a specific period means that he or she is in a poor financial shape. Companies and individuals overspend from time to time. However, such a condition cannot persist in the long-term if the company (or individual) is to survive. In the case of WYBI, OCF was a surplus of £334,000 for 2006.

FCF

This is the net cash flow resulting from a matching of inflows representing cash receipts from shareholders and lenders, and outflows representing cash repayments to lenders. FCF is positive when inflows exceed outflows. This is a normal situation for a company seeking to fund new investment by a combination of cash from FCF and OCF. However, in the long-term, a company cannot survive when FCF is positive and has become the predominant source of funding. As with the individual, this means there is a dependence on debt particularly and there is a limit to the size of debt a company or individual can sustain. However, there should also be periods in the typical economic cycle of a company when FCF is negative and outflows exceed inflows (i.e. repayments of debt are greater than new funding received). This situation arises when investment projects mature and their profitability generates cash to permit the reduction of debt acquired at the initial stages of the projects. This corporate phase is similar to individuals who reach middle age, a settled career, and less family demands for financing. In the case of WYBI, FCF is positive because the company has borrowed an additional £100,000 to assist its expansion. It has also repaid £20,000 of an existing loan, resulting in a net FCF of £80,000.

ICF

This is the net cash flow resulting from a matching of inflows representing cash disposal proceeds from sales of long-term assets and outflows representing cash payments for long-term assets. ICF is positive when inflows exceed outflows. In many cases, this is not a normal situation because it reveals that the company is selling off its long-term assets and not fully replacing them. The more typical situation is negative ICF in which new investment exceeds asset sales because a company needs to renew its asset base and, if sufficiently successful, expand it with new projects in new markets. In the case of WYBI, ICF is negative because of the purchase of new stores and equipment of £566,000. This cash outflow has been off-set by the sale of a store and other long-lived assets for £121,000. Such re-locating is typical of a retail store business.

△CR

The combination of OCF, FCF, and ICF in a period result in a change in cash resources over the period. Cash resources are defined as bank and cash balances and deposits, plus cash equivalents such as short-term investments of surplus cash, minus bank overdrafts repayable on demand. The direction of the change in cash resources depends on the relationship of the three main cash flows. In some periods, for example, a surplus of OCF and lack of ICF can result in CR increasing. Alternatively, high ICF and low OCF can produce a decrease in CR. In the case of WYBI, the surplus OCF and additional FCF are less than was spent on ICF resulting in cash assets being used to fund the difference of £31,000.

Lesson 5.2 Composition of cash flow

The overall cash flow of a company during a defined period of time results either in an increase or decrease in its CR in the same way that the bank balance of an individual changes.

Illustration 8 Would-You-Believe-It Ltd ● **107**

The composition of the overall cash flow is a combination of OCF (hopefully positive over the long-term), FCF (typically positive due to occasional injections of capital funding to the company), and ICF (typically negative due to occasional investments by the company in cash-generating resources). The magnitude of each cash flow and whether it is positive or negative will vary from period to period and result in different changes to CR.

Each of these points is expanded later in the chapter. Meantime, the cash flow statement should be seen as part of the accountability process required of senior managers and boards of directors. It is therefore important to the process of corporate governance. Over the long-term, if a company's cash inflows exceed its outflows, it is reasonable to assume its financial condition or health has improved because its cash resources have increased. Alternatively, if cash outflows exceed inflows, then its CR have reduced and its financial health is impaired. Just like an individual, a company must pay its bills, meet its contractual obligations, and maintain and enhance its generation of OCF. There is a continuous requirement in corporate business to manage the cash-generating asset base efficiently, effectively, and economically. This means that shareholders and other stakeholders need a cash flow statement to provide information about cash inflows and outflows generated from corporate business activities. In other words, a successful company is one in which its management invests in operational projects that generate profits that, through proper financial management, convert into equivalent cash flows to meet tax obligations, pay dividends to shareholder, repay debt, and invest in new operational projects. Earning profits is an important first step in successful management. Ensuring that profits translate to cash flow is a necessary second step. The cash flow statement discloses the achievement of corporate managers in this respect.

The basic message of this chapter is that cash flow is a vital part of the corporate governance story. Profits earned and recognized by a company in its profit statement should eventually translate into an equivalent realized OCF in the cash flow statement. If this does not happen then something is drastically wrong. Either the reported profit numbers are suspect—e.g. there could be creative accounting practices involving fictitious sales transactions that never generate equivalent cash inflows. Or the competence of managers with respect to financial management is suspect—i.e. they have failed to ensure that there are mechanisms in place to ensure the routine recovery of cash from customers, the timeous payment of suppliers of goods and services, and the minimization of inventory levels consistent with efficient trading. The cash flow statement can therefore reveal the extent to which reported profits are *not* realized in OCF terms. Legitimate long-term profit and OCF numbers must converge unless the former are fictitious numbers or there is incompetence in the financial management of the company—or a combination of these factors. Meaningful use of accounting information disclosed by companies should therefore always include an analysis of its realized cash flows as stated in the cash flow statement and supporting disclosures.

Lesson 5.3 Cash flow and corporate survival
Cash flow is crucial to the long-term survival of a company. In effect, it is its life blood. Without cash flow, the company could not pay for the costs of its daily operations or the purchase of

its long-term investments. The ability of the company to survive also depends on effective corporate governance of the management of its operations, investments, and funding. The cash flow statement is an important source of information about the effectiveness of that aspect of corporate governance.

SOLVENCY, LIQUIDITY, CASH FLOW, AND PROFITABILITY

To understand the role of the cash flow statement, it is important to understand the business context in which it provides financial information to shareholders and other stakeholders. Survival and prosperity in a company are not just matters dependent on profitable trading of products and services demanded by its customers. Any business owner or manager who believes that success is solely a matter of providing customers with what they want at the right quality, time and price is taking a restricted view of good management. Of course business success needs all of these ingredients. But it also requires effective financial management of trading activities and, in particular, it requires corporate managers to maintain a state of solvency in the company. This is a most crucial dimension of corporate governance.

Solvency

The term solvency means the ability of the company to pay its debts when these become due. Debts include short, medium, and long-term obligations of the company. Solvency is therefore a broad financial and legal term referring not just to the assets that the company currently holds and has available to meet its obligations, but also to its potential to raise new share and loan capital funding as and when this becomes necessary to maintain its capacity to pay.

Insolvency

A company may be in a position where its obligations exceed its assets but this does not necessarily mean that it is insolvent. If its trading prospects are believed to be favourable, then suppliers, lenders, and shareholders may provide further funds to enable current and future obligations to be met. However, if its trading prospects are unfavourable, and further funding is not possible because potential funders are put off by these prospects, senior managers will not be in a position to maintain solvency and repay obligations when due. This is what is called insolvency. It is regulated in the UK by the Insolvency Act 1986 and is usually associated with later court processes of bankruptcy, in which the company is either voluntarily or compulsorily liquidated in order to provide some return to its lenders and suppliers from the sale of its assets.

Receivership

The Insolvency Act 1986 permits a stage prior to insolvency called receivership, in which the company may be put under the control of a receiver in order to reorganize its asset base, recover its solvency, and prevent complete liquidation of the entity. In effect, this is a court-controlled way of providing the company with sufficient time and space to rethink its strategies, plans, and management, and put its house in order to take advantage of favourable trading conditions. It is a way of attempting to protect a company's creditors by allowing the company to reorganize in such a way that it can meet its obligations.

Liquidity

Solvency is distinguishable from the related financial state of liquidity. This exists when corporate assets are available in sufficiently realizable form to pay short-term obligations when they become due. Liquidity is therefore a much narrower concept than solvency and refers to a basic requirement of good business management to have enough cash assets (e.g. bank balances and deposits) and near-realizable assets (e.g. inventories of goods for resale) available to pay for immediate obligations (e.g. payments due suppliers).

Working capital

Management of liquidity in companies is usually referred to as working capital management because it involves monitoring and controlling working capital—i.e. the relationship of cash and realizable assets to immediate obligations. More specifically, working capital (WC) is defined as a combination of inventory of goods for production and sale, amounts due by customers, and cash resources minus obligations to suppliers of goods and services and short-term debt owed to banks.

Interest in these matters

Solvency and liquidity should be of interest to most stakeholders in a company. For example, its suppliers and lenders need to know about its short-term and long-term ability to meet obligations because the latter are their stake in the entity. If the company is illiquid then suppliers will not be paid when due. Equally, if the company is insolvent then both suppliers and lenders will suffer. Shareholders also have an interest in solvency and liquidity because their shareholdings are most at risk if suppliers and lenders are not paid. Shareholders are effectively the last to be paid on the liquidation of a company. It is rare in a liquidation to find that asset sales generate sufficient cash to repay shareholders. Solvency and liquidity are also matters that affect employees and customers as shortages of financial funding impact jobs and the supply of goods and services. Even government has an interest—particularly if the company is crucial to the national interest (e.g. as in defence contracting).

> **Lesson 5.4 Profitability, solvency, and liquidity**
> What corporate senior managers need to do consistently well is make sure that business trading is not only profitable but also generates sufficient cash to meet its known obligations (i.e. the company is solvent) and, more immediately, its current obligations (i.e. the company is liquid). There is therefore a clear relationship between profitability, solvency, and liquidity. Profitable trading generates the short-term assets required to maintain liquidity in the short-term and solvency in the longer-term.

The following Illustration 9 develops the main points stated above.

ILLUSTRATION 9 HAD-ENOUGH LTD

Had-Enough Ltd (HE) commenced trading on 1 January 2006 with a share capital of £8,000 and an equivalent bank balance. During the year to 31 December 2006, HE had the following trading transactions and purchased a machine for £4,500 with an estimated three-year life and a zero end value.

Inventory units	1	2	3	4	5	6	Total
	£	£	£	£	£	£	£
Credit purchases	2,000	2,000	2,500	2,500	3,000	3,000	15,000
Cash payments	2,000	2,000	2,500	2,500	—	—	9,000
Credit sales	2,800	2,800	2,800	3,600	—	—	12,000
Cash receipts	2,800	2,800	—	—	—	—	5,600

Assuming the earliest units purchased were the first to be sold by the company, equal annual depreciation of the machine, no other transactions or taxation, HE's profit statement for 2006 would be:

Profit statement	£	Notes
Sales	12,000	Inventory units 1–4
Less: cost of sales	9,000	Inventory units 1–6 less unsold inventory units 5 and 6
Gross profit	**3,000**	
Less: depreciation	1,500	
Net profit	**1,500**	

HE earned a GP of £3,000 on sale items 1 to 4 (£800 on each of items 1 and 2, £300 on item 3, and £1,100 on item 4) and depreciated one-third of the machine to give an NP of £1,500. The company's balance sheet is as follows:

Balance sheet	£	Notes
Machine	3,000	£4,500 − 1,500
Inventory	6,000	Inventory units 5 and 6
Debtors	6,400	Inventory units 3 and 4
Bank	100	See cash flow statement below
	15,500	
Less: creditors	6,000	Inventory units 5 and 6
	9,500	
	£	
Share capital	8,000	Initial capital
Retained profit	1,500	See profit statement above
	9,500	

Items 5 and 6 remain in as items of inventory and cash has not been recovered from the sale of items 3 and 4. The purchase of items 5 and 6 is unpaid. The opening bank balance of £8,000 has reduced by £7,900 to £100—as reflected in the following CFA statement.

Illustration 9 Had-Enough Ltd ● **111**

Cash flow statement	**£**	**Notes**
Cash inflows	5,600	Stock units 1 and 2
Less: cash outflows	9,000	Stock units 1–4
Cash deficit from operating activities	***3,400***	
Less: investment in machine	4,500	
Reduction in cash resources	***7,900***	
	£	
Bank account at beginning of period	8,000	
Bank account at end of period	100	
Reduction in cash at bank	***7,900***	

HE was profitable during 2005 with NP of £1,500 and appeared to be solvent with total assets of £15,500 covering total obligations of £6,000. Despite this, however, there is a question to be asked about its liquidity. The end-of-year bank balance of £100 does not cover the amount due to suppliers of £6,000, and much depends on the recoverability of cash due from customers and the saleability of its unsold inventory. For example, £6,400 needs to be recovered from the sale of items 3 and 4. If customers do not pay in full and the unsold inventory is not saleable, then not only is HE illiquid, it is also insolvent. A key to these concerns is the information provided by the cash flow statement, particularly when compared to the profit statement. GP is £3,000 and there is an OCF deficit of £3,400. The difference of £6,400 is due to the lack of recovery of cash on the sale of items 3 and 4.

This situation is not particularly worrying in the short-term. Companies typically manage the leads and lags resulting from the timing and completion of specific business transactions—e.g. purchases of goods and services often precede sales to customers, and cash inflows therefore typically follow outflows. Nevertheless, in the longer term, if these conditions persist and grow, there is a danger of the company's liquidity and solvency being compromised despite its profitability. Moreover, if HE is taxed on its NP of £1,500 and distributes any of the after-tax profit to its shareholders, then the danger to liquidity and solvency is exacerbated. For example, in the above illustration and assuming tax of £600 and a dividend of £500:

(1)   The profit retained reduces to £400 (£1,500 − 600 − 500).
(2)   Total assets of £15,500 would then have to cover obligations of £7,100 (£6,000 + 600 + 500).
(3)   Capital would reduce to £8,400 (£9,500 − 600 − 500).
(4)   The increase in obligations of £1,100 (£600 + 500) therefore places the company's liquidity and solvency in greater jeopardy.

Illustration 9 reveals not only the links between profitability, liquidity, and solvency, but also the relationship between profit and the equivalent OCF. More specifically, a comparison of the profit and cash flow statements emphasizes how misleading it is to focus on the former and to ignore the latter. In this case, HE is profitable and earning a return of £1,500 or 19% on opening capital of £8,000. Assuming £1 share units, EPS is 19 pence per share. The company also appears to be liquid and solvent if an optimistic view is taken of the cash recoverability of its unsold inventory and amounts due by customers. But the cash flow statement provides an additional message that there has been a cash reduction of £7,900.

Its importance is apparent when the operations of HE are examined in its second year of trading (as in Illustration 10).

ILLUSTRATION 10 PROFITABILITY, LIQUIDITY, AND SOLVENCY

HE continues to trade through the year to 31 December 2007. The transactions for this year are as follows:

Items traded	3 £	4 £	5 £	6 £	7 £	8 £	9 £	10 £	11 £	12 £	Total £
Credit purchases	—	—	—	—	3,500	3,500	4,000	4,000	4,000	4,000	23,000
Cash payments	—	—	3,000	3,000	3,500	3,500	4,000	4,000	4,000	—	25,000
Credit sales	—	—	4,000	—	—	4,000	4,500	4,500	—	4,500	21,500
Cash receipts	2,800	—	—	—	—	4,000	4,500	—	—	—	11,300

Purchase prices rise during 2007 and the company's suppliers are strict with their credit terms. HE has difficulty passing on cost increases to customers and recovering cash from the latter. Inventory unit 6 has become difficult to sell and inventory units 7 and 11 are also unsold by the end of 2007. The profit statement and balance sheet are as follows (again ignoring tax and dividends):

Profit statement	£	£	Notes
Sales		21,500	Inventory units 5, 8, 9, 10 and 12
Less: cost of sales:			
Opening inventory	6,000		Inventory units 5 and 6
Add: purchases	23,000		Inventory units 7–12
	29,000		
Less: closing inventory	10,500	18,500	Inventory units 6, 7 and 11
Gross profit		**3,000**	
Depreciation		1,500	
Net profit		**1,500**	

Five stock units were sold and, despite reduced profit margins on individual items, a GP was earned of £3,000, although depreciation expense reduced this to an NP of £1,500.

Balance sheet	£	£	Notes
Machine		1,500	£3,000 − 1,500
Inventory		10,500	Inventory units 6, 7, and 11
Debtors		16,600	Inventory units 4, 5, 10, and 12
		28,600	
Less: creditors	4,000		Inventory unit 12
Bank overdraft	13,600	17,600	See cash flow statement below
		11,000	
		£	
Share capital		8,000	As per 2006
Retained profit		3,000	As per 2006 + £1,500
		11,000	

Illustration 10 Profitability, Liquidity, and Solvency ● 113

The balance sheet position suggests that assets of £28,600 are sufficient to cover obligations of £17,600—thus making the company solvent. However, there is no cash available to meet payments to suppliers (£4,000) and much depends on cash recoveries made from customers (a maximum of £16,600). One customer (inventory unit 4 sold for £3,600) has been overdue for at least a year. The company's liquidity is therefore in question and the cash flow statement reveals why:

Cash flow statement	**£**
Cash inflows	11,300
Less: cash outflows	25,000
Cash deficit from operating activities	**−13,700**
	£
Bank account at beginning of 2007	100
Bank overdraft at end of 2007	−13,600
	−13,700

(1) There is an OCF deficit of £13,700 despite the GP of £3,000.

(2) The difference of £16,700 is mainly due to the acceleration of supplier payments and the lack of recovery from customers.

(3) The bank account reduces from a balance of £100 to an overdraft of £13,600 due to the £13,700 of OCF deficit.

(4) Add taxation and dividend matters to this case, and the dangers are obvious.

Illustrations 9 and 10 provide numerical examples of the accounting relationship between NP and OCF. As previously mentioned, the latter is a matching of cash inflows and outflows from trading activities and makes no accounting accrual and allocation adjustments for the timing leads and lags associated with the completion of business transactions (e.g. for amounts due to suppliers and from customers, unsold inventory, and the longer-term depreciation of the machine). These leads and lags, however, are accounted for in the calculation of NP in order to have a complete matching of sales and the various costs of these sales. The basic relationship between OCF and NP involves various accrual and allocation adjustments that take the following form:

Working capital

The periodic change in working capital (WC)—where WC is defined as the aggregate of unsold inventory and amounts due from credit customers (debtors) minus amounts due to credit suppliers (creditors).

Depreciation

The depreciation (DP) of long-term assets.

The full relationship is explained in Illustration 11 using the accounting numbers from Illustration 10.

ILLUSTRATION 11 ACCOUNTING PROFIT, WORKING CAPITAL, AND OPERATING CASH FLOW

The basic relationships are as follows:

When WC increases (↑) from beginning to end of a reporting period, then:

NP − ↑ WC + DP = OCF

When WC decreases (↓) from beginning to end of a reporting period, then:

NP + ↓ WC + DP = OCF

Thus, in Illustration 10:

Where NP is £1,500;

Opening WC is £6,400 (£6,000 + 6,400 − 6,000) (taken from the balance sheet in Illustration 9);

Closing WC is £23,100 (£10,500 + 16,600 − 4,000); and

DP is £1,500.

↑ WC = £23,100 − 6,400 = £16,700.

Then NP £1,500 − ↑ WC £16,700 + DP £1,500 = OCF £ − 13,700.

Alternatively, OCF £ − 13,700 + ↑ WC £16,700 − depreciation £1,500 = NP £1,500.

In other words, NP is a positive £1,500 and OCF is a negative £13,700.

It is crucial for users of corporate financial statements (particularly the profit statement and cash flow statement) to understand these basic relationships in order to avoid the pitfall of assuming that NP is a cash flow. Although NP and OCF are related, they have different accounting magnitudes dependent on the size and changes in the company's WC and the non-cash allocations such as depreciation. In other words, when reading a profit statement, the profit number must not be confused with its cash flow equivalent.

> **Lesson 5.5 Profit and cash flow**
> NP is a combination of accounting numbers that takes OCF and adjusts it to allow for unpaid credit transactions and past paid transactions for which benefit is currently being received. Thus, it is possible to take the calculated NP number and strip out the various accrual and allocation adjustments that are made by the accountant and to reveal OCF.

CASH FLOW REPORTING

The formal public reporting of CFA numbers began in the US in 1987 with an accounting standard from the FASB. Similar standards then appeared in most other Western countries (e.g. "Cash Flow Statements," *Financial Reporting Standard* 1, 1991 [amended 1996] in the UK). Cash flow statements are now a significant part of corporate financial reporting and are regulated by relevant accounting standards such as that of the IASB in 1993 ("Cash Flow Statements," *International Accounting Standard 7*). It is this standard that is used here to explain the disclosure of a cash flow statement of a listed company. Disclosure differences between listed and unlisted companies concern taxation and financial flows such as interest and dividends. These are explained in the text at appropriate points.

As previously mentioned, the simplest cash flow relationship is one that matches all inflows and outflows and reconciles the difference to a periodic change in cash resources. A financial statement in such terms resembles a receipts and payments account with which most individuals are familiar in their daily domestic lives. In the context of corporate businesses, however, receipts and payments take several distinct forms that require separation for purposes of meaningful reporting. These distinctions relate to OCF, ICF, and FCF as defined previously. In combination, these cash flows reconcile to the periodic change in cash resources (ΔCR) and the universal financial reporting relationship in this respect is as follows:

$$OCF \pm ICF \pm FCF = \Delta CR$$

Cash flows from operating activities

OCF has been explained previously and reflects the net periodic cash change resulting from the inflows and outflows associated with trading operations. It is useful as a signal of the company's capacity to generate surplus cash to maintain trading operations, repay debt, pay dividends, and make new additional investments without recourse to further external capital financing. The OCF of a listed company is stated with tax payments and receipts included, unless these matters can be identified with investing or financing activities (under ICF and FCF). For an unlisted company, taxation flows are disclosed as a separate section for taxation in the cash flow statement. For listed companies, there is no consensus on the reporting treatment of interest and dividend payments and receipts, except for financial institutions where they are treated as part of OCF. In the case of non-financial institutions, there is an argument to be made that interest payments are operating outflows related directly to the consequences of trading activities (and therefore part of the calculation of OCF), and dividends are a return on capital and should be regarded as financing outflows (and therefore part of the calculation of FCF). For unlisted companies, interest payments and receipts are disclosed in a separate section and dividends paid are also separately disclosed.

OCF can be reported in terms of actual cash flows (i.e. what is called the direct method) or as a derivative of accounting profit NP adjusted for accounting accruals and allocations during the period (i.e. what is called the indirect method). The direct method is preferable as the numbers come directly from the company's cash records and should present no problem other than the need for careful classification. The indirect method, on the other hand, is less desirable as it depends on reversing the accounting effects of accruals and allocations made in the calculation of NP. It follows the relationships and adjustments between NP, WC, and OCF as explained in Illustration 11 above. The cash flow statement under the indirect method typically discloses these relationships and adjustments. However, not all accounting numbers comprising WC necessarily relate to trading transactions and therefore to NP and OCF. Some accruals, for example, may concern investment transactions (and therefore ICF) (e.g. equipment purchased on credit). Thus, when calculating OCF by adjusting NP for changes in WC, it is essential that the latter excludes any accrual that should be associated with either ICF or FCF calculations. The following example demonstrates this point.

Johnny-Be-Good Ltd (JBG) has prepared its cash flow statement for the year 2006. NP for the period is £12,000 (after DP of £3,000) and ΔWC is an increase of £5,000. The company acquired a machine on 1 January 2006 for £9,000, £3,000 of which remained unpaid and due on 31 December 2006. The creditor is included in the ΔWC number. FCF is a net inflow of £2,000 and ΔCR is £3,000. If JBG uses the indirect method to calculate OCF and ignores the association of the £3,000 credit obligation with the investment in the machine, then the cash flow statement discloses the following accounting numbers:

(1) OCF is calculated at £10,000 (NP £12,000 − ΔWC £5,000 + DP £3,000).

(2) Therefore OCF £10,000 + FCF £2,000 − ICF £9,000 = ΔCR £3,000.
However, if the outstanding credit obligation of £3,000 for the purchase of the machine is properly adjusted in calculating ICF, then:

(3) The number for OCF is calculated as £7,000 (NP £12,000 − ΔWC £8,000* + DP £3,000).

(4) Therefore OCF £7,000 + FCF £2,000 − ICF £6,000** = ΔCR £3,000.

$*\Delta$WC = £5,000 + 3,000; $**$ICF = £9,000 − 3,000

In other words, in the first calculation, OCF and ICF are both overstated by £3,000 as the credit obligation for that amount is wrongly treated as an operating rather than investing obligation. JBG's ability to generate OCF is therefore overstated and the level of invest-ment it has paid for in 2006 is similarly inflated. This does not provide reliable cash flow information for report users and does not permit reliable comparisons between periods and with similar companies.

Cash flows from investing activities

ICF describes cash inflows and outflows relating to the acquisition and sale of longer-term assets such as land and buildings, plant and machinery, and investments in other enti-ties (including subsidiary and associated companies, joint ventures, and partnerships). It also includes loans and advances (unless the reporting entity is a financial institution), and various financial contracts dependent on future outcomes. As suggested above, the major accounting problem with the calculation of ICF is one that also affects the calculation of NP—i.e. determining whether a cash outflow is capital expenditure (and therefore to be included in ICF and depreciated for NP purposes) or an operating expense (and therefore to be included in OCF and matched against sales revenues in NP calculations). Deliber-ate or inadvertent errors of classification in this area can have significant effects on both NP and OCF—particularly inflating both numbers if the transaction is regarded as capital expenditure. The following situation illustrates this effect.

Fly-Me-To-The-Moon Ltd (FMM) is a travel firm and prepares its financial statements for the year 2006. NP for the period is £10,000 (after treating a major renovation expense of £4,000 as an operating cost). The renovation has an estimated life of four years. OCF is £8,000, having treated the cash outflow for the renovation in a manner consistent with NP. The following are the NP and OCF numbers as they should have been reported (assuming depreciation DP on an equal annual basis):

(1) The NP of £10,000 should have been £10,000 + renovation £4,000 − DP £1,000 = £13,000.

(2) The OCF of £8,000 should have been £8,000 + renovation £4,000 = £12,000.

In other words, NP is overstated by £3,000 and OCF by £4,000. ICF is understated by £4,000. None of the original numbers in the cash flow statement provide shareholders and other users of FMM's corporate financial report with reliable information about the company's capacity to generate cash flow. The corporate governance process is not served well by such a statement in this case.

Cash flows from financing activities

FCF relates to cash inflows and outflows concerning the proceeds and repayments of share capital and loans. These matters may appear straightforward with regard to classification. However, even here, there is room for manipulation. A particular concern is with respect to transactions that are deliberately written into contracts as if they were sales when, in reality, they are effectively loans to the reporting company. The following case provides an example of the effect of such deliberate misclassification on NP, OCF, and FCF.

During the year 2006, Sideward Mobility Ltd (SM) enters into a contract with There-For-You Bank (TFYB) to sell the bank goods worth £50,000 (their purchase cost was £20,000, incurred during 2005). The contract stipulates that, at the end of 2010, TFYB will resell the goods to SM for £70,000. TFYB paid cash for the goods and they remained on the premises of SM. The transaction was treated as a sale in the accounting records of both entities and as unsold inventory in the balance sheet of TFYB. In the financial statements of SM for 2006, the following accounting numbers appears in its profit statement and cash flow statement:

(1) NP includes the gain on the sale of the goods of £30,000 (£50,000 – 20,000).

(2) OCF includes the cash inflow of £50,000 and CR increases by £50,000. There is no cash outflow as the cash payment for the goods took place in the previous year of 2005.

The problem, however, is that the transaction is not a sale. In fact, it is a loan by TFYB of £50,000 and SM can regain ownership of the goods in 2010 at a cost of £70,000. What this means is that SM received a loan of £50,000 and will repay £70,000, £20,000 of which is interest on the loan. In the cash flow statement of SM for 2005:

(3) OCF should be £50,000 less than is reported, and FCF £50,000 more. CR will remain the same as £50,000 of cash was deposited in SM's bank account.

(4) NP should be £30,000 less than reported. The company's balance sheet should continue to report the goods of unsold inventory at a cost of £20,000 and the loan of £50,000 should be disclosed as a liability.

The effect of the misclassification by SM of the cash inflow from TYB is that the company:

(5) Overstates OCF and deflates FCF in the cash flow statement.

(6) Overstates NP in the profit statement.

(7) Understates unsold inventory and liabilities in the balance sheet.

By constructing a loan agreement as if it were a sale, significant misreporting takes place. The extent of the accounting error emphasizes the inter-dependence of profit and cash flow accounting calculations and statements.

DISCLOSURE OF CASH FLOW STATEMENTS

The previous sections of this chapter concentrate on outlining the basic structure and accounting for the cash flow statement. This section focuses on disclosure and contrasts cash flow statements of unlisted and listed companies. In doing so, it also emphasizes the differences between the direct and indirect methods of accounting for cash flows, and introduces two additional routine matters of disclosure (i.e. corresponding figures and notes to the cash flow statement). The following cash flow statement is that of It-Could-Only-Happen Ltd (ICOH). It assumes the direct basis of accounting for cash flows and includes comparative figures.

It-Could-Only-Happen Ltd
Cash Flow Statement for Year Ending 31 December 2006

2005 (£)		£	£
	Cash flows from operating activities		
1,657,000	Cash received from customers		2,068,000
1,348,000	*Less*: cash paid for supplies of goods and overheads		*1,617,000*
309,000			**451,000**
	Investment income and financing costs		
9,000	Dividends received	12,000	
8,000	*Less*: interest paid	*10,000*	
1,000			**2,000**
	Taxation		
60,000	Taxation paid		*70,000*
	Cash flows from financing activities		
—	Long-term loan received	150,000	
120,000	*Less*: repayment of long-term loan	*70,000*	
120,000			**80,000**
	Cash flows from investing activities		
24,000	Cash paid for buildings and equipment	*849,000*	
—	*Less*: sale of buildings	231,000	
24,000			*618,000*
	Dividends		
50,000	Dividends paid to shareholders		*50,000*
	Net increase/*reduction* in		
56,000	**cash assets**		*205,000*
145,000	Opening cash assets	201,000	
201,000	*Less*: closing cash assets	*4,000*	
56,000	**Change in cash assets**		*205,000*

Unlisted companies

The cash flow statement for ICOH as an unlisted company has seven main sections. These include OCF (£451,000), FCF (£80,000), ICF (£618,000), and ΔCR (£205,000). There are also separate sections for investment income and financing costs (£2,000), taxation paid (£70,000), and dividends paid (£50,000). For listed companies, these last three items are included appropriately in OCF, FCF, and ICF. In 2006, ICOH generated OCF of £451,000 and, supplemented by other net income of £2,000, used this to pay for tax and dividends of £120,000 (£70,000 + 50,000). This left £333,000 (£451,000 + 2,000 − 70,000 − 50,000) to augment FCF (£80,000) and fund ICF of £618,000. The difference of £205,000 was funded by available cash assets of £201,000 and a bank overdraft of £4,000.

Corresponding figures

It is normal financial reporting practice, legislated in the UK under the Companies Act 1985, to provide not only the accounting numbers for the year of reporting but also the corresponding figures for the previous period. These provide the reader of financial statements with a means of making comparisons between one period and the next to determine significant changes and thus to ask pertinent questions, thus improving the process of managerial accountability inherent in corporate financial reporting. The practice of comparative figures extends to the cash flow statement. The comparative figures for ICOH reveal that, in 2005, the company generated OCF of £309,000 and other net income of £1,000 to pay for tax (£60,000) and dividends (£50,000), and repay loans of £120,000. This left £80,000 (£309,000 + 1,000 − 60,000 − 50,000 − 120,000) to pay for ICF of £24,000 and increase cash resources by £56,000.

Notes to cash flow statement

Financial statements such as the cash flow statement are complex sources of financial information based on established and accepted accounting relationships. Because of their inherent complexity, and the need to both provide required information and understanding of that information, companies disclose additional explanations and disclosure in notes to the main financial statements. These notes affect the cash flow statement and would typically aim at improving understanding of the main cash flows and their relationship over the designated period. In the case of ICOH above, such notes could be provided to explain for 2006 the additional borrowing to fund the new investment and the use of existing cash assets to also assist in such funding.

Listed companies

The disclosure of cash flow information for listed companies is governed by the IASB and is less complex than for unlisted companies. It effectively focuses on sections for OCF, FCF, ICF, and ΔCR. The following example uses the case of ICOH above by assuming it is a listed company. It also assumes the indirect basis of accounting for cash flows in which NP is adjusted for the periodic ΔWC to obtain OCF. Other differences compared to an unlisted company put the net other income (£2,000 for 2006) and taxation (£70,000 for 2006) under OCF and dividends paid (£50,000 for 2006) under FCF.

It-Could-Only-Happen plc
Cash Flow Statement for Year Ending 31 December 2006

2005 (£)		£	£
	Cash flows from operating activities		
415,000	Net profit before taxation		611,000
	Add: depreciation of buildings and		
60,000	equipment		65,000
475,000			**676,000**
160,000	*Less*: increase in inventory		*206,000*
102,000	Increase in debtors		*151,000*
97,000	Add: increase in creditors		134,000
60,000	*Less*: taxation paid		*70,000*
250,000			**383,000**
	Cash flows from financing activities		
—	Long-term loan received	150,000	
120,000	*Less*: repayment of long-term loan	*70,000*	
120,000		**80,000**	
50,000	*Less*: dividends paid	*50,000*	
170,000			**30,000**
	Cash flows from investing activities		
	Cash paid for buildings and		
24,000	equipment	*849,000*	
—	*Less*: sale of buildings	231,000	
24,000			*618,000*
	Net increase/*reduction* in cash		
56,000	**in cash assets**		*205,000*
145,000	Opening cash assets	201,000	
201,000	*Less*: closing cash assets	4,000	
56,000	**Change in cash assets**		*205,000*

The cash flow statement for ICOH as a listed company does not result in substantial differences in the main accounting numbers disclosed as compared to an unlisted company. The assumption of the indirect method of accounting means that OCF is calculated by taking NP (from the company's profit statement), adding depreciation (again from the profit statement), and deducting the change in working capital in 2006 (from the balance sheet). Details of these adjustments are disclosed in the OCF section of the cash flow statement. In addition, numbers for interest received and paid and taxation paid are included in the OCF section. This means that, for ICOH as an unlisted company, OCF is £451,000 in 2006. As a listed company, OCF is £383,000. The difference of £68,000 is due to other net income of £2,000 and taxation paid of £70,000. The only other major difference is with FCF where dividends paid are deducted in the listed company format.

ISSUES WITH CASH FLOW STATEMENTS

There are a variety of accounting issues that affect the preparation of corporate cash flow statements. These include coping with foreign currencies and non-cash transactions, defining cash resources, additional disclosures required to support the statement, and smoothing disclosures.

Foreign exchange

Cash inflows and outflows in foreign currencies are normally converted at exchange rates recorded at the time of the flows or at rates approximating the actual rate (e.g. the weighted average for the reporting period). This is a similar practice to equivalent transactions and records affecting the profit statement.

Non-cash transactions

Non-cash transactions (e.g. the receipt of an asset as payment for an obligation) are usually disclosed separately as a note to the financial statements rather than as cash flow equivalents in the cash flow statement. Their significance with respect to assessing solvency and liquidity, however, suggests that it would be prudent for the statement user to treat non-cash transactions as if they were cash-based and incorporate them as cash flow equivalents in any analysis.

Cash resources

OCF, ICF, and FCF are reported separately and in detail before they reconcile to the periodic change in cash resources ΔCR. CR is typically defined as a combination of cash and cash equivalents—where cash comprises cash on hand and on deposit, and cash equivalents include short-term and highly liquid investments that are readily realisable. Defining CR can be problematic in practice as there are many forms of monetary assets. It is essential therefore that there is consistency over time as far as preparation of the cash flow statement is concerned if its users are to be sure of the comparability of the cash flow numbers over time and between companies.

Other disclosures

In addition to the cash flow statements, there are other disclosures to report in order to ensure that the cash flow message to report users is as clear and as comprehensible as possible. These additional disclosures mainly focus on information that brings clarity and understanding to a reading and analysis of the cash flow statement. They can include reporting the existence of cash resources that cannot be accessed easily due to exchange controls imposed by a foreign government. Disclosure should also be made about the amount of unused borrowing facility (FCF) available to the reporting company for future investing activity (ICF).

Smoothing

Cash flow statements are disclosed each year and contain current and previous year accounting numbers. However, cash flow data are volatile due to the timing of cash transactions and the lack of accounting accrual and allocation techniques that have the affect of smoothing the trend of profits reported in the profit statement. In particular, ICF and FCF are naturally lumpy because company managers invest, disinvest, finance, and repay when specific projects and contracts either come on stream or reach completion. OCF can also be affected by cash flow fluctuations due to the timing difference between the cash payment at the start of a transaction cycle and the cash receipt at its completion. For this reason, it is possible for cash flow statement users to construct cash flow data bases for individual companies that not only contain OCF, ICF, FCF, and ΔCR for several years, but also multi-period rolling totals that avoid the inherent lumpiness in cash flows for the reasons stated above and permit trends to be detected without the undue distortions of annual peaks and troughs in cash flow data. This matter is examined further in Chapter 10.

CORPORATE GOVERNANCE AND CASH FLOW STATEMENTS

One of the most fundamental aspects concerning the survival of a company is the ability of its management to generate sufficient cash—particularly OCF—to enable it to meet its debt obligations and invest in the future. More specifically, failure to translate profits into OCF is ultimately one of the most basic failures of corporate management. The history of companies is full of examples of companies that had excellent products or services, viable markets and good marketing strategies, and prices and costs that ensured profits. However, they also had managers who neglected the crucial financial management function in which control of inventory levels, speedy cash collections from customers, and prompt payments to suppliers are key factors in corporate success. For these reasons, the cash flow statement is an important source of information for shareholders and other stakeholders concerning the ability of managers to generate and manage cash flows. It therefore is a significant part of the accountability exercise that financial reporting fulfils and should be regarded as material part of corporate governance. In this respect, it focuses on a very specific dimension of management—i.e. the ability of senior managers to control the cash flow of the company.

LEGISLATIVE AND REGULATORY REQUIREMENTS

There is no specific provision in the Companies Act 1985 in the UK that requires companies to publish a cash flow statement. However, the accounting standards of the ASB apply to all companies required to provide a true and fair view of their financial results. Therefore, "Cash Flow Statements," *Financial Reporting Standard 1* (1996) applies in the UK to unlisted companies. As previously stated, listed companies are required to adhere to the equivalent IASB standard of 1993—"Cash Flow Statements," *International Accounting Standard 7*.

LEARNING OBJECTIVES

Please review the learning objectives at the beginning of this chapter and ensure they have been achieved before proceeding to Chapter 6 on the nature and purpose of the balance sheet.

Exercise 1   Profit and cash flow statements

What are the main accounting differences between a profit statement and a cash flow state-ment? Students should discuss with their instructor the relative utility of the two statements. For example, if investment decisions are based on forecasts of cash flow returns in the form of dividends, why do investors pay so much attention to profit-related information?

Exercise 2   Cash flow elements

Explain what is meant by OCF, FCF, and ICF, and how they relate to each other in the cash flow statement. Students should explore further with their instructor the idea of personal cash flows in order to better understand the relationships in a corporate cash flow statement.

Exercise 3   Cash flow statement use

To what uses can a cash flow statement be put? When answering, distinguish between profitability, liquidity, and solvency. Students should revisit the sections of Chapter 5 dealing with the definition of solvency and liquidity before leaving this exercise.

Exercise 4   Cash flow calculations

Assume the following transactions take place in a company—purchase of goods on credit for £4,000 (A), £7,000 (B), and £2,000 (C); payment for goods A and B of £4,000 and £7,000; and sale of goods A for £6,500 on credit of which £2,500 has been recovered. Calculate the GP and OCF of the company from these transactions.

Exercise 5   Cash flow calculations

Assume that all cash transactions in Exercise 4 are completed in the next accounting period. Calculate the GP and OCF for the period. Goods B and C are sold for £10,000 and £3,000 respectively. All cash is recovered from customers.

Exercise 6   Indirect method

Explain what is meant by the indirect method of calculating the accounting numbers in the cash flow statement. Discuss its strengths and weaknesses. Use Exercise 4 to illustrate your points.

ADDITIONAL READING

There are numerous sources in the literature on cash flow accounting and reporting. The following are given as a selection.

Accounting Standards Board (1996), "Cash Flow Statements," *Statement of Financial Reporting 1*, Accounting Standards Board, London. This is the current UK requirement for cash flow reporting and is additional to legal requirements for disclosure of a profit statement and balance sheet.

A J Arnold and R T Wearing (1991), *A Report on Cash Flow Statements/Accounting*, Institutes of Chartered Accountants in England and Wales and of Scotland, London and Edinburgh. This monograph provides a review of cash flow statements and CFA at the time of the introduction of the UK accounting standard.

Financial Accounting Standards Board (1987), "Cash Flows Statement," *Statement of Financial Accounting Standards 95*, Financial Accounting Standards Board, Stamford, CT. This is the US equivalent to the UK and international accounting standard on cash flow statements.

L C Heath (1978), "Financial Reporting and the Evaluation of Solvency," *Accounting Research Monograph 3*, American Institute of Certified Public Accountants, New York, NY. This monograph precedes the introduction of CFA in the US and focuses particularly on the related issues of solvency and liquidity.

International Accounting Standards Board (1993), "Cash Flow Statements," *International Accounting Standard 7*, International Accounting Standards Board, London. This is the current international standard as referred to in this chapter.

T A Lee (1996a), "Cash Flow Accounting," in M Chatfield and R Vangermeersch, *The History of Accounting: An International Encyclopedia*, Garland Publishing, New York, NY, 101–04. This is a brief history of CFA and cash flow statements.

T A Lee (1996b), "Cash Flow Accounting," in M Warner, *International Encyclopedia of Business and Management*, Routledge, London, 602–11. This is a comprehensive explanation of CFA and cash flow statements to supplement this chapter.

P B W Miller and P R Bahnson (2000), "Quality Financial Reporting: Cash Flows or Cash Flaws?" *Accounting Today*, October 23–November 5, 14 and 15. These writers discuss the flaws and limitations inherent in the current reporting of cash flows by companies.

CHAPTER 6

Corporate Balance Sheet

Learning Objectives

This chapter explains the structure and content as well as the main objectives, uses, conventions, and regulations of the corporate balance sheet in the UK. The balance sheet is alternatively titled the statement of financial position in countries such as the US. The term balance sheet, however, is used throughout this chapter. By the end of the chapter, you should be able to identify and understand:

- The purposes of the corporate balance sheet.
- The major decisions assisted by the corporate balance sheet.
- The relation of time to the corporate balance sheet.
- The main sections and components of the corporate balance sheet, particularly those dealing with assets, liabilities, and shareholders' equity.
- The accounting basis of the balance sheet and its relationship to the profit statement and cash flow statement.
- The main accounting conventions used in the production of the balance sheet.
- The subjective nature of accounting for assets, liabilities, and shareholders' equity.
- The major accounting issues affecting the corporate balance sheet.
- In general terms, the legislative and regulatory provisions governing the preparation and disclosure of the corporate balance sheet.
- The relationship of the balance sheet to the function of corporate governance.

At the end of this chapter, please refer to these learning objectives before moving on to Chapter 7 on other financial statements.

INTRODUCTION

Chapters 4 and 5, respectively, explain two statements of financial flow—i.e. the profit statement and the cash flow statement. Both statements reflect the financial consequences of various operating, investing, and financing decisions made by corporate management over a defined period of time. They attempt to describe the financial progress of the reporting company through time by capturing the financial consequences of a continuous stream of business contracts and transactions. They therefore report on the financial outcome of managerial activity and can be used to judge the performance of the reporting company and its managers. The profit statement and the cash flow statement are relevant to the exercise of managerial accountability and the wider function of corporate governance.

Financial descriptions of corporate progress such as profitability and cash flow, however, should be accompanied by a statement of the condition of the company at the end of each reporting period. These statements of position are a necessary link between one reporting period and the next and permit an assessment of the financial health of the company as a result of the progress or lack of progress it has achieved. In other words, accounting flow and position statements provide a balanced and comprehensive financial picture of the company. This is little different from information used in other aspects of human activity. For example:

Travel

When making a journey between two cities or towns, a car driver usually has a variety of information sources that in combination provide knowledge about the "dynamics" and the "state of play" in the journey. For example, the odometer records miles travelled. The clock states the current time. The fuel gauge indicates petrol consumed and still to be consumed. Oil pressure and water temperature provide signals of engine condition. External signposts indicate geographical locations. By using these sources in combination, the driver knows something about the condition of the car, where he or she is located at any particular time, how much of the journey has been completed, and how much has still to come. A car with integrated computer and satellite navigation systems provides its driver with even more flow and condition information.

Education

Children educated in a school system are continually assessed in order to determine their educational progress over defined periods of time. They are also judged by examinations at specific points of time for purposes of moving to the next stage of the system, another system such as university, or employment. Scores achieved provide a comparative basis to measure the progress over time of the individual student. When aggregated, however, they also provide an overall picture of the current state of the educational achievement of the student in relation to specific skills such as literacy and numeracy or particular subjects and syllabi. When aggregated further, student scores enable specific classes, schools, and educational systems to be ranked and compared.

Sport

Sportsmen and women compete in individual games or competitions over time and achieve specific scores or results in each game or competition in which they participate. For example, a professional golfer competes in a number of tournaments over a year, achieves a specific score for each round completed in each tournament, and obtains a specific place and monetary reward in each tournament in which four rounds are completed. These scores, places, and rewards are performance outcomes and let the interested observer know how the golfer has performed in each tournament. However, unless they are processed further, the scores, places, and rewards do not provide information about the status of the golfer in relation to his or her rivals at a specific point in time. For this reason, professional golfers are ranked on the basis of an aggregation of individual tournament scores and places. These rankings reflect overall status as well as status within specific sub-disciplines such as driving and putting.

Employment

Adults in employment are rewarded for their efforts in the workplace by contracted remuneration based on the number of hours worked or specific targets met. This remuneration provides the income from which these individuals pay for daily household expenses, longer-term obligations, and luxuries. When quantified, the relevant numbers reflect cash flowing to and from the individual. They do not, however, provide a numerical picture of the financial state of the individual at a specific point in time (e.g. at the end of the month or year, or at retirement). For information about that condition, the individual needs numbers on resources available (e.g. cash in the bank or value of home owned) and obligations due (e.g. credit card balance or mortgage outstanding).

What these examples illustrate is a human need to take stock of things at a particular point in time in addition to being informed about how things have progressed over time. In this sense, such information is similar to a still photograph during a video sequence. The video tells the story over time but, occasionally, there is a need to freeze the frame and look at the position at that point. The most obvious example of this type of information is in sporting activity where stopping the video record permits an informed decision to take place. This typically happens when there is doubt about a decision by a referee or judge in relation to the behaviour of participants in a game. For example:

(1) In a soccer game, the ball is passed from one player to another and there is doubt about whether the latter player was in a permitted position to receive the pass.

(2) In a cricket or baseball game, the ball is hit by a batsman to a fielder and there is doubt about whether it was grounded before the catch was taken.

(3) In a sprint race, several runners cross the finishing line and there is doubt as to which runner was the winner.

In each of these illustrations, the video portrays the pass, hit, or finish in the context of a continuous stream of action. But, unless the frame is frozen at the point of the pass, hit, or finish, there is often insufficient information on which to base a decision. The still photograph is therefore a useful additional source of information in a continuous stream of activity.

In accounting, the balance sheet is the still photograph that relates to the video record represented in the profit and cash flow statements. As in other aspects of human activity, corporate shareholders and other stakeholders benefit from financial information about the current condition of the company with which they are associated. In this sense, current condition represents the financial position of a reporting company calculated in accounting terms at a specific point in time—i.e. the end of the financial period to which the profit statement and cash flow statement relate. In other words, with respect to a defined financial period of time such as a year:

(1) The period starts with a statement of the financial position of the reporting company in terms of resources and obligations available for use in business (i.e. the balance sheet accounted for at the end of the previous period).

(2) The period contains various management actions and decisions in relation to resources and obligations that produce business contracts and transactions forming accounting outcomes reported in the profit statement and cash flow statement.

(3) The period ends with a statement of the financial position of the reporting company in terms of resources and obligations as a result of the contracts and transactions accounted for in profit and cash flow terms (i.e. the closing balance sheet).

The balance sheet is therefore a quantified stepping stone in the financial stream of profitability and cash flow achieved by the reporting company.

BASIC ACCOUNTING RELATIONSHIP

As a static portrayal of the reporting company, the balance sheet reflects a simple relationship that is often difficult to account for in accurate or realistic terms. The relationship is intended to represent the financial position or condition of the company at a precise point in time—e.g. on the last day of an annual reporting period. It describes three related financial features of the company:

Assets

The resources held in order to undertake its business operations. Assets are the cash and non-cash resources controlled by the company as a result of past contracts and transactions and from which profits and cash are expected to flow through use.

Liabilities

The obligations contracted in order to fund these resources. Liabilities are obligations arising from past contracts and transactions with lenders and creditors which, when settled, result in an outflow of cash assets from the company.

Equity

The capital attributable to its shareholder owners. Shareholders' equity is the residue of assets remaining after deduction of liabilities. It represents the capital provided by the shareholders together with any profits retained in the company and any other gains and losses not reported

Illustration 12 Jim Jones Insurance Ltd ● **129**

through the profit statement. Shareholders' equity is the term used by listed companies in the UK. Non-listed companies use the alternative term of capital employed. For purposes of simplicity in further explanations, the term shareholders' equity is used throughout except in numerical illustrations of balance sheets of non-listed companies.

The relationship is one of numerical equivalence in the form of assets − liabilities = shareholders' equity.

The three basic elements of the balance sheet relationship can be seen in the following Illustration 12.

ILLUSTRATION 12 JIM JONES INSURANCE LTD

Jim Jones is employed by an insurance company and has personal savings of £60,000 deposited in a bank account. On 1 January 2006, he opens an insurance agency, Jim Jones Insurance Ltd (JJI), and invests his savings in shares in the company. The initial balance sheet is as follows:

Balance Sheet as at 1 January 2006

	£
Asset	
Cash in bank	60,000
Capital employed	
Share capital	60,000

This balance sheet describes the financial position of JJI prior to any business contract or transaction. The company has a single asset (the bank account of £60,000) and share capital of the same amount held by Jim Jones.

On 3 January 2006, JJI purchases office accommodation for £100,000 and office equipment and furnishings for £20,000. A mortgage loan of £70,000 is negotiated with the company's bank and cash of £30,000 is used to complete the purchase of the office. The balance sheet of the company after these transactions is as follows:

Balance Sheet as at 3 January 2006

	£
Assets	
Office	100,000
Equipment	20,000
Cash in bank	10,000
Total assets	**130,000**
Less:	
Liability	
Mortgage loan	70,000
Net assets	**60,000**
	£
Capital employed	
Share capital	60,000
	60,000

The balance sheet after completion of the purchase of the office and equipment follows the basic accounting equation of assets minus liabilities equating with equity. JJI has three specific assets—office £100,000, equipment £20,000, and bank account £10,000 (i.e. £60,000 − 30,000 − 20,000). It also has a liability of £70,000. The balancing figure is its share capital of £60,000 (as before). In other words, the company has acquired £70,000 of additional assets by borrowing that sum and re-allocating the cash asset of £60,000 to assist in the purchase of the office (£30,000) and equipment (£20,000).

The format used in presenting the balance sheet is of a vertical structure that starts with assets and moves to liabilities before arriving at shareholders' equity (capital employed). This is the format that is almost universally adopted in the UK and elsewhere. An alternative format discloses the same information horizontally. This involves two columns—the first includes shareholders' equity and liabilities, and the second deals with assets. This was the typical way of presenting a corporate balance sheet prior to the 1970s and that for JJI would appear in that style as follows:

Balance Sheet as at 3 January 2006

	£		£
Capital employed		**Assets**	
Share capital	60,000	Office	100,000
Liability		Equipment	20,000
Mortgage loan	70,000	Cash in bank	10,000
Total capital and liability	**130,000**	**Total assets**	**130,000**

BALANCE SHEET ELEMENTS

The above illustration reveals the structure of the balance sheet. However, it also points to its basic elements that are discussed in more detail later in the chapter.

Assets

The illustration lists three assets (i.e. office, equipment, and cash). These are owned by the company, under the control of its management, and available for use in its business operations as an insurance agency in order to produce future economic benefits. In effect, future economic benefits mean future cash flows from either business activity with customers or resale. The office is owned by the company although this ownership will be used as security for the mortgage loan (i.e. ownership will transfer to the bank should the company default on its loan repayment obligations). The office will be used to generate insurance business contracts with customers seeking insurance protection. The equipment is owned by the company and will assist in the generation of business with customers. The cash in the bank is in the name of the company and is available for making business payments.

Each asset is clearly of a different type and is classified accordingly for accounting and reporting. The classification is made in terms of the relative realizability of the assets (i.e. their availability for use to fund cash outflows in the business):

(1) The office has been purchased for long-term use as business accommodation and is not regarded as currently available for resale although it may be highly realizable on the property market. It is likely to facilitate the generation of NP and OCF for the company and to appreciate in value rather than to depreciate. Such long-term assets are described in the corporate balance sheet as fixed assets and disclosed as such in the UK in the balance sheets of non-listed companies. The alternative term used in listed companies is non-current assets.

(2) Equipment is also purchased for long-term use in the generation of NP and OCF rather than for resale and is therefore categorized as a fixed asset or non-current asset. However, its value is likely to diminish over time through use and technological obsolescence. It is often not readily realizable because of its specific operational use.

(3) Cash in the bank is an asset that is available for immediate use in the generation of NP and OCF—e.g. the payment of daily expenses or the repayment of liabilities such as the mortgage. Such assets are described as current assets in corporate balance sheets.

Thus, in most corporate balance sheets, the asset component of the accounting relationship comprises two main elements disclosed in order of realizability—i.e. fixed (or non-current) assets and current assets. In the case of JJI, fixed assets are £120,000 (office and equipment) and current assets are £10,000 (cash in bank).

Liabilities

The illustration reveals only one type of liability—the mortgage loan. In most corporate situations, however, there are two main categories of liability and these are described in terms of their repayment timing.

(1) A mortgage loan is usually repaid over a period of several years and can be described as either a long- or medium-term liability. In the UK, these liabilities are reported as long-term liabilities in non-listed companies and non-current liabilities in listed companies. Long-term liabilities are legally recognized as liabilities that fall due in a year or more.

(2) Long-term liabilities are distinguishable from short-term liabilities that require repayment in less than one year. The latter are described in the UK as current liabilities in both non-listed and listed companies. They are legally defined as liabilities that fall due within one year. If JJI had purchased some of its equipment on credit, this would create a liability to be repaid in the short-term.

Thus, in a corporate balance sheet, the liability component of the accounting relationship comprises two elements—liabilities due in more than one year and liabilities due in less than one year. In the case of JJI, the mortgage loan is a liability due in more than one year of £70,000.

Shareholders' equity (capital employed)

This accounting number is arithmetically a residual, being the difference between total assets and total liabilities. It attempts to represent the remaining assets if all the liabilities were repaid. Shareholders' equity represents two parts—the shares issued to and held by the shareholder owners, and the accumulated profits from previous periods that have not been distributed to the shareholders. In the case of JJI, share capital is £60,000 and there are no retained profits as the company has not commenced trading.

> **Lesson 6.1 Balance sheet**
> A balance sheet describes the financial position of a reporting company at a specific point in time. That position is dependent on the assets and liabilities accounted for by the company, the share capital it issues, and the profits it accounts for in the profit statement.

> **Lesson 6.2 Assets and liabilities**
> There are different types of asset and liability for reporting purposes by a company. The normal convention with assets is to distinguish assets held for long-term operational use (fixed or non-current assets) from assets held for short-term use and resale (current assets). For disclosure purposes within these two main categories, assets are presented in order of realizability—from the least to the most realizable. The normal convention with liabilities is to distinguish liabilities to be repaid in the long-term (non-current) from liabilities to be repaid in the near future (current liabilities).

BALANCE SHEET NUMBERS

The accounting numbers used to describe assets, liabilities, and shareholders' equity in a corporate balance sheet are derived from the business transactions that created them. They therefore typically describe the transaction value at the date of each transaction. For example:

(1) The office owned by JJI above cost £100,000 on 3 January 2006. This figure is normally used by accountants to describe it in the balance sheet. It represents what accountants describe as the historical cost of the office. Should the market value of the office appreciate to, say, £125,000 by the end of 2006 accountants will not normally recognize the unrealized appreciation in value of £25,000. The effect over the long-term is that the disclosed historical cost significantly understates the value of the fixed asset. Some companies provide a note to the balance sheet that discloses the unrecorded appreciation.

(2) The equipment owned by JJI cost £20,000 on 3 January 2006 and this forms the basis for its disclosure in the balance sheet as a fixed asset. However, unlike property such as the office, equipment quickly reduces in value due to use in

the business and, increasingly, due to technological obsolescence. At the year-end of 31 December 2006, for example, when the first company balance sheet for publication is prepared, the initial cost will be reduced by an amount that represents depreciation of the equipment due to use and/or obsolescence. The depreciation reduction is based on the initial cost (i.e. £20,000) reduced by any expected residual value (say, £2,000) spread over the expected useful life (e.g. three years). In the case of JJI, assuming an equal depreciation each year, the annual reduction would be £6,000 (i.e. £20,000 − 2,000 = £18,000 divided by three). The net amount of £14,000 (i.e. cost minus depreciation written off to date or £20,000 − 6,000) appears in the balance sheet and the depreciation in the profit statement as an expense in calculating NP. The balance sheet amount of £14,000 seems to represent a current market or resale value. However, it is only coincidently that this is the case. Instead, it is nothing more than the undepreciated portion of the purchase cost of the fixed asset.

(3) The mortgage loan of £70,000 is disclosed as a long-term liability of the company. It reduces through time due to contracted repayments. For example, assume the loan agreement held by JJI provides that the loan is to be repaid over seven years in annual amounts of £10,000. Then, in the company's balance sheet at 31 December 2006, the loan will be disclosed at £60,000. A note to the balance sheet will normally reveal that the loan is secured over the title deeds of the office, thus warning shareholders that the fixed asset is not completely at the disposal of the company.

(4) Cash in the bank is arguably the easiest asset to account for and disclose in the balance sheet. It is represented at its face value and changes according to the business transactions that JJI processes through the account. Should the company with the agreement of its bank take out of the bank account more cash than was put in then the account ceases to be a current asset and, instead, becomes a current liability. It is described in the balance sheet as a bank overdraft.

(5) Shareholders' equity is an accounting residual comprised of share capital issued to shareholders and profits retained by the company rather than distributed to shareholders. In accounting terms, it equates to the difference between total assets and total liabilities of the reporting company. In the case of JJI, this amounts to £60,000 at 3 January 2006 and will change by 31 December 2006 according to how profitable the company has been and what proportion of its profits it has not distributed. Shareholders' equity does not represent the market value of the company's capital. This can be very different from the disclosed amount. For example, in the case of JJI, although shareholders' equity is £60,000, it is unlikely that this reflects the market value of it shares. A buyer could assess it at a much larger figure on the basis of an optimistic view of the company's potential. Alternatively, a buyer may be willing to pay less than £60,000 because of a more pessimistic view of that potential.

Lesson 6.3 Original costs and market values

The corporate balance sheet comprises accounting numbers that purport to represent the current state of the assets, liabilities, and shareholders' equity. In fact, these numbers are based on the various originating transactions and values and do not necessarily represent current market values. Even if adjustments are made to the originating values (termed historical costs), the net effect should not be regarded as equivalent to current market values.

BASIC BALANCE SHEET

The basic accounting relationship identified above can be summarized as follows:

Fixed (non-current) assets + current assets = **total assets**

−

Long-term (non-current) liabilities + current liabilities

=

Net assets

=

Share capital + retained profits

=

Shareholders' equity or **capital employed**

The relationship's basic structure does not vary from company to company, particularly as it is inherent in legislative disclosure requirements in the Companies Act 1985. However, there will be differences in the content disclosed under each heading and in the precise details of the formatting and disclosure in order to accommodate the different asset and liability structures of companies. Illustration 13 provides an example of a corporate balance sheet that uses the relationship described above.

ILLUSTRATION 13 RUNALOT SPORTS LTD

Runalot Sports Ltd is a manufacturer of running shoes for men and women. The company has been in operation for several years and is owned by a number of former professional runners and their families. The balance sheet reveals several pieces of accounting information not previously mentioned or dealt with in detail in this chapter. These are the distinction between tangible and intangible fixed assets, accumulated depreciation, different types of current asset and liability, and the separate disclosure of liabilities. These are discussed appropriately following the illustration.

Illustration 13 Runalot Sports Ltd ● 135

Runalot Ltd
Balance Sheet as at 31 December 2006

	£	£	Notes
Assets			
Fixed intangible assets			
Patents and trade marks at cost	50,000		
Less: accumulated amortisation to date	*40,000*	10,000	1
Fixed tangible assets			
Factory building at cost		265,000	2
Machinery and equipment at cost	179,000		
Less: accumulated depreciation to date	*100,000*	79,000	3
Motor vehicles at cost	55,000		
Less: accumulated depreciation to date	*30,000*	20,000	4
		374,000	
Current assets			
Inventory of finished goods, work-in-progress, and raw materials at lower of cost or market value	561,000		5
Trade debtors	390,000		6
Prepayments	16,000		7
Investments in market securities	23,000		8
Cash in bank	15,000	**1,005,000**	
Total assets		**1,379,000**	
Less:			
Current liabilities			
Trade and other creditors	*256,000*		9
Accruals	*36,000*		10
Taxation payable	*61,000*	*353,000*	11
		1,026,000	
Less:			
Long-term liabilities			
Bank loan		*223,000*	12
Net assets		**803,000**	
Capital employed			
Called up share capital		300,000	13
Profit and loss account		503,000	14
		803,000	

Notes

(1) Costs of patents and trade marks on running shoes manufactured by the company are amortized over their estimated useful life.

(2) The company's factory building is disclosed at its original cost. The board of directors estimates its current market value is £406,000 at 31 December 2006.

(3) The original cost of the company's machinery and equipment, minus its estimated residual sale value, is depreciated over its estimated useful life using the straight-line basis of depreciation.

(4) The original costs of the company's motor vehicles, minus their estimated residual sale values, are depreciated over their estimated useful lives using the reducing balance basis of depreciation.

(5) The company's inventory comprises:

	£
Finished goods	235,000
Work-in-process	201,000
Raw materials	125,000
Total	**561,000**

These figures are based on the lower of cost or market value for each type of shoe manufactured by the company. Cost is defined for finished goods and work-in-process as the original cost of raw materials and a relevant proportion of manufacturing wages and overhead expenses.

(6) The amount due by customers for sales on credit after an estimated provision for uncollectible debts.

(7) Prepayments relate to payments made for overhead expenses in advance of the delivery of the services concerned.

(8) Stated at market value on 31 December 2006.

(9) The amount due to suppliers for raw materials and related supplies, together with unpaid wages and other invoiced overhead expenses.

(10) Estimated overhead expenses incurred but not invoiced by 31 December 2006.

(11) Estimated unpaid liability for corporation tax on profits for the year ended 31 December 2006.

(12) Loan repayable in eight equal instalments between 2007 and 2014, and secured over all the assets of the company.

(13) Share capital comprises 300,000 ordinary share units of £1 each fully paid up. The authorized share capital of the company comprises 500,000 ordinary share units.

(14) Comprises profits retained and brought forward at 1 January 2006 of £323,000 together with retained profits for the year to 31 December 2006 of £180,000.

Illustration 13 Runalot Sports Ltd ● **137**

The following explanations are offered of each of the main sections of the balance sheet in Illustration 13.

Types of fixed asset

The Companies Act 1985 and the accounting standards of the ASB and IASB require companies to distinguish several types of fixed asset. These distinctions include long-term investments and loans in other companies and ventures, and intangible and tangible fixed assets.

Long-term investments   An example of a long-term business investment would be a joint venture or partnership between two or more companies in order to manage a particular business project or control a specific asset without requiring the participants to merge their companies—e.g. a joint venture between two oil companies to build a pipeline to deliver oil from its extraction source to a refinery. Once the project is complete, the partnership can be dissolved. A company involved in such a venture can report its investment by including an appropriate proportion of the assets and liabilities of the venture in its balance sheet. Alternatively, in the fixed assets section of the balance sheet, it can disclose the investment in terms of an appropriate proportion of the current ownership equity of the venture. Runalot Sports Ltd does not hold joint venture investments.

Intangible assets   Intangible assets cover a variety of types that have a non-physical form. They include legally-protected rights such as patents, copyrights, and trademarks that can be purchased from individuals and companies or internally generated through research and development. There are specific regulations affecting the accounting for intangible assets. Current IASB regulations, for example, require intangible assets of listed companies to be disclosed in the balance sheet in one of two ways. The first is at their cost less accumulated amounts written off evenly over their estimated useful lives—i.e. a process called amortization. Amortization amounts appear in the profit statement as an expense. Alternatively, intangible assets can be accounted for on a revaluation basis using fair values derived from active markets in the intangible assets. Revaluation losses are treated as expenses in the profit statement. Revaluation surpluses are added directly to shareholders' equity. The amortization method has been used in the case of Runalot Sports Ltd. The cost of patents and trade marks relating to its running shoes is £50,000 and £40,000 has been written off by 31 December 2006, indicating that 20% of useful life remains under legal protection. Note 1 of the Runalot balance sheet explains the basis of accounting for this fixed asset.

Goodwill   Intangible assets reported in a corporate balance sheet can also include an asset which arises from a corporate merger or takeover (i.e. a business combination) where the purchased or merged company is valued in excess of the aggregate fair value of its tangible assets minus its liabilities. The excess value is called goodwill and represents a variety of corporate resources that do not necessarily have a physical form—e.g. customer loyalty, employee skills, and the location of business premises. Current IASB regulations require goodwill to be recognized as a fixed asset when it is purchased in a business combination and to have its accounting value assessed annually for any impairment in value. An impairment loss is written off against profits. Runalot Sports Ltd has not acquired another company and there is no goodwill in its balance sheet.

Tangible assets Tangible assets disclosed in a corporate balance sheet are stated at their purchase cost minus any accumulated depreciation that has been written off as an expense in the profit statement. In the case of Runalot Sports Ltd, there are three types of tangible fixed asset—i.e. the factory building in which the manufacturing takes place, machinery and equipment required for manufacturing, and motor vehicles for delivery of supplies and finished goods as well as for sales staff and management. Accounting convention requires these assets to be depreciated over their useful lives (which have to be forecast by management). The basic formula is to take the original cost, reduce it by the forecast residual value when the asset ceases to be used (again requiring managerial judgment), and allocate the net figure over the estimated useful life in years. The process of allocation can be done in a variety of ways. The two most familiar methods are straight line (as per the machinery and equipment in Runalot) and reducing balance (as per Runalot's motor vehicles). Runalot Sports Ltd has a factory building with a cost that is exceeded by its current market value. The company does not need to depreciate the building and, rather than revalue it, it prefers to disclose the fixed asset at it cost with a note indicating the market value. Notes 2, 3, and 4 of the Runalot balance sheet explain the basis for its accounting for tangible fixed assets.

Leased assets Companies do not always purchase their fixed assets. They can determine that it is more organizationally and economically viable to rent or lease these assets. If the lease is short-term, the rental cost is treated as an expense in the profit statement. However, if the lease is long-term and effectively the asset is substantially as if it were owned by the company except for the actual title, it is accounted for as a tangible fixed asset. The cost is calculated as the present value of the future rental payments and is recalculated at the end of each reporting period. The annual difference between present values is treated as an expense in the profit statement. Runalot Sports Ltd does not have long-term leased fixed assets.

Types of current asset

As the balance sheet of Runalot Sports Ltd indicates, there are several categories of current asset. The five main categories are inventories of goods for resale, debtors or amounts due by credit customers, prepayments, market investments and cash resources such as bank accounts and deposits.

Inventories These are alternatively described in the UK as stock. However, for listed companies, IASB standards use the term inventory and this has been used throughout the

Illustration 13 Runalot Sports Ltd ● 139

text on the grounds of simplicity and avoidance of confusion with the term stock when related to market investments. Inventory is held by a company such as Runalot in a variety of forms. Some of it is readily convertible into cash flow through sale, and other categories are far less saleable. The different forms reflect various stages in the manufacturing process. At each year-end, there are goods that are finished and ready for resale. In the case of Runalot, these amount to £235,000 or 42% of the total inventory. There are also goods that are partly manufactured and therefore still in progress to completion, amounting to £201,000 or 36% of Runalot's inventory. And there are raw materials that are yet to be used in the manufacturing process—£125,000 or 22% of Runalot's inventory. The usual accounting convention used by accountants is what is termed the lower of cost or market value—i.e. inventory items are disclosed at their cost unless their market value is a lesser amount. This comparison can be done for each category, each sub-category within categories, or for the inventory as a whole. Cost is typically defined as raw material cost together with appropriate amounts of wages and overheads used in the manufacturing process. It is essential for the reporting company to be consistent from period to period in its application of the cost or market convention and in the definition of cost. Note 5 to the Runalot balance sheet explains these matters to its shareholders.

Debtors The figure for debtors is the accounting number that represents the cash flows expected from the reporting company's customers who have purchased goods on credit terms. It is therefore highly realizable but accounting convention dictates that provision is made for any expected losses in collection. These are normally described as bad debts and represent the expected proportion of debtors that will not be recovered as cash flow. Any calculated amount for irrecoverable debtors is treated as an expense in the profit statement. Any subsequent recoveries following the writing off of a bad debt to the profit statement is disclosed in the latter as sundry income. The Runalot balance sheet has Note 6 to explain its treatment of bad debts.

Prepayments Companies can pay for services for matters such as utilities, rentals, and insurance prior to receiving the services concerned. In these circumstances, it is inappropriate to treat the full cost as an expense of the period and any proportion relating to services not delivered is carried forward as a current asset to the next reporting period when the services should be delivered. The prepayment is then treated as an expense of the period. Prepayments are explained in Note 7 of the Runalot balance sheet.

Market investments Investments in market securities such as shares and bonds are highly realizable and usually reflect the investment of cash that is surplus to operational requirements. As is the case with most standard setters, the IASB requires listed companies to account for these investments at their current market value, as stated in Note 8 to the Runalot balance sheet.

Cash Cash amounts such as bank accounts and deposits are the most realizable of all assets disclosed by a reporting company. They are stated at the amount in the accounting records of the reporting company. The balances may differ from the equivalent amounts in the records of the company's banks due to cash deposits and payments in transit through the banking system at the date of the balance sheet.

Current liabilities

A reporting company such as Runalot Sports Ltd usually has several different types of liability or obligation to third parties. These can be divided into two main categories determined in the UK by the Companies Act 1985. These categories are, first, creditors that are due for payment within the next year (i.e. short-term or current liabilities) and, second, those repayable in more than one year (i.e. long-term or non-current liabilities). This distinction can be seen in the balance sheet of Runalot. Notes 9, 10, and 11 to its balance sheet provide explanations of the three current liabilities—i.e. amounts due to suppliers of goods and services contracted on credit and invoiced to the company, estimated amounts due to suppliers that have yet to be invoiced by them (e.g. utilities and local business taxes), and amounts due to the Inland Revenue for corporation tax due on profits (normally disclosed less any payments made to account).

Long-term liabilities

Note 12 to the Runalot balance sheet provides details of the long-term debt of the company. In this case, repayment will take several years. The security of the loan over the company's assets reveals that, should it default in repayment, the lender can recover the amount due by resort to a court-supervised process involving the sale of the company's assets.

Capital employed

The final section of a reported balance sheet contains information about the shareholders' equity or capital employed—i.e. the capital received from its shareholders and any profits retained in the company rather than distributed as dividends. Notes 13 and 14 to the Runalot balance sheet deal with these two aspects. In Note 13, it is disclosed that the share units have what is termed a par value of £1 and that 300,000 have been issued and paid for by shareholders. They paid £1 a share. Had they paid more—e.g. £1.50 a share unit, the share premium of 50 pence (i.e. £150,000) would appear as what is called a reserve in shareholders' equity. In the case of Runalot, 60% of the authorized share capital has been issued. This means that, if required, the company could issue a further 200,000 share units to its shareholders.

Market value

Note 14 of the Runalot balance sheet explains the other reserve amount in shareholders' equity—i.e. accumulated profits retained from the profit statement. This accounting number reminds the reader of the balance sheet that shareholders' equity is a residual or balancing figure. The combination of share capital and profits retained (i.e. £803,000) does not represent the market or sale value of Runalot Sports Ltd. Most of its assets are expressed in terms of their original costs rather than market values, and not all of its assets are disclosed in its balance sheet. For example, should the company be offered for sale, the existence and value of its goodwill (due to factors such as the reputation of its running shoes, research programme, and customer base) would be required to be evaluated and calculated in order to determine the full sale price.

Lesson 6.4 Balance sheet categories
Each of the three main categories in the corporate balance can be sub-divided into different types of asset and liability, and different aspects of shareholders' equity. The sub-categories of asset and liability are reported, respectively, according to order of realizability and payability.

OTHER BALANCE SHEET MATTERS

The previous section outlines the main components of a corporate balance sheet and explains their various bases of accounting. The illustration refers to a single company. There are, however, other reporting matters that require explanation having established the basic model. The areas covered in this section include the use of comparative figures for corporate balance sheets, a balance sheet for a group of companies, notification of accounting principles used in the balance sheet, the use of separate notes of disclosure to support the corporate balance sheet, post-balance sheet events, segmental reporting, contingencies, and related party transactions.

Group balance sheets

As previously mentioned, should a reporting company also control other companies (through shareholdings or a board of directors), it is required under the Companies Act 1985 to produce a balance sheet that combines the assets and liabilities of itself and all other controlled companies (i.e. subsidiaries). The accounting procedures for doing this are complex and not required in a text such as this. However, the general effect is to achieve a number of objectives.

(1) All assets and liabilities of subsidiary companies are combined irrespective of the degree of control of the holding company. For example, if a subsidiary company is 80% controlled, then 100% of its assets and liabilities appear in the group balance sheet and the 20% of its shareholders' equity owned by other shareholders is recognized as a liability in the balance sheet and titled "minority interests."

(2) Merging the assets and liabilities of the holding and subsidiary companies results in the inclusion in the group balance sheet of goodwill (i.e. that part of the cost of investing in a subsidiary in excess of the fair value of its tangible assets and liabilities at the date of investment). Goodwill and its accounting treatment have been explained previously in this chapter.

(3) Any assets and liabilities resulting from transactions between the holding and subsidiary companies are cancelled out in the consolidation of accounting numbers for the group balance sheet.

Group balance sheets (and profit statements) are subject to the same disclosure requirements as for single companies. The following group balance sheet reflects a holding company and several subsidiary companies in which there is a controlling investment of less than 100%. The comments explain each of the accounting numbers disclosed in the balance sheet.

Peas-And-Queues Ltd
Balance Sheet as at 31 December 2006

	Note	£	£
Intangible fixed assets			
Goodwill on acquisition of subsidiaries	1	100,000	
Trademarks	2	20,000	120,000
Tangible fixed assets			
Land and buildings	3	220,000	
Motor vehicles	4	126,000	
Joint ventures	5	50,000	396,000
Current assets			
Inventory	6	309,000	
Debtors	7	56,000	
Cash	8	21,000	386,000
Less: **current liabilities**			
Creditors and accruals	9	*277,000*	
Taxation	10	*51,000*	*328,000*
Less: **long-term liabilities**			
Bank loans	11		*200,000*
Net assets			**374,000**
Capital employed			
Share capital	12		100,000
Profit and loss account	13		230,000
			330,000
Minority interests	14		44,000
Total capital employed			**374,000**

The following comments provide an explanation of the accounting numbers in the group balance sheet. In practice, much of these explanations would appear as formal notes to the financial statements. They would include more detailed accounting breakdown of the numbers concerned. In effect, what the group balance sheet is saying is that the shareholders of the holding company control its assets and liabilities and those of its subsidiaries, and therefore these are disclosed in full under the headings required in corporate legislation. Any portion of assets and liabilities not owned by the holding company is recognized as a single figure liability of that entity (i.e. minority interests).

Note	Comment
(1)	This amount represents the premium paid by the holding company when it acquired its subsidiary companies. The figure is the excess of the amounts paid to acquire control of the subsidiaries and the fair value of their tangible net assets at the dates of acquisition. The amount disclosed in the balance sheet is the acquisition cost minus any amortization or reduction due to impairment in value.

Note	Comment
(2)	This amount is the cost to the holding company of purchasing or producing the trademarks minus any amortization to date.
(3)	Land and buildings are those of the holding company and its subsidiaries and are usually stated at their original cost.
(4)	Motor vehicles are those of the holding company and its subsidiaries and are stated at their original cost minus accumulated depreciation to date.
(5)	This amount represents the holding company's share of the net assets of joint ventures with other companies.
(6)	Inventory is held by the holding company and its subsidiaries and stated at the lower of its cost and market value.
(7)	Debtors are those due to the holding company and its subsidiaries and are stated at their recoverable amount—i.e. after deductions for estimated irrecoverable sums.
(8)	This amount represents cash in the bank of the holding company and its subsidiaries.
(9)	These are the amounts due to suppliers of the holding company and its subsidiaries.
(10)	This amount represents the estimated tax due on profits of the holding company and its subsidiaries.
(11)	These loans are due by the holding company and its subsidiaries.
(12)	This is the issued share capital of the holding company.
(13)	This amount is the accumulated retained profits of the holding company and its subsidiaries that are attributable to the holding company shareholders.
(14)	This amount represents the share capital and retained profits of subsidiary companies that are not attributable to the holding company shareholders. They represent outside shareholdings not acquired by the holding company.

Lesson 6.5 Group financial statements

For purposes of adequately informing shareholders about the financial results achieved by a reporting company's managers, it is necessary to include the financial results of all the companies for which the managers are responsible. Rather than provide separate financial statements for each company they effectively manage, legal requirements permit a consolidation of financial results as if all the companies were one entity. In doing so, it is necessary to recognize outside shareholders in companies controlled but not wholly owned by the holding company.

Comparative amounts

In the UK and elsewhere, legislative or regulative requirements require reporting companies to provide the prescribed accounting numbers for the current reporting period and for the previous period. As previously explained, this also applies to profit statements and cash flow statements. The idea is to permit shareholders and other readers of these financial statements to compare accounting numbers over time and to deduce significant changes. In practice, many larger companies provide voluntary summary statements containing comparative figures for several years. The following balance sheet is that of Peas-And-Queues Ltd above with the 2005 accounting figures disclosed.

Peas-And-Queues Ltd
Balance Sheet as at 31 December 2006

	£	2006 (£)	2005 (£)
Intangible fixed assets			
Goodwill on acquisition of subsidiaries	100,000		100,000
Trademarks	20,000	120,000	22,000
Tangible fixed assets			
Land and buildings	220,000		220,000
Motor vehicles	126,000		138,000
Joint ventures	50,000	396,000	50,000
Current assets			
Inventory	309,000		292,000
Debtors	56,000		54,000
Cash	21,000	386,000	36,000
Less: **current liabilities**			
Creditors and accruals	*277,000*		*260,000*
Taxation	*51,000*	*328,000*	*45,000*
Less: **long-term liabilities**			
Bank loans		*200,000*	*250,000*
Net assets		**374,000**	**357,000**
Capital employed			
Share capital		100,000	100,000
Profit and loss account		230,000	217,000
		330,000	**317,000**
Minority interests		44,000	40,000
Total capital employed		**374,000**	**357,000**

The addition of comparative accounting numbers in the group balance sheet permits its reader to learn that there have been no major changes in the balance sheet headings between 2005 and 2006. All of the changes affect assets and liabilities relating to routine trading operations.

Lesson 6.6 Comparative figures
The accounting numbers in a balance sheet (and its accompanying profit statement and cash flow statement) only start to make sense to their user when they are compared to other equivalent numbers. A first step in this comparative exercise is to disclose the accounting numbers for the previous year of the reporting company.

Accounting principles affecting balance sheet

In the UK, the Companies Act 1985 specifies the application of certain accounting principles that also have a related affect on the profit statement. The detail of these principles goes beyond the remit of this text, but the following general explanations are appropriate.

(1) Fixed assets are typically disclosed at their original or historical cost and this should form the basis for the depreciation expense in the profit statement. Where the fixed asset is an investment, its original cost is also the preferred basis and any fall in value should be recognized and written off to the profit statement. Where the fixed asset is goodwill, the original cost should be written off over its useful economic life as determined by the board of directors.

(2) Current assets should also be reported at their original amount unless their realizable value is less than this figure. Any difference in value should be written off to the profit statement. The Companies Act 1985 specifies in detail the accounting definitions possible for inventory.

(3) It is permitted to include intangible fixed assets (other than goodwill), investments, and inventory at their current replacement cost and to depreciate on that basis. Investments can also be reported at their current market value. The confusion resulting from this mix of possible accounting bases for assets is addressed in the section following on current balance sheet issues.

In the case of Peas-And-Queues Ltd above, the main accounting principles that would require disclosure are evident in the various noted comments. For example:

(1) The historical cost basis of accounting would be explained as would the company's adherence to the requirements of prescribed accounting standards and the Companies Act 1985.

(2) The basis for consolidating the balance sheets (and other financial statements) of the holding company and its subsidiaries would be explained if the accounting periods for the companies did not coincide.

(3) There would be an explanation of the calculation of goodwill as part of the acquisition cost of subsidiaries together with its subsequent reduction due to a policy of regular amortization or ad hoc impairment assessment. The impairment policy would be explained in relation to the requirements of a specific accounting standard on the subject.

(4) The amortization policy relating to trademarks would be explained.

(5) The company would be required to explain the lack of depreciation on land and buildings—presumably due to the fact that these assets are appreciating in value.

(6) The basis of depreciation of motor vehicles as tangible fixed assets would be given in terms of annual percentages of cost.

(7) There would be disclosure of joint venture investments as a proportion of the recorded assets and liabilities of these partnerships.

(8) The company would explain its use of the lower of cost or market value in its accounting for inventory.

(9) It is not usual to disclose the basis of debtors as their recoverable amount.

Lesson 6.7 Accounting principles
As with the profit statement, each accounting number in the balance sheet is governed by the general principles of accounting. The main principles in the UK are spelt out in the Companies Act 1985 and their implementation is governed by accounting standards such as those of the ASB and IASB.

Notes to balance sheets

Companies typically disclose additional information in reported balance sheets in support of the total figures given there. For example, in relation to Peas-And-Queues Ltd above, it would be normal for the company to produce notes giving greater detail on subsets of matters such as tangible fixed assets (e.g. cost less accumulated depreciation), inventory (particularly if the company was a manufacturer with raw materials and work-in-progress in addition to finished goods), and debtors (e.g. distinguishing trade debtors from other amounts due such as prepayments). Companies are also expected to provide notes on matters that are related to these documents but not necessarily incorporated into the accounting used in their construction. The Companies Act 1985 requires additional disclosures on post-balance sheet events, segment reporting, contingent assets and liabilities, and related party transactions. Again, the detailed provisions are complex and only a brief explanation is given here.

Lesson 6.8 Supporting notes
Balance sheet disclosure is assisted by the reporting of the basic accounting numbers in the financial statement, with the underlying detail in supporting notes. The latter should not be ignored by the user of the balance sheet.

Post-balance sheet events   There may be significant events that affect the performance and condition of a reporting company occurring between the balance year-end and the date at which the balance sheet is authorized for publication. These post-balance sheet events fall into two categories—i.e. those that clarify a position at the balance sheet year-end (e.g. the result of an outstanding court case or evidence of the impairment of an asset), and those that do not affect the balance sheet position but clearly influence the future of the company and therefore require some disclosure by note as to their nature and financial effect (e.g. the unexpected termination of a significant customer contract or the destruction of a significant manufacturing facility). An IASB accounting standard regulates this area of accounting and reporting for listed companies.

Lesson 6.9 Post-balance sheet events
The current financial state or condition of a reporting company is not always disclosed fully in the balance sheet. Later events that relate to the balance sheet should be reported where possible in order to fully inform the balance sheet user.

Segments   For many larger companies, business operations consist of distinct segments relating to matters such as business types and products and geographical locations. If this is the case then, for larger companies, additional information relating to assets, liabilities, sales, expenses, and profits should be disclosed on an appropriate segmental reporting basis. This accounting and reporting is regulated, for example, by an IASB accounting standard. In the case of Peas-And-Queues Ltd, the following segmental report could support the main balance sheet (and the related profit statement):

	2006			**2005**		
£000s	**Sales**	**Profits**	**Assets**	**Sales**	**Profits**	**Assets**
Segments						
UK operations	1,125	188	801	968	164	821
US operations	750	−175	101	792	−85	91
Total operations	**1,875**	**13**	**902**	**1,760**	**79**	**912**

The disclosure of segmental information as above provides the reader of financial statements with a level of detail that improves the knowledge gained from the aggregate accounting numbers. For example, in the case of Peas-And-Queues Ltd, the following additional information becomes available:

(1)   There are two main segments in the business—the UK and the US.

(2)   The largest proportions of sales and assets are in the UK.

(3)   The US operations are not profitable and are having a significant negative effect on overall profitability.

Lesson 6.10 Detailed information

Aggregate financial results, as in a company balance sheet, hide detail that could be useful to report users when trying to identify and distinguish strong and weak parts of the reporting company's operations.

Contingencies   For most reporting companies, accounting and reporting procedures are directed for balance sheet purposes at assets and liabilities within the control of the company. However, particularly for the largest companies, there may be contracts entered into with other companies that seek to minimize future risk in trading or secure future supplies or customers. These contracts do not create assets or liabilities at the time of reporting a balance sheet because no specific transactions have taken place on which an accounting for assets or liabilities could take place. However, they do contain legal provisions that in effect create contingent assets and liabilities—i.e. assets and liabilities that will appear if certain economic and legal conditions prevail. An IASB accounting standard, for example, requires listed companies affected by such legal contracts to make full disclosure in notes to the balance sheet of their contingent assets and liabilities. In addition, there are regular contingencies such as commitments to pay amounts for future capital expenditure such as property acquisitions not complete by the balance sheet date. In the case of Peas-And-Queues Ltd above, it is possible that the company could have entered into an agreement to guarantee bank loans or overdrafts entered into by the joint ventures in which it has invested. A note to this effect would then be required.

Lesson 6.11 Contingencies

A company can enter into a legal contract and properly disclose its immediate effect on its balance sheet and other financial statements. However, within that contract there may be provisions that could impact the profitability, cash flow, and financial position of the company in the future. This impact can be positive or negative. It is only fair to shareholders and other users of the financial statements that the reporting company discloses information on such contingent assets and liabilities.

Related party transactions   A reporting company may be related to another entity it does business with and, because of the relationship, the terms of the business transactions are different from normal business terms. For example, a company controlling a subsidiary company may buy or sell with that entity at prices less than normal. These transactions can affect both the profitability and financial position of the reporting company and, for example, if it is a listed company, an IASB standard requires it to disclose related parties that it may trade with and the financial effects of such trading on profits and financial position. This is a common feature of corporate business activity and such disclosures attempt to assist the user of corporate balance sheets (and other financial statements) determine the extent to which reported profits, cash flows, assets, liabilities, and shareholders' equity are over or understated by related party transactions. In the case of Peas-And-Queues Ltd, for example, if this was a family-controlled company, it would not be surprising to have a note to the balance sheet explaining any transactions between members of the family and the company.

Lesson 6.12 Related parties

If a reporting company enters into business transactions that are not contracted with the normal terms and conditions, full disclosure requires it to report these transactions and their effect on profitability, cash flow, and financial position.

ISSUES IN BALANCE SHEET REPORTING

There are numerous unresolved issues concerning the accounting and disclosure that underpins the corporate balance sheet. They can be categorized in two ways—i.e. as problems concerning asset and liability recognition, and problems concerning the representation of recognized assets and liabilities. Because of the introductory nature of this text, they are explained and discussed here only in broad terms to enable the reader to appreciate the limitations of the reported balance sheet.

Recognition issues

There are a number of problems affecting the balance sheet with respect to the assets and liabilities that are recognized in it for accounting purposes. The most significant are as follows:

(1) The assets and liabilities that appear in a reported balance sheet are typically those that arise from contracted transactions involving the reporting company. In the case of assets, for example, there is plant acquired or leased on a long-term basis, inventory manufactured from raw materials, and cash due from credit customers. In the case of liabilities, on the other hand, there is a long-term loan from the company's bank and amounts due to its credit suppliers. These assets are relatively easy to recognize as such and therefore record in the accounting system. Other assets and liabilities, however, are less easy to recognize. As previously mentioned, for example, goodwill can represent considerable intangible resources that generate profits and cash flows for the reporting company. In the case of some companies (e.g. a public accountancy or marketing services firm), they can be the single most important asset. Yet, unless acquired during a merger or takeover of another company, goodwill does not appear in the reported balance sheet.

(2) A liability issue in recent years has been concerned with obligations of reporting companies arising out of employee benefits such as pension and health care plans. Until recently, these were hidden liabilities. Currently, however, companies are required to disclose the expense of providing for these benefits and any liability in excess of any assets it has set aside to meet its obligations.

(3) Also in recent times, companies have attempted to hide significant assets and liabilities from their shareholders by excluding them from the balance sheet by means of the creation of complex entities in which they invest and for which they are not required to account for in full in the reported balance sheet. These are called special purpose entities (SPE) and are usually constructed in such a way that the reporting company can have a minimal investment but complete control over the SPE, including the transfer of significant assets to it and its ability to borrow considerable sums. Typically, these investments use complex financial instruments to make their detection difficult. The case of Enron cited in an earlier chapter was a prime example of this type of activity. The result is that significant assets and liabilities can be taken "off-balance sheet" and shareholders are unaware of their existence except for a small financial investment reported in the balance sheet. The IASB requires listed companies with these arrangements to fully disclose the "hidden" assets and liabilities in situations where there is effectively control of them by the reporting company.

Representation issues

There are several problems concerning the way in which accounting numbers are used to represent assets recognized in a reported balance sheet.

(1) The first problem concerns the use of historical cost accounting as the primary basis for representation. Historical costs represent the cost of the asset at the time it was transacted. However, as time moves on and the asset is held over the long-term, this number becomes irrelevant and misleading as a means of representing its current condition. For example, a motor vehicle purchased in 2003 for £10,000 may have a replacement cost in 2006 of £14,000 and a resale value in 2006 of £2,000. Neither of these current conditions can be adequately represented by

the £10,000—even if depreciated. The problem also affects current assets such as inventory which are held for shorter periods of time. For example, goods for resale may have a historical cost of £20,000 when their current replacement cost is £23,000 and current resale value £30,000. The paradoxical situation is that, if the current resale value was less than £20,000 then it would be reported in the balance sheet.

(2) The second representation problem is the policy of legislators and accounting standard-setters such as the IASB to permit reporting companies to use a mix of numbers in their balance sheets. For example, in the UK it is possible to have a company use a mix of historical costs, historical costs minus accumulated depreciation, current replacement costs, current resale values, and present values (discounted cash flows). When this occurs, the figure for total assets is arithmetically correct but representationally uninterpretable. It is similar to reporting intangible fixed assets in Euros (€100,000), tangible fixed assets in US dollars ($300,000), current assets in pounds sterling (£200,000), adding them up (600,000), and pretending they are all Euros, $s or £s. If the mix of accounting numbers for assets is difficult to interpret then the related figure for shareholders' equity is equally problematic. This is a problem that has been unresolved for nearly four decades when the FASB in 1976 first suggested an assets and liabilities accounting approach with the use of current values to represent assets. The idea was later taken up by the IASB in 1989 and the ASB in 1999 in their conceptual frameworks. However, no body has followed through on the recommendation in their accounting standards although each has recommended the use of particular current values for specific assets. The result is the current incoherence of multiple valuations in the balance sheet.

(3) Companies are required by regulators such as the IASB to continuously assess the assets disclosed in the balance sheet to consider whether their recorded accounting numbers reflect their current financial condition. The latter is defined as the recoverable amount—i.e. the lower of the asset's fair value (an approximation for market value) and its value in use by the company (an approximation of the present value of future cash flows from use). This particular practice has precedents in a long-standing accounting practice (e.g. the use of the lower of cost or market value rule for inventory and, less obviously, the depreciation of fixed assets). Impairment review is intended for fixed assets and intangible assets particularly. However, estimating fair and present values is problematic in practice as is the judgment that impairment is permanent. Balance sheet disclosures subject to impairment reviews should be treated with considerable care by their users.

(4) In recent times, company managements have been conducting what are called restructuring exercises—i.e. reviewing their operations and asset structures, selling off or closing unprofitable operations, and generally revaluing assets. The loss used to be disclosed in the profit statement as an exceptional item. However, in doing this, there was a danger that normal trading losses on balance sheet assets could be reclassified by management as exceptional and therefore effectively inflate normal profits. Restructuring losses cannot now be disclosed as exceptional or extraordinary. However, the figures disclosed from the restructuring of the balance sheet

in this way need to be treated with care and caution. The signal of a restructuring having taken place will be given in the disclosed loss in the profit statement.

Lesson 6.13 Recognition and representation
A user of a corporate balance sheet needs to understand that its relevance and reliability depend on what the accounting system recognizes for reporting and how it represents in accounting terms what it recognizes. All balance sheets contain issues with respect to recognition and representation. Part of the problem in this respect is that a statement such as a balance sheet is numerical and therefore appears to be precise.

CREATIVE ACCOUNTING

As explained in Chapter 4 with respect to the profit statement, the balance sheet is also subject to potential creative accounting in order to improve what is disclosed as the current financial state of the reporting company. Because of the accounting relationship between the profit statement and the balance sheet, any creative accounting perpetrated in one is bound to affect the other. The three general areas discussed in Chapter 4 are false or dubious business transactions, misclassification, and over-optimism. A further area discussed in this chapter is the deliberate omission of assets and liabilities by complex legal contracts. Each of these areas of creative accounting has a potential impact on the corporate balance sheet and the following example illustrates this.

Jingle-Jangle plc is a retailer of popular music on compact disks. It has been in business for a number of years, grown rapidly both nationally and internationally, but experienced diminishing profitability and cash flow and increasing debt. Its CEO and CFO have been under pressure from the capital markets regarding poor EPS figures and, in response, have introduced the following creative accounting practices prior to the end of the financial year to 31 December 2006.

(1) Inventory has been reduced by dispatching goods to customers without prior orders and invoicing them. The cost of the inventory is £575,000 and the invoiced amount is £725,000.

(2) A major repair to the packing equipment amounting to £650,000 has been treated as new equipment in the accounting records. £130,000 of depreciation was written off.

(3) Inventory at 31 December 2006 costing £800,000 and with a resale value of £400,000 has not been adjusted to reflect this unrealized loss.

In addition, the CEO and CFO set up a SPE in their names during the year. The SPE borrowed £1,300,000 from a bank, secured by a guarantee from Jingle-Jangle. The guarantee was not disclosed to the board of directors. Cash of £1,300,000 was transferred from the SPE to Jingle-Jangle and recorded as a cash sale. A repayment of £500,000 on the loan due to the bank has been made by Jingle-Jangle to the SPE and recorded as a return of goods sold in its records.

The balance sheet of Jingle-Jangle plc at 31 December 2006 after the above creative accounting is as follows:

Jingle-Jangle plc
Balance Sheet as at 31 December 2006

	£	£
Assets		
Non-current assets		
Plant and equipment at cost	1,453,000	
Less: accumulated depreciation	707,000	746,000
Motor vehicles at cost	305,000	
Less: accumulated depreciation	178,000	127,000
Current assets		
Inventory	3,862,000	
Debtors	1,355,000	
Cash	1,000	5,218,000
Total assets		**6,091,000**
Liabilities		
Current liabilities		
Creditors and accruals	*1,471,000*	
Other liabilities	*53,000*	*1,524,000*
Non-current liabilities		
Bank loans	*520,000*	
Retirement benefits	*326,000*	*846,000*
Total liabilities		**2,370,000**
Net assets		**3,721,000**
Equity		
Capital and reserves		
Share capital	1,500,000	
Profit and loss account	1,921,000	
Other reserves	300,000	
Total equity		**3,721,000**

The balance sheet that should have been reported (i.e. without the creative accounting) is
as follows:

Jingle-Jangle plc
Balance Sheet as at 31 December 2006

	Notes	£	£
Assets			
Non-current assets			
Plant and equipment at cost	1	803,000	
Less: accumulated depreciation	2	577,000	226,000
Motor vehicles at cost		305,000	
Less: accumulated depreciation		178,000	127,000

Current assets

Inventory	**3**	4,037,000	
Debtors	**4**	630,000	
Cash		1,000	4,668,000
Total assets			**5,021,000**
Liabilities			
Current liabilities			
Creditors and accruals		*1,471,000*	
Taxation		*53,000*	*1,524,000*
Non-current liabilities			
Bank loans	**5**	*1,320,000*	
Retirement benefits		*326,000*	*1,646,000*
Total liabilities			***3,170,000***
Net assets			**1,851,000**
Equity			
Capital and reserves			
Share capital		1,500,000	
Profit and loss account	**6**	51,000	
Other reserves		300,000	
Total equity			**1,851,000**

Notes

(1) £1,453,000 − 650,000 (the misclassification of repairs as capital expenditure)

(2) £707,000 − 130,000 (removing the depreciation on the misclassified repair)

(3) £3,862,000 + 575,000 − 400,000 (including the cost of the false sales and reducing the cost of impaired inventory to market value)

(4) £1,355,000—725,000 (removing the false sales)

(5) £520,000 + 1,300,000 − 500,000 (including the false sale as debt minus the repayment made)

(6)

Retained profits after creative accounting	£1,921,000
Depreciation on repair treated as capital expenditure	130,000
Cost of goods falsely sold	575,000
Debt repayment treated as sales return	500,000
	3,126,000
False sales	*725,000*
Debt treated as sale	*1,300,000*
Repair treated as capital expenditure	*650,000*
Write down of inventory to market value	*400,000*
Adjusted retained profits	**51,000**

In summary, when comparing the disclosed accounting numbers in the two balance sheets, the effect of the creative accounting in Jingle-Jangle plc has been as follows:

Balance Sheet Item	Accounting Effect £
Plant	520,000
Inventory	*175,000*
Debtors	725,000
Long-term debt	800,000
Profit	*1,870,000*

Plant is overstated by £520,000 (£746,000 − 226,000). Inventory is understated by £175,000 (£3,862,000 − 4,037,000). Debtors are overstated by £725,000 (£1,355,000 − 630,000). Long-term debt is understated by £800,000 (£520,000 − 1,320,000). The overall combined effect of these over and under-statements is to overstate profits and profits retained by £1,870,000 (£1,921,000 − 51,000). In other words, assets need to be corrected by a net reduction of £1,070,000 (i.e. £−520,000, £+175,000, and £−725,000), and liabilities and capital have to be reduced by the same amount (i.e. £+800,000 and £−1,870,000). These are obviously extreme forms of creative accounting to make in one year. However, they are consistent with those actually detected in practice and could take place over a number of years—thus making them less noticeable. They emphasize the manipulative nature of accounting numbers in balance sheets and other financial statements and the importance of effective auditing of these numbers.

CORPORATE GOVERNANCE AND BALANCE SHEETS

The balance sheet is arguably the most obvious corporate financial statement to be associated with the functions of corporate governance and managerial accountability. Corporate directors and managers are entrusted by shareholders with funds that finance assets to put to work in generating profits and cash flows that, in turn, provide returns for the shareholders. The balance sheet as a statement of assets, liabilities, and shareholders' equity at a specific point in time is effectively letting shareholders know what assets are held on their behalf for use in the company's operations and trading activities, the liabilities that have been incurred as a result of these operations and activities, and the capital that has been generated through asset use. In effect, the balance sheet "takes stock" of the company's financial position. The board of directors and senior managers are saying to the shareholders—this is where the company is financially as a result of our efforts on your behalf. However, there are drawbacks to the balance sheet in terms of its use in the accountability aspect of corporate governance.

First, the balance sheet is a statement of a financial position at a single point in time. That position can be radically different one day either side of the balance sheet date because of business transactions that significantly affect it. Second, the balance sheet is an incomplete portrayal of the financial position of the company. It lacks certain assets not reported because they have not been acquired in a business transaction. It may lack liabilities deliberately taken off-balance sheet. And it reports assets in an incomprehensible mixture of historical costs, replacement costs, market values, and present values. Accountability and corporate governance are not assisted by these characteristics of reporting financial position.

OTHER LEGAL AND REGULATORY REQUIREMENTS

The reporting of the balance sheet is governed in the same way as the profit statement by provisions of the Companies Act 1985 (as amended by the Companies Act 1989). Specific sections of this chapter make reference to the 1985 Act when relevant in order to provide an appreciation of where such legislation impacts the accounting and disclosure of balance sheet information. Similar broad references are made to pertinent IASB accounting standards. In addition, in Chapter 4 relating to the profit statement, there are explanations of legislative provisions affecting both the balance sheet and the profit statement. With this background in mind, the following explanations deal with other legislative and regulative matters affecting the balance sheet that have not been dealt with previously in detail or with aspects of corporate financial reporting generally not examined in earlier chapters.

Form and content

The Companies Act 1985 specifies alternative formats for the required balance sheet. As previously mentioned in this chapter, and in Chapter 4 in relation to the profit statement, companies are permitted to use a horizontal or vertical format for presentation of the balance sheet. The vertical format is almost universally used in the UK and has been adopted throughout this chapter.

As explained in Chapter 4, the Act specifies accounting principles that affect the balance sheet. These essentially require companies to apply historical cost accounting to fixed and current assets. However, the Act also permits alternative rules (e.g. the use of current replacement cost for intangible fixed assets [other than goodwill] and inventory; replacement cost or market value for tangible fixed assets, and market value for short-term investments). With the exception of the latter, companies rarely stray from historical cost in practice. The previous sections of this chapter, and the numerical illustrations, conform to the requirements of the Companies Act 1985.

IASB accounting standards

In the UK, as previously mentioned, the principal authority for accounting standards is the FRC and its standard-setting body, the ASB. Financial reporting standards (FRS) are prescribed for all companies and are particularly important for public companies. The standards of the ASB, however, are expected to be compatible with the standards of the IASB and the latter are required for listed companies. For this reason, IASB accounting standards typically have been cited where relevant throughout this chapter and the remainder of the text. As this chapter completes explanations of the main financial statements in this text, it is relevant to examine IASB accounting standard setting generally. The IASB requirements divide into four main areas.

Framework for preparation and presentation of financial statements   Originally published in 1989, the purpose of the framework is to assist the IASB in preparing accounting standards, auditors in giving an opinion on financial statements, and report users in interpreting published information. Such assistance is in the framework by the specification of the basic qualities that corporate financial statements should meet (e.g. relevance and reliability); the main elements of published financial statements (e.g. assets and liabilities); and the primary principles governing the recognition and measurement of these elements (e.g. the idea of future economic benefits underlying assets). In brief, the framework represents the theoretical structure underpinning individual accounting standards mandated in the preparation of balance sheets and other financial statements.

International financial *reporting* standards   These are statements issued by the IASB to govern the reporting (as distinct from accounting) of financial information. There are relatively few and the main one deals with the financial reporting of groups of companies (as dealt with in this chapter and Chapter 4 relating to the profit statement).

International *accounting* standards   These are the main pronouncements of the IASB and each standard deals with a specific prescription for accounting in a particular area of corporate financial reports. Many of these areas have already been touched on in this and earlier chapters—e.g. accounting for inventory, cash flows, post balance sheet events, segmented information, fixed assets (including leased assets), sales, related party disclosures, joint ventures, earnings per share, impairment of assets, and intangible assets.

Interpretations   The final area of IASB standard-setting relates to the interpretation of specific issues by preparers, users, and readers of corporate financial statements. These are particularly helpful in technically-difficult areas such as determining the nature of a contract for a leased asset, a special purpose entity for purposes of group accounting, and unusual transactions when accounting for sales.

ASB standards

The ASB in the UK produces various accounting prescriptions and recommendations affecting corporate financial reporting. It has a framework of basic principles (*Statement of Principles*, 1991), various accounting standards on specific matters (currently 40 in number), one best practice statement (on the operating and financial review), and various recommended practices for specific industries (called *Statements of Recommended Practices* or SORPs).

Readers of this chapter should take this section in conjunction with its equivalents in Chapters 3, 4 and 5 in order to obtain a comprehensive overview of the legislative and regulatory provisions affecting the three main financial statements (i.e. profit statement, cash flow statement, and balance sheet). Because of the general and comprehensive nature of these provisions, it is difficult to isolate specific provisions for particular statements without becoming repetitive in their explanation.

LEARNING OBJECTIVES

Please review the learning objectives at the beginning of this chapter and ensure they have been achieved before proceeding to Chapter 7 on the nature and purpose of other reported statements.

Exercise 1 Assets, liabilities, and equity

The balance sheet has been stated in this chapter as a statement describing a relationship between assets, liabilities, and shareholders' equity. Taking these ideas, construct a balance sheet of your personal assets, liabilities, and equity. Be prepared to justify what you include and exclude from this balance sheet.

Exercise 2 Constructing a balance sheet

Assuming the following descriptions and numbers, construct a balance sheet from them. Be prepared to defend your particular choices in such a construction.

The year-end is 31 December 2006 and the company is called Terra-Firma Products Ltd. It manufactures products for bathrooms such as baths and showers.

The company has received a statement from its bank stating a balance of £5,000 at 30 November 2006. According to the company's cash records for December, it received £126,000 from customers and paid £87,000 to suppliers and employees.

Plant and equipment owned by the company cost £365,000 on 1 January 2004. It is estimated it will last ten years and have a residual value of £5,000. The company has been writing off an equal amount of depreciation each year since the purchase of the plant.

The company leases its factory premises from a property company. It pays an annual rental of £80,000 and the lease agreement is renewable annually. The factory was built for a cost of £210,000 five years ago and has a current market value of £333,000.

There is a loan from the bank to the company of £100,000 that is secured over all its assets.

Customers of the company owe it £182,000 at 31 December 2006. Two specific customers have debts outstanding of £15,000. These have been unpaid for nine months and both customers appear to be in financial difficulty.

The company owes suppliers and employees £67,000 at 31 December 2006.

There are no other assets and liabilities of the company although it was approached recently by a competitor to sell its product designs for a sum of £600,000.

Exercise 3 Tangible and intangible assets

Contrast and discuss the concepts of tangible and intangible assets. In your discussion, explain the problems of accounting for and reporting on each category of asset. Give examples of each category in your discussion and explanation. Students should also consider their personal circumstances and relate these to the idea of preparing a personal balance sheet. What intangible assets would you include in your personal balance sheet and why?

Exercise 4 Depreciating fixed assets

A company reports its fixed assets at a cost of £100,000 and reduces this by accumulated depreciation of £40,000. Explain the meaning of the cost figure, the depreciation reduction, and the net amount in the balance sheet. Also explain the factors that are considered in making a reduction in cost for depreciation. Students can also consider their personal assets. If you were required to calculate annual depreciation on each item, how would you do this?

Exercise 5   Inventory

What is inventory in a company balance sheet and what comprises the total figure reported? Contrast a retail store and a manufacturing facility to illustrate your answer. What is the accounting basis commonly used in the reporting of inventory in the balance sheet. Explain some of the main issues associated with this accounting basis. Students should identify with their instructor a specific manufactured product with which they are familiar (e.g. a personal computer) and discuss the problem of identifying and associating particular costs with its manufacture.

Exercise 6   Debtors

You are looking at the accounting number in the balance sheet described as debtors. What does this number represent and what is the accounting basis commonly used to calculate it for reporting purposes?

Exercise 7   Balance sheet content

The following balance sheet has been presented to you. Review its contents and make any changes you think are appropriate. Provide reasons for the changes you make.

Balance Sheet as at 31 December 2006

	£	£
Assets		
Fixed assets		
Goodwill at cost		100,000
Machinery and equipment at cost	57,000	
Less: accumulated depreciation to date	*25,000*	32,000
Motor vehicles at cost	55,000	
Less: accumulated depreciation to date	*60,000*	*5,000*
Land and buildings at cost		260,000
Inventory for resale at cost		333,000
		720,000
Current assets		
Patents and trademarks at cost	25,000	
Trade debtors	126,000	
Investments in market securities	23,000	
Cash in bank	1,000	175,000
Total assets		**895,000**
Less:		
Creditors		
Bank loan	*50,000*	
Trade and other creditors	*201,000*	
Accruals	*15,000*	
Taxation payable	*12,000*	
Profit and loss account	*217,000*	*495,000*
Net assets		**400,000**
Capital and reserves		
Called up share capital		400,000
		400,000

ADDITIONAL READING

There are numerous publications dealing with specific aspects of accounting for the corporate balance sheet. The following are a mix of UK and US contributions listed alphabetically by author.

M Davis (1992), "Goodwill Accounting: Time for an Overhaul," *Journal of Accountancy*, June, 75–83. The problem of accounting for goodwill as an intangible asset is discussed by this author.

J L Goodfellow (1988), "Now You See Them, Now You Don't," *CA Magazine*, December, 16–18 and 20–3. The problem of significant assets and liabilities that do not appear in the reported balance sheet is examined in this article.

S Henderson and J Goodwin (1992), "The Case Against Asset Revaluation," *Abacus*, March, 75–87. The general issue of revaluing assets in a reported balance sheet is considered in detail, particularly the inconsistency of revaluation within the historical cost accounting system.

P Holgate and M Gaul (2005), "A Solution in Search of a Problem," *Accountancy*, November, 90–1. This article looks at recent proposals regarding the balance sheet for a group of companies and includes commentary on the nature of the reporting entity, the use of fair value, and accounting for goodwill.

J Kruger (2005), "Shaping Hedges," *Accountancy*, December, 76–7. This is a brief review of current required practice regarding the reporting by companies of financial instruments to hedge against financial risk.

P B W Miller and P R Bahnson (2001), "Inventory and Cost of Goods Sold: Getting Them Both Right," *Accounting Today*, February 26–March 18, 14 and 16. These writers discuss the problem of accounting for inventory as a current asset.

P B W Miller and P R Bahnson (2001), "Using Goodwill to Placate Ill Will Shows FASB Has Lost Its Will," *Accounting Today*, April 16–May 6, 14 and 16. These writers discuss the problem of reporting goodwill in the balance sheet until it is impaired.

P B W Miller and P R Bahnson (2001), "GAAP for PP&E is Surely Museum Quality Accounting," *Accounting Today*, November 26–December 16, 14 and 16. These writers discuss the problem of accounting for a long-lived asset such as plant in the historical cost accounting system.

R Paterson (2002), "Impairment," *Accountancy*, December, 105. He reviews the requirement to account for losses on fixed assets including goodwill when their book value is greater than their present value.

R Paterson (2003), "Hidden Strengths," *Accountancy*, June, 98–9. This article reviews the problem of not accounting for hidden intangible assets.

R A Samuelson (1993), "Accounting for Liabilities to Perform Services," *Accounting Horizons*, 7 (3), 32–45. This article uses the example of payments made by customers in advance of services provided to examine the nature of liabilities for accounting purposes.

W P Schuetze (1993), "What is an Asset?" *Accounting Horizons*, 7 (3), 66–70. This is a critical examination of the nature of an asset for accounting purposes by a leading accounting regulator.

J L Zucca and D R Campbell (1992), "A Closer Look at Discretionary Writedowns of Impaired Assets," *Accounting Horizons*, 6 (3), 30–41. These authors examine the problem of accounting for impairment of assets, in which corporate management exercises subjective judgment in decisions about the reportable value of assets.

A specialist publication that analyzes corporate financial reports, *Company Reporting* (www. companyreporting.com) has specific sections on balance sheet matters—e.g. impairment of fixed assets (January 2003, 3–8; and April 2004, 3–8); and intangible assets including goodwill (January 2002, 3–8; February 2004, 3–8; December 2005, 3–8; and January 2006, 3–8).

Additional descriptions and explanations of the balance sheet and related matters can be found in a number of introductory accounting texts. One that is relevant to most readers of this text is M Jones

(2006), *Accounting*, John Wiley & Sons Ltd., Chichester. The specific parts of Jones relevant to this chapter are pages 92–112. These include discussion topics comparable to the exercises in this chapter.

An institutional view of the profit statement can be found in the IASB's (2004) "Presentation of Financial Statements," *International Accounting Standard 1*, International Accounting Standards Board, London, paras. 51–77 and in the Appendix.

CHAPTER 7

Other Corporate Statements

Learning Objectives

This chapter expands on the introduction in Chapter 3 to a variety of supplementary statements that are typically contained in a corporate annual report in the UK. Some of these statements support the main financial statements dealt with in Chapters 4, 5, and 6. Others are required under legislative or regulative provisions. The remainder are voluntary. Whatever their nature, however, it is important that the reader of financial statements can access the information in these additional statements. In combination, they represent the total communication of annual financial information by a company as part of its managerial accountability and corporate governance.

By the end of the chapter, you should be able to identify and understand:

- The additional statements that reporting companies typically report in support of their main financial statements.
- The nature and purpose of each additional statement.
- The prescriptive to voluntary range of these additional statements.
- In broad terms, the content of each of these additional statements.
- The various legislative and regulatory provisions prescribing these additional statements.
- The part played by these additional statements in the overall function of corporate governance.

At the end of this chapter, please refer to these learning objectives again before moving on to Chapter 8 on the audit of the main corporate financial statements.

INTRODUCTION

As stated in Chapter 3, there are a number of statements included in the annual corporate financial report additional to the main financial statements explained in Chapters 3, 4, 5, and 6. Some of these additional statements are prescribed by corporate legislation or accounting and stock exchange regulations. Others are recommended and voluntary. All, however, have a role to play in the discharge of the corporate governance function. The following sections deal with each statement in turn. The first section relates to statements that directly support the main financial statements, and the second section includes various statements from the board of directors and senior management.

SECONDARY FINANCIAL STATEMENTS

The following statements effectively provide additional information to that in the main financial statements.

Statement of total recognized gains and losses

This statement is required in the UK as part of the regulations of the FRC and the ASB. Its purpose is to report on all profits and losses recognized by the reporting company during the designated period. These include operating or trading profits and losses (as reported in the profit statement), and other gains and losses not reported in the profit statement—e.g. gains and losses from treasury functions (e.g. the purchase and sale of currency). The major impact is therefore to require corporate management to disclose all recognized operating and non-operating profits and losses, even if they have not been realized. For example:

(1) Corporate management recognizes unrealized revaluation surpluses and deficits when it has assets such as properties and investments valued if their historical costs become outdated and irrelevant.

(2) Reporting companies encounter gains and losses as a result of foreign currency transactions associated with operational trading and the acquisition of foreign assets and liabilities. A business transaction is contracted in monetary units and, when a foreign currency is involved, this means that monetary units have to be bought or sold in order to comply with the terms of the contract. For example, when a UK reporting company buys raw materials for manufacture from the US, it has to pay for these goods in US dollars. This means selling £s in order to purchase the required $s. If these transactions are regular and repeated, companies enter into forward contracts to purchase foreign currencies at fixed and pre-determined exchange rates and times. If an exchange rate varies from the agreed fixed rate, unrealized and realized gains or losses arise. In addition, there can be sundry accounting gains and losses that result from currency translation when combining the financial statements of companies in different countries for purposes of producing group financial statements.

(3) Companies report profits and losses, assets and liabilities, and shareholders' funds and then find that subsequent information requires adjustments to be made to the financial results of prior years. Reasons for these adjustments vary. The discovery of fraud or significant creative accounting practices are typical causes. Alternatively, accounting errors may be found. Whatever the reason, prior-year adjustments or corrections for these matters are common and typically appear in the statement of total recognized gains and losses.

The following is an example of a statement of total recognized gains and losses.

Blue Moon Construction Ltd
Statement of Total Recognized Gains and Losses
Year to 31 December 2006

	2006	2005
	£	£
Gains and losses		
Profits as per profit and loss account	123,000	118,000
Realized and unrealized foreign currency gains and *losses*	5,000	*12,000*
Unrealized gain due to revaluation of land and buildings	—	37,000
Reduction in 2004 profits due to accounting error in inventory	*7,000*	—
Total gains and losses	**121,000**	**143,000**

The company has earned trading profits in both years (i.e. £123,000 and £118,000). It has a currency gain of £5,000 in 2006 and a loss of £12,000 in 2005. The company revalued its properties in 2005 by £37,000 and there should be a separate note detailing the reasons for the revaluation. Management discovered an error with inventory in 2004 resulting in an overstatement of reported profits in that year of £7,000. The overall statement reminds users of the main financial statements that the profit statement relates to trading activity and that other associated gains and losses are possible and need to be considered when reviewing the performance of the reporting company and its management. Such reporting enhances the accountability of corporate management to shareholders and is therefore consistent with good corporate governance.

Statement of movements in shareholders' funds

This statement is also required by the ASB in the UK. It is an extension of the previous statement of total gains and losses, and reconciles the total equity or funds attributable to shareholders at the beginning and close of the reporting period. It therefore includes total gains and losses as reported in the statement of total gains and losses.

The statement of movements in shareholders' funds starts with the shareholders' funds at the beginning of the reporting period. This is defined broadly as share capital received from shareholders (i.e. from shares issued) plus reserves (i.e. accumulated net gains of previous periods, including trading profits undistributed to shareholders). The total net gains reported for the current period are added to this sum. So, too, is any additional share capital issued during the period. Such share capital includes the nominated or par value of each share unit plus any premium permitted under the regulations of the company (e.g. a £1 share unit issued for £1.50 has a par value of £1 and a premium of £0.50). The residual figure is the shareholders' funds at the end of the period as it appears in the balance sheet.

The objective of the statement is to provide shareholders and other users of the financial statements with an understanding of the overall reported change in shareholders' funds as stated in the balance sheet. The following is an example of the reconciliation required by the ASB.

Blue Moon Construction Ltd
Reconciliation of Movement in Shareholders' Funds
Year to 31 December 2006

	2006	2005
	£	£
Changes in shareholders' funds		
Distributable profits as per profit and loss account	140,000	133,000
Proposed dividend to shareholders	*17,000*	*15,000*
Profit retained for period	**123,000**	**118,000**
Realized and unrealized foreign currency gains and losses	5,000	*12,000*
Unrealized gain due to revaluation of land and buildings	—	37,000
Adjustment to 2004 profits due to accounting error in inventory	*7,000*	—
Total gains and losses for period	**121,000**	**143,000**
New issue of share capital at par value	100,000	—
Share premium received on new issue of shares	20,000	—
Shares issued in lieu of cash for dividends	10,000	10,000
Total change in shareholders' funds	**251,000**	**153,000**
Shareholders' funds at beginning of period:		
Share capital issued	1,350,000	1,340,000
Profits retained	866,000	748,000
Other reserves	121,000	96,000
Opening shareholders' funds	**2,337,000**	**2,184,000**
Shareholders' funds at close of period:		
Share capital issued	1,460,000	1,350,000
Profits retained	989,000	866,000
Other reserves	139,000	121,000
Closing shareholders' funds	**2,588,000**	**2,337,000**
Total change in shareholders' funds	**251,000**	**153,000**

The statement of movements in shareholders' funds divides into three main sections. The first section concerns the total change in funds during the reporting period for various reasons—i.e. because of profits retained rather than distributed, other realized and unrealized gains and losses (as explained in the statement of total gains and losses) (a total of £121,000 in 2006), and issued capital (including the premium received) (a total of £130,000 in 2006). The second section discloses the various elements comprising funds at the beginning of the period (a total of £2,337,000 in 2006) and the third section repeats this disclosure at the period end (a total of £2,588,000 in 2006). The total for the first section reconciles to the difference between the second and third sections (i.e. £251,000 in 2006). The overall effect of the statement is to remind financial statement users that shareholders' equity changes because of profits retained in the business, other gains and losses that have been recognized even though they may not have been realized, and new capital received from shareholders.

As was the case with the reporting of shareholders' equity in the balance sheet, the total change in funds reported by the company may not and is not intended to represent the periodic change in the market value of its shares. For example, using the above figures, assume there are 1,460,000 £1 share units issued by the company in 2006 and these are quoted on a stock exchange at the period end at £3.60 per unit. The statement of movement in shareholders' funds reports that these shares have a period-end book value in the company's records of £2,588,000 or £1.77 per share unit (£2,588,000/1,460,000). But the stock market value is £3.60 or £5,256,000 in total (£3.60 × 1,460,000). The reason for the difference of £1.83 per unit is a combination of factors—e.g. the use by the company of historical cost instead of market value for assets, non-recognition of unrealized gains, and the lack of internally-generated goodwill in the balance sheet. These problems are discussed in more detail in Chapter 9.

Statement of accounting policies

In the UK, this statement is a consequence of the Companies Act 1985 requirement for reporting companies to adhere to legally prescribed accounting practices. The latter are augmented by the requirements of the ASB and the IASB, and the statement of accounting policies contains descriptions and explanations of the main accounting practices used in the preparation of the reported financial statements. This disclosure is particularly relevant for expert users of financial statements such as financial analysts because they are capable of considering the impact of specific practices on disclosed accounting numbers. This is important when comparing the financial results of two similar companies that use different practices. Expert users can estimate accounting numbers using different practices in order to assess the effect of the latter on comparative financial results such as profits. The statement is also a significant means for company directors and managers to demonstrate their compliance with prescribed accounting standards, and therefore their adherence to this aspect of the function of corporate governance.

Each statement of accounting policies varies according to the circumstances of the reporting company and the particular accounting standards applicable to it. The following example is offered as an illustration of a statement relevant to a non-listed manufacturing company.

Blue Moon Construction Ltd
Statement of Accounting Policies
Year to 31 December 2006

Basis of financial statements
The financial statements have been prepared in accordance with the historical cost accounting convention and related standards prescribed by the Companies Act 1985.

Basis of consolidation
The profit statement and the balance sheet consist of the financial results of the holding company and its four subsidiary companies. All companies have the same year-end.

Intangible fixed assets

Goodwill on acquisition of subsidiary companies is amortized on a straight-line basis over 15 years.

Tangible fixed assets

Depreciation has been provided on a straight-line basis over the estimated economic lives of the following assets at the stated rates: buildings 10%; plant and equipment 20%; and motor vehicles 25%.

Impairment of fixed assets

Intangible and tangible fixed assets are constantly reviewed for impairment of value and any impairment recognized is written off in the profit and loss account in the year in which it occurs.

Inventory

Inventory comprises raw materials, work-in-progress, and finished goods. Each category is disclosed at the lower of its cost and net realizable value. Raw materials are disclosed at purchase cost, and work-in-progress and finished goods at the cost of raw materials plus a relevant percentage of manufacturing wages and overheads.

Investments in market securities

Market securities are disclosed at their current market value. Income on these securities is included in the profit and loss account as other income.

Pensions and post-retirement benefits

The cost of providing pensions and post-retirement health benefits to employees is charged to the profit and loss account over the working lives of the employees as advised by the company's actuaries.

Foreign currencies

Foreign assets and liabilities are translated into pounds sterling at year-end exchange rates. Profits and losses are translated at the average exchange rate for the year. Gains and losses on such translation are disclosed in the statement of total gains and losses.

The statement above therefore explains that the main financial statements are for a group of five companies and use historical cost as the primary basis for preparing accounting numbers. The historical costs of fixed assets are depreciated on a straight-line basis (giving an equal amount of depreciation each year) and reviewed for further impairment. Inventory is reported at its historical cost (including wages and overheads where relevant) and reduced to market value when necessary (therefore unrealized value increases are not recognized). Investments are also disclosed at market value (unrealized gains and losses are therefore recognized). The basis of translating profits, losses, assets, and liabilities from foreign currencies to pounds sterling is explained, as is the provision of pension and post-retirement obligations to employees. Such disclosures assist financial statement users to judge the quality and appropriateness of key accounting practices used in the preparation of the profit statement and balance sheet.

Statement of principal subsidiaries

The final statement that supports the main financial statements in the annual report is the statement of principal subsidiaries. This statement is one that has been developed by companies as a means of satisfying legislative requirements to inform shareholders and others about the nature of the reporting company and its principal activities. It discloses the companies included in the consolidated financial statements of a group of companies. These companies are subsidiaries controlled either through a majority share ownership of a holding company, or membership of subsidiary company boards of directors held by holding company directors. Share ownership in this respect refers to voting shares. The statement also discloses voting share ownerships that do not constitute control and therefore do not justify consolidation. These are holdings of between 20% and 50% of voting capital. Such associated companies do not have their assets, liabilities, and profits included in the group financial statements (other than as investments and investment income received). However, users of financial statements need to be aware of all significant investments in other companies. The following is an illustration of the type of information provided in this statement. The company is again non-listed.

Blue Moon Construction Ltd
Statement of Principal Subsidiary and Associated Companies
Year to 31 December 2006

Company	Business Type	% of Equity Capital	Country of Registration
Jim-Jams Ltd	Retail	100	England
King-John Ltd	Public relations	85	Ireland
My-Man Ltd	Manufacturing	60	England
Simply-Solid Ltd	Retail	51	Scotland
Tweet-Tweet Ltd	Distribution	25	England

The first four companies concern investments controlled by the holding company. Their assets (minus liabilities), profits, and cash flows are aggregated fully with the equivalent accounting numbers of the holding company as if the investment was 100% in each case. Due allowance is also made for the appropriate proportion of net assets and profits owned by outside shareholders or minority interests (i.e. 15%, 40%, and 49%, respectively, for the second, third and fourth companies). In the case of the fifth company, consolidation does not take place because there is not control of the entity. However, statement users are entitled to know the reporting company has a significant investment of 25%.

Lesson 7.1 Additional financial statements
The main financial statements provide shareholders and other stakeholders with information about the profitability, cash flow, and financial position of the reporting company. However, this information is enhanced by disclosures in other statements that support the main financial

statements. These additional statements provide information about gains and losses recognized but not incorporated in the profit statement, the periodic change in shareholders' equity in the balance sheet, the main accounting practices used to calculate the accounting numbers in the main financial statements, and the identity of subsidiary and associated companies whose financial results are included in the main financial statements to a greater or lesser extent depending on whether or not there is control by the holding company. The annual financial report should therefore be seen as a structure of inter-related statements—some major and some supportive in nature.

STATEMENTS FROM BOARD AND OTHERS

There are also a variety of statements in the annual financial report that are produced by the board of directors and senior managers. They contain financial information related to the contents of the main financial statements such as the profit statement, cash flow statement, and balance sheet. However, their principal objective is to disclose more general information about the reporting company and its business operations. There are six statements that meet this objective.

CHAIRMAN'S REPORT

This is a voluntary statement which means that there is no legislation or regulation in the UK that mandates its appearance or content in the annual financial report. Despite this lack of prescription, the chairman's report has a long history in the UK as a means of permitting the senior director of the reporting company an opportunity to provide a commentary and opinion on its financial performance during the reporting period as well as its future. Increasingly, particularly in public and listed companies, the chairman's report has become a source of clues about the future direction of the reporting company—e.g. its operational and financial strategies and plans. The statement is not subject to verification or audit opinion, although auditors typically review it for inconsistencies between the reported financial results and the chairman's comments.

The statement is used by the chairman of the board of directors to provide a broad review of the reporting company's financial results in the context of its trading and related activities. It is a personal rather than collective statement and its tone and focus are typically positive and optimistic—unless there are issues that are so obvious as to prevent such an approach. As well as the financial and operating activities of the reporting company, the chairman often takes the opportunity to provide personal thoughts on wider issues such as conditions in the industry generally, the state of the economy, and the impact of government interference in corporate affairs such as taxation and legislation. Because of the nature of these comments, they should be treated with caution by users of the main financial statements. They are given from a particular and privileged position. For this reason, there has been concern in the financial community for some years about the need to regulate the contents of the chairman's statement in order to reduce its bias and therefore improve its quality. Its role also needs to be evaluated in light of the disclosure of information in the directors' report and the operating and financial review explained below.

The content of the chairman's report is not subject to a prescribed model and varies from annual report to annual report. However, in broad terms, it has specific features that appear in most statements. These are illustrated by the following chairman's statement. It should be noted that the comments have been deliberately abbreviated. The company is a listed entity.

Over-The-Rainbow plc
Chairman's Report
Year to 31 December 2006

General comments
This has been a year of satisfactory progress during a period of considerable difficulty due to unfavourable economic trading conditions and unnecessary government interference in employment matters such as health and pension provision.

Financial results
Sales increased this year by 15%, and profitability (including earnings per share) improved by 12%. These results were about what was expected and due to a combination of increased market share in the company's main products and rigorous cost control procedures initiated by management. The company acquired two subsidiary companies in North America and financed these by long-term debt. Operating cash flow continued to enable the company to re-invest and repay existing debt obligations. The increased level of profitability enabled the proposed dividend to be raised from 10 to 12 pence per share.

Operating strategy
The company's success has been grounded in an operating strategy that regards the core of its business to be products that appeal to customers of both sexes aged between 20 and 40 in the UK and Continental Europe. However, the increasing prosperity of countries on the Pacific Rim has focused management's attention on developing market share in countries such as China. The deteriorating value of the US dollar has created further trading opportunities in America.

Board changes
The board lost the services of John Smith, chief executive officer of Play-Your-Cards plc, due to ill health. John served the board for 20 years and chaired its audit committee for most of that period. The company wishes John well in his retirement and is fortunate to have William Brown as his replacement. William is a former trade and industry minister in the last government and he brings a wealth of experience to our board table.

General outlook
The recent change in government has led to various legislative and fiscal measures that threaten the financial viability of the corporate sector in this country. The company has an able senior management team that is currently looking for ways to minimize the unfavourable effects of this level of interference in the corporate sector.

The above illustration reveals the interpretive and therefore subjective nature of the chairman's statement. The chairman is not usually an accountant or economist. Yet the statement contains personal reflections on accounting-based results within an economic environment. Both features are complex and the contents of the statement need to be read with caution. The chairman will typically accentuate the positive and diminish the negative aspects of the reporting company's financial performance and condition. However, the statement typically includes mention of future performance and condition. Given the historical nature of the main financial statements and the interest of shareholders and others in the company's future, the chairman's statement is therefore a significant part of the annual financial report.

> **Lesson 7.2 Chairman's report**
> The main financial statements are based on actual business transactions described in accounting terms as objectively as possible. However, the accounting process contains elements of considerable subjectivity and the reported accounting numbers are subject to audit verification and report. The chairman's report, on the other hand, is in part a personal commentary on these verified numbers and is typically presented in a positive but biased manner. Readers of the statement need to take care when relying on the personal interpretations of the chairman. They are not subject to audit verification and report. The chairman is rarely a qualified accountant.

REPORT OF BOARD OF DIRECTORS

This is a statement by the board of directors of the reporting company and is mandated under the Companies Act 1985. It includes a combination of information prescribed by legislation and stock exchange regulation, supplemented by voluntary information from the board. The objective of the statement is to enable the board to provide a prescribed narrative on aspects of the reporting company's financial results, information about directors and employees, and explanations about corporate governance procedures (including audit). In this sense, it is the one statement in the annual financial report that explicitly addresses the issue of corporate governance.

A typical statement from the board of directors has several distinct sections. The first section is mandated by legislation and refers to the principal business activities of the company and any subsidiary companies that it controls. This section is intended to inform shareholders and others about the nature of the business or businesses that the company operates and any significant changes in these matters that have occurred during the reporting period. The section is therefore a means of identifying the nature and type of company underlying the reported financial results.

The second section of the directors' report deals with significant developments in the company's business operations during the reporting period. This is effectively a review of business and an opportunity for the board to comment on the financial results of the company in terms of its sales and profits, and to explain material matters such as exceptional items. Other changes that can be explained in this section include changes in share capital, debt, fixed assets, and investments in other companies. Many of these matters may also be presented within the operating and financial review explained later in the chapter.

The third section of the directors' report is devoted to information about the board and its individual members and its content is mandated by the Companies Act 1985. It is essential that shareholders are informed about the directors who act on their behalf and such information includes not only the identity of each director but also the specific financial interests they have in the company. Directors and their families may have contracted relationships with the reporting company that constitute potential conflicts of interest—i.e. relationships that may influence their decisions and actions and which may not be in the best interests of the shareholders and other stakeholders. This section attempts to provide transparency in these matters and required disclosures include the identity of each director (boards typically provide employment details as well as names), financial interests in the company of each director and their spouses and children (including shares, loans, and credit facilities), and the emoluments of each director (including remuneration, share options, and pension and other benefits). This part of the directors' report relates specifically to corporate governance and the legislation distinguishes between listed and non-listed companies—the greatest disclosure is required of listed companies. The following tabulation is typical of a listed company's compliance with the Companies Act 1985 requirement.

Directors	Salary	Pension benefits	Other benefits	Incentive bonuses	Total
	£	£	£	£	£
John Brown (E) (chairman)	125,000	12,000	7,000	234,000	378,000
Leonard Blue (E)	100,000	10,000	8,000	112,000	230,000
Joe Green (E)	80,000	8,000	4,000	60,000	152,000
Helen Redwing (NE)	20,000	—	3,000	—	23,000
James Blackstone (NE)	20,000	—	5,000	—	25,000
Rupert White (NE)	10,000	—	1,000	—	11,000
Tim Yellowstone (NE)	5,000	—	1,000	—	6,000
Total	**360,000**	**30,000**	**29,000**	**406,000**	**825,000**

These details and accounting numbers reveal the names of the directors, whether they are executive (E) or non-executive (NE), and their remuneration packages, including benefits and bonuses (which are usually related to reported profits). In this case, the significance of incentive-based remuneration is particularly evident.

The fourth section of the directors' report contains information about the employees of the company. These form a major stakeholder group interested in the company as well as a significant resource of it. The required information may be provided in the profit statement if not in the directors' report. The information required includes the average number of employees during the reporting period (detailed over the major segments of the company's business), staff costs, and employment policy for disabled individuals (for companies with more than 250 employees). Increasingly on a voluntary basis, boards are also providing information about health and safety at work policies and practices.

The FRC's *Combined Code on Corporate Governance* of 2003 is part of the Listing Agreement of the London Stock Exchange and therefore quoted companies in the UK are required to produce a statement on the corporate governance practices in operation in the reporting company. This statement is either produced separately from the directors' report or incorporated in it as a fifth section. The objective of the corporate governance statement is to provide public reassurance that the reporting company and its board are following best practice as recommended under the *Combined Code*. These matters are numerous and complex but typically include the following:

Board responsibilities for accounting and reporting

This statement covers the board's legal responsibilities for preparing the main financial statements and ensuring their content complies with the prescribed standard of a true and fair view of profitability and financial position; maintaining a system of accounting records adequate to produce the required financial statements, safeguard assets, and prevent fraud; consistently applying suitable and prudent accounting practices in the preparation of the main financial statements by using acceptable accounting standards; and disclosing any material departures from these standards. In other words, although the appointed auditor is responsible for verifying and giving an opinion on the quality of the content of the main financial statements, it is the board of directors of the reporting company that is responsible for that quality and the underlying accounting processes and procedures. This statement of responsibility may be disclosed separately from the directors' report.

Board compliance with *Combined Code*

This statement attempts to explain the means by which the board of directors' attempts to comply with best practices recommended under the *Combined Code*. The areas covered in this respect include the composition, conduct, and procedures of the board (e.g. the numerical split between executives and non-executive directors, the lack of domination by an individual director, the chairman as a non-executive director, directors' meetings, information provided to directors, and specific matters for which the board is responsible including investment decisions, treasury policy, risk management, and financial reporting and auditing). Particular committees of the board are explained including nominations (for board appointments), compliance (to monitor for illegal acts), remuneration (for directors' emoluments), and audit (for accounting, financial reporting, and audit). Shareholder relations are also emphasized by companies. These remarks include meetings with institutional shareholders to update on company developments, the annual general meeting, and the transmission to shareholders of ad hoc price-sensitive information relating to the company's business. Boards also have responsibility under the *Combined Code* for monitoring the effectiveness of the company's internal control procedures. This is typically explained as part of the directors' report.

Other matters

There are usually other matters to be disclosed in the directors' report. These include the dividend proposed by the board for the year under report, details of any shareholding in the company in excess of 3% of the nominal or par value of voting share capital of a stock exchange-listed company, whether the auditor is aware of all relevant information likely to impact the audit, the willingness or otherwise of the auditor to be reappointed, and political and charitable donations. The first item is a straightforward information item to inform shareholders of the return they will receive on their shareholding. The second item is intended to forewarn shareholders of a shareholding that could grow to become a dominating one in the affairs of the company. In a publicly listed company, even a single digit percentage shareholding can be a potentially influential one in the management of the entity. The third and fourth items are part of the corporate governance process. Each director has to personally ensure that no relevant information has been knowingly withheld from the auditor thus preventing an effective audit taking place. In addition, should the auditor not wish reappointment then shareholders need to be informed by the board of directors of the reason for this. The fifth item relates to contributions made by the company to political parties and charitable organizations and is intended to reveal the political and social preferences of the board as a collective body. This is a sensitive area as the board is acting on behalf of the shareholders.

The following statement of the board of directors is offered as an abbreviated illustration of practice in this area. It incorporates several of the main areas mentioned above. It should be noted that it does not cover every area nor does it attempt to provide the amount of detail typically disclosed by larger companies. The company is a listed entity.

Sugar-In-The-Morning plc
Report of Board of Directors
Year to 31 December 2006

The following is the report of the board of directors of Sugar-In-The-Morning plc for the year to 31 December 2006. The board presents the audited financial statements for the year to the shareholders and debenture holders.

Principal activities
Sugar-In-The-Morning plc is a manufacturer of sugar-based products used in the confectionary industry. It has factories in the UK, US, and France. A review of the company's operating and financial activities for the year is contained separately in the operating and financial review.

Group financial results
Group sales increased by 8.6% during 2006 from £10,500,000 to £11,400,000. Profit before tax increased by 8.3% from £1,200,000 to £1,300,000. After tax of £400,000 and a proposed dividend of £200,000, profits retained for the year amounted to £700,000. Capital expenditure on fixed assets for the year totalled £3,000,000 funded in part by a new debenture issue of £2,000,000. The market value of the company's land and buildings at 31 December 2006 has been estimated at £15,000,000.

Directors' interests
The directors of the company and their interests in it are as follows:

Directors	Background	Shareholdings 2006 £	Shareholdings 2005 £
John Adam	Non-executive Chief executive officer Adam Industries plc	20,000	25,000
Graeme Eve	Executive Chief executive officer	10,000	10,000
Susan Hart	Executive Chief financial officer	5,000	—
Donald Legg	Non-executive Retired senior civil servant	16,000	16,000
Tom Burn	Non-executive Chief executive officer Sweet Treats plc	1,000	—
Frederick Sage	Non-executive Opera singer	2,000	—

None of the directors have or have had an interest in a contract with the company during the year.

Employment policies

Sugar-In-The-Morning plc is committed to the employment of staff at all levels who contribute significantly to its progress and well-being. With this in mind, the company has in place systems of recruitment, training, development, and management designed to provide first-class products to the company's customers as efficiently, effectively, and economically as possible. The company is an equal opportunity employer and careers are managed on the basis of merit irrespective of gender, class, age, or disability. Members of staff are well informed about developments in the company and share in its well-being through various incentive-based systems. The company provides all members of staff with a range of pension and health care benefits.

Corporate governance

Sugar-In-The-Morning plc complies with the principles of the *Combined Code on Corporate Governance* as part of the Listing Agreement of the London Stock Exchange. The board comprises two executive directors and four independent non-executive directors. No director can dominate the board's decision making. It meets on a monthly basis and there are regular meetings with senior executives of the company. The board deals with several matters over which it has decision making authority. These include financial statement approval, major capital expenditure, funding policy, and senior executive succession. Appointments to the board are the responsibility of the nominations committee and directors' remuneration is handled by the remuneration committee. There are regular meetings with major shareholders. The audit committee monitors internal control systems, approves accounting policies, and reviews interim and final financial statements. Each of these committees comprises non-executive directors. The board is confident that the company's internal financial controls are effective against material misstatement and loss. The board oversees an organizational structure that includes monitoring of controls including internal audit, systems of budgeting and financial performance reporting, capital investment appraisals, management policies and procedures, and staff recruitment policies and procedures. Committee members for the year 2006 were as follows (C = convener):

Non-executive directors	Nominations committee	Remuneration committee	Audit committee
John Adam	C		*
Donald Legg		C	*
Tom Burn	*	*	C
Frederick Sage	*	*	

Directors' remuneration

Sugar-In-The-Morning plc follows the remuneration principles contained in the *Combined Code*. The remuneration committee deals with executive directors' remuneration and the board handles that of non-executive directors. Remuneration is based on executive responsibilities, the financial state of the company, the competitive nature of the industry, and individual performance. The remuneration committee annually reviews base salaries and benefits of executives. Employees benefit from a profit-sharing scheme involving variable bonuses based on improvements to earnings per share and the meeting of strategic goals. Senior executives, including executive directors, benefit from a similar scheme with benefits paid in the form of company shares that must be held for at least three years. Executive directors participate in a defined benefit pension scheme administered independently and providing benefits of up to 60% of base salary on retirement at 65. The remuneration of directors for the year 2006 was as follows:

Non-executive directors	Salary or fee £	Profit-sharing £	Pensions £	Other benefits £	Total £
Graeme Eve	125,000	118,000	25,000	6,000	274,000
Susan Hart	100,000	65,000	20,000	6,000	191,000
John Adam	25,000	—	—	—	25,000
Donald Legg	25,000	—	—	—	25,000
Tom Burn	30,000	—	—	—	30,000
Frederick Sage	25,000	—	—	—	25,000
Total	**330,000**	**183,000**	**45,000**	**12,000**	**570,000**

Executive directors have service agreements including notice of one year. Non-executive directors do not have contracts but are reviewed bi-annually.

> **Lesson 7.3 Directors' report**
> The directors' report is an opportunity for the board of directors to be accountable to the shareholders beyond the accounting numbers contained in the main financial statements. In particular, it focuses on the remuneration, financial interests, and duties of each director in relation to the reporting company, and therefore improves the transparency of the board as the main mechanism for corporate governance.

OPERATING AND FINANCIAL REVIEW

This is a voluntary statement in the UK that was previously mandated under the Companies Act 1985 in the UK and regulated by the ASB in a reporting standard. Currently, there is no legislative provision and the ASB makes recommendations about the review's content in a *Statement of Best Practice*. The overall purpose of the operating and financial review is to permit the board of directors to explain in narrative style the main features of the financial results disclosed in the main financial statements. It typically has two sections. The first section deals principally with the annual performance of the reporting company and its position at the year-end. In effect, it reports on the operational matters that relate to profits and cash flows, identifying any key trends or factors affecting the company's performance and likely to influence its future performance. The second section concerns the financial funding structure and activities of the reporting company, with particular regard to share capital and long-term loans. Principal risks and uncertainties, treasury policy, and liquidity must be commented on. The contents of the operating and financial review inevitably vary from company to company—both in terms of what is disclosed and the quality of the disclosures. Typically, companies attempt to communicate in the review by means of a combination of narrative, numerical analyses, and diagrams.

Operational review

The objective of this part of the review is to explain the operational or trading features that underlie the financial results disclosed in the main financial statements. The review comments on the reporting company's operating performance in relation to sales and profits, any new initiatives concerning the acquisition and disposal of companies or operating units, and the returns achieved for shareholders from operations in terms of key performance indicators such as earnings per share and proposed dividends. Comments on sales and profits are usually made in the context of industry and market conditions (e.g. the impact of inflation or taxation), change in products and services (e.g. the launch of a new product item), new operating facilities (e.g. factories or stores), and organizational changes (e.g. different operating or sales procedures and management). The analyses often contain segmental reviews based on products, services, and markets. The aim is to identify reasons for the level of sales and profits achieved by the company during the reporting period and identify risks and uncertainties associated with these matters. This analysis is intended to assist shareholders to identify the main business strategies of the company and their potential for success.

Financial review

This part of the overall review focuses on financial aspects of the reporting company's performance and the resources available to it. These include additional long-term funding from new share issues and debt. Management can also comment on the cash flow performance of the company in terms of cash generation from operations and cash funding of capital expenditure. The liquidity of the company will be discussed in terms of available cash resources including short-term loan facilities from bankers. The review can cover the detailed aspects of the company's treasury function, including its management of credit risk, interest rates, and foreign currency exchange rates. Management can use this part of the review to reassure shareholders and other financial statement users that the company is a going concern—i.e. it is financially viable in the foreseeable future in the sense of being able to meet its financial commitments. The intention is to inform about financial strategies and their potential for success.

Because of the variability of the operating and financial review in practice, it is not possible to provide a model illustration. However, whatever the content, it should be balanced and comprehensive. The following example is offered as an abbreviated statement containing some of the main features mentioned previously. It will be noted that some of this information may also be contained elsewhere in the annual financial report—e.g. in the chairman's report. The company is assumed to be a listed entity.

Rock-Around-The-Clock plc
Operating and Financial Review
Year to 31 December 2006

The purpose of this statement is to review the company's operating performance for the year 2006 together with certain aspects of its financial structure and management.

Overall performance
Company sales increased by 11% from £3.5m to £3.9m, profit before tax from normal operating activities increased by 17% from £1.2m to £1.4m, and operating cash flow increased by 7% from £2.7m to £2.9m. Capital expenditure on new operating facilities amounted to £7m, a 40% increase compared to the year 2005. Long-term debt increased by 10% to £18m. Interest on long-term debt was £1m. This was similar to 2005 and reflects the general fall in interest rates during 2006. Taxation on operating profits amounted to an effective rate of 30%. Earnings per share increased by 14% to 25p per share. The proposed dividend of 15p per share is the same as for 2005. The total shareholder return for the year 2006, measured in terms of the annual change in share price plus the proposed dividend, amounts to 16%. This compares with 15% for 2005 and 10% for 2004.

Segmented results
The following analyses provide a breakdown of company sales and profits before tax across its main markets.

Markets	2006 Sales £000	2005 Sales £000	Change sales %	2006 Profits £000	2005 Profits £000	Change profits %
UK	1,834	1,747	5	703	661	6
Europe	1,133	1,049	8	464	396	17
North America	912	699	30	238	144	65
Total	**3,879**	**3,495**	**11**	**1,405**	**1,201**	**17**

Each of the three main markets experienced an increase in sales and profits. The smallest percentage increases were in the UK where economic conditions were poor due to increased competition from overseas products and lack of consumer confidence. Europe was little better although management improved profits significantly due to a program of effective cost cutting. The biggest success was in the North American market where economic conditions have improved after a short recession and the dollar is weak in relation to the pound sterling. Sales increased by more than one third and effective management improved profits by nearly two thirds.

Treasury management

The company operates in several countries where there is uncertainty about foreign exchange rates. Management has therefore taken steps to reduce the company's exposure to the risk of currency depreciation by entering into relevant hedging contracts. It also has a number of long-term borrowing arrangements in order to fund its five-year program of capital investment in new operating facilities. The second year of this program was 2006.

Going concern

The company reviews its financial viability on a continuing basis. Subject to the inherent uncertainty of the future, its management is confident that it is financially viable for the foreseeable future.

Lesson 7.4 Operating and financial review

The operating and financial review is an opportunity for the board of directors and senior executives of the reporting company to explain its financial performance and financial health beyond the accounting numbers contained in the main financial statements. Shareholders are typically remote from the operations and management of companies and the review can provide an important context for the accounting numbers they receive.

OTHER STATEMENTS AND CORPORATE GOVERNANCE

There are four support statements to the main financial statements covered in this chapter, together with three other statements required by the board of directors. Each statement has a particular role and each can be said to assist in the exercise of managerial accountability and the function of corporate governance.

The statement of total recognized gains and losses permits corporate management and the board of directors to provide a comprehensive statement of all the gains and losses they have recognized during the reporting period. The statement contains realized and unrealized gains and losses, and separates operational or trading gains and losses from others resulting from financial activity. The statement reminds users that managers and directors are responsible for more than operational matters and that profitability includes gains that can be recognized prior to realization. It also contains gains and losses due to financial decisions and actions.

The statement of movement in shareholders' funds is an extension of the previous statement and is intended as an explanation of the periodic change in shareholders' equity. As such it contains information not only about total gains and losses but also about new capital issued during the reporting period. It is a statement of specific interest to shareholders and, as such, reflects the managerial obligation of accountability to ownership.

The statement of accounting policies is an important source of information for the expert user of corporate financial statements. It describes the main accounting principles and practices utilized by corporate management when preparing the main financial statements. It is therefore an explanation of the calculations behind the accounting numbers and improves the transparency of the financial statements. For this reason, it is a key part of accountability and corporate governance.

The chairman's report, report of the board of directors, and operating and financial review are means by which senior managers and the board of directors can attempt to explain the operating and financial performance and position of the reporting company. They go beyond the reported accounting numbers in the main financial statements and give either additional disclosure about the numbers or explanations of them in the context of the economic environment in which the reporting company is trading. As such, they are significant tools in the process of accountability. They also contain specific information concerning the way in which the company is governed.

LEGISLATIVE AND REGULATORY REQUIREMENTS

The various statements and disclosures explained in this chapter are mainly required by various legislative and regulatory provisions. This is an introductory text and the detail of these requirements is not required to understand their significance in corporate financial reporting. Nevertheless, the following explanations form a broad review of existing provisions as they related to each statement covered above.

Total gains and losses

The statement of total recognized gains and losses is regulated by the ASB under "Reporting Financial Performance," *Financial Reporting Standard 3*, 1993. It should be noted that this standard does not recognize separations of profits and losses with respect to what is exceptional or extra-ordinary.

Reconciliation of movement in shareholders' funds

This statement is also regulated under the ASB's *Financial Reporting Standard 3*.

Statement of accounting policies

Disclosure of accounting policies is a consequence of adherence to or deviation from the disclosure provisions of the Companies Act 1985 which include several basic accounting principles and policies to be followed in the preparation of profit statements and balance sheets. The Act particularly requires disclosure of departures from any prescribed principles and policies.

Statement of principal subsidiaries

This statement is a consequence of the requirement of the Companies Act 1985 to prepare group financial statements when there are subsidiary companies.

Report of the board of directors

The Companies Act 1985 prescribes a report from the board of directors. A subsection details specific matters for reporting, including the principle activities of the company, a business review, and a statement that the auditors are aware of all relevant audit information. A schedule of the Act stipulates the disclosure of information regarding directors' remuneration and a further schedule deals with disclosures of fixed asset values significantly different from reported numbers, directors' financial interests, and political and charitable donations. It also details the specific information required about each director and his or her contract and remuneration, separating that not subject to audit from that required to be audited.

Operating and financial review

As explained above, it is no longer a requirement of the Companies Act 1985 that listed companies in the UK publish an operating and financial review. The ASB has converted its *Financial and Reporting Standard 1* of 2005 into a *Statement of Best Practice* that advises companies on how best to present an operating and financial review.

LEARNING OBJECTIVES

Please review the learning objectives at the beginning of this chapter and ensure they have been achieved before proceeding to Chapter 8 on the audit of corporate financial statements as part of the function of corporate governance.

Exercise 1   Total gains and losses

Hurry-Curry Ltd is a manufacturer of ready-made meals. It has a profit after tax for the year 2006 of £189,000 compared to a loss for the year 2005 of £56,000. Also in 2005, the company's manufacturing facility was valued at £450,000 compared to its original cost of £200,000. The revaluation was accounted for in the 2005 financial statements. During 2005, the auditors discovered an accounting error in the previous year's financial statements that resulted in profits after tax being overstated by £15,000. Prepare a statement of total recognized gains and losses for the year 2006.

Exercise 2   Total gains and losses

Explain why it is important for companies to disclose a statement of total recognized gains and losses. Students should also consider with their instructor the specific value of this statement as compared with the profit statement or cash flow statement.

Exercise 3   Movement in shareholders' funds

Red-Sails-In-The-Sunset Ltd sells boating equipment. Its balance sheet at 31 December 2005 reported that shareholders' equity amounted to £273,000. The funds comprised 100,000 £1 share units, profits retained of £143,000, and other reserves of £30,000. During the year to 31 December 2006, the company issued to its shareholders 25,000 £1 share units at £4 per unit for cash. It also issued 10,000 units to the owners of a business it acquired for £40,000. Profit after tax for the year 2006 was £61,000, the proposed dividend was £13,000, and there was a gain of £5,000 on the sale of market securities during 2006. Prepare a reconciliation of shareholders' equity for inclusion in the company's 2006 annual financial report.

Exercise 4   Movement in shareholders' funds

Explain the significance of reporting the reconciliation of movement in shareholders' funds. Students can also discuss with their instructor the disparity between reported shareholders' equity and the market value of that equity if the reporting company is a listed entity. Is their any meaning in the difference between the two figures?

Exercise 5   Accounting policies

Explain the significance of the statement of accounting policies in the annual financial report. Provide examples of accounting policies that are commonly disclosed. Students should discuss with their instructor the value of this statement for inexpert financial statement users.

Exercise 6   Chairman's statement

Sir John Winterton is the non-executive chairman of Yellow Brick Road Construction plc. He has just received the draft annual financial report from the company's CFO in order to prepare his chairman's statement. Sir John is a former Member of Parliament and transport minister and holds several non-executive directorships in listed companies. The CFO has prepared a note of the key financial results for the year ended 31 December 2006 and Sir John reviews his diary entries for 2006 to remind himself about significant events affecting the company. The following are the results and diary events he is considering before preparing his statement. What are the main issues he needs to address in his statement?

(1) Sales increased by 8.6% from £35,000,000 to £38,000,000. NP after tax declined by 2% from £3,500,000 to £3,430,000. OCF has declined by 10% to £1,780,000. Long-term borrowing increased from £75,000,000 to £100,000,000 largely due to funding necessary to acquire a US subsidiary company for £20,000,000. The subsidiary required a complete restructuring of its operations and this cost £5,000,000 to date. The dividend proposed for the year is the same as for 2005 at £1,500,000.

(2) When announcing the financial results of the company for 2005, Sir John stated an expectation that sales and NP would continue to grow at a rate similar to recent years. The average growth rate for sales and NP for 2001 to 2005 inclusive was 10%.

(3) During 2006 the company dealt with a number of unexpected events. There was a five-week strike by its construction employees over pay and pension conditions. A major supplier of construction materials entered receivership due to a series of poor financial results. The UK government announced a curtailment to its current programme of motorway renewal.

Students should also discuss the chairman's report with their instructor from the perspective of the report as an example of commercial spin. How valuable is it in such a context?

Exercise 7   Directors' report

The board of directors of Paint-Your-Wagon Ltd are meeting to discuss the contents of the company's annual directors' report to its shareholders. You are asked to advise them on the content. Provide a list of contents and explain why each item is required. Students should also discuss with their instructor the possibility of information overload because of repetition of disclosures in statements such as the chairman's report and the directors' report.

Exercise 8   Operating and financial review

Brown Sugar plc is a manufacturer of breakfast cereals and supplies markets throughout the European Union. Its CFO has drafted the following operating and financial review for the year to 31 December 2006. Explain each of the main segments disclosed in the review as if you were addressing the company's board of directors.

Brown Sugar plc
Operating and Financial Review
Year to 31 December 2006

This operating and financial review covers the financial performance of Brown Sugar plc in the year to 31 December 2006.

Overall performance
Group sales increased by 6.7% to £160m (2005 – £150m). Group profit before tax rose by 7.1% to £15m (2005 – £14m). Operating cash flow fell by 5% to £9.5m

(2005 – £10m). Capital expenditure on manufacturing facilities worldwide totalled £85m compared to £21m in 2005. This expenditure resulted in long-term borrowing increasing by 16% to £105m (2005 – £90.5m). Interest on long-term debt was £6m (2005 – £4.5m). Corporation tax of £4.2m was charged at a rate of 28% (2005—27%). Earnings per share were 10.8 pence per share, compared to 10 pence per share in 2005. The proposed dividend of 5 pence per share is the same as for 2005 and is covered more than two times by available profits. The shareholders' return for the year 2006, measured by the annual change in the company's shareholder equity together with the proposed dividend, amounts to 12% compared to 11% for 2005 and 10% for 2004.

Segmented results

The following analyses provide a breakdown of company sales and profits before tax across its main markets.

Markets	2006 Sales £m	2005 Sales £m	Change sales %	2006 Profits £m	2005 Profits £m	Change profits %
UK	75	69	8.7	7.4	7.0	5.7
EC	64	65	−1.5	6.5	6.3	3.2
Non-EC	21	16	31.3	1.1	0.7	57.1
Total	**160**	**150**	**6.7**	**15.0**	**14.0**	**7.1**

Two of the markets experienced an increase in sales and all three had increases in profits. With sales, the UK market provided an 8.7% increase in sales and a 5.7% increase in profits. This reflected improved marketing of products in an area affected by increased competition from overseas manufacturers. The EC market, however, proved to be disappointing with a 1.5% decrease in sales because of changing consumer preferences. Because of tight cost controls in manufacturing, EC profits increased by 3.2%—one percentage point above the average rate of inflation. Non-EC markets, particularly in North America, compensated for disappointments in the EC. Sales increased by nearly one third and profits more than doubled. A significant factor in this improvement was a strengthening dollar in relation to the pound.

Treasury management

Brown Sugar plc operates in countries involving major currencies that fluctuate in value in relation to the pound sterling (i.e. the Euro and the US dollar). Management has a policy of reducing the group's exposure to the risk of currency losses by entering into relevant hedging contracts. It has also a number of long-term borrowing arrangements to fund its continuing program of capital investment in new manufacturing facilities.

Going concern

The management of Brown Sugar plc reviews the group's financial viability on a continuing basis. Subject to the inherent uncertainty of the future, management is confident that the group is financially viable for the foreseeable future.

ADDITIONAL READING

Readers who wish to find the detail of legislative requirements for these statements should access specialist texts such as D French, *Blackstone's Statutes on Company Law 2005–2006*, Oxford University Press, Oxford, Ninth Edition, 2005.

There are useful descriptions and explanations of many of the statements in this chapter in P O'Regan, *Financial Information Analysis*, Wiley, Chichester, 2005. This is a book on financial analysis and the text is written with this function in mind.

There are several texts on the early voluntary use of the operating and financial review and published by the Institute of Chartered Accountants of Scotland. They are P Weetman, B Collins, E Davie, and A MacNeill, *Operating and Financial Review: A Survey of Compliance with the Spirit of the ASB's Guidance*, 1995 (a survey of corporate use of the review as a voluntary statement); P Weetman, B Collins, and E Davie, *Operating and Financial Review: Views of Analysts and Institutional Investors*, 1994 (a survey of users' perceptions of the utility of the review); and P Weetman and B Collins, *Operating and Financial Review: Experiences and Exploration*, 1996 (a survey of preparers' perceptions of the review).

Several articles in the professional accountancy press provide recent views and experiences of the supplementary financial statements in the corporate financial report.

Anonymous (2002), "Internal Controls," *Company Reporting*, July, 3–8. This analysis uses real-world examples to illustrate.

Anonymous (2004), "Operating and Financial Reviews," *Company Reporting*, August, 3–8. This analysis uses real-world examples to illustrate.

Anonymous (2005), "Non-Compliance with Combined Code," *Company Reporting*, March, 3–8. This analysis uses real-world examples to illustrate.

R Paterson (2003), "Make or Break Time," *Accountancy*, March, 100–1. This looks at the statement of total recognized gains and losses.

C Quick (2004), "Wise Words or Waffle?" *Accountancy*, June, 27. A brief overview of the operating and financial review.

N Wolstenholme (2005), "Getting Down to the OFR," *Accountancy*, November, 98–9. This is a preparer's perspective of the review.

CHAPTER 8

Corporate Auditing

Learning Objectives

This chapter expands introductory material given in Chapters 1 and 2. By the end of this chapter, you should be able to identify and understand:

- The structure and content of the corporate audit report.
- The nature and meaning of corporate audit terms such as true and fair view and fair presentation.
- The purpose, benefits, and limitations of the corporate audit.
- The major assumptions underlying the corporate audit.
- The need for an independent and competent corporate auditor.
- The legal and regulatory responsibilities of the corporate auditor.
- The corporate auditor's general duty of care.
- The corporate auditor's specific responsibility for fraud detection.
- The relationship between the corporate auditor, the internal audit, and the audit committee.
- The legal and regulatory provisions associated with the corporate audit.
- The place of the corporate audit in the function of corporate governance.

At the end of this chapter, please review these learning objectives before moving on to Chapter 9 on creative accounting and how it affects the main corporate financial statements.

INTRODUCTION

Chapters 3, 4, 5, 6, and 7 review the main financial and supplemental statements and reports that comprise the annual corporate financial report. They are produced in order to make corporate management accountable to shareholders and form an important part of the overall function of corporate governance. The annual report also acts as a significant source of information for a variety of other groups associated with or interested in companies.

These include investors, lenders, customers, suppliers, employees, and government. The main financial and supplemental statements and reports therefore attempt to assist in two related business functions—i.e. stewardship and decision making. However, the statements and reports lack credibility if their contents have not been verified or audited. The degree to which users can and will rely on the information content of corporate financial statements is dependent to a large extent on their awareness of its quality. This characteristic is determined by an expert verification process and report called an audit and has been required in the UK since the Companies Act 1900. Audits did exist before this enactment but were restricted to specific industries (e.g. banking) or individual companies on a voluntary basis as part of their internal regulations.

The purpose of this chapter is to explain the nature, purpose, benefits, and limitations of the corporate audit of financial and supplemental statements and reports. The explanations are necessarily broad because of the nature of this text and specific audit practices are not discussed in any detail. The following sections start with a consideration of the structure and content of the corporate audit report that gives an opinion on the main financial statements. From this explanation, further sections consider the purpose of the audit, the assumptions on which it is based, the need for an independent, competent, and responsible auditor, the specific issue of detecting fraud, and the relationship between the auditor and the audit committee. The place of the audit in corporate governance is argued and specific legislative and regulatory provisions are provided. The content of the chapter is predominantly focused on the position in the UK. However, where appropriate, developments in the US are discussed because of the impact of the Sarbanes-Oxley Act 2002 on UK companies and their auditors.

CORPORATE AUDIT REPORT

The content of a corporate audit report in the UK is determined by the Companies Act 1985. This focuses on the requirement that the corporate auditor give an opinion as to whether or not the reporting company or group's profit statement and balance sheet provide, respectively, a true and fair view of profitability and financial position. This quality standard is undefined and generally interpreted as a higher standard than compliance with GAAP. This situation has been complicated since 2005 with the EU requirement for listed companies to follow IASB standards. The EU requirement includes a provision that the profit statement, cash flow statement, and balance sheet are presented fairly. This term is also undefined but has been equated by the FRC as equivalent to the true and fair view. The FRC has also emphasized the primacy of the latter quality in the UK. For this reason, the following explanations of various parts of the corporate audit report in Illustration 14 focus on reporting quality in terms of a true and fair view.

ILLUSTRATION 14 TEST, TICK, & ATTEST, REGISTERED AUDITORS

The following auditor's report has been received by the board of directors of Greenhouse Blues plc:

Illustration 14 Test, Tick, & Attest, Registered Auditors ● **187**

Auditor's Report to the
Members of Greenhouse Blues plc

We have audited the financial statements on pages 15 to 30 of the annual report which have been prepared under the historical cost convention and the specific accounting policies stated on pages 18 and 19; and the information on directors' remuneration disclosed on pages 11 and 12.

Responsibilities of directors and auditors

The board of directors is responsible for the preparation of the annual report. This includes responsibility for preparing the financial statements on pages 15 to 30 in accordance with applicable accounting standards of the International Accounting Standards Board. Our responsibilities are determined by the Companies Act 1985, Auditing Practices Board, London Stock Exchange Listing Agreement, and ethical guidance from our profession.

We report to you our opinion on whether the financial statements give a true and fair view and are prepared according to the Companies Act 1985. We also report our opinion on whether the operating and financial review on pages 3 to 8 and the directors' report on pages 9 to 12 are consistent with the financial statements; proper accounting records have been maintained by the company; if we have not received all the information and explanations we required for our audit; and if the required information on directors' remuneration has not been disclosed. We have also read other parts of the annual report and considered the implications for our report on any inconsistencies with the financial statements. We have reviewed the company's report on corporate governance on page 13 and report if it has not complied with the *Combined Code*. We are not required to give an opinion on whether the company's internal controls cover all risks and controls or the effectiveness of the company's corporate governance or controls.

Basis of opinion

We have conducted our audit in accordance with the standards of the Auditing Practices Board. Our audit included an examination on a test basis of evidence related to the information in the financial statements. It also included assessments of the estimates and judgments made by the board of directors in the preparation of the financial statements, and whether the accounting policies used were appropriate, consistent, and adequately disclosed.

We planned and performed our audit to gather all the information and explanations we required to provide sufficient evidence to give us reasonable assurance that the financial statements are free of material misstatement due to fraud or error. We also reviewed the overall adequacy of the presentation of information in the financial statements.

Opinion

In our opinion, the financial statements give a true and fair view of the state of affairs of the company as at 31 December 2006 and of the profit and cash flow of the company for the year to 31 December 2006, and have been properly prepared in accordance with the Companies Act 1985.

Test, Tick & Attest, Chartered Accountants and Registered Auditors
28 February 2007

Illustration 14 demonstrates that there are four main sections of the corporate auditor's report. The first section relates to the addressees of the report and the statements subject to audit. The second section deals with the respective responsibilities of the board of directors and auditors. The third section covers the basis for the audit opinion and the fourth section states that opinion. The report is signed and dated by the auditor. The following comments relate to each of the four main sections of the report.

The addressees

The report states the persons to whom it is addressed. In every case, these are the shareholders of the reporting company. Addressing the audit report to the shareholders is an explicit signal that the corporate auditor's primary responsibility is to that group. Other groups, such as debenture-holders, may use and rely on the auditor's reported opinion but it is the shareholders for whom it is prepared.

The financial statements

The corporate auditor states which financial statements have been audited. Under the provisions of the Companies Act 1985 these are the profit statement and balance sheet of a single company or, where relevant, a group of companies. However, the accounting provisions of the IASB (alternatively, the ASB) include the cash flow statement and the auditor will audit this as well as the traditional statements of profitability and financial position. This part of the audit report relates the audit opinion to specific financial statements and therefore, by omission, identifies those statements in the annual financial report that have not been audited. This is helpful to the reader of the audit report as it separates statements whose quality has been verified (e.g. the profit statement) from those whose quality is unknown (e.g. the chairman's report). The audit report also reminds its reader that the primary accounting basis of the audited financial statements is historical cost as implemented through the various accounting practices identified by the reporting company or group. The audit also includes information on directors' remuneration as part of the process of accountability and corporate governance.

Directors' responsibility

The board of directors is legally responsible for preparing and publishing the main financial statements of the reporting company, and the auditor states this in the audit report. The specific responsibility stated is that of preparing the audited financial statements in accordance with the provisions of the Companies Act 1985 and IASB accounting standards (as a listed company). The reason for making this statement is to differentiate the responsibilities of the board and the auditor. The latter is responsible at law for verifying the main

Illustration 14 Test, Tick, & Attest, Registered Auditors • **189**

financial statements and the board for their preparation. In other words, the audited financial statements are a means by which the board is held accountable to the shareholders for the reporting company's financial performance and position.

Auditors' responsibility

The corporate auditor's responsibility for the audit of the main financial and supplemental statements is stated in the audit report. This is expressed in terms of compliance with the requirements of the Companies Act 1985, Auditing Practices Board (AUPB) auditing and ethical standards, and the London Stock Exchange Listing Agreement (where relevant). This statement makes clear the auditor's duty with respect to the audited statements and identifies the sources that govern the conduct of the audit. More specifically, the corporate auditor is required to state that the overall audit responsibility includes giving a true and fair view opinion on the audited financial statements; reporting on the consistency of the directors' report and the operating and financial review (if produced) with the audited financial statements; the adequacy of the reporting company's accounting records; the company's compliance regarding disclosure of directors' remuneration and the provisions of the *Combined Code*; and whether sufficient information and explanation was obtained to conduct the audit. In making these statements, the auditor is acknowledging a full audit was made of the main financial statements in order to give an opinion on their quality; and a more limited review was completed of supplemental statements or reports to ensure consistency and compliance. Also acknowledged is the need to obtain sufficient evidence on which to base the required audit opinion.

Audit basis

The basis for the audit opinion is explicitly stated by the corporate auditor in the audit report. This includes the use of specific auditing standards prescribed by the AUPB in the UK, test examinations of the business transactions of the reporting company, assessments of significant estimates and judgments made by the board of directors in the preparation of the audited main financial statements, and reviews of the appropriateness, consistency, and disclosure of accounting practices used by the reporting company. The statement goes further by disclosing that the audit plan was to obtain all information and explanations that were necessary to provide sufficient evidence that the financial statements were free of significant misstatement caused by fraud or error, and to ensure compliant disclosure by the reporting company. The object of this part of the audit report is to inform its reader about the structure and conduct of the audit that underlies the audit opinion and to provide comfort with respect to the possibility of the main financial statements being affected by significant accounting misstatement due to either fraud or error. The corporate auditor also gives a negative assurance that the adequacy of internal controls and corporate governance procedures is not part of the audit of financial statements. This statement assists in drawing a boundary around the corporate audit.

Audit opinion

The opinion is expressed in terms of a true and fair view of the profitability, cash flow, and state of affairs of the company as stated, respectively, in the profit statement, cash flow statement, and balance sheet. As previously explained, true and fair view is not defined in the Companies Act 1985 or in the auditing standards of the AUPB. This means that the quality of the accounting information in the audited financial statements is not subject to a static and unchanging interpretation. This matter is discussed later in the chapter but, meantime, it should be understood as a means of allowing the corporate auditor to interpret reporting quality according to the evidence obtained, the circumstances of the reporting company, as well as the specific provisions of the Companies Act 1985 or the accounting standards of the IASB (or the ASB). In this way, the expected quality of the accounting information in audited financial statements is not set in stone and can change over time as user needs change. Also, statement quality should not be interpreted in terms of a strict compliance with accounting standards prescribed by bodies such as the IASB. Such compliance tends to lead to a "checklist" mentality in auditing in which adherence to accounting rules dominates the need for relevant and reliable accounting information. Accounting rule compliance also encourages corporate managers and directors to look for ways of producing the accounting numbers they want to report within the prescribed rules.

> **Lesson 8.1 Audit report**
> The corporate audit report is the end-product of the audit process. It is addressed to the share-holders and provides an expert and independent opinion on the quality of the financial statements that are required to be audited. The report contains three main messages—the respective respon-sibilities of the directors and the auditor, the basis of the audit, and the audit opinion.

> **Lesson 8.2 Audit opinion**
> The audit opinion is expressed as an undefined and overriding quality of accounting information. It is an opinion and not a guarantee of that quality.

NATURE AND PURPOSE OF CORPORATE AUDIT

The above explanation of the end-product of the corporate audit provides clues as to the nature and purpose of the function. An understanding of these matters is necessary in order to understand the significance of the corporate audit report as part of the annual financial report to shareholders. In order to provide this understanding, this section is divided into two main parts. The first part discusses the role of the auditor within the corporate reporting context and the second part derives the principal objective of the auditor.

Social, economic, and political roles

The overall role of the corporate auditor is best explained in terms of a fundamental human need—i.e. removing doubt and uncertainty from a situation. In this case, the doubt and uncertainty is about the quality of the accounting information reported in the main financial statements. This information is prepared on behalf of the corporate managers and direc-tors who are being held to account for the reporting company's financial performance and position. It is therefore understandable that doubt and uncertainty about the quality of this information will exist in the absence of an independent verification. There is nothing new in these ideas. Verification is a familiar process that attempts to remove doubt and uncertainty in human affairs. Independent assessments are sought, for example, when a property is purchased, an unwelcome medical opinion is given, or a book manuscript is submitted for possible publication. Such assessments improve awareness and knowledge of the situation and can lead to rational and appropriate decisions. In the case of reported financial statements from a company, their potential usefulness is enhanced by their audit. Shareholders, and other users, can have comfort in the quality of the accounting information they contain, and take appropriate action without undue concern over misstatement. In this way, corporate audits assist in the processes of corporate accountability, control, and governance. They provide reassurance to the users of annual financial reports.

This is particularly important if the reported accounting information effectively becomes a public good when disclosed. For example, the annual financial statements of a listed public company are available on application or through websites to any member of the public and not just to the company's shareholders or debenture-holders. In these circumstances, there is a need to protect the public generally from sub-standard accounting information and the corporate audit satisfies that social role. This is a situation analogous to other public goods such as streets and bridges. They are all required to be safe for general public use. In the case of accounting information, however, it should be noted that audit protection is limited to certain financial statements specified for audit by legislation. It does not include all accounting information in the annual report or information disclosed under other regulations or voluntarily (e.g. quarterly profit statements).

There is also an economic dimension to the role of the corporate audit. It is an important control in a business world of agency in which owner principals (i.e. the shareholders) inevitably have to trust the manager agents (i.e. executives and directors) in all but the smallest family businesses. Managers and directors in many companies are employed by their shareholders to act on their behalf and these agents are therefore in a very powerful position to take economic advantage of their principals unless there are mechanisms such as audit to hold them to account. In other words, the corporate audit has a role of restricting the opportunity of managers and directors to take economic advantage of shareholders who are remote from the operations of the company. In economics, this situation is often described as moral hazard—i.e. the danger that managers and directors might misuse or misappropriate the economic resources entrusted to their stewardship. The probability of economic losses to the shareholders due to the immoral actions of managers and directors is lower with a corporate audit. Expert verification of and reporting on the quality of reported accounting information is a powerful part of the overall corporate governance system and can reduce potential losses within the overall corporate economic system.

Audited accounting information can also be argued to improve the quality of economic decision-making in corporate business. Investment, lending, credit, and employment decisions are all capable of becoming better grounded and more rational if they are informed by financial statements that the decision makers believe to be credible and trustworthy. Corporate auditing therefore assists in the smooth and efficient working of business activity and capital markets. It makes bad business decisions and market failures less likely. However, auditing does not automatically lead to wise, sound or successful decisions. Such outcomes are a function of the decision maker's use of the information rather than of the information itself.

Corporate audits also have a political role to play in the sense that they assist the state to demonstrate that it is working on behalf of the public by putting into place mechanisms that can curb, control or minimize the inevitable existence of corporate behaviour that is damaging to individuals. Corporate business is no different from other aspects of human activity. Within such a system there are individual managers and directors who are liable to cheat—i.e. attempt to take economic advantage of others who trust them to act on their behalf. The state exists to identify and counteract such potential moral hazard. The Companies Act 1985 provisions for a corporate audit are explicit signals of the UK government's willingness and actions to protect the public from corporate cheats.

Objective of corporate audit

The previous descriptions and explanations of the various roles of the corporate auditor provide a basis for stating an overall objective for the function as follows:

The corporate audit is an integral part of the overall corporate accountability and governance system in the UK and has the basic aim of giving an expert and independent opinion on the quality of those financial statements that are required by law to be audited. The audit also aims to report on the consistency of the information contained in these statements to that in other disclosed statements not required to be audited. The corporate report is intended for the use of shareholders and debenture-holders of the reporting company or group, although other users of corporate annual financial reports with reasonable rights of access to them may also benefit from the audit report.

The important aspects of this objective are: first, the corporate audit has a key part to play in the success of corporate governance; second, the auditor gives a professional opinion rather than a guarantee or warranty of reporting quality; third, the opinion has to be expert (in the sense of being based on competent judgments) and independent (in the sense of being neutral or unbiased); fourth, the subjects of the audit are mandated by legislation; and, fifth, the direct users of the audit report are identified with a realization that the indirect user group involves a wider public interest.

Meaning of a true and fair view

As previously stated, the required audit opinion on financial statement quality is prescribed in the undefined terms of a true and fair view (under the provisions of the Companies Act 1985) and present fairly (under the EU-inspired provisions of the IASB for listed companies). Both of these terms are undefined and their interpretation is left to the professional judgment of each auditor according to the circumstances of each reporting client. As far as can be determined, the view of the ASB in the UK is that both terms have equivalency but the true and fair view has legal primacy in the UK over the EU mandate for present fairly. Corporate audit reports may use one or other and more likely use the former rather than the latter.

Despite the lack of legislative or regulative definitions, it makes sense to provide some explanation of the equivalent terms of true and fair view and fair presentation. Therefore, it is suggested that they can be interpreted in terms of accounting information that is (a) relevant to the needs of shareholders and other users with reasonable rights of access to the information, and (b) reliable in terms of the accounting representation of the economic substance of the business transactions of the reporting company or group. The reason for making this interpretation is a recent initiative of the American FASB. It states that accounting standards of the FASB will be based on accounting concepts and principles that form its conceptual framework. They are called principles-based accounting standards and the main concepts underlying them are relevance and reliability. FASB standards are intended to be consistent with those of the IASB and therefore with those of the ASB in the UK.

The true and fair view audit opinion must be regarded as the overriding quality standard for corporate financial statements. This means that the responsibility of the corporate auditor for this opinion goes beyond ensuring that the financial statements comply with GAAP as expressed in accounting standards. In corporate auditing, there is a need to go beyond accounting standard compliance. The application of GAAP by the reporting company does not necessarily mean that its financial statements give a true and fair view of its profitability, cash flow, and financial position. Adherence to prescribed accounting standards may not produce relevant or reliable information. This may require accounting beyond GAAP by using non-prescribed standards and through additional disclosures beyond the provisions of legislation.

The true and fair view audit opinion also means that the reported financial statements are free of material accounting misstatement due to fraud or error. This is acknowledged explicitly in the corporate audit report and has made the question of deliberate accounting misstatement by corporate managers and directors a significant aspect of the corporate audit. For many decades, corporate auditors have denied responsibility for the detection of fraud. Now they are required to reassure shareholders in their report that the possibility of fraud existing and affecting the integrity of the financial statements has been built into their audit procedures. In this way, auditors are acknowledging that corporate financial statements cannot be reliable unless they are free of significant accounting misstatement.

Lesson 8.3 Audit roles
The corporate audit has several roles. Socially, it provides protection from poor accounting information in a situation when the latter is publicly available. Economically, it provides accounting information of a minimum quality to assist in informed and rational economic decision making. Politically, it allows the state to demonstrate its willingness and ability to monitor corporate managers and directors.

Lesson 8.4 Audit objective
The corporate audit is an integral part of corporate governance. It aims to determine and report on the quality of accounting information disclosed by corporate managers and directors for the benefit of shareholders directly and other financial statement users more indirectly.

Lesson 8.5 Audit opinion
The audit opinion is expressed in the undefined terms of a true and fair view (when adhering to UK legislation) and present fairly (when adhering to EU regulation). As a matter of practicality, these terms can be interpreted in the form of relevant and reliable accounting information (as defined by the FASB, IASB, and ASB).

> **Lesson 8.6 True and fair view**
> A true and fair view of profitability, cash flow, and financial position cannot be given in corporate
> financial statements if the latter contain significant accounting misstatement due to fraud or error.

FEASIBILITY OF CORPORATE AUDITING

The corporate audit can only succeed in meeting its objective of an opinion on the truth and
fairness of corporate financial statements if the audit is feasible—i.e. capable of achieving
this objective. In this respect, when the corporate auditor proceeds with the audit, there are a
number of inherent assumptions being made. If these assumptions do not hold true then the
probability of the corporate auditor providing a meaningful audit opinion are diminished. The
following are the main assumptions underlying corporate audit practice. They are divided
into three main categories—the reason for the audit, the behaviour of the auditor, and the
practice of auditing.

Reason for auditing

There are a number of assumptions behind the corporate legislation prescribing it.

(1)   Without an expert and independent audit, the quality of the accounting information
      in the main financial statements lacks sufficient credibility to be used safely by
      shareholders and other users with reasonable access to it. In other words, unaudited
      information could not be used safely

(2)   The most desired corporate audit is the expert and independent verification of
      the quality of the accounting information in the main financial statements. Other
      possible audits (e.g. the efficiency and effectiveness of corporate managers) are
      not regarded by legislators as more important or needed at the present time

(3)   The audit of the accounting information in the main financial statements is best
      achieved by legislation and regulation—i.e. a voluntary regime would not achieve
      universal corporate auditing

(4)   The true and fair view quality of the accounting information in the main financial
      statements can be determined by the corporate auditor. If this were not true then
      there would be little point in requiring such an audit

Behaviour of auditor

There are several assumptions made about the corporate auditor's behaviour.

(1)   There are no conflicts of interest between the corporate auditor and the reporting
      company and its managers and directors that prevent the satisfactory completion
      of the corporate audit. In other words, it has to be assumed that the auditor,
      senior managers, and the board of directors of the reporting company share the
      same conviction that corporate governance is best served by producing financial
      statements of an acceptable quality

(2)   There are no legal or regulatory restrictions that can hinder the satisfactory completion of the corporate audit. If legal or regulatory provisions prevent the corporate auditor from gaining access to all the information and explanation required to form an opinion on the quality of the financial statements, there is little point in undertaking such an audit

(3)   The corporate auditor is sufficiently independent in mind and appearance to give a credible and objective audit opinion. The ability of corporate managers and directors to produce accounting information that could mislead shareholders is the reason for having an independent professional to conduct its verification

(4)   The corporate auditor is sufficiently competent to give a credible and objective audit opinion. Unless the corporate auditor is sufficiently skilled and experienced to gather and evaluate the information and explanation required for the audit opinion, then the probability of the auditor being independent of managers and directors is diminished. It is essential the corporate auditor is able to ask appropriate questions and evaluate complex answers

(5)   The corporate auditor can be held accountable for the conduct of the audit and the audit opinion. Professionals can be careless or wrong in their opinions and shareholders and other financial statement users must have confidence that there are ways in which the corporate auditor can be held accountable legally and professionally

Function of auditing

The practice of corporate auditing contains several assumptions that must be held true if the audit opinion is to be credible to shareholders and others.

(1)   The quality of the accounting information in the main financial statements can be determined in terms of specific criteria of relevance and reliability. In other words, unless these qualities are defined and operational in accounting terms, the auditor cannot meaningfully verify their existence in a set of financial statements

(2)   There is sufficient competent audit evidence on which to base the audit opinion. The latter depends on a body of evidence being available to support the opinion. Too little evidence leads to a meaningless opinion

(3)   The accounting information in the main financial statements is free of major fraud and error. Although the corporate auditor is expected to plan for and assess the risk of material accounting misstatement being present in the audited financial statements, this is very different from a fraud investigation in which the auditor's attitude of mind is that fraud exists and has to be found. Fraud or forensic audits require skills and procedures that vary from those used in the conventional verification of the accounting quality of financial statements

(4)   The audit opinion on the truth and fairness of the accounting information in the audited financial statements can be reported meaningfully to the shareholders. Unless this is true—in the sense of shareholders understanding the meaning of the opinion—there seems little point in reporting it

> **Lesson 8.7 Audit feasibility**
> Every human activity based on skills depends on the simple notion of feasibility—i.e. it can be done successfully. If this were not the case, there would be little point in doing it. It is therefore important that, in understanding what the corporate audit is trying to achieve, the fundamental assumptions on which it is based are stated. Their validity can then be challenged if necessary.

INDEPENDENT AND COMPETENT AUDITORS

Arguably the most fundamental part of any explanation of the corporate audit is that the corporate auditor is competent and honest enough to provide an expert and objective opinion on the audited financial statements. Shareholders particularly and other statement users more generally need to be confident that the audit opinion comes from an independent professional who is not associated or involved with, corporate managers and directors and can give an unbiased opinion on the quality of the reported accounting information.

Auditor independence is based on a number of related factors. First, the auditor must have sufficient and appropriate skills and experience to identify, gather, and evaluate the audit evidence necessary to give an objective opinion on the quality of the reported accounting information. Second, the auditor must be honest and therefore willing to report on the truth of the audit evidence identified, gathered, and evaluated. Third, the auditor must be free of any associations or relationships that could provide perceptions of being unable to provide an unbiased audit opinion. Fourth, the auditor must not become so familiar with the client company's managers, directors, or staff that objectivity is lost by being too trusting or sympathetic about their views on the company's accounting and reporting. Fifth, the auditor must not allow client company managers, directors, or staff to intimidate in order to get the auditor to accept the company's position on accounting and reporting matters.

Fortunately, there are incentives for the corporate auditor to act competently, honestly, and free of damaging associations and relationships. These relate to a combination of economic self-interest and professional duty. The corporate auditor is typically a public accountancy firm that should have an objective of economic survival and prosperity. These firms exist to provide employment to staff and partners and to be profitable for their owners. Acting competently and honestly in corporate audits is a rational way of enhancing the firm's professional reputation for service and ensuring repeat audit engagements.

In addition, public accountancy firms acting as corporate auditors employ professionally-qualified accountants who owe a duty of care to their profession and are subject to the ethical guidelines and prescriptions of their professional bodies. The corporate auditor must be a member of a recognized professional body and registered with that body as an auditor. Acting competently and honestly is a rational means of continuing membership and registration. For this reason, any professional rules and guidance relating to the independence of the corporate auditor is focused on the audit engagement team rather than the specific public accountancy firm to which it is related through employment.

Independence in practice

Auditor independence in practice is two dimensional. The first dimension is that it is a state of mind for the individual auditor. Unless the audit engagement partner and each staff member of the audit team can think independently (i.e. honestly and without bias), then the objectivity of the audit opinion will always be in doubt. Independence as a state of mind is determined by a combination of factors relating to the individual audit partner or staff member—i.e. his or her innate character and attitude, the professional education and training received by the individual, and the extent of his or her experience in audit practice.

The second dimension of auditor independence relates to the appearance of independence—i.e. relationships and interests the individual audit partner or staff member may have that create perceptions of the possibility of his or her independence and objectivity being compromised. For this reason, it is important that conflicting relationships and interests do not exist and there are various rules in place that auditors are expected to comply with in order not to damage their position of independence. These rules take various legislative and regulatory forms (e.g. Companies Act 1985 provisions and ethical standards prescribed by public accountancy bodies). They essentially prohibit situations likely to create perceptions of bias and lack of objectivity in corporate audits.

Prohibitions and independence

In the UK, the appearance of corporate auditor independence is created by a combination of Companies Act 1985 provisions, AUPB ethical standards, and ethical guidelines from the main professional accountancy bodies. The Companies Act 1985 prohibits the auditor from being an officer or employee of the client (or a partner of an officer or employee). It also requires the company to disclose the auditor's fee and any other fees for non-audit services. In other words, no company manager, director, or other employee can be auditor, and the auditor's economic dependence on the company must be fully disclosed.

The ethical guidelines of the main bodies of public accountants in the UK contain detailed explanations of the various pressures on the appearance of corporate auditor independence. All relate to relationships that could be construed as compromising independence and the guidelines provide recommendations about relationships to avoid. These include partners and staff (and their immediate families) not having financial interests in the client company (e.g. shareholdings). Also to be avoided are personal and business relationships with a client company (e.g. the audit engagement partner married to a senior manager of the client). Other recommendations concern the avoidance of receipt of goods and services from a client company and over-dependence for fee income from a single corporate client source.

Arguably, the greatest single problem of recent times in this area has been the provision of management services to a client company in addition to the audit. More specifically, the problem relates to services that create the subject matter for the audit (e.g. the installation of systems of accounting, bookkeeping, and controls). The obvious question in this respect is how the corporate auditor can remain objective when verifying matters that were produced by his or her firm. A most recent example of this conflict concerns the outsourcing of internal audit services to the corporate auditor. When assessing the internal control systems of the company, the auditor must review internal audit procedures—meaning that there is a form of self-assessment.

Rules governing corporate auditor independence are becoming stricter. For example, the Sarbanes-Oxley Act 2002 in the US prohibits non-audit services by corporate auditors. These include management services. Corporate audit engagement partners are appointed for no more than five years. The client company's audit committee must consider and discuss any audit issues raised with it by the corporate auditor and there can be no improper influence on the auditor by corporate managers and directors. These rules affect UK audit firms working in the US. UK rules, on the other hand, are more permissive. For example, management services by the corporate auditor are allowed unless they are on a contingency fee basis. However, each audit firm must have an ethics partner to review ethical issues, engagement partners must be regularly reviewed internally, and an audit fee cannot exceed more than 10% of total fee income.

Lesson 8.8 Auditor independence

The benefits and ultimate value of the corporate audit depends on the extent to which the corporate auditor can be independent when formulating the audit opinion and also appear to be independent in that function. The auditor's state of mind is a matter of attitude, education, training, and experience. The auditor's appearance of independence is determined by a series of specific rules and guidance statements concerning the prohibition of conflicting relationships and interests, and his or her compliance with these rules and guidance statements.

Lesson 8.9 Management services

The most contentious issue over the years concerned with the appearance of independence has been the provision of non-audit services by the corporate auditor. Despite denials that such services are incompatible with an independent audit, the trend has been to prohibit them (as in the US). The UK position remains one of a continuing permissive regime.

CORPORATE AUDITOR'S DUTY OF CARE

In addition to independence, the corporate auditor's other major concern is his or her duty of care. All professionals have such a duty which means that they always apply their skills and experience in the best interests of the client while accepting a wider responsibility to protect any public interest in the situation. In the case of the corporate auditor, the principal duty of care is to the shareholders and the wider duty to a public that contains investors, lenders, creditors, employees, customers, and government. The corporate auditor's duty of care is based on a legal concept of the prudent professional. Prudence in this sense should include investigating until the quality of the reported accounting information has been adequately determined, obtaining sufficient audit evidence on which to base an opinion, acting appropriately when suspicions are aroused, and not being pressured by client managers and directors or economic self-interest.

The corporate auditor's duty of care has been determined over many decades by a mixture of education and training programmes, individual experience, legal judgments in courts of law, and ethical pronouncements by professional bodies of public accountants. The essential dictum that has emerged and remained constant during this period to the present day is that of reasonable care and skill in the circumstances. What this means is that each corporate auditor is expected to exercise sufficient care and skill in the conduct of the audit as dictated by the particular circumstances of the client company. Thus, the auditor's duty of care cannot be reduced to a formulaic standard. Instead, it varies from audit to audit depending on the complexity of the business, the attitude of managers, directors, and staff, the strengths of internal controls, and the availability of credible audit evidence. Audit research suggests that deficient audits involve failure to exercise reasonable care and skill—e.g. insufficient audit evidence to support the audit opinion, lack of scepticism by the auditor, poor interpretation of GAAP compliance, bad design and planning of the audit, and over-reliance on the client company's internal controls.

The corporate auditor's duty of care includes a number of specific tasks. These include a requirement to understand fully the operations and management of the client company in order to assess the degree of audit risk involved (i.e. the risk of significant accounting misstatement due to either fraud or error). In recent times, auditors have reviewed potential clients as a means of avoiding future audit failures and consequent litigation from shareholders and other damaged parties. The idea is to try and identify problem companies before signing an audit contract. Other tasks centre on the relatively obvious procedures of ensuring that the audit process is adequately planned, designed, executed, supervised, and recorded (in audit working papers or their electronic equivalents). The corporate auditor must fully understand the relevance and applicability of accounting standards to a client company as well as current disclosure requirements specified by legislation. Finally, the audit opinion must be based on sufficient credible audit evidence and should not be made until the corporate auditor is satisfied that the level of sufficiency has been achieved.

> **Lesson 8.10 Duty of care**
> The corporate auditor's duty of care as a professional is determined by the legal doctrine of reasonable care and skill in the circumstances. This places responsibility for its operation in practice on the individual auditor. It also creates questions regarding what is reasonable in a particular set of circumstances.

RESPONSIBLE FOR WHAT AND TO WHOM?

The corporate audit is legally responsible for formulating and communicating an opinion on the quality of certain financial statements disclosed by a reporting company. This raises a major issue of the extent to which the auditor is responsible for detecting major fraud and error. This is a long-standing issue in corporate auditing and is dealt with separately in the following section. Meantime, it is reasonable to state what the corporate auditor is *not* responsible for. For example, the audit is not intended as a warning of business inadequacies in the reporting company. Nor does it provide early warning of potential business failure. It is not a guarantee of the accuracy of financial statements, and it does not comment on the economy, efficiency or effectiveness of the reporting company's operations and management. The corporate audit is confined to an opinion on the quality of disclosed accounting numbers.

These accounting numbers are addressed specifically to the shareholders of the reporting company but may benefit other users because of their public availability. This raises the issue of to whom the corporate auditor is responsible—is it narrowly the shareholders or, more broadly, other third parties with an interest in the audited information? The issue is complex and has remained relatively unresolved over many decades. Much is determined by the attitudes of judges and juries in courts of law and these vary over time. At present, the court attitude appears to favour a narrow interpretation of shareholders to the exclusion of third parties. The current doctrine appears to be based on a number of related ideas. The first is that any person or organization apparently damaged by sub-standard auditing of disclosed accounting information must be reasonably proximate to the company. This would include many individuals and organizations with contracts with the reporting company. The list can be reduced by a further idea of forseeability—i.e. prior to the audit, the corporate auditor could predict that an individual or organization proximate to the company could rely on the audit opinion. This narrows down the third parties the corporate auditor could be responsible to. Further narrowing results from a more recent idea of prior knowledge—i.e. the corporate auditor had prior knowledge that the audit report would be used by an individual or organization. These ideas mean that the current responsibility of the corporate auditor for the audit opinion is limited to the shareholders and a relatively few additional beneficiaries previously known to be users of the opinion.

Corporate auditors in recent years have sought to limit their responsibilities for their audit opinion. This has been most noticeable in the US where litigation is frequent and expensive. It has been estimated that at least 1% of corporate audit fee income has been used to defend against litigation for alleged sub-standard auditing. US audit firms now exist as limited liability partnerships and there have been numerous and unsuccessful attempts to restrict liability by law. These arguments have been hard to sustain because of the relatively monopolistic position of the largest public accountancy firms with regard to the audit of list companies, banks, insurance companies, and defence contractors. Nevertheless, under the Limited Liability Partnerships Act 2000, UK public accountancy firms enjoy the same degree of protection from liability as auditors as their US counterparts.

Lesson 8.11 Auditor responsibility
The corporate auditor is responsible for providing an expert and independent opinion on the quality of the accounting content of a set of financial statements. This task is undertaken for the benefit of shareholders although the corporate auditor may have a responsibility to other financial statement recipients with a proximate interest in the reporting company who were known by the auditor prior to the disclosure of the audit opinion that they would use the financial statements and the audit report.

CORPORATE AUDITING AND FRAUD DETECTION

Arguably, the largest and most persistent question concerning the corporate auditor's duty of care is the extent to which he or she is responsible for the detection of major fraud or error in financial reporting. For decades there have been public expectations that fraud and error are parts of the corporate audit and corresponding denials to the contrary. This has led to what are called expectations gaps—i.e. differences between what the audit beneficiaries believe they are receiving from the auditor and what he or she is actually delivering. This causes confusion, criticism, and debate about the nature of the corporate audit.

There are two fraud types—i.e. accounting misstatement in which the reported accounting numbers are deliberately misstated in order to mislead or deceive their readers and from which they can be monetarily damaged if inappropriate decisions are taken; and the mis-appropriation of the reporting company's assets in which there is direct monetary loss to it. Either type of fraud seriously affects the reliability of the reported accounting numbers. Thus, despite years of denial, corporate auditors have gradually been forced to take more explicit responsibility for its detection. This is now done through careful assessment of the potential for fraud and corresponding planning and designing of audit techniques to increase the probability of detecting it when it exists.

Accounting error can also affect the reliability of reported numbers and the corporate auditor now needs to assess, plan, and design the audit in the same way as for detecting fraud. The key difference between fraud and error in this respect is intentionality—i.e. fraud is an intentional act by managers, directors, or staff; error is unintentional—although no less damaging in terms of consequences.

The most serious problem in recent years in corporate financial reporting and auditing has been the incidence of major accounting misstatement for fraudulent purposes by senior managers. Examples include HIH in Australia, Parmalat in Italy, BCCI and Maxwell Communications in the UK, and Cedant, Enron, and WorldCom in the US. All of these cases have involved misstatements of hundreds and sometimes thousands of millions of dollars. Each has revealed that such fraud is a result of a combination of factors usually involving dominant and risk-taking senior managers, compensation incentives for these managers to inflate profits, a managerial attitude of tolerance to dishonesty, complex organizational structures, and an economic environment of growth. The most obvious problem for corporate auditors has been assessing the accuracy and completeness of the information provided to them by the defrauding managers and the ability of the latter to override internal controls designed to prevent such abuses.

Accounting misstatements

Accounting misstatements fall into four main categories of intended omission in the corporate reporting process. The first relates to the hiding from the auditor of liabilities that are contingent on future events. They do not yet exist and cannot therefore be verified in that sense. Much depends on the auditor asking the right questions and following instincts when suspicions are aroused. The second category concerns current events that may have longer-term significant consequences (e.g. a current contract that contains severe penalties for failure to perform on time). Again, much depends on the auditor's alertness to informational detail. The third category involves deliberate accounting manipulation by senior managers in order to cover up lack of profitability (e.g. overstatement of inventory numbers, understatement of bad debt provisions, liberal depreciation policies, false sales, etc.) These are matters that can remain hidden from the auditor unless appropriate audit procedures are put in place and questions asked of management and accounting staff. The fourth category involves related party transactions between the reporting company and other organizations controlled by senior managers of the company (e.g. loans by the company to these organizations or sales to the company from them). Because senior managers of the company are at both ends of these transactions, the probability of manipulation is high. Again, the corporate auditor needs to focus on the risk of these transactions taking place.

Warning signs

The previous comments suggest that much depends on the vigilance of the corporate auditor with respect to the warning signs of fraudulent accounting misstatement. There are numerous signs of the latter and they tend to fall into two general categories—management and organization. The first category is the largest and many of the examples below are overlapping. They relate to specific characteristics of corporate senior management (including members of the board of directors). They are not given in any order of importance or incidence.

- Senior managers and directors who lie or evade questions.
- The auditor's personal experience of dealing with senior managers or directors.
- Senior managers or directors who place a considerable emphasis on the reporting company meeting earnings expectations.
- Audit disputes with individual senior managers or directors.
- Senior managers or directors willing to change the auditor when the current auditor is unwilling to give an unqualified audit opinion.
- Aggressive financial reporting practices used by senior managers and directors (i.e. financial statements that lack prudent provisions for items such as depreciation and bad debts).
- Explicit disrespect by senior managers or directors for corporate legislation and regulation.
- Particularly dominant senior managers or directors.
- Hostility to the auditor by senior managers or directors.
- Pressure placed on the auditor by senior managers or directors to accept their accounting and disclosure preferences in the financial statements.
- Senior managers or directors who are willing to take unnecessary risks in the management of the reporting company.
- Senior managers who have employment contracts with significant compensation incentives linked to profitability levels.

Organizational warning signs form the second category. They are less in number but no less serious than the managerial examples. They include:

- Complex organizational structures, often involving decentralized management and numerous companies, partnerships, and short-term ventures.
- Weak internal control systems.
- Difficult-to-audit transactions (i.e. transactions which lack available evidence or evidence that can be understood without specialist help).
- Considerable turnover in accounting staff.
- Numerous legal actions against the reporting company and its senior managers and directors.
- Unfavourable economic conditions and poor profitability.

In summary, what these warning signs suggest is that accounting misstatement for fraudulent purposes is most likely to take place in reporting companies with dominant and aggressive senior managers or directors and/or with decentralized, complex, and badly controlled organizations, and coping with difficult economic conditions. Combinations of these warning signs are particularly relevant and corporate auditors need to be aware of them and respond accordingly. In this respect, it should be noted that absolute assurance of no accounting misstatement is a virtually unattainable state and even a good audit may fail to detect it. It is therefore useful for the corporate auditor to employ forensic accountants when fraud is discovered or where there is a strong belief that there is a significant risk of material accounting misstatement. Forensic accountants are specialists with the necessary skills to investigate these matters until a conclusion has been determined.

> **Lesson 8.12 Accounting misstatement**
> A considerable part of modern corporate auditing is concerned with the possibility of financial statements being affected by fraudulent accounting misstatement. The presence of such misstatement is associated with a number of explicit warning signs to the corporate auditor. In general terms, these concern dominant senior managers and directors, and complex and badly controlled organizations.

AUDIT EVIDENCE

The corporate auditor's opinion to the shareholders on the quality of the main financial statements is based on a process of gathering, analyzing, and evaluating audit evidence. Such evidence takes the form of several types of evidential material and this requires the use by the auditor and his team of various complementary skills. For example, most generally, the auditor needs to assess the audit risk of material misstatement being faced by staff members in various parts of the audit. Such assessments are skilled activities based on considerable knowledge of the client company and its operations and management and past experience of risk assessment. Systems of internal control require mapping and evaluation. These activities depend on competence in systems design and operation. There are accounting records and documents which increasingly take electronic forms that require computer skills as well as accounting knowledge. Corporate business operations and funding are based on legal contracts and other documentation including asset ownership titles. These require legal skills to make appropriate interpretations of their meaning and consequences. The corporate auditor requires additional explanations and information resulting from specific questions asked of the reporting company's directors, managers, and other employees. Such question and answer routines demand inter-personal skills as well as interpretative ability. The auditor frequently seeks evidence from external third party sources such as banks and lawyers and, again, skills are required to make use of this material. Finally, much of the corporate audit involves members of the audit team observing the operations, assets, and staff of the reporting company. These physical observations are assisted by audit staff members who are alert, curious, and accurate in the recording of what they observe. Bringing together all of these skills and experiences into one audit team is a vital ingredient in a successful audit. In other words, without these various skills and experiences, the corporate auditor is unlikely to have the audit evidence available on which to base a sound and credible audit opinion on the quality of the audited financial statements.

> **Lesson 8.13 Audit evidence**
> The corporate audit opinion must be based on sufficient and credible audit evidence. Audit evidence comprises evidential material of various forms that require different skills, knowledge, and experience to be used meaningfully in the audit process leading to the reported opinion.

CORPORATE AUDITING AND CORPORATE GOVERNANCE

It is almost self-evident that the corporate audit is specifically designed as an important part of the overall function of corporate governance. The corporate auditor acts on behalf of the shareholders and provides a competent and independent opinion on the accounting quality of financial statements that are intended as means of holding senior managers and directors accountable to shareholders. The corporate audit is an explicit means of protecting shareholders from inappropriate behaviour by managers and directors. However, in order to maximize the effectiveness of this protective device, the corporate auditor needs to have a relationship with the reporting company that facilitates access to audit evidence, reports issues arising from the audit, and maintains auditor independence. The relationship that has gradually emerged over recent years is that between the corporate auditor and the audit committee of the reporting company's board of directors.

More specifically, audit committees are expected to comprise independent, non-executive directors and to include a director with appropriate accounting and financial expertise. They should meet regularly to consider accounting and audit issues and, particularly, be available to the corporate auditor to discuss contentious issues that are likely to affect the nature of the audit opinion. In this sense, the audit committee acts as a bridge between the board of directors (and therefore senior management) and the corporate auditor and prevents the latter being in direct conflict with senior managers. Corporate governance is therefore potentially enhanced by such an arrangement.

AUDIT EXPECTATIONS GAP

Arguably one of the largest and most long-standing problems facing the corporate auditor is the expectations gap. This concerns mismatches between what the public expects the corporate auditor to achieve and what is achieved in practice. The gap has been mentioned earlier in this chapter in relation to fraud detection. For many years, there has been a public expectation that the corporate audit is designed to detect fraud. However, so far as the auditor is concerned, all that can be done is to plan the audit so that there is a reasonable chance that major fraud is detected. The primary audit objective is to give an opinion on the accounting quality of reported financial statements. Fraud detection is not the primary activity and the auditor cannot guarantee that the planned audit will detect all major fraud. For this reason, readers of corporate financial statements should not assume that these statements are free from major fraud (or error).

The audit expectations gap is not limited to perceptual differences about fraud detection. It can also be associated with misperceptions over other possible auditable subjects and audit beneficiaries. For example, the audit is not intended to examine and report on the efficiency and effectiveness of corporate operations and management. It exists for the benefit of shareholders but, currently, courts of law are reluctant to recognize third party beneficiaries. These differences between perceptions and realities in auditing create confusions, irritations and, occasionally, costly lawsuits. Audit standard setters have attempted from time to time to clarify the expectations gap by explaining the corporate auditor's duties in written statements. This is exceedingly important in order to clarify the auditor's role within the overall function of corporate governance. In particular, it is vital that corporate stakeholders appreciate the audit in terms of:

(1) What is reasonable—i.e. what is reasonable to expect of the auditor in terms of the constraints of time and cost. The audit opinion has to be given as soon after the reporting date as possible. There are limits to what the audit can cost in terms of value for money

(2) What is feasible—i.e. what is possible to achieve in audit terms. The auditor cannot be expected to achieve particular objectives if it is not technically feasible because management can obstruct or the auditor lacks technical expertise

For these reasons, it is likely that the problem of the audit expectations gap will persist into the foreseeable future.

LEGAL AND REGULATORY PROVISIONS FOR CORPORATE AUDITING

Corporate audit requirements in the UK are contained in two main sources—the Companies Acts 1985 and 1989, and *Statements of Auditing Standards* of the AUPB. The Acts are amended from time to time (e.g. with regard to the size of company requiring audit). The Board originated in 1991 and became part of the FRC in 2001. In addition, and from time to time, the main regulators of the financial services industry in the UK (i.e. the Financial Services Authority and the Listing Authority) can impose audit requirements with the effect of statute. The following sections cover the main provisions only of the Companies Act 1985 and the AUPB. A final section briefly reviews the Sarbanes-Oxley Act of 2002 in the US that covers American corporations owned by UK companies.

Companies Acts 1985 and 1989

The requirement for companies to have their financial and supplemental statements and reports audited is contained in the Companies Act 1985. The auditor's report is mandated by the Act in a provision that the report is made to the shareholders of the reporting company and covers all the annual financial statements laid before the shareholders in general meeting. The report's content must identify the audited financial statements and the accounting bases for their preparation. The audit opinion expressed in the report should state whether a true and fair view has been given in the profit statement and balance sheet of the reporting company or group. This opinion can be either unqualified or qualified but the reason for any qualification must be stated. The auditor must also state whether or not the directors' report, including any statement on directors' remuneration, is consistent with the annual financial statements. The Act requires the audit report to state the name of the auditor and it must be signed and dated by that person.

The Companies Act 1985 also specifies the duties of the corporate auditor. The auditor is expected to ascertain whether proper accounting records have been maintained by the reporting company; these records are in agreement with the audited financial statements and (in the case of a listed company) the statement on directors' remuneration. If the accounting records are found to be inadequate or the records and statements do not agree, then the auditor must state this in the audit report. Should the auditor fail to obtain all the information and explanation required for the audit, this too must be stated in the audit report.

The Companies Act 1985 specifies provisions for the appointment, rights to information, right to attend meetings, remuneration, removal, and resignation of the corporate auditor. These include the main requirement for all companies to appoint an auditor at the general meeting at which annual financial statements are presented. Other provisions deal with specific matters relating to this appointment, including the possibility of private companies dispensing with an annual appointment, and the auditor's right of access at all times to the reporting company's accounting records and to necessary information and explanations from company directors, managers, and employees. Failure to provide access or provide information is an offence liable to imprisonment and fines. The Act covers the right of the corporate auditor to receive notices and attend and be heard at company meetings of shareholders, the remuneration of the auditor to be approved by the shareholders in general meeting, and the amount to be disclosed as a note to the main financial statements. Further sections relate to the required procedures for the removal or resignation of the corporate auditor.

The Companies Act 1989 contains the provisions specifying who can act as corporate auditor. It states that the auditor can either be an individual or firm who is not an officer or employee, or partner of an officer or employee of the reporting company. The Act also prescribes that the auditor must be a qualified member of one of six recognized qualifying bodies (e.g. a chartered accountant) and registered as a practicing auditor with one of five of these bodies (e.g. the ICAEW).

Statements of Auditing Standards

These *Statements* contain the basic auditing principles and procedures that corporate auditors are expected to follow when auditing financial statements. Compliance with *Statements* is mandatory for corporate auditors. They are contained in seven broad categories. The first category is introductory and deals with the scope and authority of AUPB pronouncements. The second category covers the corporate auditor's responsibilities. These include the objective and main principles of auditing as well as fraud detection. Category three relates to the planning, controlling, and recording of audit activities. Category four deals with the auditor's need to review and test the reporting company's accounting system and internal control. The fifth category covers a variety of auditing standards on the nature of audit evidence and includes procedures to gather and evaluate it prior to forming an audit opinion. Category six relates to the corporate auditor's need to rely on the work of others, including internal auditors. The final category concerns the auditor's reported opinion.

Ethics statements and standards

The main professional bodies of public accountants in the UK issued "Integrity, Objectivity, and Independence," *Guide to Professional Ethics Statement 1* in 1997. This statement outlines the main pressures that can compromise auditor independence. These are explained in general terms (e.g. over-familiarity with the client company) and more specifically (e.g. acting as a consultant for an audit client company). The statement gives specific guidance to remove these pressures—e.g. avoidance of financial involvement with a client company, procedures to follow when a member of the audit team joins or plans to join a client company, prohibition of acceptance of goods and services from a client company, avoidance of over-dependence of fee income from one particular client company defined as a percentage of total fee income, and the dangers of providing non-audit services. *Ethical Standard 1* from the AUPB in 2004 mandates that public accountancy firms should have a designated ethical partner to co-ordinate ethical matters, an independent review of the work of the engagement partner for each audit of listed or public companies, an economic dependence for audit fee income of no more than 10% of total fee income, and a prohibition of the provision of tax or finance services on contingency fee basis.

Sarbanes-Oxley Act 2002

This American legislation was enacted in 2002 in response to cases of fraudulent reporting such as Enron and WorldCom. Its main objective was to improve the quality of corporate governance in US public companies and its main provisions include several that relate to corporate auditors—including foreign auditors responsible for auditing subsidiaries located in the US. The Act created the PCAOB as a part of the SEC. The PCAOB is responsible for registering, monitoring, inspecting, and investigating audit firms (including foreign firms), and for establishing and adopting by rule auditing standards. The PCAOB therefore effectively controls the US audit profession and non-US auditors working in the US.

The Sarbanes-Oxley Act 2002 prohibits corporate auditors from offering non-audit services including bookkeeping and accounting, financial systems, appraisals, and actuarial, management and investment services. Corporate audit engagement partners are required to rotate off the audit every five years. The corporate auditor must report audit problems to the audit committee—which is responsible for the appointment of the auditor and must have at least one financially-qualified member. There must be no improper influence on the auditor by corporate managers and directors, and the latter are expected to disclose everything that needs to be identified to the auditor. Each annual financial report is required to contain a report from corporate management on the state of the reporting company's internal controls.

Many of the provisions of the Sarbanes-Oxley Act 2002 are similar to those contained in either the provisions of the Companies Act 1985 or the auditing standards of the AUPB.

Independence Standards Board

(ISB) The ISB was set up in the US in 1997 by the AICPA and predated the Sarbanes-Oxley Act 2002. The AICPA intended the ISB to set independence standards and it had authority on issues of auditor independence over all public companies in the US. However, it ceased operations in 2001 in anticipation of its independence standards being incorporated into the rules of the SEC as a result of Sarbanes-Oxley.

LEARNING OBJECTIVES

Please review the learning objectives at the beginning of this chapter and ensure they have been achieved before proceeding to Chapter 9 on creative accounting and its impact on corporate financial statements as part of the function of corporate governance.

Exercise 1   Doubt, uncertainty, and verification

There are numerous human activities that generate doubt and uncertainty and the need for verification. First, explain what you mean by the terms doubt, uncertainty, and verification. Second, identify examples from your personal experience where doubt and uncertainty was sufficient to require verification. Third, relate these examples to corporate financial statements and auditing. Students should also discuss with their instructor examples of uncertainty and doubt with which they are familiar and for which verification would be useful.

Exercise 2   Auditing for whom and for what?

The Companies Act 1985 requires companies over a certain size to have their main financial statements audited by a suitably qualified public accountant. Answer the following questions relating to this situation.

(1) All companies used to be required to have their financial statements audited. Why is the requirement limited to those entities of a certain size?

(2) At law, for whom is the company audit legally required? Why should it be limited in this way? Does the audit benefit other groups in society?

(3) What is the company audit expected to achieve according to the current Companies Act 1985 provisions?

Students should be prepared, with supervision from their instructor, to argue positively for both sides of these arguments (e.g. the argument that all companies should be audited irrespective of size).

Exercise 3   Detection of fraud

Joe Gardiner is a shareholder in several listed public companies. He has just read in his morning newspaper that one of these companies has filed for bankruptcy as a result of the discovery of a long-standing fraud by senior managers. Joe reads the annual financial reports of his investment companies and cannot remember receiving any without an unqualified audit opinion about the quality of the financial statements. He believes corporate auditors are responsible for the detection of fraud and seeks your advice on whether he has a case for suing the auditor of the failed company for damages. You are required to provide Joe with a considered opinion on the position. Students should be prepared to argue the case from all sides of the debate.

Exercise 4   State of mind

Why is the independence of the corporate auditor essentially a state of mind and why is the auditor's professional competence an important part of independence? Students should also discuss with their instructor the utility of an idea such as auditor independence that depends on such an intangible quality as a state of mind.

Exercise 5   Corporate audit risk

Rupert St John is the senior partner of St John & Company, a firm of chartered accountants specializing in corporate audits. He has been approached by James Golightly, the CEO of Golightly & Stevens plc, a publisher of magazines for the teenage market. St John and Golightly are members of the same golf club. Golightly wants to switch auditors and states he is having difficulty with the current auditor over the accounting practice he uses for recognizing sales from magazine subscriptions. The magazine market is highly competitive and magazine titles have, on average, a short publishing life. The profitability of Golightly & Stevens in recent years has shown rapid growth. Identify and discuss the audit issues that arise from this case, and recommend what Rupert St John should do. Students should discuss with their instructor the problem inherent in this exercise of an auditor considering his or her business risk in a task where he or she is meant to be protecting the public interest. Does walking away from a potentially difficult audit protect the public interest?

Exercise 6   Corporate auditing and accounting overstatement

Donald McDonald is the audit engagement partner for Super Cars plc, a manufacturer of custom-built executive cars for the American market. The company has been an audit client for five years and the previous four audit reports have contained the normal true and fair view opinion on the company's financial statements. He is reviewing the audit papers for the year 2006 prior to issuing his audit opinion. Before signing the last audit opinion for the year 2005, Donald McDonald raised concerns about the accounting numbers for the inventory of unsold cars. Super Cars was encountering difficulties in selling its cars in the US due to an economic recession and the audit team believed its inventory was overstated at its original cost. However, the auditor's proposal to reduce inventory to its market value was rejected by the client's board of directors on the grounds that the recession was temporary. This was eventually accepted by the auditor. This year the recession has continued and the same issue over inventory has arisen. Super Cars wants inventory to be reported at its original cost and McDonald believes it should be disclosed at a lower market value. The difference would turn a small profit into a large loss. You are required to consider and explain the accounting and auditing issues involved, and recommend what the auditor should do. Students can also discuss this dilemma with their instructor more generally in the context of the provision of professional services.

Exercise 7   Corporate auditor independence

James Alderston is the audit engagement partner for Skips R'Us plc, a company providing waste removal services. He is reviewing his audit team prior to starting the 2006 audit of the company. His file notes contain the following information.

There are eight staff members of the team—a senior audit manager, two qualified assistants, and five unqualified assistants who have recently signed staff contracts following university education. The manager has ten years of post-qualifying experience but is new to this audit. The qualified assistants have worked on this audit in 2005. Three of the unqualified assistants are arts and science graduates—the remaining two have accounting and business degrees. Alderston has been the engagement partner for the last three years. He was at school and university with the company's CEO. The audit firm provides tax and computer services for Skips R'Us. One of the qualified audit assistants is married to one of the internal audit staff of the client company.

What are the audit independence issues facing Alderston and how should they be resolved? What other independence matters should he check for before finalizing his audit team? Students should also discuss with their instructor whether absolute independence is possible in the corporate audit.

Exercise 8   Corporate audit committee

Charles Finman and Henry Thickness are, respectively, the CEO and chairman of the audit committee of Have-I-Got-Food-For-You plc. They are meeting to consider a memorandum received from the company's auditor concerning outstanding audit matters prior to the reporting of the audit opinion. The memorandum has been discussed by the audit committee and contains the following matters:

(1)   The company's debtors at the end of the 2006 year contain two amounts due where recovery is problematic. An amount of £200,000 has been outstanding for more than a year and the reason for delay in payment is due to the customer being in a legal dispute with a government department over the contract payment of £800,000. The case is likely to extend for a further three months and the customer is hopeful that it will be won and the department will be required to pay. The second amount is overdue by eight months and amounts to £150,000. There is no explanation available regarding the customer.

(2)   The auditor has found serious control weaknesses in the cash collection system of the company due to lack of segregation of responsibilities. Checks on the system by the auditor have not revealed any financial impropriety.

(3)   The company has received a lawsuit for £1,000,000 of damages from a customer supplied with defective products. The company's lawyers are of the opinion that the case has merit but could be dismissed in a jury trial.

Have-I-Got-Food-For-You plc has not provided for potential bad debts or lawsuit damages and its CFO is of the opinion that it is not necessary to do so. Pre-tax profits for 2006 before any provision for these matters amount to £2,560,000. Review these matters and present what you consider to be the position of the auditor, the audit committee, and the company's senior management.

ADDITIONAL READING

The structure of this chapter is a compilation of several previous publications by the author on the subject of auditing. These include T A Lee, *Corporate Audit Theory*, Chapman & Hall, London,

1993 (a book based on a previous text first published in 1972 and which ceased publication in 2004). References to relevant chapters of the 1993 book are as follows. Each chapter contains an additional reading list as well as discussion topics.

"Doubt, Verification, and Corporate Auditing," 19–25 (a general review of the audit problem of doubt and uncertainty about corporate financial statements).

"Economic and Social Roles for Corporate Auditing," 27–43 (the economic, political and social benefits from the corporate audit).

"Prescribing an Objective for Corporate Auditing," 45–55 (the audit objective of giving an opinion on the quality of corporate financial statements).

"An Independent Corporate Audit," 93–114 (the requirement of independence in thought, deed, and appearance for the corporate auditor).

"The Corporate Auditor's Duty of Care," 115–35 (the legal and professional responsibilities of the corporate auditor).

A recent specialist audit text covering audit practice is B Porter, J Simon, and D Hatherly, *Principles of External Auditing*, Wiley, Chichester, 2003. The following are chapters relevant to this chapter. Each chapter contains an additional reading list and discussion topics.

"What is Auditing?" 1–16 (a general review of the meaning of the process of auditing).

"Threats to, and Preservation of, Auditors' Independence," 71–95 (a general review of the meaning of auditor independence).

"Legal and Professional Duties of Auditors," 98–145 (a general review of the meaning of the auditor's duty of care, with particular reference to responsibility for fraud detection).

The following suggested reading sources provide recent views on current issues.

Anonymous (2005), "Auditor Independence," *Corporate Reporting*, August, 3–8 (a review of corporate audit independence issues using real-world examples).

D Arnold, R Bernardi, and P Niedermeyer (2006), "How Auditors Reach Balance of Expediency and Independence," *CAMagazine*, February, 50–52 (a readable report of a survey of corporate auditors' attitudes to coping with the stress of pressures on their position of independence).

R Fleck (2004), "Taking an Ethical Lead," *Accountancy*, January, 127 (new proposals for corporate auditor independence).

N Heaton (2004), "Fraud, Concealment and Liability," *Accountancy*, November, 108–9 (a view of the corporate auditor's reliance on misrepresentations of management).

K Hnatt (2001), "Forge the Right Relationship," *Journal of Accountancy*, May, 49–54 (the role of the audit committee and the external audit).

J E Ketz and P B W Miller (2000), "Beyond Compliance: A New Business Model for Auditing," *Accounting Today*, 10–23 July, 14 and 16 (the need to go beyond GAAP compliance).

T A Lee (1992), "The Audit Liability Crisis: They Protest Too Much!" *Accountancy*, December, 102 (a review of corporate audit firms' attempts to limit their responsibilities in a litigious environment).

D K McConnell and G Y Banks (2003), "How Sarbanes-Oxley Will Change the Audit Process," *Journal of Accountancy*, September, 49–55 (a review of the recent position that the corporate auditor requires management to identify, document, and evaluate internal controls).

S L Menelaides and L E Graham (2003), "The Auditor's Approach to Fair Value," *Journal of Accountancy*, June, 73–6 (how the corporate auditor should assess the procedures and staff who calculate fair values).

D D Montgomery, M S Beasley, S L Menelaides and Z-V Palmrose (2002), "Auditors' New Procedures for Detecting Fraud," *Journal of Accountancy*, May, 63–6 (a comprehensive review of the US position in auditing for fraud that came into practice in 2002 as *Statement on Auditing Standards 99*).

M F Murray (1992), "When a Client is a Liability," *Journal of Accountancy*, September, 54–8 (the need for corporate auditors to screen potential corporate clients before entering into an audit contract).

V B Neiman-Hoffman, K P Morgan and J M Patton (1996), "The Warning Signs of Fraudulent Financial Reporting," *Journal of Accountancy*, October, 75–7 (the most significant signals of fraud that auditors should observe).

A Ratcliffe (2003), "Communication and the Audit Committee," *Accountancy*, July, 100 (the role of internal and external auditors, and the audit committee in corporate governance).

W J Read and S Raghunandan (2001), "The State of Audit Committees," *Journal of Accountancy*, May, 57–60 (a review of the potential effectiveness of audit committees in the US).

J T Wells (2001), "And Nothing But the Truth: Uncovering Fraudulent Disclosures," *Journal of Accountancy*, July, 47–52 (key omissions from financial statements that attempt to hide fraud).

CHAPTER 9

Creative Accounting

Learning Objectives

This chapter expands introductory comments made in previous chapters — particularly those in Chapter 8 with respect to the corporate auditor's responsibility for the detection of fraud and error (including material accounting misstatement). The purpose of the current chapter is to provide a more comprehensive understanding of the subject of accounting misstatement. It is called creative accounting and presents considerable problems in corporate financial reporting for preparers, auditors, and users alike. It is closely associated with the reporting practice that many financial commentators have labelled earnings management. By the end of this chapter, you should be able to identify and understand:

- The nature of creative accounting in practice.
- The reasons why creative accounting is practiced.
- The forms that creative accounting takes and their impact on corporate financial statements.
- The warning signs of creative accounting.
- The role of the corporate auditor with respect to creative accounting.
- The relation between creative accounting and corporate governance.

At the end of this chapter, please review these learning objectives before moving on to Chapter 10 and the analysis of corporate financial statements.

INTRODUCTION

Previous chapters in this text have explained the nature and purpose of the main financial statements that comprise the annual financial report. They outline the profit statement, cash flow statement, and balance sheet, and comment on the accounting that underlies their numerical content. Part of the various explanations and commentaries focuses on accounting problems associated with the preparation and audit of the statements. More specifically, these problems relate to the major audit problem highlighted in Chapter 8 — i.e. the impact on reported financial statements of significant accounting misstatement by corporate senior managers and directors. Such misstatement is reviewed in the context of fraudulent reporting where managers and directors intend to deceive shareholders and other users of corporate financial statements by disclosing false accounting numbers. In this chapter, accounting misstatement is examined more broadly as something that can either occur within terms of GAAP (and therefore appear to have legitimacy) or outside GAAP (and therefore raise the question of fraud). In other words, misstatement is a corporate financial reporting matter that exists on a continuum of legitimacy due to the inherent flexibility of accounting practice. This chapter looks at the phenomenon as the outcome of a practice called creative accounting with a modern objective called earnings management. The fundamental objective of this chapter is to give its reader a basic understanding of the frailty of the accounting that underlies corporate financial statements and the ways in which corporate managers and directors attempt to disclose the accounting numbers they want to reveal rather than those which should be revealed to the shareholders. In other words, this is a chapter about reporting deception. Sometimes the deceit can be practiced within the rules of accounting. On other occasions, these rules are bypassed by managers and directors. Either way, shareholders or other users of financial statements can be misled and damaged by the deceit and there is a clear failure in corporate governance.

PRELIMINARY DEFINITIONS

Before starting the various explanations and commentaries, it is useful to provide some basic definitions of the three main terms used in this chapter—i.e. accounting misstatement, earnings management, and creative accounting.

Accounting misstatement

This is an expression used by accountants to denote that reported accounting numbers are different from what they should have been if they had not been affected by either accounting error (e.g. transactions carelessly omitted from the accounting records without the intent to deceive or a misapplication of an accounting standard) or accounting fraud (e.g. the insertion of false entries in the accounting records with the intent to deceive). The accounting misstatement is usually revealed and adjusted when the error or fraud is eventually discovered. By this time, however, shareholders and others have used the misstated numbers and can be damaged as a result (e.g. in the buying or selling of shares). It is the responsibility of the corporate auditor to plan and design the audit to have reasonable assurance of discovering significant accounting misstatement. However, as previously stated, there can be no guarantee of discovery in every case.

Earnings management

This term has been used for several years to indicate an overall practice used by corporate managers and directors to manipulate reported profits (or earnings) to a level that they wish to disclose. This means that their "ideal" or "target" profits are greater or less than those generated by a conventional use of GAAP. The flexibility inherent in GAAP is then used by managers and directors to identify accounting practices that can engineer profits up to or down to the level they desire. Because there is managerial or directorial intent in earnings management, it can lead to fraudulent accounting misstatement as defined above. It also raises the question of the legitimacy of earnings management that is kept within the bounds of GAAP and has caused accounting standard setters to alter the provisions of GAAP in order to combat questionable accounting. For this reason, it is reasonable to suggest that earnings management is a very frequent and usual occurrence in companies. Only when it steps beyond the boundaries of GAAP, however, can there be questions of fraudulent intent.

Creative accounting

This label has been given to accounting practices that attempt to manage earnings and other aspects of corporate financial statements by staying within the letter of the rules contained in accounting standards but with no intention of adhering to the spirit of these rules. In other words, creative accounting by corporate managers and directors occurs when they use the flexibility of these rules in order to prepare financial statements that are not consistent with the intention of the relevant accounting standards. This goes to the heart of what is described by accountants as the "substance versus form" issue—i.e. accounting standards typically attempt to prescribe rules that permit the economic substance of business transactions to be represented by accounting numbers rather than the legal form of these transactions. For example, a lawyer can write a business contract to make a loan transaction (the economic substance) look like a sale transaction (the legal form). Creative accounting tends to focus on form rather than substance and therefore encourages dubious legal contracting.

The remainder of this chapter examines creative accounting practices as they relate to the earnings management function of corporate management and as they often lead to significant accounting misstatement in corporate financial statements. Because of the nature of this text, any explanations and illustrations are kept as simple as possible.

NATURE AND PURPOSE OF CREATIVE ACCOUNTING

The previous definitions are explicit in their focus on the use of creative accounting practices by senior corporate managers and directors to manipulate accounting numbers in financial statements. The most frequent manipulations affect reported profits or earnings and the reason for this is the use of earnings as part of various economic decisions. For example, reported profits are the basis for calculating a significant expense and liability for the reporting company—i.e. taxation. There are economic incentives to lower reported profits in order to diminish the impact on cash flow of tax payments. However, given decades of evidence of profits being manipulated upwards, corporate managers and directors practicing earnings management by creative accounting are willing to pay higher taxes than necessary. This is counter-intuitive.

Another reason for creative accounting and earnings management is to create sufficient profits to justify the payment of a dividend to the shareholders. Corporate law requires dividends to be paid out of profit rather than share capital and it is therefore important that the board of directors can demonstrate that this has happened. If profits are insufficient to maintain a certain level of dividend, there is a temptation to use creative accounting practices to make the proposed dividend legal. A third reason for earnings management is the current climate of managerial compensation based on levels of profitability or related to profits. For example, most senior managers have contracts in which bonuses will be paid if profits reach a certain level. In addition, many managers and directors can receive share options—i.e. they receive shares in the company and can exercise options to sell them when the price reaches a certain level. In both cases, there are incentives to manipulate profits higher than they would be normally. A higher profit can trigger a bonus payment or cause the share price to rise.

A final reason for the presence of creative accounting and earnings management is a more general one of corporate managers and directors wanting reported profits to be sufficient to ensure the continuation rather than failure of the company. Poor profits or lack of profits can precipitate decisions by others that endanger the health of the reporting company—e.g. shareholders may sell their shares, bankers may not lend further or call in their loans, suppliers may restrict credit terms or be unwilling to supply, and customers may not buy the company's goods or services. Again, there is a temptation to manipulate profits in order to mask the condition of the company in the hope that better economic times may appear in the future.

Creative accounting and earnings management therefore have various stimulants. Some are connected to the economic well-being of the reporting company and others are clearly to do with the economic self-interest of managers and directors. All, however, have the intention of misleading the shareholders and other users of the financial statements about the profitability, cash flow, and financial position of the reporting company. If done to excess, creative accounting can go well beyond the boundaries of GAAP in the sense of prescribed rules in accounting standards and into the realms of illegitimate practices designed to produce fraudulent accounting misstatements in the financial statements. This sadly has been the pattern not only in recent times with cases such as Enron and WorldCom but also over the decades since financial statements began to be published.

Lesson 9.1 Protection and self-interest
Significant accounting misstatement takes place for two main reasons—protecting the well-being of the reporting company, and satisfying the economic self-interest of senior managers. The first reason appears more acceptable than the second. However, both can result in corporate financial statements that mislead shareholders and other users. This can lead to inappropriate decisions and economic damage.

ACCEPTABLE ACCOUNTING PRACTICE

Creative accounting practices for purposes of earnings management and other reporting manipulation is unacceptable under any circumstances. Although it may start with the intention of assisting the reporting company to survive, it can quickly lead to accounting adjustments that are intended to be deceitful and therefore fraudulent. In other words, a bad habit can become a damaging habit. Creative accounting deliberately inflates or deflates reported profits, cash flows, assets, and liabilities in order to improve, diminish or smooth the trend of financial results disclosed to shareholders and others. Corporate managers who are intent on using creative accounting practices will try to operate within the inherent flexibility of GAAP in order to use the latter as a means of claiming legitimacy for what they are doing. This is hard for the corporate auditor to challenge—although, at least in the UK, the true and fair view directive from legislation suggests that if such a view is not being reported with the creative practices within GAAP then these practices should not be accepted. In other words, creative accounting within GAAP may not be acceptable just because the letter rather than the substance of the accounting standard concerned is being followed. For this reason, given the possibility of corporate management using creative accounting practices, GAAP compliance is not the overriding consideration for the corporate auditor.

The history of corporate financial reporting is a history of the temporary acceptability of accounting standards contained in GAAP, at first informally and then formally. For example, at the end of the nineteenth century in the UK, many companies did not depreciate fixed assets. At best, some companies would transfer lump sums from profits to other reserves but other companies would make no provision for the expense and use of fixed assets. In these cases, profits were overstated and dividends paid to shareholders were greater than should have been the case. In extreme examples, dividends were paid out and the company failed as a consequence. Consequent court cases revealed these practices and gradually accountants and corporate managers changed their accounting practices to include the systematic writing off of depreciation to profits.

Another historical example of the temporary nature of GAAP was the use by companies of so-called secret reserve accounting (Americans now call this cookie-jar accounting). In times when it was rare to publish detailed profit statements, reporting companies would understate balance sheet accounting numbers such as fixed assets and inventory in order to deflate reported profits in years when the latter were substantial. The basic idea was to create secret reserves that could be used in leaner years to augment lower profits by overstating fixed assets and inventory. Essentially what was happening was that company managers and directors were smoothing out the trend of reported profits by these secret reserve accounting adjustments. It was a generally accepted practice done in the name of protecting the financial well-being of the reporting company and with the support of auditors. It was called conservative accounting practice and removed any natural fluctuation in profitability due to economic cycles in business. However, it was also a practice abused by some managers and directors to cover up impending corporate failure. A spectacular court case in the UK at the end of the 1930s removed secret reserve accounting from acceptable practice almost overnight.

Accounting standard setters since the late 1930s have been on a continuous treadmill of catch-up as corporate financial reporting abuses are exposed in court proceedings, reveal dubious practices within GAAP, and justify amendments to GAAP to proscribe the dubious practices. The fundamental problem, however, is the inevitable flexibility of accounting practices prescribed by accounting standards and labelled as GAAP. Unless each standard is written as an unbending rule then some flexibility in the practice is allowable to cope with the different circumstances of each reporting company. Even similar companies have different characteristics and circumstances that justify some deviation from the prescription of the standard. In the jargon of accounting standard setters, these are described as exceptions and are usually explained with specific guidance in interpretation statements.

Lesson 9.2 GAAP compliance
Creative accounting has a long and not very distinguished history. It has caused accounting standard setters to increasingly respond to abuses with accounting rules that are eventually overtaken by more creative accounting. Accounting standards that form GAAP offer a shelter to the creative accountant and therefore make GAAP compliance a less than perfect reporting objective.

Lesson 9.3 Temporary GAAP

The accounting standards that comprise GAAP are temporary in nature in the sense that they reflect prevailing and contemporary attitudes to certain aspects of accounting practice. These attitudes can change over time—particularly as a result of corporate financial reporting abuses apparently within the flexible boundaries of GAAP.

FLEXIBILITY OF ACCOUNTING

The reason for the inherent flexibility of conventional accounting practice is the foundation of numerical calculation on which it is built. This focuses on the use of historical costs (i.e. the original cost of each business transaction) to record assets such as fixed assets and inventory, and the arbitrary and subjective allocation process that is applied to these historical costs in order to eventually match periodic expenses with sales when calculating periodic profit. In recent years, some attempt has been made by standard setters to regularly update historical costs to their current market value (e.g. with respect to investments in shares) or present value (e.g. leased assets). However, in the case of the former, this is done largely for assets in which there is a known market and for which market value can be determined with reasonable accuracy. With the latter case, present value is a wholly subjective number which increases rather then decreases the flexibility of the accounting numbers concerned. It is totally dependent on subjective estimates by management of future cash flows and interest rates.

The reality in accounting, therefore, is that most assets and liabilities are recorded at the value determined in the originating contract and this becomes the basis for calculating the numbers from which profit is calculated. Even though secret reserve accounting has been proscribed, historical cost accounting allocations permit a degree of secret reserve adjustment in every set of financial statements reported. These allocations are based on subjective judgments by corporate managers about the condition and life of assets particularly and the associated matching of sales and expenses more generally. Accounting standards may have attempted to reduce the degree of subjectivity in accounting due to the flexibility of historical cost allocations. However, they cannot eliminate this flexibility. So long as every set of corporate financial statements is dependent on a subjective calculation basis using historical costs there will be flexibility and room for doubt about the integrity of the reported accounting numbers. It could be argued that each set of statements published should have a health warning attached—i.e. these statements are issued subject to the inherent flexibility of historical costs allocations to determine profitability and financial position.

The following section provides several examples of historical cost accounting and the flexibility that can be harnessed by the creative accountant in order to manage matters such as earnings in corporate financial reports.

Lesson 9.4 Historical cost accounting

The inherent nature of historical cost accounting means that, given two identical companies and economic circumstances, it is possible to produce two entirely different sets of financial statement within the accounting standards comprising GAAP.

CREATIVE ACCOUNTING IN PRACTICE

Creative accounting practices of recent years suggest that the main objective of corporate managers and directors is to improve profits and assets and hide debt. This is done at times to mask the underlying performance and condition of the reporting company (i.e. because trading operations are going badly or assets have been misappropriated) and/or to enhance the profit basis for managerial compensation. The accounting methods used are rarely sophisticated and ought to be observed by diligent auditors. The simple numerical examples that follow are offered to enhance understanding of the practice and its effects. Each example has been derived from a real case in practice.

Sales recognition

Improving reported sales is a frequent task for the creative accountant and manager. The objective is to increase sales and this will in turn increase reported profits. This can be done by either recognizing false sales, accelerating the recognition of existing sales, or inducing unwanted sales. The following are examples of each.

John Dance is the CEO of JD Merchants Ltd and is reviewing draft financial statements a month before the year-end.

Profit Statement for Year Ended 31 December 2006

	£
Sales	1,230,000
Less: cost of sales	861,000
Gross profit	**369,000**
Less: overhead expenses and depreciation	345,000
Net profit	**24,000**

Balance Sheet as at 31 December 2006

	£
Fixed assets less depreciation	528,000
Inventory of unsold goods	807,000
Cash at bank	5,000
Debtors	367,000
Total assets	**1,707,000**
Less: creditors	451,000
Net assets	**1,256,000**
Share capital	1,000,000
Retained profits	256,000
Shareholders' equity	**1,256,000**

Reported profits are much lower than expected and John instructs his accountant to make improvements by (a) creating false sales of £120,000 with a cost of £86,000; (b) treating £60,000 of subscription sales in advance as completed sales (these have an associated cost of sales of £43,000); and (c) asking the sales department to dispatch unordered goods to customers with a sale value of £90,000 and an associated cost of £65,000. The accountant makes entries in the accounting records to reflect these requests.

(1) Sales increase by £120,000 + 60,000 + 90,000 = £270,000 (the three sales numbers to be created).

(2) Debtors increase by £120,000 + 90,000 = £210,000 (the two sales created that reflect credit sales to customers).

(3) Creditors decrease by £60,000 (the advance sales treated as creditors before the adjustment).

(4) Cost of sales increases by £86,000 + 43,000 + 65,000 = £194,000 (if the created sales are to appear genuine then their associated costs of sales are recognized).

(5) Inventory of unsold goods decreases by £194,000 (representing the goods that apparently have been sold).

The effect of these five adjustments on the profit statement and balance sheet is as follows:

Profit Statement for Year Ended 31 December 2006

	£	Notes
Sales	1,500,000	1
Less: cost of sales	1,055,000	2
Gross profit	**445,000**	
Less: overhead expenses and depreciation	345,000	
Net profit	**100,000**	

Balance Sheet as at 31 December 2006

	£	Notes
Fixed assets less depreciation	528,000	
Inventory of unsold goods	613,000	3
Debtors	577,000	4
Cash at bank	5,000	
Total assets	**1,723,000**	
Less: creditors	391,000	5
Net assets	**1,332,000**	
Share capital	1,000,000	
Retained profits	332,000	6
Shareholders' equity	**1,332,000**	

Notes	Explanation
1	Sales increases by £270,000
2	Cost of sales increases by £194,000
3	Inventory decreases by £194,000
4	Debtors increase by £210,000
5	Creditors decrease by £60,000
6	Retained profits increase by £76,000 (i.e. £270,000 − 194,000)

The effect of the three adjustments is significant. Net profit and retained profits (and shareholder' equity) have increased by £76,000 or 317% of the original net profit of £24,000. Inventory has decreased by £194,000 or 24% of the initial number of £807,000. Both of these changes improve the reported financial results—i.e. improved profitability and liquidity. Debtors, however, have increased by £210,000 or 57% of the original figure of £367,000. This does not improve the company's financial position although the increase is to a realizable asset. Creditors, on the other hand, appear improved by the decrease by £60,000 or 13% of the original number of £451,000. In other words, of the four main changes, three represent improvements to the draft financial statements. However, none of the creative accounting practices is legitimate. The first adjustment is a deliberately false sale and will never result in cash flowing into the company in exchange for goods leaving it. The accounting entry is fraudulent. The second adjustment has more legitimacy but does not conform to GAAP. The latter requires sales to be recognized in this case when the goods are delivered to the customers, irrespective of when they paid their cash. Until the delivery is made the cash received in advance remains a liability of the company. The accounting entry contravenes GAAP and the intention is to deceive. The third adjustment is more difficult to deal with. Goods have been dispatched to customers and invoices mailed. The problem is that no orders were made. The consequences are that some customers will accept the goods and pay the amounts due on the invoices because their internal controls are weak. Others will notice the lack of orders and return the goods but probably after the year-end. Either way, the reporting company appears to have made and recorded genuine sales. But the intent was to deceive. All of these sales recognition examples of creative accounting have been used by real companies in an attempt to deceive their customers. In some cases, the auditors did not discover the practice for some time.

Inventory valuation

A familiar area in which to practice creative accounting is that of inventory of unsold goods. The reasons for this are two-fold. First, the accounting number for unsold inventory affects the calculation of profit (as part of the calculation of cost of goods sold) and the balance sheet presentation of current assets. Any inflation of the inventory number increases reported profit (and retained profits) and total assets. The opposite is true for any deflation of the inventory number. Second, the inventory number is determined by comparing the estimated original cost of the goods with their estimated market value. This permits (a) flexibility in defining cost and (b) flexibility in comparing cost with market value (e.g. either in total or with sub-totals). The following example, illustrates these effects.

Joel Cramer is the CFO of Cramer Brothers Ltd, a manufacturer of engineered parts for the car industry. He has prepared draft financial statements for his board of directors and realizes that profitability is insufficient to trigger the bonus provisions in the employment contracts of senior executives. He considers increasing the cost of inventory by £100,000 by including manufacturing overhead expense in the definition of cost. The following are the original draft financial statements before this creative accounting adjustment.

Profit Statement for Year Ended 31 December 2006

	£
Sales revenue	2,600,000
Less: cost of sales	2,090,000
Gross profit	**510,000**
Less: overhead expenses and depreciation	450,000
Net profit	**60,000**

Balance Sheet as at 31 December 2006

	£
Fixed assets less depreciation	774,000
Inventory of unsold goods	567,000
Debtors	480,000
Cash at bank	25,000
Total assets	**1,846,000**
Less: creditors	650,000
Net assets	**1,196,000**
Share capital	500,000
Retained profits	696,000
Shareholders' equity	**1,196,000**

The adjustment would decrease overheads in the profit statement by £100,000 and increase net profit by the same amount to £160,000. It would also increase unsold inventory in the balance sheet by £100,000 to £667,000 and shareholders' equity to £1,296,000. The company would appear to be more profitable and have more assets by this manipulation.

Now consider an alternative creative accounting practice to improve the company's profitability from that shown above. Joel Cramer has the following schedule relating to inventory of unsold goods at the year-end.

Type of Inventory	Cost £	Market Value £	Balance Sheet £
Raw materials	100,000	62,000	62,000
Work-in-progress	230,000	155,000	155,000
Finished goods	350,000	392,000	350,000
Total inventory	**680,000**	**609,000**	**567,000**

In arriving at the closing inventory figure of £567,000, Joel Cramer has applied the lower of cost or market rule to each of the three categories—i.e. £567,000 comprises the market value of raw materials and work-in-progress (£62,000 + 155,000) and the cost of finished goods (£350,000). However, if he applies the rule only to the total inventory, he then compares £680,000 with £609,000 and the number for closing inventory becomes £609,000. This would increase profits and assets in the balance sheet by £42,000 (i.e. £609,000 − 567,000). The GAAP rule has been applied in a different manner and the result is to increase profits from £60,000 to £102,000. GAAP appears to have been applied yet the purpose is to deceive.

Depreciation expense

Similar sleight of hand can be practiced in the calculation of depreciation of fixed assets. For example, the board of directors of Green Finger Express Ltd, a courier service provider, is considering its draft financial statements for the year ended 31 December 2006. The company's main asset is its fleet of vans and there is a schedule of these vans and their depreciation for the year. The reported profitability is not good. The draft statements and schedule are as follows:

Profit Statement for Year Ended 31 December 2006

	£	£
Sales		2,489,000
Less:		
Wages and salaries	875,000	
Van fuel and maintenance	745,000	
Overhead expenses	533,000	
Depreciation of vans	400,000	2,553,000
Net loss		*64,000*

Balance Sheet as at 31 December 2006

	£
Vans at cost less depreciation	780,000
Inventory of fuel	56,000
Debtors	321,000
Cash at bank	125,000
Total assets	**1,282,000**
Less: creditors	185,000
Net assets	**1,097,000**
Share capital	500,000
Retained profits	597,000
Shareholders' equity	**1,097,000**

Depreciation of Vans Schedule
Year to 31 December 2006

Van type	Number	Cost £	Estimated residual value £	Estimated life Years	2006 Depreci- ation £	Depreci- ation to date £	Net book value £
A	20	300,000	40,000	3	86,700	173,400	126,600
B	20	320,000	40,000	3	93,300	186,600	133,400
C	20	360,000	40,000	3	106,700	106,700	253,300
D	20	380,000	40,000	3	113,300	113,300	266,700
Total	**80**	**1,360,000**	**160,000**		**400,000**	**580,000**	**780,000**

Depreciation is calculated on a straight-line basis using the net cost (i.e. cost minus estimated residual value) over the estimated life. The annual number is calculated to the nearest £100 in the schedule. The company's CEO suggests that depreciation could be reduced by at least £100,000 (after all, these are estimates by management he argues) and this could turn a loss into a small profit (much more palatable to the shareholders). The CFO is instructed to re-calculate depreciation and he produces the following schedule. Estimated residual values for van types C and D are increased to £80,000 in each case and their estimated life to four years. These vans were purchased at the beginning of 2006.

Depreciation of Vans Schedule
Year to 31 December 2006

Van type	Number	Cost £	Estimated residual value £	Estimated life Years	2006 Depreci- ation £	Depreci- ation to date £	Net book value £
A	20	300,000	40,000	3	86,700	173,400	126,600
B	20	320,000	40,000	3	93,300	186,600	133,400
C	20	360,000	80,000	4	70,000	70,000	290,000
D	20	380,000	80,000	4	75,000	75,000	305,000
Total	80	1,360,000	240,000		325,000	505,000	855,000

The CFO's creative accounting involves manipulation of the managerial estimates that underlie the calculation. The accounting method used has not changed. The result is to improve profitability and total assets by £75,000. This turns the original loss of £64,000 into a profit of £11,000—perhaps not as much as the CEO required but probably enough to satisfy him. The intent, however, is to deceive the shareholders.

Capitalizing expenses

A favourite creative accounting practice of corporate managers and directors is to classify operating or trading expenses as capital expenditure. This has the effect of removing expenses from the profit statement and placing them in the balance sheet as depreciable fixed assets. This, of course, means that there is extra depreciation expense to reduce reported profits but the effect is much less than deducting the operating or trading expenses. The following is an example of this practice.

Ernest Bernard is the CEO of Bernard Telecommunications plc, a fast-growing cable communications provider. The company has been in operation for 15 years and its cable network has been renewed in several locations during the year ended 31 December 2006. The reason for the repairs was faulty materials used during the original installation. The total cost was £25,800,000 and this has been accounted for as an operating expense by the company's CFO. He states that this complies with GAAP as the expense is a repair to facilities. The company's engineers estimate that the replacement cable will have an operating life of ten years. Ernest Bernard is chairing a meeting of senior managers and reviewing draft and summary financial statements for the year 2006. These are given below and Bernard is not a happy man.

Profit Statement for Year Ended 31 December 2006

	£	£
Sales		139,800,000
Less:		
Maintenance of cable network	37,500,000	
Wages, salaries, and benefits	28,200,000	
Advertising expenses	33,000,000	
Overhead expenses	16,900,000	
Depreciation of cable network	10,000,000	125,600,000
Net profit		**14,200,000**

Balance Sheet as at 31 December 2006

	£
Cable network at cost less depreciation	78,000,000
Debtors	14,000,000
Investments at market value	6,700,000
Cash at bank	1,200,000
Total assets	**99,900,000**
Less: creditors	8,600,000
Net assets	**91,300,000**
Share capital	50,000,000
Retained profits	41,300,000
Shareholders' equity	**91,300,000**

The CEO is unhappy because the reported profit of £14,200,000 is approximately £2,000,000 less than he suggested it would be to financial analysts at the beginning of 2006. It also means that he and his senior managers will not receive a total bonus of £1,600,000 because a total profit of £16,000,000 has not been achieved. Ernest instructs his CFO to think of ways of improving profits to meet market expectations and trigger the bonus provision. The following are the amended financial statements produced by the CFO after some creative accounting.

Profit Statement for Year Ended 31 December 2006

	£	£	Notes
Sales		139,800,000	
Less:			
Maintenance of cable network	11,700,000		1
Wages, salaries, and benefits	28,200,000		
Advertising expenses	33,000,000		
Overhead expenses	16,900,000		
Depreciation of cable network	12,600,000	102,400,000	2
Net profit		**37,400,000**	

Balance Sheet as at 31 December 2006

	£	Notes
Cable network at cost less depreciation	101,200,000	3
Debtors	14,000,000	
Investments at market value	6,700,000	
Cash at bank	1,200,000	
Total assets	**123,100,000**	
Less: creditors	8,600,000	
Net assets	**114,500,000**	
Share capital	50,000,000	
Retained profits	64,500,000	4
Shareholders' equity	**114,500,000**	

Note	Comment
1	Maintenance reduces by £25,800,000 from £37,500,000
2	Depreciation increases by £2,600,000 (10% of £25,800,000) from £10,000,000
3	Network increases by £23,200,000 (£25,800,000 − 2,600,000) from £78,000,000
4	Equity increases by £23,200,000 (£25,800,000 − 2,600,000) from £41,300,000

The CFO explains the changes to these accounting numbers. The network renewal cost of £25,800,000 has been treated as capital expenditure and will be justified as such to the auditors as an upgrade or replacement rather than a repair. The company's engineers can provide a technical explanation. Ernest Bernard and his colleagues are delighted. Profits, total assets, and equity increase by £23,200,000. This exceeds market expectations by a considerable amount and managerial bonuses will be £2,320,000 in total. But these changes constitute reporting deceit.

Sales and debt

One way of operating a creative accounting system is to employ a lawyer to write contracts that say one thing and mean another. This is the classic form over substance situation, in which the legal form of the contract hides the economic substance of the transaction. In these cases, creative accounting is only possible if the reporting company has persuaded another company to agree to the contractual terms. This is best seen in an example. In this case, senior managers of the reporting company are looking for additional debt and improved profitability but already have too much debt. The answer is to find a friendly bank that is willing to enter into a contract that looks like a sale but is, in fact, new debt.

The senior managers of the Jewel-in-the-Crown Company Ltd are facing a funding crisis at a time when profits are falling. They ask the company's CFO to consider a way of achieving an increase in profits and additional funding without the latter appearing to add to its existing and considerable debt. The company manufactures high-value jewellery and holds precious stones for periods of up to ten years before using them in the manufacturing process. The CFO thinks about the problem and, after reading an article in a financial magazine, comes up with the following scheme.

Jewel-in-the-Crown has an inventory of jewels valued in current terms at £8,000,000 that it knows it will not use in manufacturing for at least ten years. The jewels cost £5,000,000 and their value in ten years time is estimated at £21,000,000. A private bank, Golden Bay Bank, is agreeable to entering into a contract to buy the jewels for £8,000,000, hold them, and, after ten years, give Jewel-in-the-Crown first option to buy the jewels back for £17,000,000. The contract is written with the legal form of a sale for £8,000,000. A sale of this amount is recorded, cash of £8,000,000 exchanged for the jewels, and cash resources increase by a similar sum. Cost of goods sold is £5,000,000 and inventory reduces by the same amount. The net profit on the transaction of £3,000,000 (£8,000,000 − 5,000,000) improves the company's profitability and its debt position does not change. The problem, however, is that the economic substance of the contract is not a sale. Instead, it is a debt of £8,000,000 that will last for ten years when it will be repaid by the purchase of the jewels for £17,000,000. The difference of £9,000,000 represents interest on the loan payable to the bank. When the jewels are repurchased for £17,000,000, they can be used for manufacturing or sold by Jewel-in-the-Crown for an estimated £21,000,000—giving a further realized profit of £4,000,000. The bank is not in the business of buying and selling jewels. It is a financial institution that lends money at interest and expects repayment of capital and interest. However, the creative accounting scheme has plausibility and may fool the auditor. Its intention is to deceive the shareholders of Jewel-in-the-Crown about the company's profitability and debt position.

Intangible assets

One of the biggest problems in corporate financial reporting concerns the reporting of intangible assets—i.e. assets legally-owned and without a tangible physical form but which, nevertheless, contribute significantly to the company's profitability, cash flow, and financial position. These assets include brands, trade marks, patents, copyrights, and more generally, goodwill. Their contribution to the business is difficult to determine—particularly when they cannot be separated from the business itself (as in the case of goodwill). Accounting standards typically require intangible assets to be reported if they have been purchased and for the purchase cost to be amortized over the useful life of the asset. Many companies prefer to write off such acquisitions immediately because of uncertainty about the underlying value. However, until recently, internally-generated intangible assets were not permitted to be accounted for and reported. This meant that in many businesses the most valuable assets were not disclosed to shareholders and others (e.g. professional sportsmen and women contracted as employees of a sports club as in association football).

Current accounting standards now permit internally-generated intangible assets to be reported. For example, development costs resulting from research into new products and services can be treated as an intangible asset if the project is identifiable, viable, and potentially profitable (e.g. as in software development in information technology businesses). However, such permissiveness can be used to advantage by the creative accountant. For example, consider the following case:

Jet Speed Technology Ltd provides search engines to access the internet. It has been in business for seven years and written off its software development costs as operating expenses against sales. The company has earned small profits in each of the first six years and will do so again in 2006 according to its CFO. Its bankers are concerned about its growing debt and lack of profit growth. Average annual profit over the first six years has been £1,500,000. The CFO is considering ways to improve profitability by earnings management techniques he has read about in the financial press. He is particularly interested in the possibility of capitalizing the company's development costs for 2006 as this appears to be permissible according to accounting standards. Development costs for 2006 amount to £9,000,000 and cover five projects. Past experience in the company and with its competitors suggests that, of every five developed projects, only two turn out to be commercially viable long-term. Successful projects produce products with a shelf life of no more than three years. And here lies the problem with creative accounting. There is a temptation for the CFO in this case to treat the £9,000,000 of costs in 2006 as a depreciable asset. With a useful life of three years, this would result in annual amortization of £3,000,000. The effect on 2006 profits (assuming the average of £1,500,000 after deduction of development costs) is as follows:

	£
2006 profit before adjustment	1,500,000
Add: development costs capitalized	9,000,000
	10,500,000
Less: annual amortization	3,000,000
Adjusted profit on new basis	**7,500,000**

Profit has therefore increased five times to £7,500,000 and the balance sheet will contain additional assets of £9,000,000 less amortization £3,000,000, i.e. £6,000,000. No doubt the CFO and his engineering managers could provide the company's auditors with a convincing argument of the suitability of this accounting manipulation. The company is more profitable and its asset structure has improved to cover its debt liability. However, in reality, there is a flaw and that is not all of the £9,000,000 of development costs may represent commercially viable projects and products. Past experience suggests that arguably 60 percent of the costs, on average, are not likely to generate sufficient sales and profits. There is therefore a strong argument not to capitalize a substantial proportion of the £9,000,000. There is also a very strong temptation for companies under pressure such as Jet Speed Technology to capitalize all development costs in the hope that future sales and profits on the viable projects will more than compensate for the losses on the unsuccessful ones. Meantime, shareholders will have been deceived about the profitability and financial position of the company.

Off-balance sheet entities

In recent years, corporate financial reporting has seen significant instances of reporting companies attempting to hide loss-making assets and mounting debt from their shareholders by use of the creative accounting practice of off-balance sheet transactions. The basic idea of these transactions is to remove assets and liabilities from the reporting company's balance sheet in such a way that it appears to be more profitable and financially healthier than is the case. The vehicle for off-balance sheet transactions is what is called a special-purpose entity or SPE. An SPE is typically a partnership between the reporting company and at least one other entity. The reporting entity investment is less than 50%, at risk in a commercial sense, but under its control. In this way, the reporting company's senior managers and board attempt not to have to consolidate the SPE assets, liabilities, profits, and cash flow in its financial statements—other than a note disclosing the investment. The following example illustrates these matters and the effect on a reporting company's financial statements.

During the year to 31 December 2006, the board of directors of Turnbull Energy Provision plc agreed to the creation of an SPE (Crocodile Tears) in which it had a 40% investment of £1,000,000. The other investors were the company's bankers (Ace-in-the-Hole Bank) with 30% and a consortium of company employees with the remaining 30%. Each of these investments amounted to £750,000 in cash. The managers of Crocodile Tears were Turnbull Energy Provision's CEO and CFO. The 40% investment was funded by the transfer of Turnbull's assets of £3,000,000 minus long-term debt of £2,000,000. The transferred assets are loss-making and the debt is secured by guarantee from Turnbull. The following are the outline balance sheets of the company before and after the creation of Crocodile Tears.

	Balance Sheet Pre SPE £	Balance Sheet Post SPE £
Profitable assets	9,000,000	9,000,000
Unprofitable assets	3,000,000	—
Investment in SPE	—	1,000,000
Total assets	**12,000,000**	**10,000,000**
Current liabilities	*2,000,000*	*2,000,000*
Long-term debt	*4,000,000*	*2,000,000*
Total liabilities	***6,000,000***	***4,000,000***
Shareholders' equity	**6,000,000**	**6,000,000**

Two changes have taken place as a result of the creation of the SPE:

(1) The unprofitable assets of £3,000,000 have been removed from the balance sheet. Any losses and negative OCF attributable to these assets will not appear in the company's profit statement and cash flow statement. Company NP and OCF in the future will be enhanced by this process.

(2) One-half of the company's long-term debt has been removed from the balance sheet, thus making it appear to have less debt than it actually has. In addition, the company's profit statement and cash flow statement in the future will have one-half of the interest expense on the debt, thus making profitability and cash flow appear better than is the case.

Shareholders' equity is unchanged. Crocodile Tears' balance sheet after its creation would appear as follows:

	£
Assets from Turnbull Energy Provision	3,000,000
Cash from other investors	1,500,000
Total assets	**4,500,000**
Long-term debt from Turnbull Energy Provision	*2,000,000*
Partnership equity	**2,500,000**

The SPE has £4,500,000 of assets and £2,000,000 of long-term debt, giving it equity of £2,500,000 (comprising £1,000,000 from Turnbull, £750,000 from the bank, and £750,000 from Turnbull employees). However, there are a number of problems with this:

(1)   The Turnbull assets acquired by the SPE are unprofitable and probably overvalued. Total SPE assets are therefore overstated.

(2)   The SPE has long-term debt that will require capital repayments and interest payments on a regular basis. These will drain any profits and cash flow to be generated from the existing assets. Turnbull's board will hope that the cash from the other investors of £1,500,000 can be invested in projects that are sufficiently profitable to cover the servicing of the debt obligation and provide a reasonable return for the investors.

In the meantime, the SPE can borrow further money as long-term debt so long as Turnbull Energy Provision is willing to provide security for it.

One further transaction between Turnbull and the SPE should be considered in this context. It is a fraudulent transaction seen in actual frauds involving SPEs in the past. Suppose Turnbull Energy Provision needs cash to pay for its obligations. With the SPE off-balance sheet and under the control of the Turnbull CEO and CFO, there is the temptation to transfer cash funds from the SPE to Turnbull. This could be done legally as a long-term loan and it would be disclosed as such. However, Turnbull wants to remove debt from its balance sheet rather than add to it. A transfer that is quasi-legal would be to treat it as a short-term loan that would appear under current liabilities. But it cannot stay there forever. The fraudulent approach would be to treat the cash flow from the SPE to Turnbull as a sale, thus inflating its sales, profits, OCF, and cash resources. As the transaction is controlled at both ends, it would be difficult to audit.

Lesson 9.5 Creative accounting and fraud
Creative accounting practices range from accounting manipulations within GAAP to obvious fraud. The danger is that, once practiced within GAAP, creative accounting is extended by corporate management to the fraudulent end of the creativity range.

Lesson 9.6 Simplicity of creative accounting
Creative accounting practices are typically simple in their construction and do not require complex accounting skills. They may require the assistance of lawyers and bankers to help in the organizational and contractual structures within which accounting operates. The corporate auditor should never be drawn into agreeing to these structures or practices.

CREATIVE ACCOUNTING AND REPORTING ISSUES

Creative accounting emphasizes a number of accounting and auditing issues that are unresolved by accounting and auditing standard setters. They damage the integrity of the corporate financial report and militate against the safe use of reported accounting information in decision making. They are offered here as a warning against any over-reliance on the credibility of reported accounting numbers and as a reminder of the frailty of the accounting and auditing process. Perhaps there is no convincing solution to any or all of these issues. Nevertheless, the reader ought to be aware of them. They are not presented in any order of importance.

Classification and relation

Corporate financial statements are based on a set of agreed classifications (e.g. assets, liabilities, sales, and expenses) and associations (e.g. assets minus liabilities equating to shareholders' equity; and sales minus expenses equating to profit). Agreement is implicit in a number of accounting standards and, at least in theory, appears unproblematic. However, in practice, due to looseness in definition and prescription, accounting classifications and relationships are not definitive. They can be manipulated by the creative accountant acting on behalf of corporate managers and directors who wish to mislead or deceive shareholders. Manipulation is assisted by the cooperation of lawyers who can write appropriate legal contracts and bankers and others willing to assist in the manipulation. For this reason, accounting regulators need to revisit the apparently simple notions of accounting classification and relationship to tighten up the current ambiguity. The role of lawyers, bankers, and others in creative accounting schemes also requires investigation if corporate governance is to be more effective.

Accounting choice

The process of producing corporate financial statements is essentially one of accounting choice—i.e. in order to produce accounting numbers required in the financial statements, corporate managers and directors have a choice of accounting methods (e.g. in the depreciation of fixed assets or the costing of unsold inventory). Such choice leads to the inevitable reality that based on a given set of economic circumstances and transactions, several different sets of financial statements are possible. This possibility is potentially confusing and incomprehensible to non-accountants. The task for accounting standard setters is to minimize choice in accounting without ignoring the need to accommodate the differing economic circumstances of reporting companies that appear similar because they operate in the same markets and industries.

Historical cost

The basis for corporate financial reporting is historical cost. It appears to have the advantage of being verifiable—i.e. each business transaction can be observed for its historical or original cost. In other words, it can be evidenced and this is important from an audit perspective. However, historical costs are not a reasonable representation of assets particularly after the date of the original transaction. In particular, historical cost is a poor representation of current value—either in use or for sale. In addition, historical costs require to be allocated to particular periods in the quest for proper matching of sales and expenses in order to calculate profit. Such allocation is a subjective process that assists the creative accountant in managing earnings.

Substance and form

Arguably the greatest issue facing accountants today is that concerning the clash between economic substance and legal form in corporate financial reporting. Associated with each business transaction is the underlying economic substance or reality it represents—e.g. the economic substance of a sales transaction is the exchange of goods or services by a willing seller to a willing buyer. However, a careful legal crafting of a transaction can make its legal form appear different from the underlying economic substance—e.g. a debt transaction appearing to be a sale or vice versa. Recent initiatives by accounting standard setters worldwide suggest they are addressing this problem. Whether they will be successful is debatable.

Economics and politics

Accounting cannot be regarded as purely a technical process that demands skills and experience from its practitioners. It is also a means of representing the performance and condition of reporting companies and their management. Reported accounting numbers therefore have an economic impact through decisions and actions that result from their use. For example, they are used to decide on dividends and managerial compensation, buying and selling shares, and loans and overdrafts. Corporate taxation is based on reported profits. Particular accounting standards can impact companies directly in the sense they can alter the accounting numbers they report. For example, in recent times, companies have been required to disclose previously hidden matters such as leased assets or pension liabilities. This, in turn, reveals the political side of accounting in which companies lobby legislators and regulators in order to prevent or revise proposed standards that might affect their profit statements and balance sheets.

International accounting standards

Accounting standards that affect corporate financial statements are increasing becoming homogenized through the activities of the IASB. Countries such as the US and the UK have agreed to adopt or be consistent with IASB standards. However, this raises the issue that accounting standards should reflect the culture, attitudes, and laws of individual countries. IASB standards are essentially based on those of the FASB in the US and may not be appropriate to companies in countries as diverse as Nigeria and New Zealand. International homogeneity may appear to be useful but may result in masking essential differences in the financial statements of companies from different countries.

Feasibility of financial reporting

The utility of corporate financial reports is limited by a number of factors, several of which have been mentioned previously (i.e. classification and relational problems, accounting choice and flexibility, historical choice and allocation, economic substance versus legal form, and political and cultural considerations). The most fundamental limitation is that financial statements are expected to relevantly and reliably represent the outcomes of numerous business transactions and events over a relatively short period of time of one year in a relatively few accounting numbers. This is a complex task of balancing compression and comprehension—i.e. compressing the complexity of business activity into a summarized numerical form that is understandable to its readers. Users of financial statements therefore need to understand that, due to necessary compression, comprehensibility may be compromised. This is true irrespective of the size and complexity of the reporting company. It is most true in the largest and most complex organizations (as evidenced in cases of fraudulent reporting by companies such as Enron and WorldCom in the US and BCCI and MCC in the UK).

Audit issues

Corporate financial reporting is not just about the calculation and disclosure of accounting numbers. It also concerns the verification and reporting on the quality of these numbers and these audits also raise issues that affect the overall utility of corporate financial reports. For example, throughout the history of corporate auditing there have been persistent concerns about the ability of the auditor to provide a competent and independent opinion. There are numerous pressures on the auditor created by a variety of factors—e.g. the complexity and variety of audit evidence to examine, the short time period with which to audit and give an opinion, and the conflicts created by providing management services in addition to the audit. There is also the problem of the expectations gap—in which the expectations of shareholders and others with respect to what the auditor does in the audit is different from what is actually done. This is particularly obvious with respect to fraud detection, with public expectations of this as a primary audit objective and auditors claiming it as an incidental benefit of the audit. A more recent issue has arisen with respect to the role of the audit committee in relation to the audit. This is a key component of modern corporate governance. Recent regulations require audit committees and auditors to work closely together with respect to matters such as the adequacy of internal controls and the quality of financial statements. However, the effectiveness of this relationship depends to a considerable extent on the competence of the audit committee to deal with such matters. Unless there is an overall understanding of accounting, reporting, and auditing problems within the committee, then it cannot satisfactorily carry out its function in this respect.

> **Lesson 9.7 Reporting issues**
> Corporate financial reporting involves a number of unresolved and persistent problems or issues that affect its ability to be an effective part of overall corporate governance.

CREATIVE ACCOUNTING AND CORPORATE GOVERNANCE

It seems self-evident that creative accounting is inconsistent with the objectives of corporate governance defined in Chapter 2. Corporate governance is a structure of formal mechanisms to direct, supervise, and control the decisions and actions of senior managers within a reporting company and to ensure these are compatible and consistent with the specific interests of shareholders and other stakeholders who contribute to its operations. Financial reporting forms part of corporate governance and its credibility depends on the quality of the accounting practices used to produce the numbers and narratives contained in the reported financial statements. Any attempt to massage or manipulate these numbers by creative accounting runs counter to the aims of corporate governance. It is not in the interests of shareholders and other users of financial statements to receive accounting numbers that do not reflect the underlying economic substance of the business transactions on which they are based.

More specifically, because of creative accounting, shareholders and others are deceived about the financial performance and position of the reporting company and may make inappropriate decisions—e.g. buying or holding shares when they should be selling, or lending money long-term when it is imprudent to do so. Creative accounting practices are not excused because they appear to operate within the existing system of GAAP. Such a situation suggests that the flexibility of GAAP is inappropriate and needs tightening up to prevent creative accounting. This is not an argument for strict and inflexible accounting rules. Instead, it is an argument for GAAP that permits a relevant and reliable production of accounting numbers that assist rather than diminish efforts at effective corporate governance.

Lesson 9.8 Creative accounting and corporate governance
The effectiveness of corporate governance is negatively affected by creative accounting—whatever the motivation for such practices.

LEARNING OBJECTIVES

Please review the learning objectives at the beginning of this chapter and ensure they have been achieved before proceeding to Chapter 10 on the analysis of corporate financial statements.

Exercise 1   Nature and purpose of creative accounting

What is creative accounting and how does it affect the quality of corporate financial reports? In order to better understand this topic, students should discuss it with their instructor from the perspective of senior managers and directors that are pressured to be creative in their accounting. Try to think of the problem from this perspective. This will also assist with the next topic.

Exercise 2   Motivation for creative accounting

What motivates corporate managers and directors to use creative accounting practices in corporate financial reporting? Students should discuss this topic with their instructor by thinking about situations in their personal lives in which they have had to be creative with the information they provided. Did the creativity work and how beneficial was it to all concerned?

Exercise 3   Place of GAAP

Given the inherent flexibility of GAAP and the ability of corporate managers and directors to manipulate within and outside it, what role does GAAP play in corporate financial reporting? GAAP implies there has been general acceptance of the standards concerned. Students should discuss with their instructor whether or not this is true in practice.

Exercise 4   Examples of creative accounting

Creative accounting can take many forms. Some are more subtle and complex than others. Without requiring the specific details in each case to be stated, what are the favourite areas of accounting practice for corporate managers and directors to apply creativity?

Exercise 5   Warning signs

Because creative accounting is endemic in corporate financial reporting to a greater or lesser extent, it is important that users of financial statements are aware of warning signs that may indicate the presence of creative accounting practices. What are these warning signs?

Exercise 6   Observing accounting numbers

James Creak is a financial analyst with a firm of stockbrokers. He is examining the financial statements of Your-Mail plc, a company that provides a letter delivery service throughout the UK. This is based on an annual subscription plan involving a contracted monthly number of deliveries. The company was founded in 1980 and operated at a relatively modest level of activity until 2001 when its shares became publicly available. James has summarized the company's financial statements for the years 2002 to 2006 inclusive and these summaries are given below. You are required to identify any unusual features in these summaries and offer explanations.

Your-Mail plc
Profits Statements 2002–2006

	2002 £000	2003 £000	2004 £000	2005 £000	2006 £000
Sales	25,000	30,000	36,000	43,000	52,000
Less:					
Operating costs	*13,000*	*15,000*	*18,000*	*20,000*	*24,000*
Administrative and financial costs	*2,000*	*3,000*	*4,000*	*3,000*	*3,000*
Depreciation of vans	*4,000*	*5,000*	*6,000*	*3,000*	*4,000*
Total costs	**19,000**	**23,000**	**28,000**	**26,000**	**31,000**
Profit before tax	**6,000**	**7,000**	**8,000**	**17,000**	**21,000**

Balance Sheets 2002–2006

	2002 £000	2003 £000	2004 £000	2005 £000	2006 £000
Vans at cost	16,000	20,000	24,000	28,000	32,000
Less: depreciation	*8,000*	*13,000*	*19,000*	*22,000*	*26,000*
	8,000	**7,000**	**5,000**	**6,000**	**6,000**
Debtors	2,000	3,000	4,000	9,000	12,000
Cash in bank	1,000	1,000	1,000	1,000	1,000
Total assets	**11,000**	**11,000**	**10,000**	**16,000**	**19,000**
Less: subscriptions in advance	*2,000*	*3,000*	*3,000*	*4,000*	*4,000*
Less: long-term debt	*2,000*	*2,000*	*3,000*	*3,000*	*3,000*
Total liabilities	**4,000**	**5,000**	**6,000**	**7,000**	**7,000**
Net assets	**7,000**	**6,000**	**4,000**	**9,000**	**12,000**
Shareholders' equity	**7,000**	**6,000**	**4,000**	**9,000**	**12,000**

ADDITIONAL READING

There are several texts that can be consulted in order to understand the nature and role of creative accounting and the corporate function of earnings management. They include the following:

A Berenson (2004), *The Number: How America's Balance Sheet Lies Rocked the World's Financial Markets*, Pocket Books, New York: NY. This is a text that chronicles the boom and bust cycle of the 1990s and the increasing reliance by corporate senior managers and directors on creative accounting and earnings management because of the capital market's predilection for the single accounting number of earnings per share. Although American, its story has global relevance.

F Clarke, G Dean, and K Oliver (2003), *Corporate Collapse: Accounting, Regulatory, and Ethical Failure*, Cambridge University Press, Cambridge, 25–42. This chapter deals specifically with the issue of creative accounting in the context of corporate business failure. The book contains numerous Australian examples of creative accounting.

I Griffiths (1995), *New Creative Accounting*, Macmillan, London. This is one of the original texts on creative accounting and covers all aspects of it, particularly from a British perspective.

M Jones (2006), *Accounting*, John Wiley & Sons Ltd, Chichester, 328–49. This is a relatively simple introductory coverage of creative accounting and has been written to assist non-accounting readers.

P O'Regan (2001), *Financial Information Analysis*, John Wiley & Sons Ltd, Chichester, 335–53. This is also a relatively simple introductory coverage and is written in the context of analyzing corporate financial statements.

There are a number of articles that can be read on the subject of creative accounting and earnings management. Most were written during the time of greatest creativity in American accounting. Their message, however, is just as relevant today and knows no geographical boundaries.

P R Brown (1999), "Earnings Management: A Subtle (and Troublesome) Twist to Earnings Quality," *The Journal of Financial Statement Analysis*, Winter, 61–3. This is a brief review of earnings management from the perspective of the expert financial analyst.

W J Bruns and K A Merchant (1990), "The Dangerous Morality of Managing Earnings," *Management Accounting*, August, 22–5. This is a brief report on a research project on corporate managers' views about earnings management; it reveals the prevalence of such activity, and a wide range of views concerning its legitimacy in order to improve short-term profits.

J A Byrne (1999), "Chainsaw: He Anointed Himself America's Best CEO: But Al Dunlap Drove Sunbeam Into the Ground," *Business Week*, October 18, 128–34, 140, 142, 147 and 149. This article examines the case of a large electrical goods manufacturer and its CEO who dominated the management structure to such an extent that managers were forced to misstate earnings in order to meet targets set by the CEO.

N Byrnes (1998), "Earnings Hocus-Pocus: How Companies Come Up With the Numbers They Want," *Business Week*, October 5, 134–6, 138, 140 and 142. This is a useful review of the main creative accounting practices with specific corporate examples.

D R Carmichael (1999), "Hocus-Pocus Accounting," *Journal of Accountancy*, October, 59–65. A leading US regulator looks at the specific and popular creative accounting practice of early recognition of sales in order to inflate reported profits.

D Henry (2001), "The Numbers Game," *Business Week*, May 14, 100–104, 106, 108 and 110. A comprehensive review of creative accounting in the US, which cites specific cases and methods, and also covers the response of regulators.

A Levitt (1998), *"The Numbers Game,"* American Accounting Association, Rutgers University, New York. The SEC chairman of the time voices his frustrations about creative accounting practices in the US.

M Maremont (1995), "Blind Ambition: How the Pursuit of Results Got Out of Hand at Bausch & Lomb," *Business Week*, October 23, 79–82, 86 and 90–2. A case study of a large and well-known US corporation that practiced creative accounting worldwide at the behest of dominant senior managers.

P Rosenfield (2000), "What Drives Earnings Management?" *Journal of Accountancy*, October, 106 and 109–10. A leading US accounting regulator blames earnings management and creative accounting on the basic structure of the conventional accounting system—i.e. realization and allocation practices.

M Schroeder (1992), "The Accounting Questions at Terex," *Business Week*, October 12, 148–50. An article that examines a US company that has experienced rapid growth and where accounting practices appear to be at the boundaries of legality.

CHAPTER 10

Corporate Financial Statement Analysis

Learning Objectives

This chapter builds on previous chapters by introducing the objectives and basic techniques of financial analysis — i.e. the process of using accounting numbers disclosed in corporate financial statements to provide numerical indicators of a reporting company's financial performance and position. These indicators are presented in two forms — first, standardized percentages for comparative overviews; and, second, specific ratios using generally accepted calculations. Each set of indicators is based on reported accounting numbers taken from the financial statements explained in previous chapters. They are as strong or as weak as these numbers. Many of the explanations and commentaries in previous chapters are relevant to this chapter (particularly those made in Chapter 9 in relation to creative accounting and current weaknesses of accounting practice).

This chapter is structured in several sections. First, there is an introductory section dealing with the use of the main financial statements in a common-size format of percentages that provides broad and interpretable reviews of corporate financial performance and position. Second, the next section outlines the nature and purpose of financial statement ratio analysis, focusing on the use of calculated ratios in decision making. Third, key accounting ratios are defined as financial indicators of specific aspects of corporate performance and position, and explained in terms of interpretations of these matters that can be construed from them. The ratios cover areas of interest to shareholders and other users such as corporate profitability, solvency and liquidity, managerial effectiveness, and investment. By the end of this chapter, you should be able to identify and understand:

- The need to reduce corporate financial statements to a common-size format.

- The transformation of accounting numbers in corporate financial statements into numerical indicators of performance called financial ratios.

- The various decisions to which financial ratios can be applied in order to put these decisions on an informed and rational basis.

- The methods of calculating each main financial ratio.

- How to interpret each main financial ratio.

- The use of financial ratios in comparative analyses.

- The strengths and limitations of each main financial ratio.

● The impact of creative accounting on financial ratios.

● The relationship between financial ratios and corporate governance.

At the end of this chapter, please review these learning objectives.

COMMON-SIZE ANALYSIS

It is useful to start this chapter with an introductory example of summary financial statements. This permits the reader to appreciate the position of a financial analyst attempting to create an overall impression of the reporting company's financial performance and position from the accounting numbers in these summaries. They cover profit, cash flows, assets, liabilities, and shareholders' equity. The analysis is called common-size analysis because the accounting numbers are reduced to a common size of percentages.

The reporting company is Simple Simon Pies Ltd, a manufacturer of meat pies for several large national food stores. The accounting numbers summarize the company's profits statements for the three years 2004, 2005, and 2006.

Simple Simon Pies Ltd
Summary Profit Statements 2004–2006

	2004 £	2005 £	2006 £
Sales	250,000	280,000	300,000
Less: cost of goods sold	170,000	180,000	210,000
Gross profit	**80,000**	**100,000**	**90,000**
Less: overhead expenses and depreciation	40,000	45,000	50,000
Net profit before tax	**40,000**	**55,000**	**40,000**
Less: taxation	15,000	20,000	17,000
Net profit after tax	**25,000**	**35,000**	**23,000**
Less: dividend	10,000	10,000	7,000
Retained profit	**15,000**	**25,000**	**16,000**

The profit summary is straightforward and discloses (a) the accounting relationship of each number to the next (e.g. sales minus cost of goods sold gives GP); and (b) the trend of each number over time (e.g. sales for 2004 compared to sales for 2005 and 2006). The financial analyst can therefore determine certain broad conclusions from reading these numbers. For example:

(1) In each year, Simple Simon Pies Ltd has been profitable—i.e. sales exceed cost of goods sold, GP is greater than overheads, NP exceeds taxation, and profit after tax covers dividends.

(2) There are differences in profitability when each year is compared with the next. GP increases from £80,000 to £100,000 and then decreases to £90,000. NP before tax increases from £40,000 to £55,000 and then drops back to £40,000. Retained profit increases from £15,000 to £25,000 and reduces to £16,000.

Some knowledge of profitability can therefore be gained from reading the summary in this way. However, it is difficult to interpret except in the broadest of terms. One means of going beyond this simple level of financial analysis is to introduce a structure that provides greater readability, comprehension, and therefore better interpretation for the analyst. This is called common-size analysis and it converts the reported accounting numbers to percentages—i.e. in the first instance using sales as the base and in the second instance using 2004 numbers as the base. The first percentage presentation permits individual years to be examined in isolation. The second presentation permits a comparison to be made over time and between periods. The objective is to avoid analytical distortions caused by accounting numbers of different sizes. Thus, common-sizing based on sales produces the following percentage summary:

Simple Simon Pies Ltd
Common-Sized Profit Statements 2004–2006

	2004 %	2005 %	2006 %
Sales	100	100	100
Less: cost of goods sold	68	64	70
Gross profit	**32**	**36**	**30**
Less: overhead expenses and depreciation	16	16	17
Net profit before tax	**16**	**20**	**13**
Less: taxation	6	7	6
Net profit after tax	**10**	**13**	**7**
Less: dividend	4	4	2
Retained profit	**6**	**9**	**5**

The percentages above are effectively simple ratios based on sales (e.g. in 2004, GP of £80,000 is 32% of sales of £250,000, and retained profit of £15,000 is 6% of sales of £250,000). Putting the accounting numbers in percentage form creates a more interpretable format. For example, the GP percentage increased from 32% to 36% and then decreases from 36% to 30%. A similar trend occurred with NP before tax, NP after tax, and retained profit (e.g. retained profit rose from 6% to 9% before dropping to 5%). These percentage comparisons allow a general conclusion to be arrived at—that the profitability of the company increased between 2004 and 2005 and then fell in 2006 to below 2004 levels. This should invite the financial analyst to ask relevant questions about why profitability in 2005 was different from that in the previous and succeeding years.

A second common-size presentation assists with these questions by facilitating trends over time—i.e. in this case, from 2004 to 2005 to 2006. Accounting numbers for 2004 are used as the base (e.g. sales in 2006 of £300,000 are 120% of sales of 2004, and taxation of £17,000 in 2006 is 113% of taxation of £15,000 in 2004).

Simple Simon Pies Ltd
Summary Profit Statements 2004–2006

	2004 %	2005 %	2006 %
Sales	100	112	120
Less: cost of goods sold	100	106	124
Gross profit	**100**	**125**	**113**
Less: overhead expenses and depreciation	100	113	125
Net profit before tax	**100**	**138**	**100**
Less: taxation	100	133	113
Net profit after tax	**100**	**140**	**92**
Less: dividend	100	100	70
Retained profit	**100**	**167**	**107**

Creating the above inter-period percentage comparison for Simple Simon Pies Ltd reveals several interesting features not previously obvious in the raw accounting numbers or the percentage presentation year by year. Over the three years, sales increased by 12% and then 20% but cost of goods grew by 6% and then 24%. The net effect was to increase GP by 25% and 13%. Overheads increased by 13% and 25% and taxation by 33% and 13%. Retained profit increases were 67% and 7%. Again, the differences between 2005 and 2006 need further investigation by the analyst but at least common-sizing has provided a basis for doing so.

> **Lesson 10.1 Common-size analysis**
> The analysis and interpretation of reported accounting numbers is assisted by common-size standardization to permit comparisons within a particular period or between periods. Common-sizing is a fundamental form of standardization and converts accounting numbers into percentages.

COMPARISONS OF ACCOUNTING NUMBERS

The previous section emphasizes the importance of standardizing reported accounting numbers for use by financial analysts and implies that standardization is necessary for comparative purposes. In other words, accounting numbers become meaningful in use through a process of comparison. There are two types of comparison.

Inter-period comparisons

These comparisons reflect the reported accounting numbers of a company over several periods (as illustrated above). The objective of inter-period comparisons is to detect significant changes in financial performance and position over time that could influence decisions such as investing and lending. Examining the financial results of a single period in the life of a reporting company has limited utility because it is effectively trying to look at the entity in isolation. Few expert examinations in human activity are made without some form of comparison. For example, a medical doctor responsible for an ill patient will not depend on a single and isolated series of tests and readings of matters such as temperature and blood pressure. Instead, these characteristics of health will be measured several times over a period of time until a trend is determined from which an opinion can be made about the development of the illness and the health of the patient. The same is true in financial analysis and an example is given below—in this case, of cash flow accounting numbers over several periods.

One-For-The-Road Concrete Ltd is a company that manufactures concrete mixes for road construction projects. It has produced the following summary cash flow statement for the years 2002 to 2006 inclusive (negative cash flows are shown in italic script).

One-For-The-Road Ltd
Summary Cash Flow Statements 2002–2006

	2002 £	2003 £	2004 £	2005 £	2006 £
Operating cash flow	121,000	245,000	90,000	*68,000*	23,000
Investment cash flow	*50,000*	*164,000*	*118,000*	*45,000*	*27,000*
Financing cash flow	*10,000*	*77,000*	*23,000*	100,000	50,000
Change in cash resources	**61,000**	**4,000**	***51,000***	**13,000**	**46,000**

These numbers reveal several aspects of the company's cash flow performance:

(1) OCF is positive for 2002, 2003, 2004, and 2006—with a single negative contribution in 2005. Although this is not unusual or particularly surprising, the overall trend appears to be downwards—i.e. from £121,000 in 2002 to £23,000 in 2006.

(2) ICF is consistently negative, indicating that the company was reinvesting or making new investment in capital expenditure in each of the five years. This too is not unusual and, indeed, is to be expected in a company that is considering the future. ICF provides the basis for future OCF. Fixed assets wear out or become obsolete and need to be changed or replaced.

(3) FCF shows that the company repaid long-term debt in 2002, 2003, and 2004 and receiving new debt in 2005 and 2006. Again, this is unsurprising as a company will go through cycles of receiving and repaying long-term funding.

(4) The change in cash resources in each year is the balancing figure—i.e. cash resources increased in 2002 and 2003 as a result of OCF surpluses, and decreased in 2004 and 2005 because of negative flows. There was an increase in 2006.

These changes can be reviewed in these general terms but are seen more clearly in detail by a formal trend analysis incorporating three-yearly totals of cash flows. In this analysis, the three-year totals are calculated by adding the current period to a three-year aggregate and deleting the oldest year—e.g. above, 2002 + 2003 + 2004 is the first aggregate (e.g. OCF £121,000 + 245,000 + 90,000 = £456,000). 2003 + 2004 + 2005 is the second aggregate (e.g. ICF £164,000 + 118,000 + 45,000 = £327,000). 2004 + 2005 + 2006 is the third aggregate (e.g. FCF £23,000 + 100,000 + 50,000 = £127,000).

One-For-The-Road Ltd
Summary Cash Flow Statements 2002–2004 to 2004–2006

	2002–4	2003–5	2004–6
	£	£	£
Operating cash flow	456,000	267,000	45,000
Investment cash flow	*332,000*	*327,000*	*190,000*
Financing cash flow	*110,000*	—	127,000
Change in cash resources	**14,000**	*60,000*	**18,000**

The above three-year rolling trend provides greater insight into the cash flow results. For example, OCF is diminishing—from £456,000 to £45,000. So, too, is ICF (from £332,000 to 190,000). FCF, on the other hand, has changed from a repayment situation of £110,000 to new debt of £127,000. Overall, therefore, the company is increasingly relying on external cash funding rather than internally-generated funds and is reducing its investment programme. This is not good news with respect to future OCF. The trend analysis has permitted this to be seen despite the yearly fluctuations in the reported figures.

Lesson 10.2 Trends
The financial analyst needs to look for ways to reduce the complexity and volatility of reported accounting numbers into a simple form that assists interpretation. Putting numbers into rolling trends is one way of doing this. The length of the trend period is a matter of judgment. But three to five years is usually acceptable.

Inter-company comparisons

A further type of comparative financial analysis can involve reporting companies. In addition to monitoring the financial performance and position of a single company over several periods (as above), the financial analyst can compare similar companies in the industry or commercial sector in order to determine significant differences that signal whether the company is under or out-performing its competitors. As with inter-period comparisons, inter-company comparisons permit informed decisions to be made by financial statement users such as shareholders and lenders. The comparisons are consistent with other areas of human activity. For example, when a doctor completes a health check on a middle aged woman, he can relate the medical results to his experience or database of other middle aged women. More specifically, he may be able to compare his patient's results to norms that are averages constructed from studies of numerous middle aged women.

Inter-company comparisons of financial results are intended to detect significant differences in profitability, cash flow, and financial position that ought to be of interest or concern to the financial analyst. The following example compares balance sheets in a summarized format. The comparison could have been of profit statements or cash flow statements. It could also have been more detailed if necessary.

Comparative Analysis of Balance Sheets 2006 (£)

Company	A £000	B £000	C £000	D £000	E £000	Total £000
Fixed tangible assets	25,000	34,000	35,000	30,000	44,000	168,000
Intangible assets	5,000	—	8,000	—	4,000	17,000
Current assets	18,000	23,000	20,000	37,000	24,000	122,000
Total assets	**48,000**	**57,000**	**63,000**	**67,000**	**72,000**	**307,000**
Current liabilities	12,000	10,000	19,000	15,000	14,000	70,000
Long-term liabilities	12,000	24,000	6,000	30,000	15,000	87,000
Shareholders' equity	24,000	23,000	38,000	22,000	43,000	150,000
Total obligations	**48,000**	**57,000**	**63,000**	**67,000**	**72,000**	**307,000**

The above summary analysis is expressed in monetary amounts taken from the published balance sheets of each company. There are five companies and each has business operations that are classified in the same industry. This makes comparisons easier as each company should be dealing with similar economic circumstances and problems. The numerical size of each company, however, varies—from total assets of £48,000,000 to £72,000,000. There is an overall difference of 50%. However, it does not necessarily mean that Company A is two-thirds the size of Company E. The assets (particularly fixed assets) of E could be more recent than those of A, and A's use of its assets could be more productive than that of E.

The comparison reveals differences not only in the numerical amounts for each asset and obligation type but also in the numerical totals. This makes comparisons difficult to read. Therefore, one means of assisting the financial analyst is to translate the numerical amounts to percentages and to provide percentages for the total (to give some form of average for the five companies as a whole). This translation is made below. The percentages are based on the numerical totals for each company.

Comparative Analysis of Balance Sheets 2006 (%)

Company	A %	B %	C %	D %	E %	Total %
Fixed tangible assets	52	60	55	45	61	55
Intangible assets	10	—	13	—	5	5
Current assets	38	40	32	55	34	40
Total assets	**100**	**100**	**100**	**100**	**100**	**100**
Current liabilities	25	18	30	22	19	23
Long-term liabilities	25	42	10	45	21	28
Shareholders' equity	50	40	60	33	60	49
Total obligations	**100**	**100**	**100**	**100**	**100**	**100**

Translating accounting numbers to percentages removes the problem of numerical size differences for individual assets and obligations and their totals. The comparison becomes easier to make. The following comments relate first to assets and then to liabilities and equity.

(1) On average, the companies have 55% of their assets in fixed tangible assets, 5% in intangibles, and 40% in current assets. This can be used as a broad comparative benchmark. Companies B and E have the greatest proportions of fixed assets and Company D the least, indicating that it may have the oldest set of fixed assets. Companies B and D have no reported intangible assets. This may mean that they write off these assets more quickly than the other companies or that they do not invest in such resources. Company D has the highest proportion of current assets (perhaps indicating poor financial management due to overstocking or slow debtor collection) and Company C the least. The financial analyst needs to investigate all of these differences appropriately. This could be done, in part, by reference to industry averages in an attempt to have a benchmark for comparison.

(2) On average, these five companies fund their assets in the proportions of approximately one-half from shareholders' equity, one-fifth from current liabilities, and the remainder from long-term debt. Again, these data form a benchmark to compare with individual companies. Companies B and E seem to depend less on current liabilities than the other companies and Company C more so. Companies B, C, and D have differing long-term debt situations—B and D have proportionally more debt and C has proportionally less. Companies C and E are proportionally funded more by equity than the others—particularly D with one-third. Again, these differences could be bench-marked with industry averages.

(3) From these comparisons, Company D seems to be very different from the other four companies in terms of asset composition and funding. It has proportionally more current assets and long-term debt. Companies C and E are predominantly funded by equity and investment is predominantly in fixed tangible and intangible assets. These differences need to be used in conjunction with similar studies of profitability and cash flow. Reasons for the differences need to be found. The main point at this stage is that differences have been identified for further investigation. The latter will involve the use of calculated financial ratios.

Lesson 10.3 Comparisons
The analysis of corporate financial statements is essentially a comparative exercise in which the financial results of a reporting company are compared with those of previous periods, similar companies, and industry averages. Financial results therefore cannot be examined in isolation. They need to be seen in a context—either within the recent past of the reporting company or its competitors.

Inter-company comparisons of reported financial results make sense when the comparisons are of reasonably similar companies. It makes no sense to compare the financial results of different companies because their inherent structural, organizational, and economic differences create accounting differences that are hard to interpret—i.e. how much of an inter-company difference in profits is due to the companies being different and how much is due to differences in the quality of their operations, products, and management. Again, this is little different from comparisons in other aspects of human activity. A doctor, for example, would not compare the health characteristics of a 20-year-old male with those of a 90-year-old female. Instead, he would wish to compare the characteristics of 20-year-old males or 90-year-old females.

However, in corporate financial analysis, finding comparable companies is not without its problems. No two companies are exactly identical. As shown above, there are differences in size that may influence the comparison—e.g. larger companies may have economies of scale not enjoyed by smaller companies. Two companies can be in the same business and of the same size but have asset structures of different ages—e.g. in relation to fixed tangible assets. Two companies can be in the same business and of the same size and age of asset but produce and sell different mixes of goods or services—e.g. two newspaper companies can produce different newspaper types. For these reasons, it is important that the financial analyst is aware of the limitations of comparative exercises and is therefore willing to determine not only the numerical differences between apparently similar companies but also the reasons for these differences.

> **Lesson 10.4 Interpreting differences**
> It is rare to find two absolutely identical companies with which to apply financial analysis. It is therefore difficult to isolate differences in financial results that are due to superior products, services, operations, and management.

NATURE AND PURPOSE OF FINANCIAL RATIOS

Having examined the use of reported accounting numbers to provide an overview of corporate performance and position by means of common-sizing, it is now relevant to look at financial analysis in a more specific way. Much of this concerns the production and interpretation of individual financial ratios that are designed to assist a variety of decisions. Before explaining these ratios, it is necessary to explain what is meant by a decision in this context and the main decisions that require analyzed financial information in ratio form.

Decisions

A decision typically involves the use of information in order to formulate options regarding courses of action (e.g. whether or not to eat, dress, shower, etc.). The decision itself is the choice of a particular option. The decisions that relate to the financial analysis of calculated ratios are generally to do with the optimal use of scarce economic resources. Investors want to invest in shares that provide the greatest amount of dividend return and capital appreciation. Lenders want to lend to customers who will pay the interest and capital payments in full and on time. Suppliers want to provide goods and services on credit to customers who will pay cash due in full and within the credit period agreed. In these circumstances, there are certain basic principles relating decisions to financial ratios.

(1)   In order to make rational decisions such as investing, lending, and credit, decision makers must assess the future. They therefore need reliable information that provides insights into the future. For example, the investor is interested in future dividends from a company and uses financial information to estimate or predict these dividends. Financial ratios form part of that information. In other words, financial ratios assist in the predictions on which decisions are based.

(2)   In order to monitor the success or failure of prior decisions such as investing, lending, and credit, decision makers need reliable information to determine the outcomes of these decisions. For example, the investor who is a shareholder examines the financial statements of a reporting company in which he has invested in order to obtain information with which to assess its financial performance and position, and therefore the wisdom of continuing to be a shareholder in it. In other words, financial ratios should assist in the evaluation of past decisions.

Lesson 10.5 Decisions, ratios, and consistency
Financial ratios are based on reported financial information describing past corporate business activity. However, they are used to satisfy two dimensions of decision making. The first is the making of decisions based on predictions of the future, and the second is the monitoring of outcomes of past decisions. For this reason, it is important that reported financial information and financial ratios are calculated on the same bases over time in order to ensure numerical consistency between prediction and outcome.

Decision types

As suggested above and in earlier chapters, there are various decisions that can be informed by reported accounting information and the financial ratios derived from them. Existing and potential shareholders are interested in dividend returns and capital appreciation, and data reflecting profitability are important in these matters. Profits are the basis for dividends and share price movements. Investors are also concerned about the financial viability of the reporting company and data concerning cash flow and financial position are equally of interest to them. Lenders are interested in interest and capital repayments and cash flow data are of primary concern. But so too are ratios reflecting profitability (from which OCF is generated) and financial position. Similar arguments can be made for other decision types such as supplying goods on credit and it can be concluded that most financial ratios are potentially useful to most types of decision makers with an interest in corporate financial performance and position.

Objectives

Financial ratios are calculated and interpreted in order to provide relevant information for decision making purposes. Ratios attempt to standardize financial information in a way that is comprehensible and useable. They are also calculated in order to assist in making comparisons (over time and between companies) that contain differences that ought to be considered when making decisions.

Ratio process

There are several stages in the process of calculating and using financial ratios. These are as follows:

(1)   The accounting numbers that can be related in a ratio form need to be identified. In particular, it must make sense to associate numbers in this way. For example,

the accounting numbers for sales and GP profit can be linked in the GP ratio. Sales are the means of generating profit and GP is the outcome from selling after taking into account the cost of the goods or services sold. The ratio of GP to sales can also be converted into a percentage by multiplying by 100. The GP percentage is a familiar means of assessing profitability over time and between similar companies. A ratio that does not make sense in terms of association is not likely to be a good basis for a decision. For example, relating sales to the height of the CEO may be possible numerically but does not provide a meaningful interpretation or prediction of corporate performance (unless there is a prior and accepted theory associating sales performance with the height of senior managers).

(2) The associated numbers can be related as a ratio by a process of arithmetical division and then multiplication by 100 if they are to be expressed in percentage form. There is nothing judgmental or controversial in this stage.

(3) The calculated ratios need to be placed in a context of other similar ratios—either for the same company (in the form of an inter-period analysis) or for different companies in the same industry or location. As previously stated, this part of the process is much more subjective and requires care and awareness of the need for consistency in the underlying accounting. Overall, this stage is concerned with providing the financial analyst with a series of ratios to interpret.

(4) The series of inter-period or inter-company ratios are then reviewed with the objective of identifying significant differences in financial performance and position that could influence a decision. This stage in the process is judgmental and much depends on the experience of the financial analyst with respect to (a) identifying differences and (b) realizing their decision significance.

(5) The final step is to make the decision based on the analyzed and interpreted ratios. This part of the process can be done by the financial analyst but, more likely, it will be the responsibility of others who have been given the ratio-based evaluation by the analyst. For example, in share investment, decisions are usually taken by investment managers who rely on ratio analyses from professional financial analysts.

The overall process described above is commonly described as fundamental analysis. The idea behind such a process is that it focuses on the fundamental aspects of a company's financial performance and position—i.e. various aspects of its profitability, cash flow, and financial position. The rational for such a focus is that, if these fundamentals are not in order, then the viability and survivability of a company must be in doubt. Fundamental analysis can be applied to all decisions relating to a company, including investing, lending, and supplying. It is to be contrasted with another form of analysis that is applied solely to the investment decision. This is technical analysis, in which the financial analyst examines market-based data such as share prices. Examining the movement and trend in share prices provides the analyst with the basis for predicting future movements and trends. Justification for the use of technical rather than fundamental analysis relates to an argument that share prices are determined by decisions informed by the analysis of corporate fundamentals.

FINANCIAL RATIO CRITERIA

Financial ratios are arithmetic calculations but they need to conform to certain criteria if they are to have meaning. These criteria include the following:

(1) Financial ratios only have meaning if they can be compared over time, between companies (as in common-size analysis), and with industry averages. This means that they need to be based on comparable accounting numbers in which there has been consistency in calculation. A ratio that has been prepared from accounting numbers dependent on certain accounting methods is going to be different from a ratio based on other methods. Such a difference may mislead the financial analyst into believing that differences reflect operational and managerial performance differences. For example:

Two-Is-Company Ltd has sales of £100,000 for the year 2006. The cost of these sales using a particular accounting method of inventory calculation is £75,000. Three-Is-A-Crowd Ltd also has sales of £100,000. However, using another accounting method of inventory calculation, cost of sales is £85,000. Both companies have made identical sales and bought identical goods for sale at the same price and time. GP should be identical. However, with Two-Is-Company Ltd, GP is £100,000 − 75,000 = £25,000. This gives a GP margin (GPM) on sales of £25,000/100,000 or 25%. With Three-Is-A-Crowd Ltd, the GP is £100,000 − 85,000 = £15,000 and the GPM is £15,000/100,000 or 15%. The first company appears to be much more profitable than the second with a margin of 25% compared to 15%. Yet, in reality, operational performance has been identical. The difference has been caused by the accounting choice of method.

Consistency is also a limiting factor with respect to comparable financial ratios. For example, assume the above situation is entirely for Two-Is-Company Ltd—i.e. the sales, cost of sales, and GP numbers are for 2006 and 2007. If so, the GPM for 2006 is 25% and that for 2007 is 15%. This appears to reveal a deteriorating profit performance. GP has fallen by 40% or (25 − 15)/25 but this is due to a change in inventory accounting method rather than to operational or managerial performance changes. The financial analyst therefore needs to ensure that ratios are based on consistent accounting method.

(2) One of the most intractable problems in financial ratio analysis is that of materiality—i.e. judging the significance of a change in ratio or a difference between ratios. Materiality concerns whether such a change or difference would be likely to influence the particular decision to which it is applied. This is also a problem for accountants, managers, directors, and auditors when making decisions about disclosing information in corporate financial statements. Would the disclosure make a difference to an investment or a lending decision? For example, assume the CEO of a company defrauded it of £500 of travelling expenses. The company's profit before tax was £1,000,000. In relative terms, the fraud is an immaterial percentage of profit. However, in absolute terms, it reflects a lack of honesty in a senior manager that ought to be known by the shareholders. Financial ratios create similar

questions. For example, assume the EPS of a company is calculated at £3.50 and the stock market was expecting a figure of £3.60. The absolute difference of ten pence and the relative difference of 3% appear immaterial. However, investors in markets such as this take a different view and even a small difference is regarded as material. The financial analyst needs to be sensitive to these matters.

(3) One of the most obvious features of financial ratio analysis is that it is possible to prepare a considerable number of different ratios from the available accounting numbers. Many of these ratios are reflecting a slightly different dimension to a particular aspect of corporate financial performance (e.g. profitability). For this reason, there is a danger to the financial analyst that a proliferation of ratios may prevent key features of performance being detected—a case of too much information clouding the issue. It is therefore important for the analyst to concentrate on sufficient ratios to determine the key features of corporate performance and only to use others if more information can be derived from them.

Lesson 10.6 Comparable ratios
Financial ratios must be comparable over time and between companies, consistently calculated, and avoid the confusion of too much information preventing the message being understood.

FINANCIAL RATIO LIMITATIONS

Before proceeding to explain and use financial ratios, it is important to provide a reminder or health warning about them. In fact, they have several limitations that militate against their usefulness. These are as follows:

(1) Financial ratios are mainly based on reported accounting numbers in corporate financial statements. They therefore contain all the accounting limitations of these numbers including the flexibility and subjectivity of GAAP, the possible presence of creative accounting practices, and the inherent limitations of historical cost accounting. If there is a problem in GAAP application or senior managers have manipulated the numbers, this will be absorbed into the ratio. The financial analyst must therefore not over-rely on reported accounting numbers and must examine them carefully before use in order to detect any sign of these problems. Most of the most significant accounting frauds of recent times have produced numbers that financial analysts have used without questioning. That is one reason why the frauds were allowed to continue for so long undetected.

(2) Financial ratios are essentially used in a comparative context—i.e. over time and between companies. If the ratio-based analyses are to make sense to the financial analyst, then it is necessary that the accounting numbers and the ratio calculations are produced using consistent practices. For this reason, the financial analyst should be reasonably certain that the basic accounting numbers are calculated on the same GAAP basis and that the ratio calculations follow a similar treatment. GAAP consistency is problematic because the financial analyst has nothing to do with the preparation of the accounting numbers in the financial

statements. However, it is essential that the analyst examines these statements in order to determine for the statement of accounting policies which practices have been used in key areas such as inventory and fixed asset depreciation. What to do if there are differences between periods and, particularly, companies is a problem unless the financial analyst attempts to recalculate the numbers using the same accounting practice. Consistency in calculating ratios is less of a problem as the analyst is making the calculations. Thus, when interpreting financial ratios for decision making purposes, it is possible that differences may be due to inconsistency in the application of GAAP by the reporting companies concerned.

(3) Financial ratios attempt to standardize reported accounting information in such a way that the analyst and decision maker can find it easier to assess the financial performance and position of reporting companies. However, standardization of this nature tends to mask the effect of size in corporate business activity. The ratios for companies A and B can be identical and yet A can be many times larger than B and therefore have opportunities of economies of scale in purchasing, manufacturing, and selling which should translate into superior performance and position. The financial analyst needs to be aware of this hidden problem and take it into account when interpreting ratios prior to taking decisions.

(4) Financial ratios are arithmetical calculations that contain particular distorting features and assumptions that may invalidate their use in comparative analyses. The detail of these problems is beyond the scope of the book but the reader should be at least aware of their existence. For example, negative accounting numbers such as losses create problems when calculating profit-based ratios (i.e. what does a negative percentage mean in a GPM calculation?). Also, ratios assume a linear relationship between numerator (e.g. GP) and denominator (e.g. sales) (i.e. if sales increase by 5% then GP will increase by 5%). In corporate business, such linearity is rare and accounting numbers may increase or decrease at different rates due to economies and diseconomies of scale.

(5) As indicated in earlier sections of this chapter, one safeguard against the problems of comparing financial ratios of individual companies is to assess them in relation to industry averages. Professional analysts working for investment and financial news organizations provide these averages as a service that can be purchased by individual analysts. Industry averages have the advantage of large numbers of companies being incorporated into the calculations and differences in accounting method and size being countered by this factor. The danger, however, of industry averages is that they do not represent the performance or position of any specific company. This is a similar problem to the use of a retail price index to indicate price inflation. The change in the index rarely matches the inflation with which an individual consumer has to cope.

Lesson 10.7 Limiting factors
Financial ratios can be limited by a variety of factors of which accounting practice flexibility and lack of consistency are the most serious.

COMPUTATION AND INTERPRETATION OF FINANCIAL RATIOS

This section introduces the calculation and interpretation of financial ratios. The primary emphasis is on interpretation. However, it is necessary to provide a basis for understanding through the fundamental steps of calculation. The financial ratios described can be divided into two main categories of calculation. These are:

Internal ratios

These are ratio calculations that use numerators and denominators taken directly from the reported financial statements. They are therefore derived from the same database and have been subject to the same set of accounting practices. An example already met in the text is the GPM—where the GP is related to sales. Both accounting numbers are disclosed in the reported profit statement.

External ratios

These are ratio calculations that use a mixture of numerators and denominators taken from the reported financial statements and external databases such as stock market price lists. These ratios therefore use numbers that are not derived from the same database and it is essential that they are related. An example dealt with in an earlier chapter is the PER that compares share price with reported EPS as an indicator of ROI.

The financial ratios covered in the following sections of this chapter deal with three main areas of corporate financial performance—i.e. profitability, liquidity, and financial structure.

Profitability

These are ratios that examine how profitable the reporting company has been in relation to such matters as sales (e.g. the amount of profit earned per £1 of sales) and capital employed (e.g. the amount of profit earned per £1 of shareholder capital employed). These ratios allow the financial analyst to assess the relative success of corporate management to generate profitability for purposes of providing funding for future replacement and growth of business projects and returns to shareholders. They also include the use of cash flow data where relevant.

Liquidity

These are ratios that focus on the ability of corporate management to generate liquid funds to meet immediate obligation such as payments to suppliers and employees, and longer-term obligations such debt repayments. These ratios aid the financial analyst interested in determining the quality of the reporting company's management of cash resources and include the use of cash flow data where relevant.

Financial structure and performance

These are ratios that particularly are concerned with the quality of the financial management of the reporting company. This deals mainly with the financing of the company's operations by share capital and debt, and the impact this has on the market performance of these funding sources when shares and debt are traded on a recognized stock exchange.

FINANCIAL RATIOS AND PROFITABILITY

The aim of these financial ratios is to assist in determining how successful the reporting company has been in terms of profitable trading activity. In particular, the ratios attempt to indicate how successful the company's managers have been in utilizing the assets with which they have been entrusted by the shareholders. This is usually referred to as efficiency analysis in the sense that the profitability ratios attempt to signal how efficiently corporate resources have been used. The absolute size of the accounting number for profit is not, of itself, sufficient to gauge such success or efficiency. It has to be related to other relevant matters to provide signals of performance.

Return on investment

This financial ratio is alternatively called the return on capital employed and relates a defined profit number (as numerator) to a defined capital number (as denominator) in order to determine the yield or return on shareholders' investment in the reporting company. The ratio ROI is:

$$(\text{Defined periodic profit} \div \text{defined capital employed}) \times 100$$

Defined periodic profit is typically taken as either NP before tax or NP after tax, and defined capital employed is usually year-end shareholders' equity (i.e. paid-up share capital plus reserves, including profits retained). For example, assuming reported NP after tax for the year 2006 is £126,000 and year-end shareholders' equity is £578,000, then ROI for 2006 is:

$$(£126,000 \div 578,000) \times 100 = 21.8\%$$

In other words, in approximate terms, for every £1 of capital employed in the company, 22 pence of after-tax profit has been earned. This indicator of profitability can then be compared to previous indicators for the same company or similar indicators for companies in the same industry or who are potential sources of investment. In this respect, the financial analyst is looking for changes or differences that could affect share investment decisions. For example, if the average ROI for this type of company was 25% then this company's return at less than 22% could precipitate a decision to sell shares or not buy shares in it.

Capital employed can also be defined as total assets in this financial ratio. If this is the case then it is important that the numerator and denominator are comparable. Capital is defined in terms of all resources used by the company irrespective of type of funding. Therefore profit must be defined in the same way—i.e. before deduction for any interest return to lenders. For example, following the previous numbers and assuming total assets were £823,000 and profits before interest and tax were £161,000, then ROI would be:

$$(£161,000 \div 823,000) \times 100 = 19.6\%$$

Again, this indicator needs to be compared with previous numbers for the company and with those for other similar companies in order to judge its merit.

Because the defined periodic profit number covers an annual period, it is sensible to define capital employed for that period. The above examples have used the year-end figure rather than an average for the period. What needs to be done is calculate the average capital employed for the year by taking the opening and closing numbers and dividing by two and then relating the result to the profit number. For example, assuming opening capital for 2006 is £492,000 and closing capital is £578,000, and NP after tax is £126,000, then:

Average capital is $(£492,000 + 578,000) = £1,070,000 \div 2 = £535,000$; and

ROI is $(£126,000 \div 535,000) \times 100 = 23.6\%$

Alternatively, the denominator can be averaged using total assets. For example, assuming profits before tax and interest of £161,000, opening total assets of £784,000 and closing total assets of £823,000, then:

Average total assets are $(£784,000 + 823,000) = £1,607,000 \div 2 = £803,500$;

and; ROI is $(£161,000 \div 803,500) \times 100 = 20\%$

In other words, taking an average capital employed perspective, ROI is 23.6%— compared to 21.8% on a year-end capital employed basis, and taking an average total assets approach, 20% compared to 19.6%. All of these indicators are valid but must be used consistently to be meaningful comparatively.

Lesson 10.8 Multiple returns

There is no absolute definition for financial ratios such as ROI. This means that there are several possible returns to be calculated and assessed based on the same set of accounting numbers. Varying the definition of these numbers in the ratio provides different returns. It is vital that the financial analyst uses the same definitions on a consistent basis otherwise differences in returns may be due to ratio definitional differences rather than operational or managerial factors.

Financial ratios such as ROI can be affected by creative accounting practices. Such practices change the accounting numbers that form the defined numerator and denominator in a ratio. For example, assuming the profit and total assets numbers above (i.e. £161,000 and £823,000) and further assuming corporate management has created year-end sales by sending goods to customers without prior orders (sales and debtors increase by £50,000, cost of sales increases and inventory decreases by £35,000), then ROI becomes:

$$(£161,000 + 50,000 - 35,000) \div (£823,000 + 50,000 - 35,000) \times 100 = 21\%$$

In other words, the original return of 19.6% has been inflated to 21% by the additional £15,000 of profit on the creative sales transactions. Such an increase may be sufficient to meet market expectations or appear consistent with returns of previous periods, similar companies, or industry averages.

> **Lesson 10.9 Creative accounting**
> Creative accounting hidden in published financial statements also impacts the reliability and credibility of financial ratios based on manipulated accounting numbers.

Earnings per share

This particular ratio has been covered previously in Chapter 4 when explaining the profit statement. However, it is useful to provide a brief review of its nature, purpose, and calculative basis. EPS is typically defined in terms of NP after tax divided by the number of ordinary share units issued by the reporting company. For example, assuming that after-tax NP is £256,000 and 200,000 ordinary share units of £1 each have been issued, then:

$$EPS = £256,000 \div 200,000 = £1.28 \text{ per share unit}$$

Thus, if an individual shareholder owns 30,000 ordinary share units, then the after-tax NP attributable to that shareholding is:

$$£1.28 \times 30,000 = £38,400$$

EPS is therefore an indicator of share investment performance in the sense of identifying profitability associated with share capital. It has the advantage of apparent simplicity and is therefore capable of being compared over time and between companies. However, as with all accounting-based ratios, comparability depends on consistency in accounting method. EPS is also subject to creative accounting—probably more directly than any other financial indicator of performance because it focuses entirely on reported profit. Any attempt to manipulate profit up or down immediately affects earnings and inflates or deflates EPS accordingly. For example, assuming the above accounting numbers for reported profit and share units, also assume that profit has been inflated by £75,000 due to understating fixed asset depreciation by this amount. The EPS calculation then becomes:

$$£256,000 + 75,000 = £331,000 \div 200,000 = £1.66$$

In other words, EPS has increased from £1.28 to £1.66 as a result of an accounting manipulation and shareholders are misled about the reporting company's profitability. The calculation of EPS is subject to prescribed accounting standards throughout the world. The calculational rules vary through time and their detail is outside the scope of this book. However, reporting companies with accounting standard prescriptions are required to report EPS calculations and these should be used by the financial analyst in calculating further indicators of corporate performance such as the PER (explained in a later section of this chapter).

Profit margins

ROI and EPS are the broadest and most inclusive of profitability indications. Profit margins, on the other hand, are a set of ratios that constitute a subset of ROI and EPS. They are basic indicators of corporate management's ability to maximize sales and profit per £1 of sale or profit per £1 of assets. It should be noted, however, that margins are only one dimension of assessing managerial capability. They ignore, for example, the size of the capital investment in business operations needed to generate sales and profits. The most basic profit margin or ratio is that between sales and GP—i.e. GPM or profits before deduction of administrative, selling, and financing costs. The ratio is calculated as GP divided by sales and multiplied by 100. For example, assuming sales are £874,000 and cost of goods sold is £624,000, then:

$$\text{GPM} = £874{,}000 - 624{,}000 = (£250{,}000 \div 874{,}000) \times 100 = 28.6\%$$

In other words, the GPM earned on sales for the period was 28.6% or for every £1 of sales, the company earned nearly 29 pence of GP to cover administrative, selling, and financing costs. Such an indicator is relatively unique to specific business operations. For example, restaurants have typical GP percentages, as do car dealers, cement manufacturers, grocery stores, etc. The GP percentage of a specific company can therefore be compared by the financial analyst to industry norms in order to assess the company's performance. For example, if the industry average was 40% then approximately 29% is low in comparison and indicates probable weakness in the company's operations and management.

GPM is not the only margin that can interest the financial analyst. Any of the profit numbers reported in the profit statement can be related to the sales number. For example, NP after tax to sales describes the amount of profit available for dividend that has been generated from each £1 of sales. Assuming reported sales are £874,000 and after-tax NP is £89,000, then:

$$\text{Net profit margin (NPM)} = (£89{,}000 \div 874{,}000) \times 100 = 10.2\%$$

This means that approximately ten pence of every £1 of sales is available either for dividends to shareholders or retention in the reporting company.

> **Lesson 10.10 Profit margins**
> Profit margins are the most fundamental indicators of corporate profitability as they focus on the generation of profits through sale of goods or services.

Sales turnover

There is a further ratio that can be calculated using data derived from two of the above ratios—i.e. ROI (using after-tax profit and total assets) and profit margin (using after-tax profit and sales). Taking the four ingredients in these ratios and eliminating after-tax profit as common to both, what are left are total assets and sales. These can be related in a single ratio called sales turnover—i.e. sales divided by total assets (preferably based on the average assets for the year). This ratio provides an indication of how fast or slow assets are turned over each year in the generation of sales. For example, assuming sales of £874,000, after-tax profits of £126,000, and average total assets of £803,500, the following ratios can be calculated:

$$\text{NPM} = (£126,000 \div 874,000) \times 100 = 14.4\%$$

$$\text{ROI} = (£126,000 \div 803,500) \times 100 = 15.7\%$$

$$\text{Sales turnover} = £874,000 \div 803,500 = 1.088$$

What these ratios indicate is that, with a sales turnover of little more than one, an ROI of approximately 15% needs a NPM of about the same percentage. If the sales turnover had been two, on the other hand, an ROI of 15% could be obtained with a NPM of about 7%. In other words, the higher the turnover of sales, the smaller the NPM needs to be to obtain a specific ROI (and vice versa).

> **Lesson 10.11 Sales turnover**
> Corporate profitability is a function of two related matters. The first is the use of total assets to generate sales, and the second is the generation of profit from these sales. The more efficient the use of assets, the less the margin on sales that is necessary to achieve a particular return on these assets.

FINANCIAL RATIOS AND LIQUIDITY AND CASH FLOW

There are a number of ratios that provide indicators of a reporting company's ability to manage its liquid assets and generate cash flow. They mainly bear upon the issue of the company being able to meet its obligations in full and on time. They also relate to its ability to generate cash flow from its business operations (i.e. OCF) and use this in its various investment (ICF) and financing (FCF) activities. In other words, being a profitable company is insufficient for long-term viability and survival. Corporate management must be capable of using all of the resources at its disposal to generate profits that translate to cash flows useable in meeting debt obligations and financing new investment.

Working capital

The most basic ratio in the financial management of corporate assets is called the working capital ratio. Working capital is a term used in corporate financial management to denote the overall topic of managing a company's current assets and current liabilities. The working capital ratio is therefore an indicator of that management and takes the form of a numerator (current assets) and a denominator (current liabilities). By dividing the former by the latter, the ratio indicates how short-term obligations are covered by realizable assets. The objective of management is to ensure that there are sufficient current assets available to enable current liabilities to be paid when due. Shareholders and other financial statement users are interested in such information because it provides knowledge about management's ability to manage a viable and surviving company. If current liabilities are not paid in full and on time, this puts the continuing existence of the company at risk. Bankers and other creditors can take it to court for such failure and, in extreme cases, seek to have the company declared bankrupt. The following example illustrates the working capital ratio.

Jeepers Creepers Ltd is a company that owns several dance studios. In its published balance sheet for the year 2006 it discloses the following information:

	£
Current assets	
Inventory of unsold clothing and shoes	345,000
Amounts due by customers	271,000
Investments in stock market securities	23,000
Amount at bank	1,000
	640,000
Current liabilities	
Amount due to suppliers	285,000
Amount due to Inland Revenue	65,000
Bank loan repayable in 2007	100,000
Provisions for unpaid utilities	24,000
	474,000

The working capital ratio in this case is:

$$£640,000 \div 474,000 = 1.35$$

In other words, at the end of the year 2006, Jeepers Creepers Ltd had £1.35 of current assets available to meet every £1 of current liabilities that are due in the short-term (usually interpreted as the next 12 months). The company is therefore apparently solvent—i.e. there are sufficient realizable assets available to meet its immediate obligations. However, if current liabilities had exceeded current assets, then the company would be insolvent and unable to meet its obligations. For example, if current assets had been £340,000 and current liabilities £474,000, then:

$$£340,000 \div 474,000 = 0.72$$

That is, the company has 72 pence available to repay every £1 of immediate obligation. It is not apparently able to meet its current obligations in full. Not only does it not have a margin of safety (in the sense of surplus current assets), it has a deficiency of the latter. This does not reflect well on the quality of the financial management in the company. However, it should be noted that a positive working capital ratio need not always be an indicator of good financial management in the company. High current assets can be due to over-stocking inventory and not collecting cash from customers quickly. In other words, a high working capital ratio can indicate poor financial management.

The working capital ratio has the advantage of simplicity. It compares one accounting number with a seemingly related number and the interpretation of the ratio appears straight-forward. However, it also has several deficiencies of which the financial analyst ought to be aware.

(1) It is over-simplistic as it assumes all current assets are available to meet all current liabilities. First, not all current assets are available to be converted into cash needed to repay liabilities. In the example above, not all inventory can be sold immediately. Indeed, it is probable that not all goods held will ever be sold. Second, the amounts due by customers may be associated with credit terms and, again, the cash inflow may take some time as these terms are activated. Third, in contrast to the previous points, not all current liabilities require to be repaid immediately. In the above example, amounts due to suppliers and for utilities will probably be due according to contracted credit terms and the bank loan is repayable in the next year. Thus, the working capital ratio is only a broad-brush indicator of the reporting company's ability to repay its obligations.

(2) The reliability of the working capital ratio depends in large part on the sound-ness of the accounting classifications made in producing the accounting numbers for current assets and liabilities. Any errors in classification are bound to affect the magnitude of either the numerator or denominator in the ratio. In the above example, assume that in the unsold inventory number there is £100,000 for storage and display furniture. This is not a current asset and, instead, should be classi-fied as a depreciable fixed asset. The effect on the working capital ratio is that the numerator is overstated by £100,000 (it should be £540,000) and the ratio should be:

$$£540,000 \div 474,000 = 1.14$$

In other words, there is £1.14 rather than £1.35 of realizable assets available to repay each £1 of current liabilities. In addition, profits of the company are overstated by the amount of depreciation that should be written off the depreciable fixed asset. Such misclassifications are either erroneous or fraudulent. They should be discovered by a diligent auditor.

Misclassification can also affect the denominator in the working capital ratio. This particularly relates to the classification of loans in the balance sheet. Long-term loans can become part of current liabilities as they near repayment. If they are not reclassified, then the working capital ratio overstates the reporting company's ability to meet its obligations. For example, in the above example, assume that a loan of £50,000 (additional to that stated at £100,000) is also repayable in 2007 but has not been reclassified as a current liability. Current liabilities should be £524,000 and not £474,000 and the working capital ratio should be:

$$£640,000 \div 524,000 = 1.22$$

This compares to the original 1.35. As before, the misclassification can be erro-neous or fraudulent.

(3) The working capital ratio is dependent on accounting numbers generated by the historical cost accounting system. This particularly affects the numerator of current assets and typically this number is understated by a combination of factors—first, unsold inventory is usually disclosed in terms of its original cost and not sale value; and, second, debtors may be reduced to a conservative estimate of recovery due to provisions for possible bad debts. For example, in the above case, assume that the realizable value of unsold inventory is £518,000 and amounts due by customers eventually recovered £292,000. Given that investments and the bank balance are disclosed at their realizable values, this means that the realizable value of current assets is £518,000 + 292,000 + 23,000 + 1,000 = £834,000 and the working capital ratio becomes:

$$£834,000 \div 474,000 = 1.76$$

In other words, instead of £1.35 of available current assets for every £1 of current liability, there is £1.76.

(4) It is possible through creative accounting practices to manipulate the working capital ratio. This is a problem when there is an incentive to inflate the ratio—i.e. when key stakeholders in the reporting company look for specific ratio numbers before making crucial decisions. For example, bankers have been known to look for a specific level of working capital before lending (e.g. a working capital ratio of 2.00). In these cases, there is a temptation to inflate current assets or deflate current liabilities or both. In the above example, assume that the stated accounting numbers were draft figures and the board of directors knows that the company's bankers look for a ratio of 1.50 before lending. The company is negotiating a new loan of £150,000 to replace the loan of £100,000 repayable in 2007. The draft working capital ratio is 1.35. In order to inflate it to 1.50, the directors need to "find" additional current assets of £71,000—i.e. current assets of £711,000 (£640,000 + 71,000) to cover current liabilities of £474,000:

$$£711,000 \div 474,000 = 1.50$$

In order to increase current assets by £71,000, the directors could adopt a number of creative accounting practices—e.g. a more liberal provision for bad debts, an exaggeration of the costs of unsold inventory, or additional or false sales (selling to customers without prior orders). Alternatively, they could reduce current liabilities by delaying the recognition of credit purchases in 2006 to 2007. Sales at the beginning of 2007 could be accounted for at the end of 2006 to improve current assets. Obviously, diligent auditing ought to discover these manipulations. This does not prevent managers and directors trying and sometimes succeeding.

Quick ratio

A major problem with the working capital ratio is that it does not reflect the current ability of the reporting company to repay its current liabilities because not all of the current assets are in realized or readily realizable form (e.g. unsold inventory may take some time to convert into cash). For this reason, financial analysts prefer the quick ratio to assess a reporting company's ability to pay. The quick ratio is similar in structure to the working capital ratio with current assets as the numerator and current liabilities as the denominator. The difference is that current assets are defined as realized or readily realizable assets and therefore conventionally exclude inventory of unsold goods. Therefore, in the above example, current assets are redefined as £295,000 (£640,000 − 345,000 and with current liabilities as £474,000, then:

$$£295,000 \div 474,000 = 0.62$$

This means that, as at the end of the year 2006, Jeepers Creepers Ltd had 62 pence of realized or readily realizable assets to cover each £1 of current liabilities. This is a much more conservative indicator of the company's ability to pay (compared to a working capital ratio of £1.35), although it must be stated that:

(1) Not all current liabilities will be repayable immediately.
(2) Not all current assets are, in fact, readily realizable immediately (e.g. debtors).

The quick ratio is therefore a fallible indicator of corporate financial management and is subject to the same limitations as the working capital ratio (e.g. regarding matters such as classification and creative accounting). It needs to be interpreted with care and also within context—i.e. particularly in comparison to ratios for previous periods and for other similar companies and industries.

Lesson 10.12 Working capital and quick ratios I
It is important to assess how well or badly a reporting company is being managed financially. In this respect, the ability of managers and directors to ensure that the company has sufficient assets available to meet its known obligations when these become due. The working capital and quick ratios are designed to give general indications of the financial management of current assets and liabilities.

Lesson 10.13 Working capital and quick ratios II
There are no absolutely right or wrong numbers for working capital or quick ratios. As with all financial ratios, the analyst is looking for significant differences in the computed value of the ratio over time (for the same company) or between similar companies.

Cash flow generation

So far in this section, corporate liquidity has been examined in terms of static financial ratios. More specifically, the working capital and quick ratios provide information about corporate liquidity and ability to pay but are associated with the position of the reporting company at a specific date (i.e. typically the last day of the reporting period). Consequently, it is possible that an apparently liquid company at the end of 2006 can become illiquid at the beginning of 2007 as further events and transactions erode current assets or enlarge current liabilities or both.

For example, in the case of Jeepers Creepers Ltd, assume at the end of 2006 that £200,000 of the unsold inventory relates to dancing shoes and three months later it is discovered that there is a design flaw in the shoes that can seriously injure a dancer's foot. Also assume that there has been fundamentally no change in the other current asset and liability numbers as a result of business transactions in the three months. The unsold shoes are worthless. Current assets become £440,000 (£640,000 − 200,000) and the working capital ratio of £1.35 becomes:

$$£440,000 \div 474,000 = 0.93$$

In other words, the current (and quick) ratio is subject to the limitation of being static rather than dynamic in nature as a financial indicator. For this reason, it is useful for the financial analyst to examine indicators of cash flow as these typically indicate performance over time rather than at a point in time.

There are a number of relevant indicators of cash flow generation.

(1) **Cash flow conversion** The first cash flow indicator relates to the conversion of reported profits into cash flow (i.e. OCF). It takes the simple ratio OCF divided by NP after tax and attempts to describe how much OCF is generated from each £1 of equivalent NP. The idea behind the ratio is to provide an indicator of the effectiveness of corporate management in ensuring that profits are converted into cash flow that is usable for purposes of financing new investment or repaying long-term obligations. Accounting profits are based typically on credit transactions and involve adjustments for unsold inventory and provisions for unbilled expenses and revenues received in advance. Effective cash flow management ensures customers pay on time, unsold inventory is kept to a minimum, and suppliers are paid according to the terms of credit. There will always be differences between NP after tax and OCF but, over time, profits should generate an equivalent amount of OCF. If this does not occur, then the ratio may indicate that creative accounting practices are manufacturing profits that will never generate OCF. For example, assume the following reported accounting numbers for Jeepers Creepers Ltd for the years 2002 to 2006 inclusive.

	2002 £	2003 £	2004 £	2005 £	2006 £	Total £
OCF	125,000	136,000	15,000	−63,000	80,000	293,000
NP after tax	75,000	85,000	95,000	30,000	45,000	330,000

A simple examination of the two streams of accounting numbers reveal that profits have risen steadily before falling in 2005 and recovering somewhat in 2006. OCF has followed a similar but much more volatile trend. Overall, NP exceeds OCF for the five years. This is not unusual or surprising. The cash flow conversion ratios supplement this general conclusion.

Year	Ratio Calculation	Ratio
2002	£125,000 ÷ 75,000	1.67
2003	£136,000 ÷ 85,000	1.60
2004	£15,000 ÷ 95,000	0.16
2005	£−63,000 ÷ 30,000	−2.10
2006	£80,000 ÷ 45,000	1.78
Total	**£293,000 ÷ 330,000**	**0.89**

Overall, Jeepers Creepers Ltd has generated 89 pence of OCF for every £1 of after-tax NP between 2002 and 2006. In other words, management has converted approximately 89% of profits into cash flow. Its annual success in this regard reveals a downward trend from £1.67 of OCF per £1 of profit in 2002 to −£2.10 to £1 in 2005. In 2006, the ratio reverts to a level above that for 2002 at £1.78 to £1. These ratios indicate a cycle of economic activity as old projects wind down in the early years of the period and new projects come on stream later.

(2) **Operating to investment cash flow** Companies need to convert profits into OCF in order to assist in the financing of new investment (either to replace old projects or grow). The ratio relationship between OCF and ICF reveals the extent to which management of the reporting company has used OCF to fund ICF. Being able to fund ICF with internally-generated cash flow avoids the need to raise funds externally through share capital or long-term debt. In other words, OCF divided by ICF indicates the use by the company of internally-generated cash flow. For example, assume the previous OCF numbers for Jeepers Creepers Ltd and the following ICF numbers for the five years:

Year	£
2002	17,000
2003	21,000
2004	139,000
2005	106,000
2006	52,000
Total	**335,000**

The ratio OCF to ICF is as follows for each year and in total:

Year	Ratio Calculation	Ratio
2002	£125,000 ÷ −17,000	7.35
2003	£136,000 ÷ −21,000	6.48
2004	£15,000 ÷ −139,000	0.11
2005	£−63,000 ÷ −106,000	—
2006	£80,000 ÷ −52,000	1.54
Total	**£293,000 ÷ −335,000**	**0.87**

Over the five years, the company has had £0.87 of OCF available for every £1 of ICF needed. This means that it has had the capacity to finance its investment programme from internally-generated funds. This is particularly the case in 2002 and 2003 when capital expenditure was low (i.e. £7.35 and £6.48 of OCF per £1 of ICF), less so in 2004 and 2005 when it was much higher (£0.11 and £1.54 respectively), and not at all in 2005 because of negative OCF.

(3) **Operating to financing cash flow** Companies fund their investment needs from a combination of OCF and FCF. OCF is also required for helping to repay long-term debt when this becomes due. The ratio of OCF to FCF provides an indicator of the reporting company's relative dependence on internally-generated funds as compared to externally-generated cash flow. For example, in addition to the above OCF numbers for Jeepers Creepers Ltd, assume the following FCF numbers:

Year	£
2002	−55,000
2003	−45,000
2004	65,000
2005	45,000
2006	10,000
Total	**20,000**

These numbers indicate that the company repaid debt in 2002 and 2003, borrowed £120,000 over the next three years, and had a net new borrowing of £20,000 overall. The ratio OCF to FCF is as follows:

Year	Ratio Calculation	Ratio
2002	£125,000 ÷ −55,000	2.27
2003	£136,000 ÷ −45,000	3.02
2004	£15,000 ÷ 65,000	0.23
2005	£−63,000 ÷ 45,000	−1.40
2006	£80,000 ÷ 10,000	8.00
Total	**£293,000 ÷ 20,000**	**14.65**

Over the five years, Jeepers Creepers Ltd generated £14.65 of OCF for every £1 of FCF, revealing it was largely self-financing in terms of cash flow. In 2002 and 2003, the company used OCF to reduce long-term debt (i.e. it had £2.27 of OCF to cover every £1 of debt repayment in 2002 and £3.02 in 2003). In 2004, the company has £0.23 of OCF for every £1 of new loan. In 2006, the figure was £8.00. In 2005, there was £1.40 of OCF deficit for every £1 of new loan.

Lesson 10.14 External funding dependence
The analysis of cash flow is a complex exercise in determining how effective corporate management is in converting profits into needed OCF, how OCF is used to fund ICF and reduce debt, and therefore how dependent the company is on externally-generated funding.

(4) **Working capital management** There are three further ratios used by financial analysts to assess the quality of the working capital and cash flow management of

the reporting company. These relate to control of inventory, debtors, and creditors. Minimizing current assets such as inventory and debtors is crucial to maximizing OCF. Unsold inventory typically involves prior cash outflow due to payments for raw materials, wages, and overheads. Reducing inventory quantities therefore reduces cash outflow. It also increases cash inflow if the reduction is due to sale. Debtors represent uncollected cash inflow. Reducing debtors through smaller credit periods and efficient collection procedures increases cash inflow. The inventory and debtor turnover ratios provide indicators of how successful management has been in minimizing inventory and debtor levels. In addition, maximizing current liabilities such as creditors assists in improving OCF due to delays in paying creditors. The creditors' turnover ratio indicates management's performance in this regard.

Inventory turnover

This ratio calculates the average holding time for unsold inventory (including work-in-progress where relevant) during a reporting period. The calculation has a numerator of cost of sales for the period (representing the volume of inventory sold during the period) and a denominator of the average inventory for the period (representing the average volume of inventory held during the period). The arithmetical result is a figure that represents the number of times that inventory has been turned over and replaced during the period. The faster the turnover of inventory, the quicker the cash flow cycle from outflow to inflow. By dividing the inventory turnover figure into 365 days (or the number of operational days in the year), an indication is given of the average number of days of inventory held in the period. Corporate management should be attempting to reduce this figure to the minimum conducive to efficient business operations—i.e. the physical level necessary to satisfy customer orders promptly. Many businesses attempt to operate in what is called a just-in-time environment in which inventory is delivered to the premises in time for manufacture or sale. The financial analyst looks for an inventory turnover figure that reflects efficiency norms in the industry concerned. A turnover that is slower than in previous years or compared to similar companies indicates ineffective management of inventory levels and therefore a negative impact on OCF. The following example, illustrates these points.

Bright-Lights Ltd is a manufacturer of light fittings for homes and offices. The following accounting numbers have been extracted from its published financial statements for the years 2004, 2005, and 2006.

	2004 £	2005 £	2006 £
Opening inventory	304,000	389,000	421,000
Closing inventory	389,000	421,000	475,000
Cost of goods sold	1,670,000	1,892,000	2,116,000

These numbers are the basis for calculating the stocks turnover ratios for each of the three years.

	2004	2005	2006
	£	£	£
Cost of goods sold	1,670,000	1,892,000	2,116,000
÷			
Average inventory*	347,000	405,000	448,000
=			
Inventory turnover	4.81	4.67	4.72
365			
÷			
Inventory turnover	76 days	78 days	77 days

*(Opening inventory + closing inventory) ÷ 2

In each of the three years, inventory turned over approximately less than five times annually or once every 76 to 78 days. There is relative stability in these numbers and the analyst would be required to judge them in terms of comparable figures for similar companies and from industry sources. For example if the industry inventory turnover for 2006 was 9.25 this indicates that, on average, companies in that industry turned over their inventory once every 39 days (i.e. 365 ÷ 9.25). This is approximately twice as much as Bright-Lights Ltd and indicates a negative effect on its OCF.

Debtors turnover

A similar exercise can be done with debtors. In this case, the analyst is attempting to determine how often debtors are turned over or how many days of credit on average are given to customers. The greater the turnover of debtors, the less credit is being given, and the speedier the cash inflow from customers—thus improving OCF. The numerator of the ratio is sales for the reporting period and the denominator is the average debtors for the period. By dividing the ratio number into 365, the analyst derives the average number of days credit given to customers. For example, the following accounting numbers relate to the sales and debtors of Bright-Lights Ltd for 2004, 2005, and 2006.

	2004	2005	2006
	£	£	£
Opening debtors	187,000	201,000	258,000
Closing debtors	201,000	258,000	310,000
Sales	2,356,000	2,668,000	2,984,000

The debtors turnover ratios for each year are calculated as follows:

	2004 £	**2005** £	**2006** £
Sales	2,356,000	2,668,000	2,984,000
÷			
Average debtors*	194,000	230,000	284,000
=			
Debtors turnover	12.14	11.60	10.51
365			
÷			
Debtors turnover	30 days	31 days	35 days

*(Opening debtors + closing debtors) ÷ 2

In this case, the company appears to have a slowing debtors turnover and credit period—from approximately 30 days in 2004 to 35 days in 2006. This is not good news for OCF as cash is flowing into the company more slowly. It should be noted that debtors turnover does not apply to companies operating retail businesses with no credit to customers.

Creditors turnover

This ratio provides similar information to that for debtors. Using cost of goods sold and average creditors for the period, then dividing the result into 365, the ratio indicates the average credit period taken by the company from its suppliers. The basic idea here is that the company ought to be maximizing these credit terms without causing upset to suppliers and therefore endangering the flow of needed supplies of goods and services. This aspect of financial management is designed to minimize cash outflow and improve OCF. Assume the following accounting numbers for Bright-Lights Ltd for the years 2004, 2005, and 2006.

	2004 £	**2005** £	**2006** £
Opening creditors	195,000	217,000	301,000
Closing creditors	217,000	301,000	395,000
Cost of goods sold	1,670,000	1,892,000	2,116,000

The creditors turnover ratios for each year are calculated as follows:

	2004 £	**2005** £	**2006** £
Cost of goods sold	1,670,000	1,892,000	2,116,000
÷			
Average creditors*	206,000	259,000	348,000
=			
Creditors turnover	8.11	7.31	6.08
365			
÷			
Creditors turnover	45 days	50 days	60 days

*(Opening creditors + closing creditors) ÷ 2

The above ratios indicate that Bright-Lights Ltd was taking 45 days of credit from suppliers in 2004. This increased to 50 days in 2005 and 60 days in 2006, indicating potential problems with suppliers. Although the increased credit is useful for improving OCF, it is done at a risk of alienating suppliers and creating supply problems in the future. It should be noted that creditors turnover does not apply to companies operating retail businesses that purchase for cash only.

Lesson 10.15 Working capital management

Companies survive because they are profitable in the long-term and able to convert profits into OCF. A great deal of the conversion process is due to effective management of working capital—specifically inventory, debtors, and creditors. By reducing inventory and debtors to a minimum and increasing creditors to a maximum, OCF is improved. Ratios reflecting inventory, debtors, and creditors turnover are useful indicators of the reporting company's management of working capital and OCF.

ILLUSTRATION 15 JUST-IN-CASE LTD AND ON-THE-BUTTON LTD

The management of short-term corporate assets and liabilities, and the need to be profitable and to generate cash flow, are brought together in this illustration. Just-In-Case Ltd and On-the-Button Ltd are small trading companies that buy and sell materials and goods for the home sewing and quilting market. They both compete in the same town. Just-In-Case Ltd operates with inventory of materials and goods which it buys on credit and provides credit terms to its customers. On-the-Button Ltd operates with no inventory and has no credit transactions. When a customer makes an order the goods are purchased for cash and delivered to the customer for cash. The following transactions are typical of each company during the year 2006.

	Just-In-Case Ltd £	On-the-Button Ltd £
Purchased 1,200 units @ £10 per unit	12,000	
Purchased 1,000 units @ £10 per unit		10,000
Sold 1,000 units @ £15 per unit	15,000	15,000
Cash paid to suppliers	11,000	10,000
Cash received from customers	12,000	15,000

The following draft financial statements can be produced from the above transactions. They ignore other transactions, assets, and liabilities that each company would have in order to focus the reader's attention on the financial management of working capital in companies.

Illustration 15 Just-In-Case Ltd and On-the-Button Ltd ● **269**

	Just-In-Case Ltd	On-the-Button Ltd	Notes
Profit statement	£	£	
Sales	15,000	15,000	
Cost of sales	10,000	10,000	
Net profit	**5,000**	**5,000**	
Cash flow statement	£	£	
Cash inflow	12,000	15,000	
Cash outflow	11,000	10,000	
Operating cash flow	**1,000**	**5,000**	
Balance sheet	£	£	
Inventory	2,000	0	1
Debtors	3,000	0	2
Cash	1,000	5,000	3
Total assets	**6,000**	**5,000**	
Creditors	*1,000*	0	4
Net Assets	**5,000**	**5,000**	
Shareholders' equity			
Retained profits	**5,000**	**5,000**	5

Note	Explanation
1	£12,000 – 10,000
2	£15,000 – 12,000
3	Equal to OCF
4	£12,000 – 11,000
5	Equal to net profit

These financial statements clearly reveal the effects of two different approaches to the financial management of current assets and current liabilities. Just-In-Case Ltd has inventory of unsold materials and goods (£2,000) which reduces OCF because of the cash payments required to be made for these items (£1,000—i.e. £2,000 of inventory funded by credit of £1,000). It has debtors (£3,000) which reduces its OCF because of this amount of cash uncollected from customers. The result is net profit of £5,000 and OCF of £1,000. On-the-Button Ltd, on the other hand, has no inventory, debtors, and creditors. It has a net profit of £5,000 and OCF of the same amount. The financial ratios of the two companies based on these accounting numbers are as follows:

Financial Ratios	Just-In-Case Ltd	On-the Button Ltd	Notes
Working capital ratio	6.00	5.00	1
Quick ratio	4.00	5.00	2
Cash flow conversion	0.25	1.00	3
Inventory turnover	5.00	10,000.00	4
Debtors turnover	5.00	15,000.00	5
Creditors turnover	10.00	10,000.00	6

Note	Explanation
1	£6,000 ÷ 1,000; £5,000 ÷ 0
2	£(3,000 + 1,000) ÷ 1,000; £5,000 ÷ 0
3	£1000 ÷ 5,000; £5,000 ÷ 5,000
4	£10,000 ÷ 2,000; £10,000 ÷ 0 (using year-end inventory)
5	£15,000 ÷ 3,000; £15,000 ÷ 0 (using year-end debtors)
6	£10,000 ÷ 1,000; £10,000 ÷ 0 (using year-end creditors)

Both companies have good working capital ratios with current assets comfortably covering current liabilities. However, On-the-Button Ltd has a better quick ratio of five compared to four because of the amount of cash at the bank. Cash flow conversion is 100% at On-the-Button Ltd compared to 25% at Just-In-Case Ltd. This is due to On-the-Button's policy of no inventory and no credit transactions. The detail of this difference is seen in the inventory and debtors turnover ratios of Just-In-Case (five in each case representing, respectively, 73 days of inventory and customer credit). These have been alleviated by supplier credit (creditors turnover of 10 or 37 days). On-the-Button effectively turns over inventory, debtors, and creditors immediately because of the cash basis of its transactions.

Obviously, On-the-Button Ltd is an exaggerated situation for illustrative purposes. In practice in most situations, there would be inventory of unsold goods and credit terms for customers and suppliers. The lesson of the illustration for the financial analyst is that by keeping inventory and debtors to a minimum and taking as much supplier credit as possible then OCF is improved—as is the conversion of NP into OCF. In the above illustration, inventory and debtors levels of less than 73 days would have improved OCF and cash flow conversion for Just-In-Case Ltd.

FINANCIAL RATIOS, STRUCTURE, AND PERFORMANCE

A company is financed typically from a variety of external sources. The first source is investments by shareholders in its capital. The second source comprises long-term and short-term borrowing from institutions such as banks. The third source is credit from suppliers of goods and services. The latter has been covered in the previous section and is not dealt with further. The purpose of this section is to examine financial ratios concerning financial structure and performance as these relate to shareholders and lenders. In particular, they emphasize the relative financial risks and returns associated with these groups. The first set of ratios concerns risk and the second set deals with returns.

Gearing

Gearing, alternatively known as leverage, is a financial ratio that describes the relationship between shareholders' equity (including profits retained and other reserves) and long-term debt. It is an indicator of the relative financial risk of shareholders and lenders. Shareholders take the ultimate risk in a company as they are the last to receive a return from profitability and repayment of capital in a liquidation. Long-term lenders, on the other hand, have a known rate of return in the form of fixed rate interest and are typically repaid in a liquidation from secured assets under the terms of the loan agreement. Because of their relatively preferential position, the existence of lenders affects the financial risk of shareholders in two ways:

(1) The greater the amount of long-term debt compared to shareholders' equity, the greater the impact of interest payments on profits and the greater the risk of this affecting available profits for dividend purposes. In other words, the more debt, the less profits for dividends to shareholders.

(2) The greater the amount of long-term debt compared to shareholders' equity, the greater the risk of shareholders not being repaid on a liquidation of the company. Long-term debt contracts usually contain provisions that secure the availability of specific or all assets to repay the lenders on a liquidation—thus depriving shareholders of assets as a source of capital repayment.

Gearing ratios attempt to indicate the degree of risk to shareholders caused by long-term debt. There are, in fact, three such ratios.

(1) **Capital gearing** This ratio uses a numerator of long-term debt and a denominator of shareholders' equity. It can be expressed either in absolute or percentage terms. For example, As-You-Were Ltd is a company providing genealogical services on a global basis using the worldwide web. It has the following accounting numbers extracted from recent published financial statements.

	2004 £	2005 £	2006 £
Long-term debt	100,000	150,000	250,000
Shareholders' equity	300,000	325,000	385,000

The company's capital gearing can be shown in a variety of forms. For example, in 2004, long-term debt to shareholders' equity was £100,000 to 300,000 or 1:3. This means that for every £3 of equity, there was £1 of long-term debt. Alternatively, the same numbers can be expressed as a percentage—i.e. (£100,000 ÷ 300,000) × 100 or 33%. Long-term debt is one third of shareholders' equity in 2004. Further, the numbers can be expressed as a ratio where long-term debt is the numerator and the denominator is total capital (i.e. shareholders' equity plus long-term debt). Thus, the ratio for 2004 is (£100,000 ÷ 400,000) × 100 or 25% (i.e. debt constitutes one-quarter of the total long-term capital of the company). The following are a summary of these various ratios as they relate to 2004, 2005, and 2006.

	2004	**2005**	**2006**
Long-term debt to shareholders' equity £	1:3.0	1:2.2	1:1.5
Long-term debt to shareholders' equity (%)	33	46	65
Long-term debt to total capital £	1:4.0	1:3.2	1:2.5
Long-term debt to total capital (%)	25	32	39

All of the ratios indicate a trend in the relationship between equity and debt over the three years—i.e. debt is increasing proportional to equity (33% in 2004 and 65% in 2006) and to total capital (25% in 2004 and 39% in 2006). Such a trend should be of concern to the shareholders of As-You-Were Ltd. More debt means more interest expenses diminishing profits and OCF available for dividend payments to shareholders and capital repayments absorbing cash that could be used to finance replacement and growth investment projects.

(2) **Profit gearing** The risk to shareholders posed by long-term debt can also be described in two financial ratios that use profit statement-based accounting numbers. The first ratio of interest cover compares interest payments on long-term debt to profit available to meet these payments (i.e. NP before interest and tax). The second ratio of dividend cover associates dividends to shareholders with profits available to cover these dividends (i.e. NP after tax). The following accounting numbers illustrate these ratios.

Mississippi Mud Ltd sells beauty products for women. Its published profit statements for the years 2004, 2005, and 2006 contain the following information:

	2004	**2005**	**2006**
	£	**£**	**£**
Profit before deduction of interest	129,000	135,000	141,000
Interest expense on long-term debt	*13,000*	*26,000*	*39,000*
Profit after interest	**116,000**	**109,000**	**102,000**
Taxation on profits	*38,000*	*36,000*	*34,000*
Profit after tax	**78,000**	**73,000**	**68,000**
Dividends proposed	25,000	25,000	25,000
Profit after dividends	**53,000**	**48,000**	**43,000**

Before computing the relevant ratios, it is relevant to examine the trend in key numbers in the above statement. First, profits before interest have increased by 9% between 2004 and 2006 (i.e. [£141,000 − 129,000 or 12,000 ÷ 129,000] × 100). Interest expense has increased by 200% over the same period (i.e. [£39,000 − 13,000 or 26,000 ÷ 13,000] × 100). Dividends have remained stable at £25,000 but profits available to cover dividends have reduced by nearly 13% (i.e. [£78,000 − 68,000 or 10,000 ÷ 78,000] × 100). The ratios reflect these changes:

	2004	**2005**	**2006**	**Notes**
Interest cover	9.92	5.19	3.62	**1**
Dividend cover	3.12	2.92	2.72	**2**

Note	**2004**	**2005**	**2006**
1	£129,000 ÷ 13,000	£135,000 ÷ 26,000	£141,000 ÷ 39,000
2	£78,000 ÷ 25,000	£73,000 ÷ 25,000	£68,000 ÷ 25,000

The rapid increase in interest payments on long-term debt compared to the smaller increase in profits is indicated in the interest cover which diminishes from 9.92 times in 2004 to 3.62 times in 2006. A similar effect can be seen with the dividend cover ratios—from a cover of 3.12 times in 2004 to 2.72 in 2006. In other words, increasing debt not accompanied by a similar increase in profitability puts pressure on possible dividends to shareholders. This is the gearing effect created by long-term debt.

Lesson 10.16 Gearing

 Gearing in financial analysis is a relatively straightforward issue that focuses on the impact of long-term debt on a reporting company's assets and profits. The gearing effect relates to the different rates at which debt, assets, and profits increase. If there are significant differences, then debt can seriously affect shareholders' financial interest in assets and profits. In particular, if debt increases faster than assets and profits then there will be less assets and profits available to shareholders—e.g. profits available to cover dividends will diminish putting the prospect of maintaining these dividends in the future in jeopardy. Similarly, if debt increases faster than assets then, should the company liquidate, there will be fewer assets available to repay shareholders.

Investment returns

Financial ratios dealing with returns earned by shareholders have been introduced earlier in this chapter when examining indicators of corporate profitability such as return on investment and earnings per share. The focus of these ratios is on the investment return to the shareholder. This focus can be extended to include two ratios that are commonly used by financial analysts to assess the performance of a reporting company in relation to the investment in it of its shareholders. The ratios are the dividend yield and the earnings yield. The first calculation adopts DPS as the numerator and the market price of the ordinary share as its denominator. The second yield uses EPS in association with market price. The yields can be expressed either absolutely or as percentages. The following example illustrates each ratio.

Sunshine Juices plc is a manufacturer of fruit juices. The following data have been extracted from its published financial statements for the years 2002, 2003, 2004, 2005, and 2006. Market prices are as quoted on a local stock exchange on the last day of each year.

	2002 £000	2003 £000	2004 £000	2005 £000	2006 £000
NP after tax	5,800	6,200	6,500	7,100	7,900
Proposed dividends	2,000	2,500	2,600	2,800	3,000
Share capital (£1 units)	10,000	10,000	10,000	10,000	10,000
Market price (per £1 unit)	£1.40	£1.75	£2.38	£3.00	£3.64

The dividend and earnings yields are as follows. First, the dividends and earnings are expressed in "per share" terms.

	2002 £	2003 £	2004 £	2005 £	2006 £	Notes
DPS	0.20	0.25	0.26	0.28	0.30	1
EPS	0.58	0.62	0.65	0.71	0.79	2

Note	2002 £000	2003 £000	2004 £000	2005 £000	2006 £000
1	2,000/10,000	2,500/10,000	2,600/10,000	2,800/10,000	3,000/10,000
2	5,800/10,000	6,200/10,000	6,500/10,000	7,100/10,000	7,900/10,000

Next, the "per share" data are related to market prices in the ratio form of yields.

	2002	2003	2004	2005	2006	Notes
Dividend yield	0.14	0.14	0.11	0.09	0.08	1
Earnings yield	0.41	0.35	0.27	0.24	0.22	2

Note	2002 £	2003 £	2004 £	2005 £	2006 £
1	0.20/1.40	0.25/1.75	0.26/2.38	0.28/3.00	0.30/3.64
2	0.58/1.40	0.62/1.75	0.65/2.38	071/3.00	0.79/3.64

The yields can be converted into percentages by multiplying by 100. Thus, the dividend yield moves from 14% in 2002 to 8% in 2006, and the earnings yield from 41% in 2002 to 22% in 2006. These trends indicate that the returns on the share price have steadily fallen. The actual return on price to shareholders is dividend-based and the total return is earnings-based. Dividends rose by 50% between 2002 and 2006—i.e. from £2,000,000 to £3,000,000. NP rose by 36%—i.e. from £5,800,000 to £7,900,000. However, share price increased by 160%—i.e. from £1.40 to £3.64. This indicates that investors were impressed by the company's performance between 2002 and 2006 and the price moved accordingly. However, the slower increase in dividends and earnings meant the returns fell as a percentage of market prices. In turn, this indicates that investors perceived the shares to be much less risky in 2006 than was the case in 2002. Falling percentage yields on share prices indicate decreasing risk. Increasing percentage yields suggest increasing risk.

> **Lesson 10.17 Investment yields**
> Yields based on share prices are indicators of investors' perceptions of the degree of risk associated with the shares. The greater the risk that is perceived to be associated with the shares, the greater the percentage return or yield expected from their investments. Calculated yields are therefore useful indicators of investment risk perceived by the capital market.

LEARNING OBJECTIVES

Please review the learning objectives at the beginning of this chapter and ensure they have been achieved before leaving this chapter.

Exercise 1   Common size analysis

You are a financial analyst and received the following summary profit statements. Prepare common-size summaries and identify and explain the main features contained in them. The company provides kennel services for cat and dog owners.

Bouncing Barry Kennels Ltd
Summary Profit Statements 2004–2006

	2004 £	2005 £	2006 £
Sales	156,000	145,000	137,000
Less: cost of kennel services	78,000	80,000	77,000
Gross profit	**78,000**	**65,000**	**60,000**
Less: administrative overheads	35,000	36,000	37,000
Net profit before tax	**43,000**	**29,000**	**23,000**
Less: taxation	13,000	9,000	7,000
Net profit after tax	**30,000**	**20,000**	**16,000**
Less: dividend	10,000	10,000	10,000
Retained profit	**20,000**	**10,000**	**6,000**

Exercise 2   Inter-period comparisons

Over-The-Horizon Sailing Company Ltd manufactures sailing dinghies. The following are summarized profit statements for the years 2002 to 2006 inclusive. You are required to prepare a common-size inter-period analysis of these statements and identify significant changes in the company's profit performance.

Over-The-Horizon Sailing Company Ltd
Summary Profit Statements 2002–2006

	2002 £000	2003 £000	2004 £000	2005 £000	2006 £000
Sales	1,011	1,234	1,206	1,457	1,370
Less: cost of goods sold	607	740	664	875	822
Gross profit	**404**	**494**	**542**	**582**	**548**
Less: administrative overheads	120	125	130	140	145
Net profit before tax	**284**	**369**	**412**	**442**	**403**
Less: taxation	85	111	124	133	121
Net profit after tax	**199**	**258**	**288**	**309**	**282**
Less: dividend	50	50	50	50	50
Retained profit	**149**	**208**	**238**	**259**	**232**

Exercise 3   Inter-company comparisons

Joe Hines has prepared the following summary cash flow statements for five companies of reasonably similar size and operating in the same industry. Consider the cash flow accounting numbers and provide a brief explanation of the cash flow performance of each company for the year 2006. Also compare their performances in a concluding statement.

Summary Cash Flow Statements 2006

Company	A £	B £	C £	D £	E £
Operating cash flow	440,000	215,000	373,000	8,000	123,000
Investment cash flow	650,000	710,000	50,000	500,000	127,000
Financing cash flow	200,000	800,000	118,000	490,000	5,000
Change in cash resources	10,000	125,000	305,000	18,000	1,000

Exercise 4   Ratio objectives, criteria, and limitations

Prepare a statement in which you explain the main objectives, criteria, and limitations of financial ratios.

Exercise 5   Return on investment

Assuming ROI is calculated on the basis of NP before tax to total assets, comment on the following data taken from published corporate financial statements of a book publisher and government statistics. The latter data relate to comparable companies.

Year	Companion Books Ltd %	Book Industry %	All Industry %
2002	20	18	15
2003	22	19	17
2004	24	20	19
2005	28	21	21
2006	30	22	23

Exercise 6   Working capital and quick ratios

Cement Boots Ltd is a manufacturer of footwear for the construction industry. A financial analyst has examined the company's published financial statements for the years 2002, 2003, 2004, 2005, and 2006 in order to produce the following ratios. Comment on these ratios after explaining their intended meaning and calculation.

Year	Working Capital Ratio	Quick Ratio
2002	2.25	1.18
2003	2.10	1.09
2004	1.98	0.93
2005	1.87	0.82
2006	1.75	0.65

Exercise 7   Cash flow generation

The Cuckoo's Nest Ltd is a restaurant and bar located in a high street. Its profit and cash flow figures for the last five years are as follows:

Year	2002 £	2003 £	2004 £	2005 £	2006 £
Operating cash flow	58,000	37,000	26,000	41,000	54,000
Investment cash flow	22,000	15,000	3,000	59,000	61,000
Financing cash flow	25,000	25,000	25,000	20,000	8,000
Change in cash resources	11,000	3,000	2,000	2,000	1,000
Profit after tax	65,000	42,000	31,000	45,000	60,000

Review these figures with regard to the general cash flow performance of the company and the specific conversion of its profits into cash flow.

Exercise 8   Cash flow management

A company can be profitable and yet become bankrupt because of lack of cash flow and liquid assets. Explain how this can be so and the importance of cash flow management to the survival of a company. Identify the key aspects of cash flow management in your discussion.

Exercise 9   Inventory, debtors, and creditors turnover

Hole-In-One Ltd is a golf club retailer. The following accounting numbers have been extracted from its published financial statements for years 2002 to 2006 inclusive by a financial analyst who has been asked to assess its investment potential. You are required to compute relevant financial ratios to assist in the analysis and assessment. You should also prepare a commentary on the ratios you calculate.

Year	2002 £	2003 £	2004 £	2005 £	2006 £
Sales	387,000	391,000	423,000	456,000	489,000
Cost of goods sold	225,000	227,000	245,000	264,000	284,000
Opening inventory	32,000	36,000	45,000	56,000	61,000
Closing inventory	36,000	45,000	56,000	61,000	70,000
Opening debtors	35,000	39,000	41,000	48,000	53,000
Closing debtors	39,000	41,000	48,000	53,000	59,000
Opening creditors	17,000	19,000	20,000	22,000	26,000
Closing creditors	19,000	20,000	22,000	26,000	28,000

Exercise 10   Gearing

What is gearing in corporate financial analysis and which financial ratios indicate the gearing effect in financial statements? In particular, distinguish between the different calculations of gearing. If a company was described as highly geared, what does this mean and how would it affect a decision you had to make regarding the purchase of ordinary shares in it? Illustrate your answer with numerical examples.

Exercise 11   Investment returns

You are an investor in a public company and hold 100,000 ordinary share units in it. You have extracted several pieces of financial information about it from a national newspaper and have asked your stockbroker about the significance of the numbers concerned. They are as follows:

Year	2002 £	2003 £	2004 £	2005 £	2006 £
Earnings per share	0.65	0.71	0.89	0.56	0.70
Dividends per share	0.21	0.23	0.25	0.10	0.15
Year-end market price per share	2.62	2.87	2.91	2.30	2.45

ADDITIONAL READING

It is difficult to recommend additional reading in the area of financial ratios calculation and analysis. There are many texts covering the area and most deal with similar material. Three texts that provide supporting material for this chapter are:

M Jones (2006), *Accounting*, John Wiley & Sons Ltd, Chichester, 216–56. This is a relatively simple introduction to financial ratios for non-accounting readers. It examines individual ratios in six categories (e.g. profitability), provides a fully worked example using the financial statements of a public company, and briefly looks at the use of ratios in combination.

P O'Regan (2001), *Financial Information Analysis*, John Wiley & Sons Ltd, Chichester, 185–226. The title of this text suggests that it is devoted entirely to the calculation and interpretation of financial information. However, a relatively small part deals with this subject-matter (the remainder is concerned with contextual matters, financial statements, and reporting issues). The section on analysis includes common-size analysis, liquidity and cash flow, financing, and profitability.

G I White, A C Sondhi, and D Fried (2003), *The Analysis and Use of Financial Statements*, John Wiley & Sons Ltd, Hoboken: NJ, 87–96 (cash flow analysis) and 110–39 (financial ratio analysis). This is an advanced text on the use of accounting information and the pages recommended deal with introductory material. The book is American and contains US terminology. However, most of this is compatible with that used in the current text.

Index

Marianne Jewell Memorial Library
Baker College of Muskegon
Muskegon, Michigan 49442